The Political Philosophy of Bakunin

SCIENTIFIC ANARCHISM

THE POLITICAL PHILOSOPHY OF

Bakunin: SCIENTIFIC ANARCHISM

COMPILED AND EDITED BY *G. P. Maximoff*

PREFACE BY BERT F. HOSELITZ
THE UNIVERSITY OF CHICAGO

INTRODUCTION BY RUDOLF ROCKER

BIOGRAPHICAL SKETCH OF BAKUNIN BY MAX NETTLAU

THE FREE PRESS, NEW YORK
COLLIER-MACMILLAN LIMITED, *London*

70166

printing number
2 3 4 5 6 7 8 9 10

Contents

Contents

Publisher's Preface

PHILOSOPHICAL ANARCHISM is a very old doctrine. One would be tempted to say that it is as old as the idea of government, but clear evidence is lacking which would support such an assertion. Still, we possess texts more than two thousand years old which not only describe human society without government, force, and constraining law, but which designate this state of social relations as the ideal of human society. In beautiful, poetic words Ovidius gives a description of the anarchist utopia. In the first book of his *Metamorphoses* Ovidius writes about the golden age which was without law and in which, with no one to use compulsion, everyone of his own will kept faith and did the right. There was no fear of punishment, no legal sanctions were engraved on bronze tablets, no mass of supplicants looked, full of fear, upon its avenger, but without judges everyone lived in security. The only difference between the vision of the Roman poet and that of modern philosophical anarchists is that he placed the golden age at the beginning of human history, whereas they put it at the end.

But Ovidius was not the first inventor of these sentiments. He repeated in his poetry ideas which had been cherished for centuries. Georg Adler, a German social historian, who in 1899 published an exhaustive and well-documented study of the history of socialism, showed that anarchist views were certainly held by Zeno (342 to 270 B.C.), the founder of the Stoic school of philosophy.[1] There were doubtless strong anarchist sentiments among many of the early Christian hermits, and in the politico-religious views of some, for example, Karpocrates, and his disciples, (second century A.D.), these feelings seem to have held a strong and perhaps predominant position. Such sentiments lingered on among some of the fundamentalist Christian sects of the Middle Ages and even the modern period.

Max Nettlau, the indefatigable historian of anarchism, also has gone over the field and lists a series of works composed in the two centuries before the French Revolution which contain strong libertarian views or are even outspokenly anarchist.[2] Among the most important French works

---

[1] Georg Adler, *Geschichte des Sozialismus und Kommunismus von Plato bis zur Gegenwart*, Leipzig, 1899, pp. 46-51.

[2] Max Nettlau, *Der Vorfrühling der Anarchie*, Berlin, 1925, pp. 34-66.

of this period are Etienne de la Boétie's *Discours de la servitude volontaire*, which was composed about 1550, but remained unpublished until 1577; Gabriel Foigny's *Les aventures de Jacques Sadeur dans la découverte et le voyage de la Terre Australe*, which appeared anonymously in 1676; a few short essays by Diderot; and a series of poems, fables, and stories by Sylvain Maréchal which saw the light of day in the two decades immediately preceding the Revolution. Similarly, during the same period anarchist ideas can be traced in England, where, as in France, they are expressed usually by representatives of the most radical wing of the rising middle class. Thus anarchist views can be found in some of the writings of Winstanley, and it is well-known that the young Burke in his *Vindication of Natural Society* (1756) presents an ingenious argument in favor of anarchy, even though the work was intended as a satire.

But all these, and many other writings of this earlier period, display one of two characteristics which make them differ profoundly from later anarchist works. They are either openly utopian as, for example, the books of Foigny or Maréchal, or they are political tracts directed against some directly felt abuse by a ruler or a government, or aiming at the attainment of greater freedom of action in a particular political constellation. They contain not infrequently a discussion of political theory, but this is incidental and not the major object of the work.

As a systematic theory, philosophical anarchism may be said to have begun in England with William Godwin's *Enquiry Concerning Political Justice*, which appeared in 1793. Godwin's anarchism, as well as that of his more immediate predecessors, and of Proudhon some fifty years later, is the political theory of the most radical branch of the small bourgeoisie. In the English Revolution of 1688 and the French Revolution of 1789 the bourgeoisie had broken the monopoly of political power held previously by the crown and the aristocracy. Although post-revolutionary governments were still influenced strongly by the landed nobility and the bureaucracy (which remained, for long, a *noblesse de robe*), the more powerful and wealthy middle class families gradually became associated by marriage or through political alliances with aristocratic circles; and provided the government abstained from excessive interference in its economic affairs, the *haute bourgeoisie* was willing to support it. But since it demanded and obtained greater freedom in economic matters, it was instrumental in gradually abolishing or making ineffective the old guild organizations and other protective, quasi-monopolistic associations which had survived from the Middle Ages and which had become a fetter on the full development even of small-scale trade and manufacture. By the end of the eighteenth century in England the manufacturer who had a few hands in his employ, the small shopkeeper, the petty trader, formed a mass of independent entrepreneurs. By the middle of the nineteenth century in France, the artisan and craftsman, the peasant who owned a lot just large enough to support himself and his family, also had acquired the nature of independent small entrepreneurs. All these men had only a puny amount of capital at their disposal; they were exposed to the fresh winds of competition, unprotected by guilds or other cooperative organizations; and were relegated at the same time to a state of political impotence. They received no benefits from the government, and whatever legislation they felt, appeared to be designed for the protection of large-scale property, the safeguarding of accumulated wealth, the maintenance of monopoly rights by the large trading companies, and the support of established economic and political privilege.

The more moderate elements among this group supported the trend towards parliamentary reform, the more radical ones followed Paine and later the Chartists, but a few of the most radical intellectuals held anarchist ideas. The distance beween Godwin's anarchism and the liberalism of some of his contemporaries was not very wide. Basically the two doctrines grew out of the same stream of political traditions, and the main difference between them is that anarchism was the more logical and consistent deduction from the common premises of utilitarian psychology and the conception that the greatest happiness of all and mutually harmonious social relations can be achieved only if every person is left free to pursue his self-interest. To be sure, the liberals, following John Locke, regarded property as an outflow of natural right, and hence stipulated the maintenance of a political power monopoly in the hands of the government to safeguard the security of property and life against internal and external attack. But to this the anarchists replied: The government protects the property of the rich; this property is theft; do away with the government and you'll do away with big landed and industrial property; in this way you'll create an egalitarian society of small, economically self-sufficient producers, a society, moreover, which will be free of privilege, of class distinctions, and in which government will be superfluous because the happiness, the economic security, and the personal freedom of each will be safeguarded without its intervention.

It is of the utmost importance to understand that the anarchist doctrine as propounded by Godwin, Proudhon, and their contemporaries was the apotheosis of petty bourgeois existence; that its ultimate ideal was the same as that of Voltaire's *Candide*, to cultivate one's garden; and that it ignored or opposed large scale industrial or agricultural enterprises; and that it, therefore, never became a political theory which could find real sympathy and enthusiastic support among the masses of industrial workers. It was the radical extension of the liberalist doctrine which regarded the freedom of each as the highest political good and the responsible reliance on one's conscience as the highest political duty. It was thus based on a political philosophy which is closely associated with the rise of middle-class, liberal, anti-socialist, political movements. Yet Bakunin, as is well known, regarded himself as a socialist, obtained admission as a leading member to the International Workingmen's Association, struggled for the control of this organization, and counted among his followers and adherents many genuine proletarians.

How and why did anarchism become associated so closely, around the middle of the nineteenth century, with socialism, a political philosophy which championed the aspirations of a different social stratum and which had appeal for so different a class of men? That the bedfellowship between anarchists and socialists was never very happy needs no reiteration. And yet, in spite of repeated conflicts, mutual incriminations, and bitter abuse, anarchists and socialists teamed up with one another again and again, so that by the end of the nineteenth century anarchism was quite commonly regarded as the most radical branch of socialism. The reason for the close association between socialists and anarchists can not be found in the similarity of their basic doctrines, but alone in the revolutionary strategy common to both of them.

The political philosophy of Godwin and Proudhon expressed, as already stated, the aspirations of a part of the petty bourgeoisie. With the consolidation of capitalism in western and central Europe during the nineteenth century, with the slow extension of the suffrage, and with the gradual retreat of unconditional laissez-faire and the adoption by the state of added responsibilities towards its citizens, increasingly larger portions of the middle class became staunch supporters of the existing political order, and anarchism became more and more a philosophy held only by a small marginal group of intellectuals. This development had the result that anarchist theory became more diffuse and at the same time more radical than it had been. Instead of writing fat tomes, as had been the practice of Godwin and Proudhon, anarchists turned to writing tracts, pamphlets and newspaper or magazine articles, dealing with questions of the day, points of factional or personal controversy, and problems of revolutionary tactics. Bakunin's often fragmentary writings, the high proportion of manifestoes, proclamations, and open letters among his works, are typical not merely of his personal peculiarities but even more of the great bulk of anarchist publications of his day. What was needed in this situation to save anarchist theory from falling apart completely was the appearance either of a great theorist or of a dynamic, powerful personality who would by the sheer appeal of his own convictions draw together the scattering fragments of the movement. This role was played by Bakunin. Although not a theorist of the stature of his great antagonist, Marx, in the fervor of his convictions and the elan with which he expressed them he was superior to the socialist leader.

The importance of Bakunin for modern students of political philosophy thus lies in the crucial position which his works occupy in anarchist and libertarian literature in general. In spite of his frequently unconcealed confusion, in spite of the internal contradictions in his writings, in spite of the fragmentary character of almost his entire literary output, Bakunin must be regarded as the most important anarchist political philosopher. By accident of birth—both as to time and place—in consequence of manifold early influences which embrace contact with Slavophilism, Hegelianism, Marxism, and Proudhonism, and last but not least because of his restless, romantic temperament, Bakunin is a man who stands at the crossroads of several intellectual currents, who occupies a position in the history of anarchism at the end of an old and the beginning of a new era. There is none of the ponderous common sense of Godwin, of the ponderous dialectics of Proudhon, of the ponderous thoroughness of Max Stirner in Bakunin's works. Anarchism as a theory of political speculation is gone, and has been reborn as a theory of political action. Bakunin is not satisfied to outline the evils of the existing system, and to describe the general framework of a libertarian society, he preaches revolution, he participates in revolutionary activity, he conspires, harangues, propagandizes, forms political action groups, and supports every social upheaval, large or small, promising, or doomed to failure, from its very beginning. And the type of revolt which Bakunin principally considers is the wild *Pugachevchina*, the unleashing of century-long suppressed peasant masses, who had plundered and destroyed the countryside, but had proven themselves essentially incapable of building up a new and better society. And although Bakunin was not a member of any of the nihilist action groups in Russia or elsewhere, his unconditional partisanship of the revolutionary overthrow of the existing order, provided inspiration for the young men and women who believed in the efficacy of "propaganda by deeds."

With Bakunin there appeared, therefore, two new tendencies in anarchist theory. The doctrine shifted from abstract speculation on the use and abuse of political power to a theory of practical political action. At the same time anarchism ceased to be the political philosophy of the most radical wing of the petty bourgeoisie and became a political doctrine which looked for the mass of its adherents among the workers, and even the *lumpenproletariat*, although its central cadres continued to be recruited from among the intelligentsia. Without Bakunin anarchist syndicalism, such as existed for a long time notably in Spain, is unthinkable. Without Bakunin, Europe probably never would have witnessed an organized anarchist political movement, such as made itself felt in Italy, France, and Switzerland in the thirty years preceding the first world war. And it was Bakunin's talent for and imagination in "establishing a school of insurrectionary activity which . . . contributed an important influence to the policies of Lenin."[3]

Bakunin's role in the anarchist tradition may thus be regarded as having consisted in founding a new political party with the program to end all

[3] John Maynard, *Russia in Flux*, London, 1941, p. 187.

parties and to end all politics, and in having written that new party's program and its philosophical and general political underpinnings. This is no
mean feat in itself, but in view of the peculiar constellation of intellectual
and practical political movements which affected Bakunin, his contribution to political theory should be of special interest to students of the
history of political and social ideas. In the center of Bakunin's political
thought stand two problems which have provided the subject matter for
a veritable host of arguments and debates: liberty and violence. The first
has been the main concern of philosophical anarchism ever since it origi-
nated in human thought, the second was added by Bakunin. The originality
of his contribution lies in the weaving together of both themes into a consistent whole.

Unfortunately Bakunin's thought has received very little attention up
to the very recent past in the United States. For example the well-known
text on the *History of Political Theory* by George H. Sabine mentions
Bakunin only once and even in this place makes no comment on any views
professed by him, but merely lists him as an intellectual ancestor of syndicalism. Only a very minute fraction of the original works by Bakunin have
so far been available in English translation, and hence his own opinions
expressed in his own words are scarcely known to those who do not read
foreign languages. But also the Russian, French, German, and Spanish editions of Bakunin's works are not easily available, and there are quite a
number of even large libraries in the United States which have only very
poor and incomplete collections of Bakuniniana.

The reason for this neglect to make available the works of a doubtless
important political thinker in an American edition seems to be threefold.
In part, the bad repute anarchism has had in the United States must be
made accountable for it. Since it was regarded as a set of beliefs cherished
by "criminals" or, at best, lunatics it was not felt necessary to place before
American readers the works of a man who was commonly regarded as
one of the most important intellectual forebears of this "political lunacy."
But we have seen that anarchism did not originate with Bakunin, that it
has a long and distinguished history, and that some of its roots—the quest
for human freedom, the postulate of moral self-reliance on one's conscience,
the license to use violence against tyranny—are in the Christian and the
Anglo-Saxon radicalist tradition, both of which have had a deep influence
on political thought in the United States.

A second reason for the almost complete unavailability of Bakunin's
works in English has been the persistence of a one-sided historical account
of his conflict with Marx which was built almost into a legend by later
followers and disciples of Marx. This incident, the struggle for control of
the International Workingmen's Association, is probably the best known
episode of Bakunin's life. Unfortunately there exists hardly a single truly
objective study of that conflict. The followers of Marx have imputed
sometimes the most sinister motives to Bakunin, and the followers of Baku-

nin, notably James Guillaume, have been inspired by such apparent hatred
of Marx that their descriptions of the conflict must be ruled out because
of their very obvious bias. The best and most detached history of Bakunin's
relations with Marx, that has come to my attention, is the account given
by E. H. Carr in his biography of Bakunin. It is not necessary to repeat
this account here, even very briefly. In essence the struggle between
Bakunin and Marx was one for the control of an organization which had
international ramifications and which both believed to be able to attain
great influence among large masses of the workers. Since the organization
had to have a clear and consistent political program, the struggle was
fought with bitterness and use of all the ideological weapons at the disposal of each side. There were denunciations and counter-denunciations,
there were castigations of the opponent's character and purity of motives,
and since both Marx and Bakunin could be irate, sarcastic, and violent in
their use of words, the conflict was hurtful to each side and left a large
amount of hatred, suspicion, and bad feeling. Bakunin lost out, but, as is
well known, Marx's victory was a Pyrrhic victory. The conflict between
the giants had destroyed the International. The posthumous revenge of
the Marxist movement, which was infinitely better organized and provided
with considerably larger funds than the followers of Bakunin, was the
attempt to condemn Bakunin to oblivion. But in doing this it did a
disservice even to Karl Marx himself, for he had continued to read
Bakunin's writings even after the break, and on the basis of some marginal notes which he made in his copy of *Gosudarstvennost i Anarkhiia*
(*Statism and Anarchism*) and which were published by Ryazanoff in the
second volume (1926) of *Letopisi Marksisma*, we must conclude that many
of Bakunin's ideas exerted a deep and lasting influence on Marx. And although Bakunin's influence on Russian socialism has so far only been
partially investigated, there can be no doubt that he must be counted
among the intellectual forebears of Lenin's party.

The third reason for the past neglect of bringing out Bakunin's works
in the United States must be laid at the very door of Bakunin himself. As
already pointed out most of his works are either fragmentary, or deal
with political problems of the day or factional disputes. The reader of
these works thus is either presented with an incomplete piece and/or has
to familiarize himself with a mass of historical detail of the history of
radical parties and movements of the nineteenth century to appreciate them
fully. Some aid to potential readers of Bakunin has been available since
1937 in the bulky biography, *Michael Bakunin*, by Edward H. Carr. But
the usefulness of Carr's work is strictly limited, since it deals almost exclusively with the factual incidents of Bakunin's life rather than with his
ideas. The obvious intention of Carr not to write an intellectual biography
of Bakunin is exhibited clearly by the fact that he does not even mention
Statism and Anarchism, a book that by some is judged to be Bakunin's
greatest and most mature work.

For all these reasons, it appears eminently desirable to let Bakunin speak for himself. But a publication in English of a comprehensive selection of his works in full would have presented insurmountable difficulties. Nothing less than a set of several volumes would have done justice to the voluminous output of Bakunin. Such a procedure would have been clearly impracticable—however desirable from a purely scholarly standpoint it might have been—and would probably have delayed for decades, if not forever, the appearance of Bakunin's works in English. Fortunately these difficulties are avoided by the able compilation and systematic presentation of excerpts from Bakunin's works by G. P. Maximoff, which is contained in this volume. Although Bakunin's ideas appear in a much more systematic and logically consistent form than he ever presented them, the advantage of this arrangement is obvious, since much space is saved and yet not merely the gist but the exhaustive grounding of Bakunin's thought is presented. It is believed that this work, therefore, presents at least, in a convenient fashion, the thought of an important political thinker of the nineteenth century, and certainly one of the three or four leading figures in the history of philosophical anarchism.

But there is still another reason why a publication of Bakunin's writings today may be considered timely. The bureaucratic, centralized state is everywhere on the increase. In the Soviet orbit, all personal freedoms, which even in the most democratic periods of those countries had led a very tenuous existence, are suppressed more thoroughly than ever before. In the western world, political freedoms are under attack from many quarters, and the masses, instead of loudly voicing their concern over this trend, appear to become daily more and more inert, with standardized tastes, standardized views, and, one would fear, standardized emotions. The field is wide open for demagogues and charlatans, and although it may still be true that not all the people can be fooled all the time, very many people apparently have been fooled a very long time. The garrison state of Stalin, on the one hand, and the increasing political apathy of large sections of the popular masses, on the other, have given a new impetus to some men of vision to reflect anew upon some of the principles which had been taken for granted as the foundation of western political thought. The meaning of liberty and the forms and limits of political violence are problems which agitate a good many minds today, just as they did in the days of La Boétie, Diderot, Junius, and Bakunin. In such a situation men like to turn for inspiration or confirmation of their own thought to the work of authors who have struggled with the same or similar problems. The startling and often brilliant insights of Bakunin presented in this volume should be a fruitful source of new ideas for the clarification of the great issues surrounding the problems of freedom and power.

Bert F. Hoselitz
THE UNIVERSITY OF CHICAGO

Introduction

BY RUDOLF ROCKER

MIKHAIL BAKUNIN stands out as unique among the revolutionary personalities of the nineteenth century. This extraordinary man combined in his being the dauntless socio-philosophical thinker with the man of action, something rarely encountered in one and the same individual. He was always prepared to seize every chance to remold any sphere of human society.

His impetuous and impassioned urge for action subsided somewhat, however, after the defeat of the Paris Commune of 1871, and finally—following the collapse of the revolts of Bologna and Imola in 1874—he withdrew completely from political activity, two years before his death. His powerful body had been undermined by ailments from which he had long suffered.

But it was not only the increasingly rapid decline of his physical powers which motivated his decision. Bakunin's political vision, which was later so often confirmed by events, convinced him that with the birth of the new German Empire, after the Franco-Prussian War of 1870-71, another historical epoch had been ushered in, bound to be disastrous for the social evolution of Europe, and to paralyze for many years all revolutionary aspirations for a rebirth of society in the spirit of Socialism.

It was not the disillusionment of an elderly man, ravaged by disease, who had lost faith in his ideals, which had made him abandon the struggle, but the conviction that with the change of conditions caused by the war, Europe had entered a period which would break radically with the traditions created by the Great French Revolution of 1789, and which would be superseded by a new and intense reaction. In this respect Bakunin foresaw the future of Europe much more correctly than most of his contemporaries. He was mistaken in his estimate of the duration of this new reaction, which led to the militarization of all Europe, but he recognized its nature better than anyone else. That appears particularly in his pathetic letter of November 11, 1874, to his friend Nikolai Ogarev:

"As for myself, old friend, this time I also have finally abandoned any effective activity and have withdrawn from all connection with active engagements. First, because the present time is decisively inappropriate. Bismarckianism, which is militarism, police rule, and finance monopoly, united in a system characteristic of the new statism, is conquering everything. For the next ten or fifteen years perhaps, this powerful and scientific disavowal of all humanity will remain victorious. I don't mean to say that there is nothing to be done now, but these new conditions demand new methods, and mainly new blood. I feel that I am no good any more for fresh struggles, and I have resigned without waiting for a plucky Gil Blas to tell me: *'Plus d'homélies, Monseigneur!'* " [No more sermons, My Lord!]

Bakunin played a conspicuous part in two great revolutionary periods, which made his name known throughout the world. When the February revolution of 1848 broke out in France, which he, as Max Nettlau wrote, had foreseen in his fearless speech in November, 1847, on the anniversary of the Polish revolution, Bakunin hastened to Paris, where, in the thick of the turmoil of revolutionary events, he probably lived the happiest weeks of his life. But he soon realized that the victorious course of the Revolution in France, in view of the rebellious ferment noticeable all over Europe, would evoke strong reverberations in other countries, and that it was of paramount importance to unite all revolutionary elements, and to prevent the splitting up of those forces, knowing that such dispersion would work only to the advantage of the lurking counter-revolution.

Bakunin's foreknowledge then was considerably ahead of the general revolutionary aspirations of that time, as appears from his letter of April, 1848, to P. M. Annenkov, and particularly also from his letters to his friend, the German poet Georg Herwegh, written in August of the same year. And he likewise had enough political insight to discern that existing conditions must be reckoned with, in order that the larger obstacles be removed, before the Revolution could reach for higher aims.

Shortly after the March revolution in Berlin, Bakunin went to Germany, to make contact from there with his many friends among the Poles, Czechs, and other Slavic nationalities, with the thought of stimulating them to a general revolt in conjunction with the Western and German democracy. In this he saw the only possible way to batter down the last remaining bulwarks of royal absolutism in Europe—Austria, Russia, and Prussia—which had not been much affected by the Great French Revolution. To his eyes those countries loomed as the strongest barriers against any attempt at social reconstruction on the Continent and the most powerful buttress for every reaction.

His feverish activity in the revolutionary period of 1848-49 attained its highest point during his military leadership of the Dresden uprising in May of the latter year, which made him one of the most celebrated revolutionaries in Europe, to whom even Marx and Engels could not deny their recognition. This period, however, was followed by gloomy years of long and harrowing confinement in German, Austrian, and Russian prisons, which were lightened only when he was exiled to Siberia in March, 1857.

After twelve years of prisons and exile Bakunin succeeded in escaping from Siberia and arriving in December, 1861, in London, where he was welcomed with open arms by his friends Herzen and Ogarev. It was just then that the widespread reaction in Europe, which had followed the revolutionary happenings of 1848-49, began gradually to abate. In the Sixties new trends and a new spirit were manifest in many parts of the Continent, which inspired new hope among the rebel-minded whose goal was human freedom. The exploits of Garibaldi and his gallant bands in Sicily and on the Italian mainland, the Polish insurrection of 1863-64, the growing opposition in France to the regime of Napoleon III, the beginning of a European labor movement, and the founding of the First International, were portentous signs of forthcoming great changes. All these stirring developments made not only the revolutionists of various political leanings believe that another 1848 was in the making, but even impelled reputable historians to make similar forecasts. It was a time of great expectations, which, however, was cut short by the war of 1870-71, and by the defeat of the Paris Commune and the Spanish Revolution of 1873.

This vibrant atmosphere of the Sixties was exactly what was needed by Bakunin's impetuous urge for action, a craving by no means weakened by his past gruelling imprisonment. It almost looked as if he sought to catch up with all the activity he had missed in more than a decade of enforced silence. During the long years when he was a prisoner, first in the Austrian fortress of Olmutz and then in the Peter-and-Paul fortress and in Schlüsselburg, where he was kept in unbroken solitary confinement, he was deprived of any possibility of learning what was going on in the outside world. Neither was he able to visualize during his exile in Siberia the far-flung transitions in Europe which had followed the stormy days of the two revolutionary years. Whatever he heard by accident in the exile period was only faint echoes from distant lands, of occurrences which had no relation to his Siberian surroundings.

That helps to explain why, immediately after his escape from the farthest reaches of Alexander II's domain, Bakunin tried to resume his activity where he had left off in 1849, by announcing that he was renewing his struggle against the Russian, Austrian, and Prussian despotisms, and contending for the union of all Slavic peoples on the basis of federated communes and common ownership of land.

Only after the defeat of the Polish insurrection of 1863 and Bakunin's moving to Italy, where he found an entirely new field for his energies, did his actions assume an international character. From the day he arrived in London his indefatigable inner urge drove him again and again to revolutionary enterprises which occupied the next thirteen years of his agitated life. He took a leading part in the secret preparations for the Polish insurrection, and even succeeded in persuading placid Herzen to follow a path contrary to his inclinations. In Italy he became the founder of a social-revolutionary movement, which came into open conflict with Mazzini's nationalist aspirations, and which attracted many of the best elements of Italian youth.

Later he became the soul and inspiration of the libertarian wing of the First International, and thus the founder of a federalist anti-authoritarian branch of the Socialist movement, which spread all over the world, and which fought against all forms of State Socialism. His correspondence with well-known revolutionists of various countries burgeoned to an almost unparalleled volume. He participated in the Lyons revolt in 1870, and in the Italian insurrectional movement in 1874, at a time when his health was obviously breaking. All this indicates the mighty vitality and will-power that he possessed. Herzen said of him: "Everything about this man is colossal, his energy, his appetite, yes, even the man himself!"

It will be easily understood why, in view of the tempestuousness of his life, most of Bakunin's writings remained fragmentary. Publication of his collected works did not begin until nineteen years after his death. Then, in 1895, the first volume of a French edition of those writings, edited by Max Nettlau, was brought out by P. V. Stock in Paris. That was followed by five other volumes, also issued by Stock, but edited by James Guillaume, in the period from 1907 to 1913. The same publisher announced additional Bakunin works to come, but was prevented from issuing them by conditions growing out of World War I. We know that Guillaume prepared a seventh volume for the printers, and that it was to have been brought out after the Armistice. But unfortunately it has not yet appeared. The six French volumes issued so far include, in addition to works published in pamphlet form at earlier dates, the text of numerous manuscripts never before printed.

A Russian edition of Bakunin in five volumes was issued by *Golos Truda* in Petrograd in 1919-22. Notably the first of these is *Statism and Anarchism*, which is not in the French edition. But the Russian edition lacks several of Bakunin's works which are included in the French set. In addition to these five tomes in Russian the Bolshevik government planned to bring out in its *Socialist Classics* complete editions of the works of both Bakunin and Kropotkin. The editing of the Bakunin edition for this enterprise was entrusted to George Steklov, who intended to issue fourteen volumes. But only four of these were published—containing the writings, letters, and other documents of Bakunin up to 1861. Later, however, even those four tomes were withdrawn from circulation.

Three Bakunin volumes in German were brought out in 1921-24 by the publishers of the periodical *Der Syndikalist* in Berlin. At my suggestion they undertook to produce two more volumes, the translation and preparation of which were to have been done by Max Nettlau, who also had selected the contents of and edited the second and third German volumes. But the Nazi domination of Germany prevented the publication of the additional two.

In the Nineteen Twenties a Spanish edition of Bakunin was projected by the administrators of the Anarchist daily newspaper, *La Protesta,* in Buenos Aires. Diego Abád de Santillán was commissioned to prepare the Spanish text for it, with Nettlau as editorial consultant. Of that edition five volumes had appeared by 1929, the fifth one being *Statism and Anarchism,* with a prologue by Nettlau. But issuance of the remaining five was completely blocked by the suppression of both *La Protesta* and its book publishing business by Uriburu's dictatorial regime, established in 1930.

The fifth Spanish volume included the text of *Statism and Anarchism,* which Bakunin wrote in Russian. This book, of which, in 1878, only a few short passages had been published in French in the newspaper *L'Avant-Garde* in Chaud-de-Fonds, Switzerland, so far has not been translated into any other language but Spanish. One special virtue of the Buenos Aires edition is the illuminating historical introduction written by Nettlau for each volume. . . . Afterward, in the time of the Spanish Civil War, Santillán tried to bring out Bakunin's works in Barcelona, and a few volumes in beautiful format were printed there, but the victory of Franco killed all attempts to complete that undertaking.

No complete edition of Bakunin's works has yet been issued in any language. And none of the existing editions—except the four-volume set issued by the Soviet Russian government, contains the writings of his first revolutionary period, which are of particular interest and importance for the understanding of his spiritual evolution. Some of those writings appeared in periodicals or in pamphlet form, in German, French, Czech, Polish, Swedish, and Russian. Among these were his notable and widely discussed essay, *The Reaction in Germany, A Fragment by a Frenchman,* which, under the pseudonym Jules Elysard, he wrote for the *Deutsche Jahrbücher,* published by Arnold Ruge in Leipzig; his article about *Communism* in Fröbel's *Schweizerischer Republikaner* in Zurich, 1843; the text of Bakunin's speech on the anniversary of the Polish revolution; his anonymous articles in the *Allgemeine Oderzeitung* of Breslau; his *Appeal to the Slavs* in 1849, and other writings from that period. Later on, after his escape from Siberia, there were his *Appeal to My Russian, Polish, and All Slavic Friends,* in 1862; his essay *The People's Cause: Romanov, Pugachev, or Pestel?,* which came out the same year in London, and various others.

Bakunin was a brilliant author, though his writings lack system and organization, and he knew how to put ardor and enthusiasm and fire into his words. Most of his literary work was produced under the direct influence of immediate contemporary events, and as he took active part in many of those events, he rarely had time for leisurely and deliberate polishing of his manuscripts. That largely explains why so many of them remained incomplete, and often were mere fragments. Gustav Landauer understood this well when he said: "I have loved and admired Mikhail Bakunin, the most enchanting of all revolutionists, from the first day I knew him, for there are few dissertations written as vividly as his—perhaps that is the reason why they are as fragmentary as life itself."

Bakunin had long wished to set down his theories and opinions in a large all-inclusive volume, a desire which he repeatedly expressed in his later years. He attempted this several times, but for one reason or another he succeeded only partly, which, in view of his prodigiously active life, wherein one task was apt to be shoved into the background by ten new ones, hardly could have been avoided.

The first attempt in that direction was his work *The Revolutionary Question: Federalism, Socialism, and Anti-Theologism.* He and his more intimate friends submitted to the inquiry committee of the first Congress of the League for Peace and Freedom, held in Geneva in 1867, a resolution intended to win the delegates over to these postulates, an effort which, because of the composition of the committee, was utterly hopeless. Bakunin expounded the three points in a lengthy argument which was to be printed in Berne. But after a few sheets had gone through the press, the job was stopped and the type-forms destroyed—for reasons never explained. The manuscript (or most of it) surviving, the text was published in 1895 in the first volume of the French edition of Bakunin. That work runs to 205 pages. Its conclusion, however, is missing, the final printed paragraph ending with a broken sentence. We do not know whether that part was lost, or if Bakunin never got around to completing this manuscript. But the pages which were preserved show clearly that he intended to include in one volume the basic tenets of his theories and opinions.

A second and more ambitious attempt was made by Bakunin with his *The Knouto-Germanic Empire and the Social Revolution,* the first part of which was published in 1871. A second part, of which several pages had been set up in type, was never published in his lifetime. But numerous manuscripts left by him, of which several had been prepared with great care, as is evidenced by the changes in the text, prove that he was exceedingly anxious to complete this work.

Like most of Bakunin's literary productions, this one also was inspired by the pressing events of the hour. In that instance the compelling *motif* was the Franco-German War of 1870-71. He preceded that script in September, 1870, with a kind of introduction entitled *Letters to a Frenchman About the Present Crisis,* of which only a small part of 43 pages was put into print at that time. With those letters, which he had secretly dispatched to rebel elements in France, Bakunin tried to arouse the French people to revolutionary resistance against the German invasion, and his personal participation in the insurrection of Lyons in September, 1871, bears witness that he was willing to risk his own life in that venture. Only after the insurrectionary efforts in Lyons and Marseilles failed and he was forced to flee from France, did he find time to work on his more substantial manuscript, though even then his writing was frequently interrupted. The residue of his *Letters to a Frenchman*, which was not printed while he lived, as well as most of the manuscripts he intended for his larger volume about the Knouto-Germanic Empire, were published for the first time, in French, long after his death.

Though Bakunin never succeeded in completing this intended larger volume, that attempt to concentrate on the most important points of his socio-philosophical theories, enabled him soon thereafter to confront Mazzini with brilliant arguments, when the latter launched his attacks against the First International and the Paris Commune. In fact, the polemical writings of Bakunin against Mazzini, and particularly his *The Political Theology of Mazzini and the International* are among the best he ever wrote. From various manuscripts left by Bakunin, it is evident that he meant to write a sequel to this latter pamphlet, but only a few sketchy notes on the subject were discovered.

His last important work, *Statism and Anarchism*, appeared in 1873. It was the only extensive text that he wrote in Russian. In it he incorporated many ideas which are found in one form or another in several other manuscripts, intended for inclusion in *The Knouto-Germanic Empire and the Social Revolution*. But of *Statism and Anarchism*, which, together with an appendix, comprises 332 printed pages in that Russian edition, only the first part has been published. In 1874, when Bakunin had definitely retired from both public and secret revolutionary action, he might have found time for the materialization of his life-long ambition, but his illness and worries over the problem of obtaining the bare necessities for subsistence marred the last two years of his life, though he did not suspect that he had only a short while longer to live. Yet even in those days of dire poverty he was tormented by the desire to finish the major literary task so often interrupted. In November, 1874, he wrote in the previously quoted letter to Ogarev:

"By the way, I do not sit around idle, but I work a lot. First, I am writing my memories, and second, I am preparing myself—if my forces will allow it—to write the last words concerning my deepest convictions. And I read a lot. Now I am reading three books simultaneously: Kolb's *History of Human Culture*, John Stuart Mill's autobiography, and Schopenhauer. . . . I have had enough of teaching. Now, my old friend, in our old days we want to begin learning again. It is more amusing."

But his memoirs, which Herzen had urged him so often to put on paper were never written, except for a fragment, *Histoire de ma Vie*, in which Bakunin tells of his early youth on the estate of his parents in Pryamukhino. It was published for the first time by Max Nettlau in September, 1896, in the magazine *Societe Nouvelle* of Brussels.

Even though the bulk of Bakunin's writings remained fragmentary, nevertheless the numerous manuscripts he left, which saw the light of print only in later years, contain many original and sagaciously developed ideas on a great variety of intellectual, political, and social problems. And these largely still maintain their importance and may also inspire future generations. Among them are profound and ingenious observations on the nature of science and its relation to real life and the social mutations of history. One should keep in mind that those superb dissertations were written at a time when intellectual life generally was under the influence of the reawakened natural sciences. At that time, too, functions and tasks were often assigned to science which it could never fulfill, and thus many of its representatives were led to conclusions justifying every form of reaction.

The advocates of the so-called *social Darwinism* made the *survival of the fittest* the basic law of existence for all social organisms and rebuked anyone who dared contradict this latest *scientific revelation*. Bourgeois and even Socialist economists, carried away by their fervor to give their own treatises a scientific foundation, misjudged the worth of human labor so greatly that they pronounced it equivalent to a commodity exchangeable for any other commodity. And in their attempts to reduce to a simple formula *value for use* and *exchange value*, they forgot the most vital factor, the ethical value of human labor—the real creator of all cultural life.

Bakunin was one of the first who clearly perceived that the phenomena of social life could not be adapted to laboratory formulas, and that efforts in this direction would inevitably lead to odious tyranny. He by no means miscalculated the importance of science and he never intended to dispute the place to which it was entitled, but he advised caution against attributing too great a role to scientific knowledge and its practical results. He objected to science becoming the final arbiter of all personal life and of the social destiny of humanity, being keenly awake to the disastrous possibilities of such a course. How right he was in his forebodings, we understand better now than most of his contemporaries could know. Today, in the age of the atomic bomb, it becomes obvious how far we may be misled by the predominance of exclusively scientific thinking, when it is not influenced by any human considerations, but has in mind only immediate results without regard to final consequences, though they may lead to extermination of all human life.

Among countless fragmentary notes by Bakunin there are various sketchy memoranda, which indicate that he meant to elaborate them when time might permit. And there was never enough time for him to do this. But there also are others, developed with meticulous care and vividly expressive language; for instance, the scintillating essay which Carlo

Cafiero and Elisée Reclus published for the first time in 1882—in pamphlet form—under the title *God and the State*. Since then that pamphlet has been republished in many languages and has had the widest circulation of any of its author's writings. A logical continuation of this essay, in pages penned for *The Knouto-Germanic Empire*, was found later by Nettlau among Bakunin's manuscripts, and he incorporated it under the same title in the first volume of the French edition of the Bakunin *Oeuvres*, after publishing an extract thereof in English in James Tochetti's magazine *Liberty* in London.

Bakunin's world of ideas is revealed in a diversity of manuscripts. Therefore it was no mean task to find in this labyrinth of literary fragments the essential inner connections to form a complete picture of his theories.

It was an admirable purpose on the part of our cherished comrade Maximoff, who died all too young, to present in proper order the most important thoughts of Bakunin, and thus to give the reader a clear exposition of his doctrines in the pages which follow. This work is particularly commendable because most of Bakunin's collected writings in any language are out of print and difficult to obtain. The Russian and German editions are completely out of print, and several volumes of the French edition also are no longer obtainable. It is especially gratifying that the present edition will appear in English, because only Bakunin's *God and the State* and a few minor pamphlets have been issued in that language.

Maximoff divided his annotated selections into four parts, and arranged in logical sequence the fundamental concepts expressed by Bakunin on subjects including Religion, Science, the State, Society, the Family, Property, historical transitions, and his methods in the struggle for social liberation. As a profound connoiseur of Bakunin's socio-philosophical ideas and of his literary work, he was eminently qualified to undertake this project, to which he devoted years of painstaking labor.

Gregori Petrovich Maximoff was born on November 10, 1893, in the Russian village of Mitushino in the province of Smolensk. After completing his elementary education he was sent by his father to the theological seminary in Vladimir to study for the priesthood. Though he finished the course there, he realized that he was not fitted for that vocation, and went to St. Petersburg, where he entered the Agricultural Academy, graduating as an agronomist in 1915.

At a very early age he became acquainted with the revolutionary movement. He was tireless in his quest for new spiritual and social values, and during his college years he studied the programs and methods of all revolutionary parties in Russia, until he came across some writings of Kropotkin and Stepniak, in which he found confirmation of many of his own ideas which he had worked out by himself. And his spiritual evolution was further advanced when, later on, he discovered in a private library in the Russian interior two works of Bakunin which impressed him deeply. Of all the libertarian thinkers it was Bakunin who appealed most strongly to Maximoff. The bold language of the great rebel and the irresistible power of his words which had profoundly influenced so many of Russia's youths, now also won over Maximoff, who was to remain under his spell for the rest of his life.

Maximoff took part in the secret propaganda among the students in St. Petersburg and the peasants in the rural regions, and when finally the long awaited revolution broke out, he established contacts with the labor unions, serving in their shop councils and speaking at their meetings. It was a period of boundless hope for him and his comrades—which, however, was shattered not long after the Bolsheviks seized control of the Russian government. He joined the Red Army to fight against the counter-revolution, but when the new masters of Russia used the Army for police work and for the disarming of the people, Maximoff refused to obey orders of that kind and was condemned to death. He owed it to the solidarity and dynamic protests of the steel workers' union that his life was spared.

The last time that he was arrested was on March 8, 1921, at the time of the Kronstadt rebellion, when he was thrown into the Taganka prison in Moscow with a dozen comrades on no other charge than the holding of his Anarchist opinions. Four months later he took part in a hunger strike there which lasted ten and a half days and which had wide reverberations. That strike was ended only after French and Spanish comrades, then attending a congress of the Red Trade Union International, raised their voices against the inhumanity of the Bolshevik government, and demanded that the imprisoned men be freed. The Soviet regime acceded to this demand, on condition that the prisoners, all native Russians, be exiled from their home land.

That is why Maximoff went first to Germany, where I had the welcome opportunity to meet him and to join the circle of his friends. He remained in Berlin for about three years and then went to Paris. There he stayed for six or seven months, whereupon he emigrated to the United States.

Maximoff wrote a great deal about the human struggle through many years, during which he was at various times an editor of and contributor to libertarian newspapers and magazines in the Russian language. In Moscow he served as co-editor of *Golos Truda* (Voice of Labor), and later of its successor, *Novy Golos Truda* (New Voice of Labor.) In Berlin he became the editor of *Rabotchi Put,* (Labor's Path), a magazine published by Russian Anarcho-Syndicalists. Settling later in Chicago, he was appointed as editor of *Golos Truzhenika* (Voice of the Toiler), to which he had contributed from Europe. After that periodical ceased to exist he assumed the editorship of *Dielo Trouda-Probuzhdenie* (Labor's Cause-Awakening, a name growing out of the merger of two magazines), issued in New York City, a post he held until his death. The roster of Maximoff's writings in the periodical field makes up a long and substantial bibliography.

To his credit, too, is the writing of a book entitled *The Guillotine at Work*, a richly documented history of twenty years of terror in Soviet Russia, published in Chicago in 1940; a volume called *Constructive Anarchism*, brought out likewise in that city in 1952; a pamphlet, *Bolshevism: Promises and Reality*, an illuminating analysis of the actions of the Russian Communist Party, issued in Glasgow in 1935 and reprinted in 1937; and two pamphlets published in Russian in Germany earlier—*Instead of a Program*, which dealt with the resolutions of two conferences of Anarcho-Syndicalists in Russia, and *Why and How the Bolsheviks Deported the Anarchists from Russia*, which related the experiences of his comrades and himself in Moscow.

Maximoff died in Chicago on March 16, 1950, while yet in the prime of life, as the result of heart trouble, and was mourned by all who had the good fortune to know him.

He was not only a lucid thinker but a man of stainless character and broad human understanding. And he was a whole person, in whom clarity of thought and warmth of feeling were united in the happiest way. For him, Anarchism was not merely a concern for things to come, but the *leit-motif* of his own life; it played a part in all of his activities. He also possessed understanding for other conceptions than his own, so long as he was convinced that such beliefs were inspired by good will and deep conviction. His tolerance was as great as his comradely feeling for all who came into contact with him. He lived as an Anarchist, not because he felt some sort of duty to do so, imposed from outside, but because he could not do otherwise, for his innermost being always caused him to act as he felt and thought.

Crompond, N. Y.
July, 1952.

Mikhail Bakunin:
A Biographical Sketch

BY MAX NETTLAU

MIKHAIL ALEXANDROVITCH BAKUNIN was born on May 18, 1814 in Prya-mukhino, an estate on the banks of the Osuga, in the Novotorschok district of Tver province. His grandfather, Mikhail Vasilevitch Bakunin, state counselor and vice-president of the Chamber Collegium in the time of Catherine II, had bought the estate in 1779, and after leaving government service, had lived there with his large family. His third son, Alexander, Mikhail Bakunin's father, for unknown reasons was brought up after the age of nine in Italy, where he became a doctor of philosophy at the University of Padua.

Though Alexander was slated for diplomatic service, he took up natural sciences also, and followed in general liberal philosophical and cosmopolitan ideas which were prevalent in all educated circles in the years before the French Revolution and in the period immediately follow-ing the storming of the Bastille. But the grim realities of the years of revolution quenched his platonic liberalism. One of his two brothers was a government official and the other an officer. Alexander, however, very soon left the government service, and at the request of his parents he managed the family estate, where his unmarried sisters also lived. These sisters were wholly absorbed in religious devotions, apparently because of the death of their brother Ivan, an officer who had been killed in the Caucasian war in the Eighteen Twenties.

Not before he reached the age of forty did Alexander fall in love—and then he married a young woman of the Muraviev family, Barbara Alexandrovna, who had had numerous suitors. During the years 1811-1824 she became the mother of eleven children. The oldest were daughters, Lyubov (1811) and Barbara (1812); they were followed by Mikhail

---

NOTE: Bakunin's birth-date in this sketch is given in Russian Old Style, and Nettlau's Russian dates therein evidently are all Old Style, which in the 19th century was in each instance 12 days earlier than the equivalent date in our own calendar.

(1814), the daughters Tatiana (1815), and Alexandra (1816), and five sons, born between 1818 and 1823, and a daughter who died at the age of two. This big family lived most of the time in Pryamukhino, occasionally visiting Tver and Moscow, until studies, or, in the case of the older sisters, marriage and an early death in 1838 decreased the size of the household. The parents, particularly the father, who became blind, reached a ripe old age. He died in 1856, the mother in 1864.

Mikhail Bakunin's youth and his relationships with his family circle undoubtedly had a great influence on his development, as appears from his own short account—*The Youth of Mikhail Bakunin* published in Moscow, 1911, in *Russkaya Mysl* (Russian Thought), from the letters carefully edited by A. A. Kornilov, and other material. Although Bakunin outgrew his environment so completely, nevertheless it supplied the basis, trend, and motivation for his career, while the energy of his active life and the breadth of his aims undoubtedly sprang from his individual nature. His great capacity to absorb the best thoughts and achievements of his period was combined with ability to co-ordinate their inner meaning with his own purposeful and resolute striving toward a distant goal.

While there were no radical or realistic influences in his parents' home to shape his character, there were humanistic influences there which tended to deepen his inner life. His old father, cautiously conservative as his attitude toward young people appeared to be, was however, deeply influenced by the prevailing humane ideas of the Encyclopedists and Jean Jacques Rousseau. The piety of Mikhail's aunts was transferred to the oldest of their nieces in the form of a cult of their inner life, and a striving toward unattainable truth, which they later came to look for in philosophy rather than in religion. As Mikhail grew older, his sisters soon began to see in him a co-searcher with them for the truth, and the uncontested spiritual mentor of this younger brother. Soon he became the spiritual leader of all his brothers and sisters.

That family circle was, in fact, the most ideal group to which he ever belonged, the model for all his organizations and his conception of a free and happy life for humanity in general. The absence of any economic problems, the comfortable country life among the beauties of nature, though it was based on the serfdom of so many, formed a close bond between these sisters and brothers, created a microcosm of freedom and solidarity with intimate and intensive striving toward the inner perfection of each one of them and the full expression of his inborn talents. There was, however, always present the desire that from the fulfilment of each one, the best interests of all should be forwarded. From this soon developed Mikhail's desire to serve all humanity and to give selflessly to others everything he might gain for himself.

Here undoubtedly were planted the seeds of his life-long striving toward a world in which freedom and solidarity, Anarchism and Socialism, could be united; doctrines inseparable from spiritual freedom and from that understanding of nature, free of all superstitions—atheism. What seemed to be missing then was the desire for destruction of the existing society which later filled him so completely. He felt a holy zeal and a fervent desire to work toward that aim; this logically grew into his conviction of the necessity of destruction—revolution.

Bakunin's spiritual development was interrupted but by no means stopped when on November 25, 1828, at the age of fourteen and a half, he was sent to St. Petersburg to enter the artillery school. For several years he lived in that institution—and hated it—until he was promoted to the officer class at the end of January, 1833. Now permitted to live outside the institution, he greeted his new freedom with joy. Soon he had a temporary romance with a young cousin, and later in the summer of 1833, was deeply inspired by the poems of Venevitinov. This was followed by an attachment to an old friend of his father and a relative of his mother, the former statesman Nikolai Nazarovitch Muraviev, who gave him a practical insight into Russian political and economic affairs. A younger Muraviev, Sergei Nikolayevitch, who was five years older than Bakunin, very probably helped to foster his Russian nationalist sentiments at that time. Such proclivities, though never lacking, had found little encouragement in the cosmopolitan education in his father's home.

In August-September, 1833, Mikhail visited his family in Pryamukhino, and there found a new cause to champion—the fight for justice, the struggle of youth against the older generation, and the struggle of human freedom against authority. At first this took the form of his siding with his oldest sister in her rebellion against an unhappy marriage that was hateful to her. This was his first struggle, which he fought with all his energy; consequently the illusion of general harmony, particularly of the time-honored family happiness, was destroyed.

His military career, which had never much interested him, was cut short by a violent quarrel with a general, after which he was assigned to an artillery brigade in western Russia, beginning in 1834, before he had finished his officer's training. His military service in the provinces of Minsk and Grodno was interrupted by a summer journey to Pryamukhino. He detested that service, which was a torture to him. He was also in Vilna, and there he became somewhat acquainted with Polish society and got a glimpse of Russia's policy in Poland, through another relative, M. N. Muraviev, then governor of Grodno, who later became so notorious as Poland's hangman.

Smarting under military service and feeling terribly lonesome, Bakunin at that time (December, 1834) dreamed of dedicating himself to science and some civilian occupation after leaving the service. Only in the event of war, he decided, would he remain in the Army. He hoped to be transferred to his home territory, and at the beginning of 1835 he was sent to

Tver to buy horses. From there he went to Pryamukhino, reported sick, and greatly against the wishes of his father, obtained his discharge from the Army on December 18, 1835. The father got for him a position in the civil government service in Tver, but he refused to accept it. His fond desire was to train himself for scientific work and obtain a professorship in order to disseminate the philosophical knowledge he had gained from his studies.

In March, 1835, he became acquainted in Moscow with a young man named Stankevich, born in 1813; during the summer his friend Efremov visited the family estate, and in the fall Stankevich also came there and he and Mikhail became intimate friends. Their philosophical interest at that time was concentrated on Kant. However, Stankevich, for several years a student of German philosophy, wanted to study Kant as a basis for understanding Schelling. Connection of Bakunin with Stankevich's circle of friends, established in 1831 and 1832, was easily formed through his acquaintance with the Beer family in Moscow, whose two daughters were friends of his sisters and at whose house Stankevich and his friends often visited.

In the fall of 1835 he had conceived in Tver, with his sisters and brothers and the Beer sisters in Pryamukhino, the idea of forming his own intimate circle, united in purpose and thought, as a refuge against the outside world. This was, so to speak, the first of his secret societies, which always had an inner core of his closest friends. To detail all these relationships would be a huge task. Those who are interested in the people of the Thirties and Forties and who can read Russian could be referred to numerous volumes of correspondence, memoirs, biographies, etcetera, but for those not acquainted with this special material it would be necessary to write volumes of explanation. In general, however, it can be said, that behind the philosophical literary ideology they put forward, the real life of all these diverse young men and women went on and demanded its right to be heard. Their mutual idealistic aim formed a bond between the rich and the relatively poor, and still more did the cross currents of love affairs and passions, happy and unhappy, hopeless or fulfilled. The final solution of all these entanglements and conflicts, entered into with philosophical zeal and intensively discussed, was generally a very prosaic one, wholly outside of the realm of ideas.

Naturally Mikhail was soon in the center of these surging emotions, and took upon himself not only his own affairs but also those of his sisters. It was inevitable that his friends, Belinsky included, would fall in love with his sisters, while Mikhail remained emotionally impervious, though many a girl's heart beat faster when he was around. In addition to that, there was his personal championship of his eldest sister, already mentioned, in her luckless marriage. Because of the intimate family life of his early youth he could not brush aside such worries, but had to interfere with great energy in all these matters, which might have been settled much better by themselves without his meddling, and resulted in many conflicts and enmities. This trait remained in him to the end of his life, for he was deeply convinced of his mission as a social being.

Being interested only in the remote possibility of a professorship of philosophy in Moscow as his goal in life, Mikhail came to a sharp break with his family, and at the beginning of 1836, he left his parents' home for Moscow, to establish an independent existence in the metropolis. He expected to attain this by private tutoring in mathematics while studying at the University as a non-matriculated student. The immediate reason for the quarrel with his parents was Bakunin's persistent demand to travel abroad, in order to study at a German university, which his old father, blessed with eleven children, considered an impossible extravagance. In Moscow, after February, 1836, Mikhail was entirely absorbed in the philosophical ideas of Fichte, whose *Lectures on the Destiny of the Scholar* he translated for the *Telescope* at the request of Belinsky. Fichte's *The Way to a Blessed Life* fascinated him, and became his favorite book. With Stankevich, he read Goethe, Schiller, Jean Paul, E.T.A. Hoffman, and others. But his hope for economic independence did not materialize, neither then nor at any time in all his years.

In April, 1836, he began to lecture, but by the end of May he was back in Pryamukhino, and remained there for quite a while, as the conflict with his father had somewhat subsided, though neither of them abandoned his point of view. With his sisters, who greatly deplored his brusque attitude toward the father, he had threshed out the matter by correspondence. In the spring and summer he succeeded in converting them from their formal piety, which up to that time they had considered the greatest aim in life, to the most idealistic form of Fichteanism as propounded in *The Way to a Blessed Life*. Also he strengthened his somewhat weakened influence over them and his growing brothers.

Little information is available on the following years up to the summer of 1840, during which Bakunin transferred his theoretical allegiance from Fichte to Hegel—in fact to the most rigorous Hegelianism, with its conservative-reactionary conclusions concerning the Russia of that day. That period also was marked by his relationship with Belinsky, his conflicts with the radical and Socialist circles centering about Herzen and Ogarev, and his contact with the younger Slavophiles, particularly with Konstantin Aksakov and the older P. A. Tschaadaev (1794-1856). It was for Bakunin largely a painful period of waiting because he could not obtain from his father the means to study at a German university; neither were his other hopes fulfilled.

He was only twenty-six years old when he finally left Russia, but he had begun to fear that there he would "gradually decay mentally." Probably, however, these years were useful to him spiritually, because by continuous mental activity he learned to enhance through brilliant discussions his rather small philosophical knowledge. He now faced new impressions abroad with a more mature outlook than he had had in 1836, and thus he escaped from being entirely absorbed by any one doctrine—as had happened to him in the case of Fichte and Hegel. And fortunately the evolution of the radical philosophy and of Socialism advanced rapidly in the years after 1840, while during the years 1836 to 1840 it had been only in the stages of incubation. In this respect, also, conditions favored him.

The circumstances of his leaving Russia are clear from his well-known letter (Tver, April 20, 1840) to Herzen, who finally lent him money for the journey, and also from his passport (Tver, May 29) for the journey from St. Petersburg by way of Lubeck to Berlin on June 29, 1840.

We do not know the details of Bakunin's mental growth during his sojourn in Berlin and Dresden up to the end of 1842, but in the second half of this period he did make continuous progress toward becoming a conscious revolutionary. Three documents serve as milestones of this mental evolution: Bakunin's preface to Hegel's *Lectures to High School Students*, published in the *Moskovskii Nablyudatel*, vol 16, 1838, edited by Belinsky: the article *On Philosophy* in *Otechestvennyia Zapiski*, St. Petersburg, 1849, vol. 9, section 2, the second part of which was never published; and *Reaction in Germany—A Fragment by a Frenchman* signed Jules Elysard, in the *Deutsche Jahrbücher für Wissenschaft und Kunst*, Leipzig, October 17-21, 1842. It is surprising to find in the first of these two publications that such a clear mind could still remain so profoundly influenced by empty dogmas, which Bakunin took as absolute truth, without any regard to reality. Yet the famous article in the *Deutsche Jahrbücher*, in spite of its philosophical verbiage, was a clarion call for revolution in the widest sense, including social revolution. It ended with the words: "Let us have confidence in the eternal spirit which destroys and annihilates only because it is the unfathomable and eternally creative source of life. The urge of destruction is at the same time a creative urge."

It is noteworthy also that Bakunin, after three university semesters in Berlin, preferred to move to Dresden in the spring of 1842, to enjoy the company of Arnold Ruge, who at that time was the center of the radical Hegelians, and not to prepare for a Moscow professorship. Losing interest in that, his chief concern now was awaiting the Revolution. At that time many forces were working toward the Revolution, which indeed was not far distant, as was proved in 1848. Only then did the Western world unfold to him—a world which up to that time he had viewed with disdain, partly because of his Russian nationalist point of view, which still clung to him, and partly because of the lofty philosophical knowledge he imagined he had. Socialism, as it was developing at that time in France, was introduced to the German public for the first time through the well-known book of Dr. Lorenz Stein. This book did not offer anything new, but gave a sizeable survey of many socialistic trends and the reasoning behind them; and in 1842 it introduced Bakunin, as he himself pointed out, to this subject, which fascinated him.

In Berlin in 1840, he saw his sister Barbara, who had returned from the death-bed of Stankevich in Italy. In Berlin and Dresden his younger brother and Ivan Turgeniev were his closest friends. By now his connection with Russia was finally severed and he became a true exile, fully accepting his status. The Russian government became aware of his radical evolution and demanded his return to Russia. But Bakunin had no intention of submitting, and in January, 1843, he took the decisive step of going to Zurich with Georg Herwegh, the most famous poet of the time. Herwegh returned to Zurich, then the center of literary, political, and revolutionary propaganda for Germany, and to which, that spring, Wilhelm Weitling, the German Communist, transferred his activity from French Switzerland.

During his Zurich sojourn from January 16 to the beginning of June, Bakunin, having closely observed the political activities there, lost all his republican political illusions, if he still had any. Through his personal relations with Weitling, he became acquainted with the Communist ideology, which he considered a general revolutionary factor, but which, however, never succeeded in captivating him. From that time up to 1848, he had friendly relations with German Communists in Switzerland and in Paris, and occasionally he called himself a Communist. In a letter to Reinhold Solger, dated October, 1844, and in some other letters to Solger, August Becker, and the wife of Professor Vogt, he expressed these ideas up to 1847.

Opinions voiced by Bakunin at that time were published in the *Deutsch-Französische Jahrbücher* (Paris, 1844) under the title B. to R. (Bakunin to Ruge), dated Peter Island in the Bieler Lake, May, 1843, and several articles entitled *Der Communismus* in the *Schweitzerische Republikaner*, (Zurich, June 2, 6 and 13, 1843), signed XXX. I believe also that still another article, in 1843, generally overlooked, was written by Bakunin. Closer scrutiny of the articles would show that he was sympathetic and hopefully, though not uncritically, inclined toward the expressions of Socialism then current. Those movements championed a good cause, had a very lofty goal, but they could not satisfy his aspirations for ideas and systems that would really liberate mankind. He felt instinctively the absence of freedom in these systems, and therefore he hesitated to accept completely any of the ideas embodied in them.

Shortly before the arrest of Weitling, Bakunin went to western Switzerland and lived in Geneva, Lausanne, and also in Nyon. He tramped on foot over the Alps to Berne, where he remained during the winter of 1844 until February. These travels and sojourns were influenced by his personal relations: In Zurich he knew August Follen, the brother of Professor Vogt's wife, who lived in Berne; in Dresden he knew Madame Pescantini, a German-Russian from Riga, who lived with her husband, an Italian emigré, in Promenthoux near Nyon. His lifelong friend, the musician Adolf Reichel, from East Prussia, whom he had met in Dresden, also had come to Geneva, and together with him and the German Communist, August Becker, he had crossed the Alps on foot. Reichel remained with him in Berne in order to accompany him in February, 1844, to Brussels. Bakunin's long friendship with the sons of the Vogt family began at that time. The youngest Vogt, Adolf, and Adolf Reichel were the only ones who, thirty-three years later, stood at Bakunin's bier in Berne.

On July 21, 1843, the Swiss police issued an official report, signed by State Counselor Bluntschli, quoting many letters of Weitling's in which Bakunin's name was mentioned repeatedly. This put the Russian police into motion, and in February, 1844, the Moscow ambassador in Berne ordered Bakunin to return to Russia immediately. But Mikhail preferred to move to Brussels. There he saw the first Polish emigrés, and as he knew everywhere how to meet the most important men in radical and revolutionary movements, who in turn considered him a highly interesting acquaintance, he became friendly with old Joachim Lelewel, one of the most charming Poles of that period. Thus he got acquainted with the Polish aspirations in their most exalted, but also in their most determined and intransigent ideas—the demand for the "historical Poland" of 1772, which included Lithuania, Little Russia, and White Russia.

As a Russian, but also as a democrat and internationalist, Bakunin maintained, on the contrary, the right to autonomy and independence for the non-Polish territories within these "historic" frontiers. Thus, in spite of all his sympathy for the Poles and all his efforts to bring about co-operation, it inevitably followed that the Poles always considered him an unwelcome and disturbing element in their plans and never reciprocated his sincere attempts toward solidarity with them. Since the Poles as well as Bakunin saw in each other a revolutionary factor of some real value, the subject was rarely discussed frankly, and all attempts at mutual action were destined to failure. To this was added the fact that the question of liberation of the peasants and the distribution of land naturally separated Bakunin from the powerful aristocratic Polish party, as did also their extreme clericalism.

After a short visit to Paris in 1844, Mikhail persuaded his friend Reichel to come and live with him in Paris, and they stayed there until 1847. Bakunin endeavored to get in contact with the German radicals who lived there, particularly with the circle around the weekly *Vorwaerts*, through which he got acquainted with Marx and Engels. Many disagreeable quarrels ensued between Ruge, Marx, and Herwegh, and lasted up to the time when the German circle was broken up by expulsion of its members and the suspension of the publication. Thereafter Bakunin did not take any sustained interest in the German movement, but he remained in friendly relations with Herwegh and his wife, with Karl Vogt, a few German Communists, and in general, with the Swiss acquaintances he had made in 1843-44.

He became acquainted with French Socialists and political and literary personalities of all shades of opinion, without getting very close to any of them, with the exception of Proudhon, whose ideas and personality attracted him, and who in turn showed interest in Bakunin. He also met Russians—the Dekabrist Nikolai Turgeniev, as well as many Russian visitors to Paris—Poles, Italians, and others. It was a period in which a great many advanced ideas emerged, without, however, any one idea predominating. While the bourgeois system seemed to be nearing its full development unchallenged, Bakunin sensed that, underneath, the ferment of the coming revolution was at work. "We arrived," Bakunin said in 1876, according to a French Socialist, "at the firm belief that we were witnessing the last days of the old civilization, and that the age of equality would soon begin. Very few could resist this highly charged emotional atmosphere in Paris; two months on the boulevards was usually long enough to change a liberal into a Socialist."

In spite of this active and interesting life during the years 1845, 1846, and 1847, Bakunin was not happy, because he felt more isolated than any of the others. Neither did he have a clear conception of the future. To be more exact, these various Socialist trends were all narrowly sectarian, each one opposed to the others; because they had no right of assembly nor freedom for public activity, their adherents were limited to an artificial life through books, magazines, and small groups. It is true that Bakunin did not join any of the groups, but to conclude from this fact that at that time he was no Socialist would be, in my opinion, absolutely wrong. He did not find *his* conception of Socialism in any of the sects then existing; indeed, he probably had not clearly formulated *his own* ideas, as he had no practical incentive to do so. It is impossible to imagine him as a follower of a certain trend or sect—such as being a Fourierist, Cabetist, or Marxist. The only man from whom he could derive part of *his* Socialism then was Proudhon.

One of Bakunin's Italian comrades, at the end of the Sixties, stated that Bakunin had told him that, when reading Proudhon's book, it had suddenly flashed upon him: "This is the right thing!" That is how it must have happened. Only Proudhon had at that time the idea of attaining full freedom, of really abolishing the State, without rebuilding it in a new form. This established a spiritual bond between the two men, though they differed on certain details. That Bakunin understood the basic ideas of Anarchism, which he approved, is shown by a few passages in his *Intimate Letters to Herwegh*. By pure accident he had no opportunity to express them publicly. The voice he had raised in 1842 and 1843 was now silenced (except in Slavonic affairs) and his work on Feuerbach, whose ideas he wanted to publish in French, was not completed or was lost.

In December, 1844, Tsar Nikolai I issued, at the proposal of the Senate, a decree depriving Bakunin of all his civil and nobility rights, confiscating his property in Russia and condemning him to lifelong exile in Siberia should he ever be caught on Russian soil. He wrote a long letter on this subject to the Paris *Réforme* (January 27, 1845) expressing his first free opinion on Russia and foreshadowing his future writings in many respects. His first statement on Poland was made in his letter to *Le Constitutionel* (March 19, 1846) on the occasion of Russian persecution of Polish Catholics.

Soon afterward he tried (as he also tells in his *Confession* of 1851) to enter into conspirative relations with the Polish Democratic Central Committee, the headquarters of which was in Versailles. His aim was revolution in Russia, a republican federation of all Slavic countries, and establishment of a united and indivisible Slavic republic, administered federatively for interior affairs and centralized politically for foreign affairs. But nothing came out of these deliberations, mainly because he could not offer the Poles anything except his good intentions. Before that, after the appearance of his article in *La Réforme*, the Polish aristocrats, such as Prince Adam Czartoryski, as well as the democratic Poles, welcomed him, and the Polish classical poet, Adam Mickiewicz, tried to attract him into his mystical-federalist circle, which Bakunin, however, declined to enter. Again in 1846 young refugee Poles from Cracow approached him, and it was this group which invited him to speak at the meeting of November 29, 1847, in commemoration of the Polish insurrection of 1830.

A few months before, in 1847, Bakunin again met with Herzen, Belinsky, and other Russian friends in Paris, and though that reunion was amicable, those friends did not respond to his plea that conspiratory action be planned for a revolutionary movement in Russia. There is no evidence that he knew of the efforts of the group of Petrashevsky and Speshnev at that time. Thus he could not help knowing or feeling that he was quite alone so far as Russian problems were concerned.

On November 29 he made his famous speech in Paris in favor of a revolutionary conciliation between Poles and Russians. Thereupon, at the request of the Russian ambassador, he was expelled from France, and on December 19, he went to Brussels, where he met many Poles as well as the Communist circle of Karl Marx, whom he greatly disliked. On February 14, 1848, he spoke again at a meeting called by Lelewel to form brotherly tries between Polish and Russian democrats. According to Bakunin's *Confession* he also spoke of the great future of the Slavs, destined to rejuvenate the Western world, of the break-up of Austria, etcetera. The full text of that speech was never published.

The Russian Embassy, headed by Count Kisselev, also tried to ruin his reputation by setting rumors afloat that he actually was a Russian agent, who had exceeded his orders. This slander was passed on to the French government by Polish intermediaries. Bakunin answered in an open letter of February 7, 1848, to Count Duchatel, then Minister of Interior, but after the February revolution, the same source spread this calumny in democratic circles and cast a shadow of doubt over all the rest of Bakunin's life, beginning with 1848-49, the last year of his activity at that time.

When the longed-for revolution finally came, Bakunin's joy knew no bounds. Even his crestfallen *Confession* of 1851 contained an enthusiastic description of the life and activities of the people of Paris, in which he took part up to April, 1848. *La Réforme* of March 13 carried a lengthy article by him, in which his ideas were summarized. But what grieved him most was that he saw no sign of an approaching Russian revolution, to accomplish which he felt driven to give his utmost energies. Russian power was in the service of the counter-revolution, and in fact it did intervene in Hungary in 1849, to suppress the revolution there. In 1848 a clash between the rebelling countries of Europe and the Russia of Tsar Nikolai I appeared probable, and the Poles worked toward this goal. Bakunin wanted to prevent that conflict, and the idea of a Slavic federation seemed to him the proper means.

Such a federation was intended to unite all Slavs, Poles, and Russians as well, under the battle-cry of liberating the Slavs living under the rule of Prussia, Austro-Hungary, and Turkey. Bakunin had no resources for this propaganda, so he approached Flocon, Louis Blanc, and Albert and Ledru Rollin, who reluctantly lent him 2,000 francs. For everything else he was dependent on the Poles. He went to Germany, where the slander launched by the Russian Embassy followed him, as did also the lie that he was preparing an attempt on the life of the Tsar. This brought about another expulsion. These slanders likewise affected his trial in Saxony (1849-50), and in 1851 were to help determine his fate in Russia.

His journey took him through Baden to Frankfort and Cologne, where he made the final break with Marx on account of Herwegh. From there he went to Berlin, where the police stopped him from traveling on to Posen; from Berlin he went to Leipzig and Breslau, where he again met many Poles; then he continued on to the Slav Congress in Prague, in which he actively participated. This congress was followed by the bloody but abortive Whitsun-week insurrection in June, 1848, which Bakunin wanted to promote and intensify. His return to Breslau and to Berlin was followed by his expulsion from Prussia and Saxony, but finally in the fall and winter he found a pleasant and safe refuge in Koethen, Anhalt State, at that time an oasis of freedom in Germany, where certain Cabinet ministers of that state, old friends of Max Stirner and his comrades, were his table companions in the local Rathskeller.

Later, when the conspiracy became more active, Bakunin returned to Leipzig. His life in the "underground" there was interrupted by a still more secret journey to Prague, and finally he went to Dresden to be nearer to Bohemia. While he was there the May revolution of 1849 broke out. He gave all his energy to it, and shared the fate of other leaders of the revolution, when, after several sleepless nights, totally exhausted, he was arrested in Chemnitz (Saxony) on the night of May 9. This put an end to his activities for many years to come.

Bakunin's ideas in that period can be ascertained from a few documents of the Prague Slav Congress, particularly from the *Charter of a New Slavic Policy* and from the pamphlet *Appeal to the Slavs* published in the fall of 1848, and other statements of that time and later. The most extensive account of his plans is set down in his *Confession* of 1851. To this can be added a few intimate letters, particularly to Herwegh, and his long defense plea at the trial in Saxony. I am familiar only with extracts of this plea contained in a letter to his lawyer, but the whole plea as well as the statements in the preliminary questioning are available for publication.

From these sources we see how he, who in the months immediately following February 24, certainly was inspired by the purest revolutionary spirit, gradually became more and more imbued with nationalist ideas, until, after the events in Prague and Breslau, he indulged in the most commonplace expressions of hate against everything German. This made him feel impelled, as he says in his *Confession* to Nikolai I, to write to the Tsar asking forgiveness for his sins and imploring him to put himself at the head of the Slavs as their savior and father, and to carry the banner of Slavdom into Western Europe.

His good common sense prevented him, however, from finishing this letter, and he destroyed it. Nothing compelled him to record this fact, which, by the way, is not so surprising, since nationalism unites men of all ideologies, and the revolutionist and the Tsar stood here on common ground.

Autumn in 1848 brought about a change in Bakunin's attitude. He came out in favor of common struggles of all peoples—Slavs, Magyars, and Germans—against the oppressors, their governments. By organizing and heading Czech and German secret societies to instigate a revolutionary movement in Bohemia, he made extraordinary efforts to help German democracy which, at that time, was preparing for the struggles of 1849. But only the German democrats in Saxony started a revolt (in May, 1849), while the premature Czech conspiracy was nipped in the bud by many arrests, ending in a lengthy trial and cruel sentences to long imprisonment of many young Czechs and Germans in Bohemia. In general, it can be said, however, that Bakunin's activity in 1848 lost much of its effectiveness because of its close relation to nationalism. It was therefore fortunate for the clarifying of his ideas that the May revolution in Dresden offered him such a welcome opportunity for objective revolutionary activity unmarred by nationalism.

Next, Bakunin spent one year in Saxon prisons in Dresden and in the fortress of Koenigstein, up to June 13, 1850, when a death sentence against him was commuted to imprisonment for life. That his spirit was unbroken appears in his letters from the fortress to Adolf and Matilde Reichel. He was then extradited to Austria, where for one year he was chained in his cell and had to submit to endless questioning in Prague and Olmutz till 1851—probably the grimmest experience of his life.

This was followed by a new condemnation to death with immediate commutation of the sentence—but extradition to Russia. Not knowing what to expect, Bakunin viewed his fate with dread, but was pleasantly surprised when he soon found himself treated relatively well as a state prisoner of importance, and also considered as such in the Peter-and-Paul fortress in St. Petersburg.

After two months, around August, 1851, the Tsar sent Count Orlov to see Bakunin in the fortress and to ask for a confession from him. Bakunin really did write this, as it became known in 1921. The document did not change his situation, and Nikolai's successor, Alexander II, pointed out quite correctly that he did not see any repentance in that confession. Opinions may vary concerning this document, but it contained nothing that would have endangered any person or compromised any cause, embodying, rather, details interesting to a biographer. Anything in it which may appear unsavory is the result of the nationalist psychosis that influenced Bakunin at the time, and from which few are entirely free.

Solitary confinement in the Peter-and-Paul fortress and later, during the Crimean war, in Schlüsselburg, was to him a spiritual torment, despite the fact that his manner of life and his treatment were tolerable. Life in prison caused his body to lose its youthfulness and to assume the misshapen form, which later on was one of the causes of his early death. I have no knowledge of his letters from prison, except of the one addressed to Alexander II in 1857, but even if I knew them I would not consider myself entitled to pronounce any judgement. He was near to committing suicide, when his family finally succeeded in having him sent to Siberia, after Tsar Alexander II had extorted from him the letter of February 27, 1857 which gave such a moving description of the effects of solitary confinement.

Bakunin was allowed to spend a day in Pryamukhino where he saw his mother for the last time and met again his surviving sisters and brothers after the seventeen-year separation since 1840. He was then taken to Tomsk in Western Siberia, where, within the usual limitations, he could move about freely.

He adapted himself quite well to Siberian conditions by getting interested in them and in the Russian expansion toward Eastern Siberia, down the Amur toward the sea. Envisaging a future Siberian independence, he encouraged such ideas among young men like the explorer Potanin, who later, in 1865, had to stand trial in Omsk with other youthful Siberians for separatist attempts. Bakunin became acquainted with many exiled Poles, whom he wanted to impress with the necessity of a conciliation between Poles and Russians.

While he was giving French lessons to some members of the Polish family Kwiatkowski, he came to know one of the daughters, Antonia, whom he married in 1858. There are memoirs of his relations with the Dekabrists and the followers of Petrashevsky (the latter by Emanuel Toll), though later on sharp differences arose between Petrashevsky and Bakunin. Nikolai Muraviev-Amurski, Governor-General of Eastern Siberia, also a relative of Mikhail's mother, came to see him. In 1833 he had known both Muraviev and his father well. Finally Bakunin's wish to be transferred to Eastern Siberia was granted and in 1859 he arrived in Irkutsk.

For a while that year he traveled for a business concern in the Far East, but this occupation was only temporary, because he expected a full pardon and the right to return to Russia, though if that hope failed, he dreamed of a not too difficult escape. He realized that the Governor-General was a brutal despot, but their nationalism and their hatred of the Germans united them to such a degree that Bakunin condoned Muraviev's bad characteristics. The correspondence which he resumed in 1860 with Alexander Herzen, whose periodical *Kolokol* [The Bell] was then at the peak of its influence, contains hymns of praise for Muraviev. This may be explained by Bakunin's increasing nationalist psychosis, induced and nourished by the expansionist ideas of the officials and exploiters who surrounded him in Siberia, causing him to overlook the plight of their victims.

Finally Muraviev left Siberia without being able to do anything for Bakunin, and that relieved him of any compunction which might have restrained him from escaping while a relative was Governor. He left Irkutsk on June 18, 1861, sailed down the Amur River, succeeded in boarding an American ship, and, after passing through several Japanese ports, San Francisco, Panama, and New York, he arrived in London on December 27 and went straight to the home of Herzen and Ogarev, who received him like a brother. In Yokohama he had met up with a fellow-fighter of the Dresden May revolt, and in the United States he talked with comrades of the 1848 revolution.

From San Francisco he had written to Herzen that he would continue his efforts, begun in that year, toward Slavic federalism. In short, from the first hour of his freedom he was ready to resume with unimpaired energy his activity, interrupted in 1849, aiming at a Russian peasant revolution, Slavic national wars for independence, and Slavic federation. In the Italy of 1859 and in the actions of Garibaldi he recognized the way, perceiving many symptoms of the rising tide toward liberty, and, as in 1848, Bakunin again was ready to do his share. His Socialism, however, was deeply buried beneath his nationalist psychosis.

That appears still more evident from his first "open letter" entitled *To Russian, Polish, and all Slavic Friends,* published on February 15, 1862; from the pamphlet *The People's Cause: Romanov, Pugachev, or Pestel?,* issued in London in 1863, and from shorter articles; from Herzen's account in his *Posthumous Writings;* and from Bakunin's own letters, some of which appeared in the St. Petersburg periodical *Byloe* (The Past).

There were important and impressive open movements in Russia (Tchernishevsky's and the Youth movement); secret organizations of unknown and constantly shifting scope, such as *Zemlya y Volya* (Land and Freedom), and the great liberal movement headed by Herzen and Ogarev; the Zemstvos, in which several brothers of Bakunin distinguished themselves in Tver, etcetera. Here also may be mentioned the sectarian movement of Ogarev and Kelsiev, the revolutionary possibilities of which were so extremely overrated. These movements, which needed many years to reach their full development, were suddenly followed or joined by the Polish movement in the violent form of an insurrection, which complicated the situation considerably. Only Bakunin and a Russian military organization [headed by a sympathetic officer from Warsaw named Potebnya] were willing to co-operate sincerely with the Poles. At the same time, however, the old dissensions between Bakunin and the Poles continued, and there were for example, bitter polemics with Mieroslawski.

Though this situation, in 1862 and 1863, offered innumerable opportunities for action by Bakunin, embroilments repeatedly ensued, and led more to confusion than to solutions. Thus, in spite of his good intentions, his activities produced only meager results. He conspired in all directions; had negotiations in Paris; and on February 21, 1863, he went via Hamburg and Copenhagen to Stockholm, where he remained until autumn, and where, after many vicissitudes, he was reunited with his wife, who had found her way out of Siberia. He was not connected with the Polish incursion of Lapinski, whom he met in Malmo, but he would have been willing to go to Russia, if he had sensed the beginning of any revolutionary movement there. This element lacking, he did his best to influence public opinion in Sweden about events in Finland. His speeches and articles in the large dailies created a sensation, and he was fairly lionized, but was unable to get armed assistance from the Poles.

Bakunin never abandoned his attitude in public, but he had such bad experiences with many personalities in the Polish movement and with the elusive Russian secret organizations, that in the fall of 1863 he withdrew entirely from Slavic national movements, and probably reconsidered the situation thoroughly. It also became apparent to him that further work with Herzen and Ogarev in London would be impossible. Bonapartist

France was out of the question for a permanent sojourn, but there was one country where he would be able to remain—Italy—which had an active radical party. At the end of 1863 he left London, and by slow stages, crossing Belgium, France, and Switzerland, he reached Italy. From that time onward he began anew to participate in the international revolutionary movement.

I do not know whether, during that journey, in the course of which he met Proudhon, Elie and Elisée Reclus, Vogt, Garibaldi, and other old and new friends, he intended to make direct connection with those men, or if he went just for the purpose of meeting old friends and gathering information. His new place of residence was Florence, where he stayed through the first half of 1864. In August he went to London and Sweden, and in November, going back to London and then to Brussels and Paris, he returned to Florence. While on those travels, the purpose of which is not quite clear, he was visited by Marx in London, and in Paris saw Proudhon for the last time. The summer of 1865 found him in Sorrento, and till August, 1867, he dwelt in Naples and vicinity. Bakunin enjoyed his sojourn in Italy, particularly the simple, natural life of the people, and from the fall of 1869 until his death seven years later he lived in small towns in the Swiss canton of Ticino.

He saw the defeat of the Polish revolution of 1863, which was led by the feudal lords, but he hoped to live to see a peasant upheaval and a new European revolution in the offing. Inasmuch as he maintained contacts with the leading men in the militant parties and their following among young people, especially in Italy, he undoubtedly became aware of two great obstacles: The fact that the national movements were inextricably blended with the designs of the States—Napoleon III in particular was behind these—and that the ideologies of the young people were hopelessly circumscribed by religious ideas and by the pseudo-Socialism of Mazzini. Therefore Bakunin felt compelled to assemble and educate a group of clear-thinking revolutionists freed from the fetters of religion and religious philosophy, and opposed to the idea of the State, and to establish among them close contacts which would facilitate international activities.

He tried to use the Free Mason movement for that purpose, and explained his ideas with great lucidity to Italian lodges, but failed to win them over. He then worked alone and did succeed in forming an intimate circle of able persons from various countries—a secret society, so to speak, which may be designated as the *Fraternité Internationale*. Through personal contact and extensive correspondence he worked tirelessly to clarify the ideas of his comrades, and to free them from a variety of nationalist proconceptions. Most of them made valuable contributions to the international Socialist movement in later years.

Through this activity, begun in Florence—perhaps during his first visit to that city—or even earlier in London, Bakunin systematized his anti-religious, atheist, anti-State, and Anarchist *Weltanschaung*, and of course also formulated his Socialist, national, and federalist ideas. This was done in comprehensive programs and program outlines for closely knit groups; in elaborate expositions, which he probably wrote first for the Free Masons; in occasional articles, and in his careful and widespread correspondence. Represented in these are all the ideas with which he was equipped when he joined the First International in 1868. The labor movement as such was given the least consideration because in 1864 it had hardly existed. Bakunin had no personal contact with the insignificant labor movement in London in 1862-63, and in Italy there was no such movement at all. The International, when Marx spoke to him about it in 1864, was then in its initial stage, and the followers of Proudhon in Paris were not a revolutionary element for action in Bakunin's sense. These circumstances explain why he acted alone and created by himself an international revolutionary fighting group.

When later, in September, 1867, European democrats at their Geneva Congress formed the League for Peace and Freedom, Bakunin considered this international organization an appropriate medium within which he and his friends in the *Fraternité* could forward and spread their ideas. In 1868 he submitted his thoughts to this effect to the Geneva and Berne Congresses, outlining them in his *Federalism, Socialism, and Antitheologism*. He also was notably active in the organizing committee of the League in 1867-68, while living in Vevey and Clarens. But the bourgeois Socialists proved deaf to Socialist ideas, whereupon Bakunin and some of his friends left the League, joined the [Geneva section of the] International, and founded the Alliance of Socialist Democracy, within which of course, the old secret group of the *Fraternité Internationale* would continue to exist.

Under these conditions, which came about quite by themselves, but the intrinsic nature of which remained unknown and incomprehensible to all outsiders—including Marx—Bakunin joined the labor movement of the period represented by the International. This movement developed after 1864, principally in its theories, and spread rather slowly. Only after 1868 did it show a more pronounced revolutionary spirit, as manifested by strikes and in the Congress of Brussels. Thus the time was most opportune, and between the end of 1868 and the summer of 1869 the Socialist movement in Geneva was revived, and temporarily wrested from the hands of the local politicians.

The Swiss Jura Federation was won for the anti-authoritarian Socialist concepts, revolutionary Socialism in France was considerably invigorated, particularly in Lyons and Marseilles, the International in Spain was founded and from the very beginning inspired by Anarchist ideas, the Italian International was built on the foundation laid many years before, and those ideas also had certain influence in Russia. In various articles by

Bakunin in *Egalité* of Geneva his propaganda presented to the workers the most comprehensive Socialist thought and aims with marvelous clarity and objectivity.

At the same time he worked at selecting, educating, and co-ordinating elements capable of really revolutionary initiative. It was through Bakunin that the International was revived and received its real incentive. Though the International of Belgium and Paris showed some vigor, it never rose above mediocrity. Bakunin and his friends were the first to arouse it, and the Paris Commune did the rest.

There is a wealth of documentary material and reminiscences about Bakunin's international activity in the period from the fall of 1868 to the summer of 1874. The versatility and intensity of his work can be recognized in the daily notes he wrote during two of those years, and in numerous manuscripts, publication of which began in 1895. Among his outstanding efforts were those in the sections of the *Alliance* and in the editorial office of *Egalité*, his propaganda in the Jura region of Switzerland in the spring of 1869, in the last period of the Paris Commune in 1871, and particularly during the preparation of a Commune revolt in Besancon, in order to come to the rescue of the Paris Commune.

Too, there were his attempts to initiate in the Southwest and South of France—during the Franco-Prussian War of 1871—a social-revolutionary action which would refuse to recognize the State, but would promote the creation of free Communes, to be seconded by similar movements in Spain and Italy to help that in France. These were ambitious plans for which Bakunin risked his life to no purpose in Lyons in September of that year, though he succeeded in organizing the demonstration of September 29. But after further attempts in Marseilles he had to return to Locarno.

The Russian episode of 1869-70 in connection with Nechayev makes a notable chapter in itself, which, however, should not be judged without full knowledge of the documentary material involved. More satisfactory are the reports on Bakunin's Russian propaganda in Zurich in 1872-73, the famous summer of 1872 which saw him in Zurich and in the Jura region for a longer period, and the reports on the Russian printing plants of his friends in Zurich and London, which published several important works of his, among them *Statism and Anarchism*, which, unfortunately, like so many of his writings, was never completed.

When Mazzini, the eternal enemy of Socialism, denounced the Paris Commune, Bakunin came to its defense and to that of the International in a brilliant pamphlet issued in Milan. This led many young Italians to communicate with him and to form sections of the International, which had an inner revolutionary core of militant comrades closely connected with Bakunin. That was the *Alliance Revolutionaire Socialiste*, the very soul of the Italian International. The Spanish International, the *Alianza*, had a similar core; Bakunin's intimate friend and comrade, Fanelli, had organized it in 1868 during a journey to Barcelona and Madrid, arranged by Bakunin's circle. In 1870 and again in the summer of 1873 Bakunin was on the point of going to Spain, where he would have found in Barcelona his most convinced and reliable followers, but circumstances prevented him from going there. Finally, in August, 1874, he went to Italy, where preparations for an insurrectional movement were under way in many places. He was in Bologna on the night of the *Prati di Caprara,* and after the defeat of that movement he fled to Switzerland, which was his last revolutionary peregrination.

It is well known that these activities, which aimed at the spreading and revolutionary realization of the ideas of collective Anarchism—and thus of anti-authoritarian Socialism—were bitterly resented and hated by Karl Marx and his followers. They wanted to found Social-Democratic labor movements, or if the opportunity arose—a situation which, however, they themselves did not intend to bring about by revolutionary action—to seize power as dictators of the Revolution and to establish an authoritarian people's State. They hated Bakunin because his and all other liberal-revolutionary activities opposed and thwarted these objectives. This bitter hatred, which often assumed most repulsive forms, because of their complete ignorance of Bakunin's real objectives and actions (as appears from the published correspondence between Marx and Engels), expressed itself by the spreading of slander as well as by administrative chicanery and arbitrary decisions in the International, the executive committee of which in London was dominated by Marx.

A local political party in Geneva and several henchmen such as Nicholas Utin and Paul Lafargue helped Marx in this job. These intrigues reached their peak at the Hague Congress of the International (September, 1872), where, through a majority obtained by tricks and wily maneuvers, Bakunin was expelled from the International, and, in addition, was slandered at the instigation of Marx. All those facts have been investigated fully and so thoroughly explained that the final judgement, now entirely possible, is certainly a blot on the memory of Marx and Engels.

These arbitrary dictatorial tactics at the London Conference of 1871 and the Hague Congress of 1872, which were aimed at altering completely the spirit of the International, resulted in a closer union of the anti-authoritarian sections and federations. Beginning with the answer to the Jura circular of November, 1871, this unity was emphasized by a declaration of the minority of the Hague Congress, and the Congress of St. Imier, Switzerland (September, 1872), and brought about the reorganization of the International at the Geneva Congress of 1873, while the organization of the authoritarian remnant of the International collapsed miserably. Bakunin lived to see this victory of the libertarian trend, the effects of which, however, were thwarted temporarily by the general reaction of the Seventies, following the defeat of the Commune of Paris. Nevertheless this victory led directly to the spiritual consolidation of all freedom-loving revolutionary elements, to whom the future belongs.

After his return from exile, Bakunin's personal situation, owing to some special circumstances, was somewhat better up to 1868, but later he again was beset by poverty and worries, which were mitigated only in 1872 to 1874 by the Cafiero episode. But after this he felt even more keenly his destitution and privation, from which death alone finally relieved him. His health, impaired by his various imprisonments, had broken down, causing him much suffering and bringing his life to an end at the age of not quite sixty-two. Nevertheless, up to his last years, which he spent in Lugano, he preserved the lucidity of his spirit, and all his concepts, desires, and hopes. In June, 1876, he went, hopelessly ill, to Berne and died there on July 1, attended by the friend of his youth, Professor Vogt, who was his physician, and by the musician, Adolf Reichel. His ideas remain fresh and will live forever.

The Political Philosophy of Bakunin

SCIENTIFIC ANARCHISM

PART I

Philosophy

The World-Outlook

Nature Is Rational Necessity. This is not the place to enter into philosophical speculations on the nature of Being. Yet, since I have to use this word *Nature* frequently, it is necessary to make my meaning clearly understood.

I could say that Nature is the sum of all things that have real existence. This, however, would give an utterly lifeless concept of Nature, which, on the contrary, appears to us as being all life and movement. For that matter, what is the sum of things? Things that exist today will not exist tomorrow. Tomorrow they will not pass away but will be entirely transformed. Therefore I shall find myself much nearer to the truth *if* I say: Nature is the sum of actual transformations of things that are and will ceaselessly be produced within its womb. In order to render more precise the idea of this sum or totality, I shall lay down the following proposition as a basic premise:

Whatever exists, all the beings which constitute the undefined totality of the Universe, all things existing in the world, whatever their particular nature may be in respect to quality or quantity—the most diverse and the most similar things, great or small, close together or far apart—necessarily and unconsciously exercise upon one another, whether directly or indirectly, perpetual action and reaction. All this boundless multitude of particular actions and reactions, combined in one general movement, produces and constitutes what we call Life, Solidarity, Universal Causality, Nature. Call it, if you find it amusing, God, the Absolute—it really does not matter —provided you do not attribute to the word God a meaning different from the one we have just established: the universal, natural, necessary, and real, but in no way predetermined, preconceived, or foreknown combination of the infinity of particular actions and reactions which all things having real existence incessantly exercise upon one another. Thus defined, this Universal Solidarity, Nature viewed as an infinite universe, is imposed upon our mind as a rational necessity. . . .[1]

Universal Causality and Creative Dynamics. It stands to reason that this Universal Solidarity cannot have the character of an absolute first cause; on the contrary, it is merely the result produced by the simul-

---

NOTE: The side-heads set in black-faced type at the beginning of paragraphs are Maximoff's annotations, while the light-faced text is Bakunin's.

taneous action of particular causes, the totality of which constitutes universal causality. It creates and will always be created anew; it is the combined unity, everlastingly created by the infinite totality of the ceaseless transformations of all existing things; and at the same time it is the creator of those very things; each point acts upon the Whole (here the Universe is the resultant product); and the Whole acts upon every point (here the Universe is the Creator).

The Creator of the Universe. Having laid down this definition, I can say, without fear of being ambiguous, that Universal Causality, *Nature*, *creates the worlds*. It is this causality that has determined the mechanical, physical, geologic, and geographic structure of our earth, and, having covered its surface with the splendors of vegetable and animal life, it still continues to *create*, in the human world, society in all its past, present, and future developments.[2]

Nature Acts in Conformity to Law. When man begins to observe, with steady and prolonged attention, that part of Nature which surrounds him and which he discovers within himself, he will finally notice that all things are governed by *inherent laws* which constitute their own particular nature; that each thing has its own peculiar form of transformation and action; that in this transformation and action there is a succession of facts and phenomena which invariably repeat themselves under the same given conditions; and which, under the influence of new and determining conditions, change in an equally regular and determined manner. This constant reproduction of *the same facts through the action of the same causes* constitutes precisely *Nature's method of legislation*: order in the infinite diversity of facts and phenomena.

The Supreme Law. The sum of all known and unknown laws which operate in the universe constitutes its only and supreme law.[3]

In the Beginning Was the Act. It stands to reason that in the Universe thus conceived there can be neither *a priori* ideas nor preconceived and preordained laws. Ideas, the idea of God included, exist upon the earth only in so far as they are produced by the mind. It is therefore clear that they emerged much later than the natural facts, much later than the laws governing such facts. They are right if they correspond to those laws; they are false if they contradict the latter.

As to natural laws, those manifest themselves under this ideal or abstract form of law only through the human mind, reproduced by our brain on the basis of more or less exact observation of things, phenomena, and the succession of facts; they assume the form of human ideas of a nearly spontaneous character. Prior to the emergence of human thought, they were unrecognized as laws and existed only in the state of *real, natural processes*, which, as I have pointed out above, are always determined by the indefinite concurrence of particular conditions, influences, and causes which regularly repeat themselves. The term *Nature* thus precludes any mystic or metaphysical idea of a Substance, Final Cause, or providentially contrived and directed creation.[4]

Creation. By the word *creation* we do not imply theologic or metaphysical creation, nor do we mean thereby artistic, scientific, industrial, or any other form of creation which presupposes an individual creator. By this term we simply mean the infinitely complex product of an illimitable number of widely diverse causes—large and small, some of them known, but most of them still remaining unknown—which, having combined at a given moment (not without cause, of course, but without any premeditation or any plans mapped in advance) have produced this fact.

Harmony in Nature. But, we are told, were this the case, history and the destinies of human society would present nothing but chaos; they would be mere playthings of chance. On the contrary, only when history is free from divine and human arbitrariness, does it present itself in all the imposing, and at the same time rational, grandeur of a necessary development, like the organic and physical nature of which it is the direct continuation. Nature, notwithstanding the inexhaustible wealth and variety of beings of which it is constituted, does not by any means present chaos, but instead a magnificently organized world wherein every part is logically correlated to all the other parts.

The Logic of Divinity. But, we also are told, there must have been a regulator. Not at all! A regulator, were he even God, would only thwart by his arbitrary intervention the natural order and logical development of things. And indeed we see that in all the religions the chief attribute of Divinity consists in being superior—that is, in being contrary to all logic and possessing a logic of its own: the logic of natural impossibility or of absurdity.[5]

The Logic of Nature. To say that God is not contrary to logic is to say that he is absolutely identical with it, that he himself is nothing but logic; that is, the natural course and development of real things. In other words, it is to say that God does not exist. The existence of God has meaning only in so far as it connotes the negation of natural laws. Hence the inescapable dilemma follows:

The Dilemma. God exists—hence there can be no natural laws, and the world presents mere chaos; or the world is not chaos, and it possesses inherent order—hence God does not exist.[6]

The Axiom. What is logic if not the natural course and development of things, or the natural process by means of which many determining causes produce a fact? Consequently, we can enunciate this very simple and at the same time decisive axiom:

Whatever is natural is logical, and whatever is logical is realized or is bound to be realized in the natural world: in Nature—in the proper sense of the word—and in its subsequent development—in the natural history of human society.[7]

The First Cause. But why and how do the laws of the natural and social world exist if no one created them and if no one is governing them? What gives them their invariable character? It is not within my power to solve this problem, nor—so far as I know—has anyone ever found an answer to it, and doubtless nobody ever will find one.[8]

Natural and social laws exist in and are inseparable from the real world, from the totality of things and facts of which we are the products and effects, unless we also in our turn become the relative causes of new beings, things, and facts. This is all we know, and, I believe, all we can know. Besides, how can we find the first cause if it does not exist? What we have called Universal Causality is in itself only the result of all the particular causes operating in the Universe.[9]

Metaphysics, Theology, Science, and the First Cause. The theologian and the metaphysician would forthwith avail themselves of this forced and necessary eternal human ignorance in order to impose their fallacies and fancies upon mankind. But science scorns this trivial consolation: it detests these as ridiculous and dangerous illusions. When not able to go on with its investigations, when it sees itself compelled to call them off for the time being, it will prefer to say, "I do not know," rather than present unverifiable hypotheses as absolute truths. And science has done more than that: it has succeeded in proving, with a certitude that leaves nothing more to be desired, the absurdity and insignificance of all theological and metaphysical conceptions. But it did not destroy them in order to have them replaced by new absurdities. When it has reached the limit of its knowledge, it will say in all honesty: "I do not know." But never will it draw any inferences from what it does not and cannot know.[10]

Universal Science is an Unattainable Ideal. Thus universal science is an ideal which man will never be able to realize. He will always be forced to content himself with the science of his own world, and even when this science reaches out to the most distant star, he still will know little about it. Real science embraces only the solar system, our terrestrial sphere, and whatever appears and passes upon this earth. But even within these limits, science is still too vast to be encompassed by one man or one generation, the more so because the details of our world lose themselves in the infinitesimal and its diversity transcends any definite boundaries.[11]

The Hypothesis of Divine Legislation Leads to the Negation of Nature. If harmony and conformity to law reign in the universe, it is not because the universe is governed according to a system preconceived and preordained by Supreme Will. The theological hypothesis of divine legislation leads to a manifest absurdity and to the negation not only of any order but of Nature itself. Laws are real only in so far as they are inseparable from the things themselves; that is, they are not ordained by an extraneous power. Those laws are but the simple manifestations or continuous variations of things and combinations of varied transient but real facts.

Nature Itself Does Not Know Any Laws. All this constitutes what we call Nature. . . . But Nature itself does not know any laws. It works unconsciously, representing an infinite variety of phenomena inevitably manifesting and repeating themselves. And it is only because of this inevitability of action that order can and actually does exist in the Universe.[12]

The Unity of the Physical and Social Worlds. The human mind and the science it creates study those characteristics and combinations of things, and systematize and classify them with the aid of experiments and observation, such classifications and systematizations being termed laws of Nature.[13]

Science thus far has had for its object only the mental, reflected, and, in so far as it is possible, the systematic reproduction of laws inherent in the material as well as the intellectual and moral life of the physical and social worlds—both of which, in reality, constitute but one natural world.[14]

The Classification of Natural Laws. These laws fall into two categories: those of general laws and those of particular and special laws. Mathematical, mechanical, physical, and chemical laws are, for instance, general laws which manifest themselves in everything that has real existence; in short, they are inherent to matter—that is, inherent in *the real and only universal being, the true basis of all existing things*.[15]

Universal Laws. The laws of equilibrium, of the combination and mutual interaction of forces or of mechanical movement; the law of gravitation, of vibration of bodies, of heat, light, electricity, of chemical composition and decomposition—are inherent in all things that exist. These laws make no exception for the manifestations of will, feeling, and intelligence which constitute the ideal world of man and which are but the material functions of organized and living matter in animal bodies, and especially those of the human animal. Consequently all these laws are general laws, since all the various orders—known and unknown—of real existence are subject to their operation.

Particular Laws. But there also are particular laws which are relevant only to particular orders of phenomena, facts, and things, and which form their own systems or groups; like, for instance, the system of geologic laws, the system of laws pertaining to vegetable and animal organisms, and, finally, laws governing the ideal and social development of the most accomplished animal on earth—man.

Interaction and Cohesion in Nature. Not that laws pertaining to one system are altogether foreign to the laws underlying other systems. In Nature everything is much more closely interlinked than what is generally thought—and perhaps even desired—by the pedants of science in the interests of greater precision in their work of classification.[16]

The invariable process by means of which a natural phenomenon, extrinsic or intrinsic, is constantly reproduced, and the invariable succession of facts constituting this phenomenon, are precisely what we call its law. However, this constancy and this recurrent pattern are not absolute in character.[17]*

The Limits of Man's Understanding of the Universe. We shall never succeed in envisaging, much less in comprehending, this one real system of the universe, in one way infinitely outspread, in another infinitely specialized. We shall never succeed in doing it, for our investigations are brought to a halt before two infinities—the infinitely great and the infinitesimally small.[18]

Its details are inexhaustible. Man will never be able to recognize more than an infinitesimally small part thereof. Our star-spangled sky with its multitude of suns forms only an imperceptible speck in the immensity of space, and though our eye embraces it, we know almost nothing about it; we must content ourselves with a tiny bit of knowledge about our solar system, which we assume to be in perfect harmony with the rest of the Universe. For if such harmony did not exist, it would have to be established or our entire system would perish.

We already have obtained a good idea of the workings of this harmony with respect to celestial mechanics; and we also are beginning to find out more and more about it in relation to the realms of physics, chemistry, and even geology. Only with great difficulty will our knowledge go much beyond that. If we seek more concrete knowledge, we shall have to keep close to our terrestrial sphere. We know that our earth was born in time, and we assume that, after an unknown number of centuries have passed, it will have to perish—just as everything else that is born exists for some time and then perishes, or rather undergoes a series of transformations.[19]

How did our terrestrial sphere, which at first was incandescent, gaseous matter—cool off and take definite shape? What was the nature of the prodigious series of geologic evolutions which it had to traverse before it could produce upon its surface this immeasurable wealth of organic life, beginning with the first cell and ending with man? How did it keep on being transformed and still continue its development in the historic and social world of man? Where are we heading, impelled by the supreme and inevitable law of incessant transformations which in human society are called progress?

These are the only questions open to us, the only questions that can and should be seized upon, studied, and solved by man. Forming, as we already have said, only an imperceptible speck in the limitless and undefinable question of the universe, they present to our minds a world that is infinite in the real and not in the divine—that is, the abstract—meaning of the word. It is infinite not in the sense of a supreme being created by religious abstrac-

---

* The relative character of natural laws is treated by Bakunin in a somewhat different form in *Federalism, Socialism, and Anti-Theologism*, Russian volume III, pp. 162-164.

tion; on the contrary, it is infinite in the tremendous wealth of its details, which no observation, no science, can ever hope to exhaust.[20]

Man Should Know the Laws Governing the World. [But] if man does not intend to renounce his humanity, *he has to know*, he has to penetrate with his mind the whole visible world, and, without entertaining the hope of ever comprehending its essence, plunge into an ever deeper study of its laws: for our humanity is acquired only at such a price. Man must gain knowledge of all the lower realms, of those which preceded him and those contemporaneous with his own existence; of all the mechanical, physical, chemical, geologic, vegetable, and animal evolutions (that is, of all the causes and conditions of his own birth and existence), so that he may be able to understand his own nature and mission upon this earth—his home and his only scene of action—and so that in this world of blind fatality he may inaugurate the reign of liberty.[21]

Abstraction and Analysis Are the Means Whereby the Universe is Comprehended. And in order to comprehend this world, this infinite world, abstraction alone is not sufficient. It would again lead us infallibly to God, to non-being. It is necessary, while applying our faculty of abstraction, without which we would never be able to rise from a simple to a more complex order of things—and, consequently, never comprehend the natural hierarchy of beings—it is necessary, we say, that our intelligence plunge with love and respect into a painstaking study of details and of the infinitesimal minutiae without which we could not conceive the living reality of beings.

Only by uniting those two faculties, those two apparently contradictory tendencies—abstraction and attentive, scrupulous, and patient analysis of details—can we rise to a true conception of our world (*not merely externally but internally infinite*) and form a somewhat adequate idea of *our universe*, of our terrestrial sphere, or, if you please, of our solar system. It then becomes evident that, while our sensations and our imagination are capable of giving us an image, a representation of our world necessarily false to a greater or lesser degree, it is science alone which can give us a clear and precise idea of it.[22]

Man's Task Is Inexhaustible. Such is the task of man: it is inexhaustible, it is infinite, and quite sufficient to satisfy the heart and spirit of the most ambitious men. A transient and imperceptible being lost in the midst of a shoreless ocean of universal mutability, having an unknown eternity behind him and an eternity just as unknown ahead of him, the thinking, active man, the man who is conscious of his human mission, remains proud and calm in the awareness of his liberty which he won by freeing himself through work and science and by liberating, through revolt when necessary, the men around him—his equals and brothers. This is his consolation, his reward, his only paradise.

Real Unity is Negation of God. If you ask him after that what is his intimate thought and his last word about the real unity of the universe, he will tell you that it is constituted by the *eternal transformation*, a movement which is infinitely detailed and diversified, which is self-regulated and has no beginning, limit, nor end. And this is the absolute reverse of any doctrine of Providence—it is the negation of God.[23]

CHAPTER 2 *Idealism and Materialism*

Development of the Material World. The gradual development of the material world, as well as of organic animal life and of the historically progressive intelligence of man—both individual and social—is perfectly conceivable. It is a wholly natural movement from the simple to the complex, from the lower to the higher, from the inferior to the superior; a movement in conformity with our daily experience and accordingly also with our natural logic, with the very laws of our mind, which, being formed and developed only with the aid of this same experience, is nothing else but its reproduction in the mind and brain, its meditated pattern.

The System of the Idealists. The system of the idealists is quite the opposite of this. It is the complete reversal of all human experience and of that universal and general common sense which is the necessary condition of all understanding between man and man, and which, in rising from the simple and unanimously recognized truth that two times two is four to the sublimest and most complicated scientific speculations—admitting, moreover, nothing that has not been strictly confirmed by experience or by observation of facts and phenomena—becomes the only serious basis of human knowledge.[1]

The Course of the Metaphysicians. The course followed by the gentlemen of the metaphysical school is wholly different. And by metaphysicians we mean not only the followers of Hegel's doctrine, of whom few are now left, but also the positivists, and all the present votaries of the goddess of science; likewise all those who, proceeding by various means, even if by the means of the most painstaking, although necessarily imperfect study of the past and present, have set up for themselves an ideal of social organization into which they want to force at any cost, as into a Procrustean bed, the life of future generations; and all those, in a word, who do not regard thought and science as necessary manifestations of natural and social life, but narrow down this poor life of ours to such an extent that all they can see in it is only the practical manifestation of their own thought and of their own rather imperfect science.[2]

The Method of Idealism. Instead of pursuing the natural order from the lower to the higher, from the inferior to the superior, and from the relatively simple to the more complex; instead of tracing wisely and rationally the progressive and real movement from the world called inorganic to the organic world, to the vegetable, and then the animal kingdom, and finally to the distinctively human world; instead of tracing the movement from chemical matter or activity to living matter or activity, and from living activity to the thinking being—the idealists, obessed, blinded, and pushed on by the divine phantom which they inherited from theology—take precisely the opposite course.

They begin with God, presented either as a person or as a divine substance or idea, and the first step that they take is a terrible fall from the sublime heights of the eternal ideal into the mire of the material world; from absolute perfection into absolute imperfection; from thought to being, or rather from Supreme Being to mere nothingness.

Idealism and the Mystery of Divinity. When, how, or why the Divine Being, eternal, infinite, absolutely perfect, (and who probably became weary of himself), decided upon this desperate somersault is something that no idealist, no theologian, no metaphysician, no poet, has ever been able to explain to the layman or to understand himself. All religions, past and present, and all the systems of transcendental philosophy revolve around this unique and iniquitous mystery.[3]

Holy men, divinely inspired law-givers, prophets, and Messiahs have sought life in it and found only torment and death. Like the ancient Sphinx, it devoured them, because they could not explain it. Great philosophers, from Heraclitus and Plato down to Descartes, Spinoza, Leibnitz, Kant, Fichte, Schelling, and Hegel, not to mention the Indian philosophers, have written heaps of volumes and built systems both ingenious and sublime, in which they said in passing many grand and beautiful things, and discovered immortal truths, yet they left this mystery, the principal object of their transcendental researches, just as unfathomable as before.

And if the gigantic efforts of the most wonderful geniuses the world has ever known, and who through at least thirty centuries have each undertaken anew this labor of Sisyphus, have resulted only in rendering the mystery still more incomprehensible—how can we hope that it will be unveiled for us by the uninspired speculations of some pedantic disciple of an artificially warmed-over metaphysics?—and this at a time when all vital and serious minds have turned away from that ambiguous science which came as a result of a compromise—which doubtless can be explained by history—between the unreason of faith and sound scientific reason.[4]

It is evident that this dreadful mystery cannot be explained, which means that it is absurd, for only the absurd admits of no explanation. It is evident that whoever finds it essential to his life and happiness must renounce his reason and return, if he can, to naive, blind, and crude faith, to repeat with Tertullian and all sincere believers the words which sum up the very quintessence of theology: *Credo quia absurdum.* (I believe because it is absurd.) Then all discussion ceases, and nothing remains but the triumphant stupidity of faith.[5]

The Contradictions of Idealism.　The idealists are not strong on logic, and one might say that they despise it. This is what distinguishes them from the metaphysicians of the pantheistic and deistic school, and imparts to their ideas the character of practical idealism, drawing its inspiration much less from the rigorous development of thought than from the experience,—I might almost say from the emotions, historical and collective as well as individual—of life. This imparts to their propaganda an appearance of wealth and vital power, but an appearance only; for life itself becomes sterile when paralyzed by a logical contradiction.[6]

This contradiction consists in the following: They want God, and they want humanity. They persist in linking up two terms which, once separated, cannot be conjoined without destroying each other. They say in one breath: "God and the liberty of man," or "God and the dignity, justice, equality, fraternity, and welfare of men," without paying heed to the fatal logic by virtue of which, if God exists, all these things are condemned to non-existence. *For if God is,* he is necessarily the eternal, supreme, and absolute Master, and if such a Master exists, man is a slave. Now if man is a slave, neither justice, nor equality, nor fraternity, nor prosperity is possible for him.

They (the idealists) may, in defiance of sound sense and all historical experience, represent their God as being animated by the tenderest love for human liberty, but a master, whatever he may do, and no matter how much of a liberal he may want to appear, will nevertheless always remain a master, and his existence will necessarily entail the slavery of all those who are beneath him. Therefore, if God existed, he could render service to human liberty in one way only—by ceasing to exist.

A zealous lover of human freedom, deeming it the necessary condition of all that I admire and respect in humanity, I reverse Voltaire's aphorism and say: *If God really existed, it would be necessary to abolish him.*[7]

The Contemporary Defenders of Idealism.　With the exception of the great but misled hearts and minds, to which I have already referred, who are now the most obdurate defenders of idealism? In the first place, all the reigning houses and their courtiers. In France, it was Napoleon III and his wife, Madame Eugenie; it is still all their former ministers, courtiers, and marshals, from Rouher and Bazaine down to Fleury and Pietri; the men and women of this imperial world who have done such a good job in idealizing and saving France; journalists and savants—the Cassagnacs, the Girardins, the Duvernois, the Veuillots, the Leverriers, the Dumas; the black phalanx of Jesuits and Jesuitesses in whatever garb they may appear in; the entire nobility as well as the upper and middle bourgeoisie of France;

the doctrinaire liberals and liberals devoid of doctrines: the Guizots, the Thierses, the Jules Favres, the Pelletans, and the Jules Simons—all hardened defenders of bourgeois exploitation. In Prussia, in Germany—it is William I, the current representative of the Lord God on earth; all his generals, his officers—Pomeranian and others; his entire army, which, strong in its religious faith, has just conquered France in the "ideal" way that we have come to know so well. In Russia it is the Tsar and his Court; the Muravievs and the Bergs, all the butchers and pious converters of Poland.

Idealism Is the Banner of Brutal Force. Everywhere, in short, religious or philosophical idealism, (the one being simply the more or less free interpretation of the other, serves today as the banner of bloody and brutal material force, of shameless material exploitation.

Materialism Is the Banner of Economic Equality and Social Justice. On the contrary, the banner of theoretical materialism, the red banner of economic equality and social justice, is unfurled by the practical idealism of the oppressed and famished masses who strive to bring about the greatest liberty and realize the human right of each individual in the fraternity of all men on earth.[8]

The True Idealists and Materialists. Who are the true idealists—the idealists not of abstraction, but of life, not of heaven, but of earth—and who are the materialists?

It is evident that the essential condition of theoretical or divine idealism is the sacrifice of logic, of human reason and the renunciation of science. On the other hand, we see that in defending the doctrines of idealism, one finds himself drawn into the camp of the oppressors and exploiters of the masses. These are the two great reasons which, it would seem, should be sufficient to alienate from idealism every great mind and every great heart. How does it happen that our illustrious contemporary idealists, who certainly lack neither mind, nor heart, nor good will, and who have placed their lives at the service of humanity—how does it happen that they have persisted in remaining among the representatives of a doctrine henceforth condemned and dishonored?

They must have been impelled by very strong motives. These cannot be logic nor science, for logic and science have pronounced their verdict against the idealistic doctrine. And it stands to reason that personal interests cannot be counted among their motives, because these people are infinitely above self-interest. Then it must have been a powerful motive of a moral order. Which? There could be but one: These celebrated people think, no doubt, that idealistic theories or beliefs are essential to the dignity and moral grandeur of man, and that materialistic theories reduce him to the level of the beast.[9]

But what if the opposite were true?

Every development implies the negation of its point of departure. And since the point of departure, according to the doctrine of the materialistic school, is material, the negation must necessarily be ideal. Starting from the totality of the real world, or what is abstractly called matter, materialism logically arrives at the true idealization, that is, at the humanization, at the full and complete emancipation, of society. On the other hand, and for the same reason, the starting point of the idealistic school is ideal and it necessarily arrives at the materialization of society, at the organization of brutal despotism and a vile, iniquitous exploitation in the forms of the Church and the State. The historic development of man according to the materialistic school is a progressive ascension, while in the idealistic system it can be nothing but a continuous fall.[10]

Points of Divergence Between Materialism and Idealism. Whatever question pertaining to man we may happen to touch upon, we always run into the same basic contradiction between those two schools. Thus materialism starts from animality in order to establish humanity; idealism starts from divinity in order to establish slavery and doom the masses to perpetual animality.

Materialism denies free will and ends in the establishment of liberty. Idealism, in the name of human dignity, proclaims free will and founds authority on the ruins of every liberty. Materialism rejects the principle of authority, rightly viewing it as the corollary of animality, and believing, on the contrary, that the triumph of humanity, which materialism regards as the main object and significance of history, can be realized only through liberty. In a word, when approached on any question, you will always find the idealist in the very act of practical materialism, while on the other hand, you will invariably see the materialist pursuing and realizing the most ideal aspirations and thoughts.[11]

Idealism is the despot of thought, just as politics is the despot of will. Only Socialism and positive science show due respect to Nature and the freedom of men.[12]

Marxism and Its Fallacies. The doctrinaire school of Socialists, or rather of State Communists of Germany . . . is quite a respectable school, a circumstance which, however, does not prevent it from lapsing into errors from time to time. One of its main fallacies is that it took as the basis of its theories a principle which is profoundly true when viewed in its proper light—that is, from a relative point of view—but which becomes utterly false when observed in isolation from other conditions and held up as the only ground and primary source of all other principles (as is done by that school.)

This principle, constituting moreover the essential foundation of positive Socialism, was first given its scientific formulation and developed by M. Karl Marx, the chief leader of the German Communists. It is the dominant idea of the famous *Communist Manifesto*.[13]

Marxism and Idealism. This principle is in absolute contradiction to the principle recognized by the idealists of all schools. While the idealists deduce all the facts of history—including the development of material interests and the various stages of economic organization of society—from the development of ideas, the German Communists, on the contrary, see in all human history, in the most ideal manifestations of collective as well as individual human life, in every intellectual, moral, religious, metaphysical, scientific, artistic, political, juridical, and social development taking place in the past and in the present, only the reflection or the inevitable result of the development of economic phenomena.

While the idealists maintain that ideas produce and dominate facts, the Communists, in full agreement with scientific materialism, maintain on the contrary that facts beget ideas and that ideas are always only the ideal reflection of events; that out of the sum total of phenomena, the economic material phenomena constitute the essential basis, the main foundation, while all the others—the intellectual and moral, political, and social phenomena—follow as a necessary derivative from the former.[14]

Who Are Right—the Idealists or the Materialists?   Who are right: the idealists or the materialists? When the question is stated in this way hesitation becomes impossible. Undoubtedly the idealists are wrong and the materialists are right. Yes, facts come before ideas; yes, the ideal, as Proudhon said, is but the flower, the roots of which lie in the material conditions of existence. Yes, the whole history of humanity, intellectual and moral, political and social, is but the reflection of its economic history.

All branches of modern science, of a conscientious and serious science concur in proclaiming this great, basic, and decisive truth: yes, the social world, the purely human world, in short, humanity—is nothing but the last and supreme development—at least in so far as our own planet goes—the highest manifestation of animality. But as every development necessarily implies the negation of its base or point of departure, humanity is at the same time the cumulative negation of the animal principle in man. And it is precisely this negation, as rational as it is natural, and rational precisely because it is natural—at once historical and logical, as inevitable as the development and realization of all the natural laws in the world—that constitutes and creates the ideal, the world of intellectual and moral convictions, the world of ideas.[15]

The First Dogma of Materialism.   [Mazzini] contends that we materialists are atheists. We have nothing to say to this, for we are indeed atheists, and we take pride in it, in so far as pride can be permitted to wretched individuals who like waves rise up for a moment and then vanish in the vast collective ocean of human society. We are proud of it, because atheism and materialism are the truth, or rather the actual basis of truth, and also because, above everything else, above practical consequences, we desire the truth and only the truth. And besides, we believe that despite appearances, despite the cowardly promptings of a policy of caution and skepticism, only the the truth will bring practical well-being to the people.

Such is the first dogma of our faith. But it looks ahead, toward the future, and not backward.

The Second Dogma of Materialism. You are not content, however, with pointing out our atheism and materialism. You infer from it that we cannot have love for people nor respect for their virtues; that the great things which have caused the most noble hearts to throb—freedom, justice, humanity, beauty, truth—must be altogether alien to us, and that, aimlessly dragging out our wretched existence—crawling rather than walking erect upon earth—we know of no other cares than to gratify our coarse and sensual appetites.[16]

And we tell you, venerable but unjust master [Mazzini], that this is a grievous error on your part. Do you want to know to what extent we love those great and beautiful things, the knowledge and love whereof you deny to us? Let it be known to you that our love for them is so strong that we are heartily sick and tired of seeing them everlastingly suspended in your Heaven—which ravished them from earth—as symbols and never-realized promises. We are not content any more with the fiction of those beautiful things: we want them in reality.

And here is the second dogma of our faith, illustrious master. We believe in the possibility, in the necessity, of such realization upon the earth; at the same time we are convinced that all those things which you worship as heavenly hopes will necessarily lose their mystic and divine character when they become human and earthly realities.

The Matter of Idealism. You thought you had disposed of us completely by calling us materialists. You thought that you had thereby condemned and crushed us. But do you know where this error of yours comes from? What you and we call *matter* are two totally different things, two totally different concepts. Your matter is a fictitious entity, like your God, like your Satan, like your infinite soul. Your matter is infinite grossness, inert brutality, it is an entity just as impossible as the pure, incorporeal, absolute spirit, both of whom exist only as figments of the abstract fantasy of theologians and metaphysicians—the only authors and creators of those two fictions. The history of philosophy has revealed to us the process—a simple process indeed—of the unconscious creation of this fiction, the origin of this fatal historical illusion, which the long course of many centuries has hung heavily, like a terrible nightmare, upon the oppressed minds of human generations.

The Spirit and the Matter. The first thinkers were necessarily theologians and metaphysicians, the human mind being so constituted that it must always start with a great deal of nonsense, with falsehood and errors, in order to arrive at a small portion of the truth. All of which does not altogether speak in favor of *the holy traditions of the past.* The first thinkers, I say, took the sum of all the real beings known to them, themselves included, of everything that, so it seemed to them, constituted force,

movement, life, and intelligence, and called it *spirit*. All the rest—the form-
less, lifeless mass which, as they saw it, was left after their own minds had
unconsciously abstracted it from the actual world, they named *matter*.
And then they wondered that this *matter*, which, like the same spirit,
existed only in their imagination, was so inactive, so stupid, in the presence
of their God, the pure spirit.[17]

The Matter of Materialists.   We frankly admit that we do not know
your God, but neither do we know your matter; or rather, we know that
one as well as the other does not exist, but that they were created *a priori*
by the speculative fantasy of naive thinkers of bygone ages. By these words
matter and *material* we understand the totality, the hierarchy of real
entities, beginning with the most simple organic bodies and ending with
the structure and functioning of the brain of the greatest genius: the most
sublime feelings, the greatest thoughts, the most heroic acts, acts of self-
sacrifice, duties as well as rights, the voluntary renunciation of one's own
welfare, of one's egoism—everything up to the transcendental and mystic
aberrations of Mazzini—as well as the manifestations of organic life,
chemical properties and actions, electricity, light, heat, the natural gravitation of bodies. All that constitutes, in our view, so many different but
at the same time closely interlinked evolutions of that totality of the real
world which we call *matter*.

Materialism is Not Pantheism.   And note well, we do not regard this
totality as a sort of absolute and everlastingly creative substance, as the
Pantheists do, but as the perpetual result produced and reproduced anew
by the concurrence of an infinite series of actions and reactions, by the
incessant transformations of real beings who are born and who die in the
midst of this infinity.

Matter Includes the Ideal World.   I will sum up: We designate, by
the word *material*, everything taking place in the real world, within man
as well as outside of him, and we apply the word *ideal* exclusively to the
products of the cerebral activity of man; but since our brain is wholly
an organization of the material order, its function being therefore also
material like the action of all other things—it follows that what we call
matter, or *the material world*, does not by any means exclude, but, on the
contrary, necessarily embraces the ideal world as well.[18]

Materialists and Idealists in Practice.   Here is a fact deserving attentive thought on the part of our platonic adversaries! How does it happen
that the theoreticians of materialism usually show themselves in practice
as being greater idealists than the idealists themselves? This, however, is
quite logical and natural. For every development implies to some extent a
negation of the point of departure; the theoreticians of materialism start
from the concept of matter and arrive at the idea, whereas the idealists,
taking for their starting point the pure, absolute idea, and constantly reit-
erating the old myth of original sin—which is only the symbolic expression

of their own sad destiny—relapse, in theory and in practice, into the realm of matter from which they seemingly find it impossible to disentangle themselves. And what matter! Brutal, ignoble, stupid matter, created by their own imagination as their *alter ego,* or as the reflection of their *ideal self.*[19]

In the same way the materialists, always conforming their social theories to the actual course of history, view the animal stage, cannibalism, and slavery as the first starting points of the progressive movement of society; but what are they aiming at, what do they want? They want the emancipation, the full *humanization* of society; whereas the idealists, who take for the basic premise of their speculations the immortal soul and freedom of the will, inevitably end up in the cult of public order like Thiers, in the cult of authority like Mazzini; that is, in the establishment and consecration of perpetual slavery. Hence it follows that theoretic materialism necessarily results in practical idealism, and that idealistic theories find their realization only in a coarse practical materialism.

Only yesterday the proof thereof unfolded before our eyes. Where were the materialists and atheists? In the Paris Commune. And where were the idealists who believe in God? In the Versailles National Assembly. What did the revolutionaries of Paris want? They wanted the final emancipation of humanity through the emancipation of labor. And what does the triumphant Versailles Assembly want now? The ultimate degradation of humanity under the double yoke of spiritual and secular power.

The materialists, imbued with faith and with scorn for suffering, danger, and death, want to forge ahead, for they see before them the triumph of humanity. But the idealists, gasping for breath and seeing ahead of them nothing but bloody specters, want at any cost to push humanity back into the mire from which it extricated itself with such great difficulty.

Let anyone compare both and pass judgement.[20]

CHAPTER 3 *Science: General Outlook*

The Unity of Science. The world is a unity, notwithstanding the infinite variety of its component beings. Man's reason, which takes this world as an object to be recognized and comprehended, is the same or identical, despite the infinite number of various human beings—past and present—by whom it is represented. Science, therefore, also must be unified, for it is but the recognition and comprehension of the world by human reason.[1]

The Object of Science.   Science has for its sole object the thought-out and, as far as possible, systematic reproduction of the laws inherent in the material as well as the intellectual and moral life of both the physical and social worlds, which in reality are part of the same natural world.[2]

These laws divide and subdivide into general—and into particular and special laws.[3]

The Method of Science.   In order to ascertain those general, particular, and special laws, man has no other means but attentive and exact observation of facts and phenomena which occur outside as well as within him. And in the course of this observation he distinguishes the accidental, contingent, and mutable from what occurs always and everywhere in the same invariable manner.[4]

What is the scientific method? It is the realistic method *par excellence*. It proceeds from the particular to the general, from studying and ascertaining facts to understanding them, and thence to ideas. Its ideas are but the faithful representation of the co-ordination, succession, and mutual action or causality which exist between real facts and phenomena. Its logic is nothing more than the logic of facts.[5]

The scientific or the positivist method does not recognize any synthesis which has not been preliminarily verified by experience and a scrupulous analysis of facts.[6]

Experiment and Criticism.   Man has no other means of firmly convincing himself of the reality of a given thing, fact, or phenomenon, than actually to find, recognize, and establish them in their fullness without any admixture of fantasy, conjectures, and irrelevancy brought in by the human mind. Thus experience becomes the foundation of science. And it is not the experience of the individual that we have in mind. . . . Science, therefore, has as its basis the collective experience not only of contemporaries, but likewise of all past generations. It does not admit any evidence without preliminary criticism.[7]

Wherein does this criticism consist? It consists in comparing things affirmed by science with the conclusions of my own personal experience. And wherein does the experience of every individual consist? In the evidence of his senses governed by his reason. . . . I do not accept anything which I have not found in the material state, which I have not seen, heard, or where possible, touched with my own fingers. For me personally this is the only means of becoming convinced of the reality of an object. And I trust the evidence only of that person who unconditionally proceeds in the same manner.[8]

Hence it follows that science is first of all based upon the co-ordination of a mass of personal experiences—past and contemporary—always subjected to the rigorous test of reciprocal criticism. It is impossible to imagine any more democratic basis than this. It is the essential primary foundation, and all human knowledge which in the last analysis has not been tested by such criticism, must be totally excluded as lacking any certitude or scientific value.

Science and Belief. There is nothing so unpleasant for science as belief. Criticism never says the last word. For criticism—representing the great principles of rebellion within science—is the one severe and incorruptible guardian of truth.[9]

The Inadequacy of Experience and Criticism. Science, however, cannot confine itself to this basis, which does no more than provide it with a multitude of the most diverse facts of Nature duly established by countless individual observations and experiences. Science properly begins with the comprehension of things, facts, and phenomena.[10]

The Properties of Science. The general idea is always an abstraction and therefore it is in some degree a negation of real life. I have said that human thought, and consequently science itself, can grasp and name in real facts only their general meaning, their general relations, their general laws; in short, thought and science can grasp that which is permanent in the continued transmutations of things, but never their material and individual aspect, palpitating, so to speak, with life and reality, but for that very reason transient and elusive.

The Limits of Science. Science comprehends the thought of reality, but not reality itself; the thought of life, but not life itself. That is its limit, its only insuperable limit, since it is grounded in the very nature of human thought, which is the only organ of science.[11]

The Mission of Science. It is in this nature of thought that the indisputable rights and the great mission of science are grounded, as well as its impotence in respect to life and even its pernicious action whenever it arrogates to itself, through its official representatives, the right to govern life. The mission of science consists in the following: By establishing the general relations of transitory and real things, by discerning general laws inherent in the development of the phenomena of the physical and social worlds, it fixes—so to speak—the unchangeable landmarks of the progressive march of humanity by indicating the general conditions, the rigorous observation of which is a matter of prime necessity, and the ignoring or forgetting of which leads to fatal results.

Science and Life. In a word, science is the compass of life, but it is not life itself. Science is immutable, impersonal, general, abstract, insensible, like the laws of which it is but an ideal, thought-out or mental,—that is, *cerebral*—reproduction. The word *cerebral* is used here as a reminder that science itself is only a material product of a human material organ—the brain.

Life is fleeting and transitory, but it also palpitates with reality and individuality, with sensibility, sufferings, joys, aspirations, needs, and passions. It alone spontaneously creates real things and beings. Science creates nothing; it only recognizes and establishes the creations of life. And every time scientific men, emerging from their abstract world, interfere with the work of vital creation in the real world, all they propose or produce is poor, ridiculously abstract, bloodless and lifeless, still-born, like Homunculus, created by Wagner, the pedant disciple of the immortal Dr. Faust. It follows that the only mission of science is to enlighten life and not to govern it.[12]

Rational Science. By *rational science* we understand a science which has rid itself of all the phantoms of metaphysics and religion, but which differs at the same time from purely experimental and critical sciences. It differs from the latter, first in not confining its investigations to a definite object but in trying to encompass the whole world—in so far as that world is known, for rational science is not concerned with the unknown. Second, rational science, unlike experimental science, does not confine itself to the analytical method, but has recourse to the method of synthesis as well, and often proceeds by analogy and deduction, although it attaches only a hypothetical significance to syntheses, except where they have been thoroughly confirmed by the most rigorous experimental or critical analysis.

The Hypotheses of Rational Science and Metaphysics. The hypotheses of rational science differ from those of metaphysics in that the latter, deducing its hypotheses as logical corollaries from an absolute system, pretends to force Nature to accept them—whereas the hypotheses of rational science follow not from a transcendental system, but from a synthesis which is in itself only the resumé or the general inference from a variety of facts, the validity of which has been proven by experience. That is why those hypotheses can never have an imperative and obligatory character, being presented, on the contrary, in such a manner as to make them subject to withdrawal as soon as they are refuted by new experiences.[13]

Theological and Metaphysical Survivals in Science. Since in the historic development of the human intellect, science comes always after theology and metaphysics, man arrives at this scientific stage already prepared and greatly corrupted by a certain kind of abstract thinking. He carries over many abstract ideas worked out by theology as well as by metaphysics, ideas which on the one hand were the object of blind faith, and on the other the object of transcendental speculations and more or less ingenious play of words, explanations, and proofs of a kind that do not prove nor explain anything—because they are beyond the sphere of concrete experiment, and because metaphysics has no other guarantee of the very objects about which it reasons than the affirmations or categorical dictates of theology.[14]

From Theology and Metaphysics Toward Science. Man, at first theologian and metaphysician, and then tired of both theology and metaphysics—because of their theoretical barrenness and their baneful results in practice—carries over, as a matter of course, all those ideas into science. Yet he introduces them not as fixed principles to be used as points of departure but as questions to be solved by science. He came to science because he began to doubt these ideas. And he doubts them because his long experience with theology and metaphysics, which fathered them, showed him that neither of the two gave him any certainty about the reality of their creations. And what he doubts and rejects in the first place is not so much those creations, those ideas, as the methods, means, and ways by which theology and metaphysics created them.

He rejects the system of revelations and *the theologians' faith in the absurd because it is absurd;* and he no longer wishes to be imposed on by the despotism of priests nor by the butchers of the Inquisition. And above all, he rejects metaphysics because it took over, either without criticism or with illusory and much too complacent and mild criticism, the creations, the basic ideas of theology: the idea of the Universe, of God, and of a soul or spirit separated from matter. It was upon those ideas that it built its system, and inasmuch as it took the absurd for its starting point, it inevitably ends up with the absurd. Thus emerging from theology and metaphysics, man first of all seeks a truly scientific method which above all gives him complete certitude about the reality of the things on which he reasons.[15]

The Great Unity of Science is Concrete. Vast as the world itself, it [science] exceeds the capacities of the individual man, even though he may be the most intelligent of all humans. No one is capable of encompassing science in all its universality, and in all its infinite details. He who clings to the general and neglects the particular lapses therewith into metaphysics and theology—for *the scientific generalization differs from the generalization in theology and metaphysics in that the former is built not upon an abstraction from all particulars, as is the case with metaphysics and theology, but, on the contrary, solely by relating the particulars into an ordered whole.*

The great unity of science is concrete. It is unity in infinite diversity, whereas the unity of theology and metaphysics is abstract; it is a unity in the void. In order to grasp scientific unity in all its infinite reality, one would have to be able to understand all the beings whose natural, direct, and indirect inter-relations constitute the universe. And manifestly this task exceeds the capacities of any one man, one generation, or of humanity as a whole.[16]

The Advantage of Positive Science. The immense advantage of positive science over theology, metaphysics, politics, and juridical right consists in this—that instead of the false and baneful abstractions, upheld by those doctrines, it sets up true abstractions which express the general nature and logic of things, their general relations, and general laws of development. This is what separates it [positive science] from all preceding doctrines and what will always assure it an important and significant place in human society.[17]

Rational or Positive Philosophy. Rational philosophy or universal science does not proceed aristocratically or authoritatively as the defunct metaphysics does. The latter, always organized from the top downward, by deduction and synthesis, also pretended to recognize the autonomy and freedom of particular sciences, but in actuality it greatly cramped them, by imposing upon them laws and even facts which often could not be found in Nature, and preventing them from applying themselves to experimental researches, the results of which might have reduced to naught all the speculations of metaphysics.

Metaphysics, as you can see, acted according to the method of centralized states. Rational philosophy, on the contrary, is a purely democratic science. It is organized freely, from the bottom upward, and it regards experience as its only basis. *It cannot accept anything which has not been analyzed, or confirmed by experience or by the most severe criticism.* Consequently God, Infinity, The Absolute, all those subjects so much beloved by metaphysics, are entirely absent from rational science. Indifferently it turns away from them, regarding them as phantoms or mirages.

But phantoms and mirages play an essential part in the development of the human mind, and man usually has arrived at the comprehension of simple truths only after conceiving and then exhausting all sorts of illusions. And since the development of the human mind is a real subject matter for science, natural philosophy assigns to these illusions their true places. It concerns itself with them only from the point of view of history and at the same time it tries to show us the physiological as well as the historic causes accounting for the birth, development, and decay of religious and metaphysical ideas, and also their relative and transitory necessity for the development of the human mind. Thus it renders them all the justice to which they are entitled and then turns away from them forever.

Co-ordination of Sciences. Its subject is the real and known world. In the eyes of the rational philosopher, there is only one existence and one science in the world. That is why he aims to unify and co-ordinate all the particular sciences. This co-ordination of all the positive sciences into one single system of human knowledge constitutes the *positive philosophy* or the universal science. The heir and at the same time the absolute negation of religion and metaphysics, this philosophy, which had been anticipated and prepared a long time ago by the noblest minds, was first conceived as a complete system by the great French thinker, Auguste Comte, who boldly and skilfully traced its original outline.[18]

The co-ordination of sciences established by positive philosophy is not just simple juxtaposition; it is a sort of organic concatenation which begins with the most abstract science—mathematics, which has for its subject matter facts of the simplest order, and gradually ascends toward comparatively more concrete sciences which have for their subject matter facts ever growing in their complexity. And thus from pure mathematics one passes to mechanics, to astronomy, and then to physics, chemistry, geology, and biology, including here the classification, comparative anatomy, and physiology of plants, and then of animals, and finally reaches sociology, which embraces all human history, such as the development of the collective and individual human existence in political, economic, social, religious, artistic, and scientific life.

There is no break of continuity in this transition from one to the other followed by all sciences, beginning with mathematics and ending with sociology. One single existence, one single knowledge, and always the same basic method, but which necessarily becomes more and more complicated in the measure that the facts presented to it grow in complexity. Every science forming a link in this successive series rests largely upon the preceding science and, in so far as the present state of our real knowledge permits it, it presents itself as the necessary development of the antecedent science.[19]

The Order of Sciences in the Classifications of Comte and Hegel. It is curious to note that the order of sciences established by Auguste Comte is almost the same as the one in the *Encyclopedia* [*of Sciences*] by Hegel, the greatest metaphysician of past or present times, whose glory was that he brought the development of speculative philosophy to its culminating point, from which, impelled by its own peculiar dialectics, it had to follow the downward path of self-destruction. But between Auguste Comte and Hegel there was an enormous difference. The latter, true metaphysician that he was, spiritualized matter and Nature, deducing them from logic; that is, from spirit. Auguste Comte, on the contrary, materialized the spirit, grounding it solely in matter. And therein lies his greatest glory.

Psychology. Thus psychology, a science which is so important, which constituted the very basis of metaphysics, and which was regarded by speculative philosophy as practically absolute, spontaneous, and independent from any material influence—this science is based in the system of Auguste Comte solely upon physiology and is but the continued development of the latter. Thus what we call intelligence, imagination, memory, feeling, sensation, and will are nothing else in our eyes but the sundry faculties, functions, and activities of the human body.[20]

The Starting Point of Positive Science in Its Study of the Human World. Considered from the moral point of view, Socialism is the *self-esteem of man* replacing the *divine cult;* envisaged from the scientific, practical point of view, it is the proclamation of a great principle which permeated the consciousness of the people and became the starting point for the investigations and development of positive science as well as for the revolutionary movement of the proletariat.

This principle, summed up in all its simplicity, runs as follows: "Just as in the so-called material world, inorganic matter (mechanical, physical, chemical) is the determining base of organic matter (vegetable, animal, cerebral, and mental), so in the social world—which can be regarded as the last known stage of development of the material world—the development of economic problems has always been the determining base of religious, philosophical, and social development."[21]

Considered from this point of view, the human world, its development and history, will one day appear to us in a new and much broader light, more natural and humane, and pregnant with lessons for the future. Whereas formerly the human world was envisaged as the manifestation of a theological, metaphysical, and juridico-political idea—now we must renew the study of it by taking Nature as the starting point and the peculiar physiology of man as the guiding thread.[22]

Sociology and Its Tasks.   In this way one can already foresee the emergence of a new science: *Sociology*, that is, the science of general laws governing all the developments of human society. This science will be the last stage and the crowning glory of positive philosophy. History and statistics prove to us that the social body, like any other natural body, obeys in its evolutions and transformations general laws which appear to be just as necessary as the laws of the physical world. The task of sociology should be to clear those laws from the mass of past events and present facts. Aside from the immense interest which it already presents to the mind, it holds out a promise of great practical value for the future. For just as it is possible for us to dominate Nature and transform it in accordance with our progressive needs, owing to our acquired knowledge of Nature's laws, so shall we be able to realize freedom and prosperity in the social environment only when we take into account the natural and permanent laws which govern that environment.

Once we recognize that the gulf which in the imagination of theologians and metaphysicians was supposed to separate spirit from Nature actually does not exist at all—then we will have to regard the social body as we would any other body, more complex than the others but just as natural and obeying the same laws, in addition to those which apply to it exclusively. Once this is admitted, it will become clear that knowledge of and rigorous observance of those laws are indispensable in order to make practicable the social transformations we shall undertake.

But, on the other hand, we know that Sociology is a science which has only recently emerged, and that it is still seeking out its elementary principles. If we judge this science—the most difficult of all sciences—by the example of others, we shall have to admit that centuries will be needed—or at least one century—in order that it may constitute itself in definite form and become a serious and more or less adequate and self-sufficient science.[23]

History Not Yet a Real Science.   History, for example, does not yet exist as a real science, and for the present we are only beginning to catch glimpses of the infinitely complex tasks of this science. But let us suppose that history as a science had already constituted itself in its final shape. What could it give us? It would reproduce a faithful and rational picture of the natural development of the general conditions—material and spiritual, economic, political, and social, religious, philosophical, aesthetic, and scientific—of societies which have had a history.

But this universal picture of human civilization, however detailed it might be, would never present anything more than a general and consequently *abstract* evaluation—in the sense that the billions of individuals who make up the *living and suffering materials* of this history, at once triumphant and dismal (triumphant from the point of view of its general results and dismal from the point of view of the gigantic hecatomb of human victims "crushed beneath its chariot wheels")—that those billions of obscure individuals without whom none of the great abstract results of history would have been attained (and who, it should be well borne in mind, have never benefited from any of these results) will not find even the slightest place in history. They lived and were sacrificed, crushed for the good of abstract humanity, that is all.

The Mission and Limits of Social Science. Should the science of history be blamed for it? That would be ludicrous and unjust. Individuals are too elusive to be grasped by thought, by reflection, or even by human speech, which is capable of expressing only abstractions; they are elusive in the present as well as in the past. Therefore social science itself, the science of the future, will necessarily continue to ignore them. All that we have a right to demand of it is that it shall faithfully and definitely point out *the general causes of individual suffering.* Among those causes it will, of course, not forget the immolation and subordination (alas, still too common even in our time) of living individuals to abstract generalizations—and at the same time it will have to show us *the general conditions necessary to the real emancipation of the individuals living in society.* That is its mission and those are its limits, beyond which its activity can be only baneful and impotent. For beyond those limits begin the pretentious doctrinaire and governmental claims of its licensed representatives, its priests. It is time to do away with all popes and priests: we want them no longer, *not even if they call themselves Social Democrats.*

I repeat once more: the sole mission of science is to light the way. Only life itself, freed from all governmental and doctrinaire fetters and given the full liberty of spontaneous action, is capable of creation.[24]

CHAPTER 4 *Science and Authority*

Science and Government. A scientific body entrusted with the government of society would soon end by devoting itself not to science but to quite another interest. And that, as is the case with all established powers, would consist in its endeavor to perpetuate itself in power and consolidate its position by rendering the society placed in its care even more stupid and consequently ever more in need of being governed and directed by such a body.[1]

Hence it follows that the only mission of science is to illumine life but not to govern it.

Government by science and men of science, even if they style themselves positivists, the disciples of Auguste Comte, or even the disciples of the doctrinaire school of German Communism, cannot fail to be impotent, ridiculous, inhuman, cruel, oppressive, exploiting, and pernicious.[2]

What I preach then is, up to a certain point, *the revolt of life against science*, or rather against *government by science*, not against the destruction of science—for that would be a high crime against humanity—but the putting of science in its rightful place so that it would never forsake it again.[3]

The Authoritarian Tendencies of the Scientists. Though we can be almost certain that no scientist would dare to treat a man today as he treats rabbits, nevertheless there remains the fear that scientists as a body, if permitted to do so, might submit living men to scientific experiments, doubtless less cruel but none the less disastrous to their human victims. If scientists cannot perform experiments upon the bodies of individuals, they are eager to perform such experiments upon the collective body, and it is in this that they must be unconditionally stopped.

The Savants as a Caste. In their present organization the monopolists of science, who as such remain outside of social life, undoubtedly form a separate caste which has much in common with the caste of priests. Scientific abstraction is their God, living and real individuals their victims, and they themselves the licensed and consecrated priests.

Science, in Contradistinction to Art, is Abstract. Science cannot go outside of the realm of abstractions. In this respect it is vastly inferior to art, which, properly speaking, has to do with general types and general situations, but which, by the use of its own peculiar methods, embodies them in forms which, though not living forms in the sense of real life, none the less arouse in our imagination the feeling and recollection of life. In a certain sense it individualizes types and situations which it has conceived; and by means of those individualities without flesh and bone—and consequently permanent and immortal—which it has the power to create, it recalls to our minds living, real individuals who appear and disappear before our eyes. Art therefore is, as it were, the bringing back of abstraction to life. Science, on the contrary, is the perpetual immolation of fugitive and passing, but real life on the altar of eternal abstractions.[4]

Science and the Real Man.   History, however, is not made by abstract individuals, but by real, living, and passing individuals. Abstractions do not move by themselves; they advance only when borne by real people. But for these beings who are composed not of mere ideas but of flesh-and-blood reality—science has no heart. It considers them at most as material for intellectual and social development. What does it care for the particular conditions and the ephemeral fate of Peter or James?[5]

Since by its very nature science has to ignore both the existence and the fate of the individual—of the Peters and Jameses—it must never be permitted, nor must anyone be permitted in its name, to govern Peter and James. For science in that case would be capable of treating them much the same as it treats rabbits. Or perhaps it would continue to ignore them. But its licensed representatives—men who are far from being abstract but on the contrary quite active men with real interests, yielding to the pernicious influence which privilege inevitably exercises upon men—would finally end up by fleecing those individuals in the name of science, just as they have hitherto been fleeced by priests, politicians of all shades, and lawyers, all of whom did it in the name of God, or of the State, or of Juridical Right.[6]

The Inevitable Results of a Government by Savants.   But until the masses have reached a certain level of education, will they not have to let themselves be governed by men of science? God forbid! It would be better for those masses to dispense with science altogether than to allow themselves to be governed by men of science. The first effect of the existence of such a government would be to render science inaccessible to the people. For such a government necessarily would be aristocratic, because existing scientific institutions are aristocratic by their essential nature.

An aristocracy of intellect and learning! From a practical point of view, this would be the most implacable and from the social point of view the most arrogant and offensive aristocracy. And such would be the power established in the name of science. Such a regime would be capable of paralyzing all life and movement in society. The scientists, ever presumptuous, conceited and impotent, would want to meddle with everything, and as a result the sources of life would dry up under their abstract and learned breath.[7]

Picture to yourself a learned academy composed of the most illustrious representatives of science. Suppose that this academy were charged with the task of legislating and organizing society, and that, inspired by the purest love of truth, it dictates to society only laws which are in absolute harmony with the latest discoveries of science. I maintain that such legislation and such organization would be a monstrosity, and this for two reasons:

First, because human science is always and necessarily imperfect, and when we compare what it has discovered with what remains to be discovered we can say that it is still in its cradle. That is true to such an extent that were we to force the practical life of men—collective as well as individual—into rigorous and exclusive conformity with the latest data of science, we would thus condemn society as well as individuals to suffer martyrdom on a Procrustean bed, which would soon dislocate and stifle them, since life is always an infinitely greater thing than science.

The second reason is this: A society obeying legislation emanating from a scientific academy, not because it understood the *rationale* of this legislation—in which event the very existence of this academy would become useless—but because the legislation, emanating from the academy, was imposed in the name of a science venerated without being understood—such a society would be a society not of men but of brutes. It would be a second edition of the wretched Paraguayan Republic which submitted so long to the rule of the Society of Jesus. Such a society would sink rapidly to the lowest stage of idiocy.

And there is a third reason which makes such a government impossible. It is that a scientific academy, invested, so to speak, with absolute sovereign power, were it composed even of the most illustrious men, would inevitably and quickly end by becoming morally and intellectually corrupted. Such has been the history of the academies even with the limited privileges they have enjoyed up to the present.[8]

Government by Savants Ends in Repulsive Despotism. The metaphysicians or positivists, all those knights of science and thought, in the name of which they consider themselves entitled to dictate laws to life, all of them are reactionaries—consciously or unconsciously so. And it is quite easy to prove it.

Apart from metaphysics in general, which, even at the time of its most flourishing condition, was studied by only a few people, science, taken in its wider connotation, the more serious science, deserving such a name to any extent, is within the reach of only a small minority. For instance, in Russia, with its eighty million population, how many serious scientists are there? Yes, there are thousands who hold forth on science, but people who have a real knowledge of it can be counted only in hundreds.

But if science is to dictate its laws to life, the vast majority—millions of men—will have to be governed by only a few hundred savants. And this number would have to be reduced still further, for it is not every science that renders one capable of governing society; and sociology, the science of sciences, presupposes on the part of the fortunate scientists a serious knowledge of all other scientists.

How many such scientists have we got not just in Russia but throughout Europe? And so all these twenty or thirty savants are to rule the whole world! Can one conceive a more absurd and repugnant despotism? The chances are that those thirty scientists would fall out among themselves, but if they did work together it would be only to the woe of humanity. . . . To be the slaves of pedants—what a fate for humanity!

Give them [the scientists] this full freedom [to dispose of the lives of others] and they will submit society to the same experiments which they now perform, for the benefit of science, upon rabbits, cats, and dogs.

Let us honor the scientists on their proper merits, but let us not accord them any social privileges lest we thereby wreck their minds and morals. Let us not recognize on their part any other rights but the general right freely to advocate their convictions, thoughts, and knowledge. Neither to them nor to any one else should be given power to govern, for by the operation of the immutable law of Socialism, those invested with such power necessarily become oppressors and exploiters of society.[9]

Science and the Organization of Society.   How could this contradiction be solved? On the one hand, science is indispensable to the rational organization of society; on the other hand, being incapable of interesting itself with that which is real and living, it must not interfere with the real or practical organization of society. This contradiction can be solved in only one way: Science, as a moral entity existing outside of the universal social life and represented by a corporation of licensed savants, should be liquidated and widely diffused among the masses. Called upon to represent henceforth the collective consciousness of society, science must in a real sense become everybody's property. In this way, without losing thereby anything of its universal character, of which it can never divest itself without ceasing to be science, and while continuing to concern itself with general causes, general conditions, and general relations of things and individuals, it will merge in fact with the immediate and real life of all individuals.

That will be a movement analagous to that which made the Protestants at the beginning of the Reformation say that there was no further need of priests, for henceforth every man would be his own priest, each man, thanks to the invisible and direct intervention of the Lord Jesus Christ, at last being able to devour the body of God.

But here the question is not of Jesus Christ, nor of the body of God, nor of political liberty, nor of juridical right—all of which come as metaphysical revelations and, as is known, are all alike indigestible. And the world of scientific abstractions is not a revealed world; it is inherent in the real world, of which it is only the general or abstract expression and representation.

So long as it forms a separate domain, specially represented by a corporation of savants, this ideal world threatens to take the place of the Eucharist in relation to the real world, reserving for its licensed representatives the duties and functions of priests. That is why it is necessary, by means of general education, equally available for all, to dissolve the segregated social organization of science, in order that the masses, ceasing to be a mere herd, led and shorn by privileged shepherds, may take into their own hands their historic destinies.[10]

CHAPTER 5 *Modern Science*
Deals in Falsities

The Seats of Modern Science. At present the science and scientists of European schools and universities are in a state of systematic and premeditated falsification. One might think that these schools were established especially to poison bourgeois youth intellectually and morally. For the schools and universities have become marts of privilege where falsehood is sold both at wholesale and retail.

We are not going to point to theology, the science of divine falsehood; to jurisprudence, the science of human falsehood; to metaphysics, or idealistic philosophy—which are sciences of all kinds of half-lies. But we shall point here to such sciences as history, philosophy, politics, and economic science, which are falsified by being deprived of their true basis, natural science, and are based to an equal extent on theology, metaphysics, and jurisprudence. One can say without fear of exaggeration that any young man who is graduated from these universities and is imbued with those sciences, or rather with systematized lies and half-lies which arrogated to themselves the name of science, is lost unless special circumstances arise which may save him from that fate.

The professors—those modern priests of licensed political and social quackery—poison the university youth so effectively that it would need a miracle to cure them. By the time a young man is graduated from the university, he has already become a full-fledged doctrinaire, full of self-conceit and contempt for the rabble, whom he is quite ready to oppress, and especially to exploit, in the name of his intellectual and moral superiority. The younger such a person is, the more pernicious and reprehensible he becomes.

The Revolutionizing Character of Natural Sciences. It is altogether different with the faculty of exact and natural sciences. Those are genuinely scientific. They are foreign to theology and metaphysics and are inimical to all fictions, being exclusively based upon exact knowledge, upon conscientious analysis of facts, and upon pure reasoning, that is to say upon the individual's common sense, broadened by the well co-ordinated experience of all. As much as the idealistic sciences are aristocratic and authoritarian, so are the natural sciences democratic and extensively liberal. And therefore what do we see in practice? Young men who have studied the idealistic sciences eagerly enter the party of exploiters and reactionary doctrinaires, while those who have studied natural sciences join, with equal eagerness, the party of the Revolution, and many of them are frankly revolutionary Socialists.[1]

Education and Science Are Now the Privilege of the Bourgeoisie. In all the European States it is only the bourgeoisie, an exploiting and dominating class—including the nobility, which today exists only in name —that receives a more or less serious education. Apart from that, a special minority is produced from the midst of the bourgeoisie, one which devotes itself exclusively to the study of the greater problems of philosophy, social science, and politics. It is this minority that, properly speaking, constitutes the newest aristocracy of the licensed and privileged "intellectuals." It is the quintessence and the scientific expression of the spirit and interests of the bourgeoisie.

Science and Its Progress at the Service of the Bourgeoisie. The modern universities of Europe, which form a sort of scientific republic, render in the present day the same services to the bourgeoisie which at one time the Catholic church rendered to the nobility; and just as Catholicism once sanctioned the violence perpetrated by the nobility upon the people, so does the university, this church of bourgeois science, explain and legitimize the exploitation of the same people by bourgeois capital. Is it any wonder that in the great struggle of Socialism against bourgeois political economy, the official science of today has decisively taken and continues to take the side of the bourgeoisie?[2]

Most of all we blame science and the arts for extending their benefits and exercising their influence only over a very small section of society, to the exclusion and therefore to the detriment of the great majority. In this connection one can now say about progress in science and art the same that has already been said with so much reason about the amazing development of industry, commerce, and credit—in a word, of the social wealth in the most civilized countries of the modern world.[3]

Technical Progress Under Capitalism Paralleled by Growth of Poverty Among the Masses. The progress is stupendous—that is true. But the more it grows, the more does it become the cause of intellectual and consequently of material slavery, the cause of poverty and mental backwardness of the people; for it constantly deepens the gulf separating the intellectual level of the privileged classes from that of the great masses of the people.[4]

The Proletariat Must Take Possession of Science. Let us not lay the blame on consequences, but turn instead to root-causes. The science of the schools is the product of the bourgeois spirit; and the representatives of this science were born, grew up, and were educated in a bourgeois environment, under the influence of the spirit and exclusive interests of the latter. Therefore it stands to reason that this science, as well as its representatives, should be inimical to the real and full emancipation of the proletariat, and that their economic, philosophical, political, and social theories, consistently worked out in the same spirit, should have for their aim only to prove the incapacity of the working masses and accordingly the mission of the bourgeoisie to govern them to the end of time, since wealth gives it knowledge and knowledge in turn affords it the opportunity to grow still richer.

How can the workers break this vicious circle? They must, of course, acquire knowledge and take possession of science—this mighty weapon without which, it is true, they can make revolutions, but lacking which they will never be able to erect upon the ruins of bourgeois privileges the equality of rights, justice, and liberty which constitute the true basis of all their political and social aspirations.[5]

CHAPTER 6 *Man: Animal and Human Nature*

The Unity of Man and Nature.   Man forms together with Nature a single entity and is the material product of an indefinite number of exclusively material causes.[1]

Monism and Dualism: the Universal Consciousness of Humanity.   To people who think logically and whose minds function on the level of modern science, this unity of the Universe or of Being has become a well established fact. One must recognize, however, that this fact, which is so simple and self-evident that anything opposed to it appears to us as being absurd, finds itself in flagrant contradiction to the universal consciousness of humanity. The latter, manifesting itself in the course of history in widely diverse forms, always unanimously recognized the existence of two distinct worlds: the spiritual and the material world, the divine and the real world. Beginning with the crass fetichists who worshiped in the world surrounding them the action of a supernatural power embodied in some material object, all the peoples believed and still believe in the existence of some kind of a divinity.

The Irrefutability of Dualism.   This imposing unanimity, in the opinion of many people, carries more weight than the proofs of science; and if the logic of a small number of consistent but isolated thinkers contradicts this universal assent, the worse — so these people declare — for that logic. . . . Thus the antiquity and universality of belief in God have become, contrary to all science and all logic, irrefutable proofs of the existence of God. But why should it be so? Until the age of Copernicus and Galileo, the whole world, with the exception of the Pythagoreans, believed that the sun revolved around the earth. Did the universality of such a belief prove the validity of its assumptions? And always and everywhere, beginning with the origin of historic society down to our own period, a small conquering minority has been, and still is, exploiting the forced labor of the masses of workers—slaves or wage-earners. Does it follow that the exploitation of the labor of someone else by parasites is not an iniquity, robbery, and theft?

Absurdity is Old—Truth is Young. Here are two examples which show that the arguments of our Deists are utterly worthless. And indeed: There is nothing more universal, more ancient, than absurdity; it is truth, on the contrary, that is relatively much younger, always being the result, the product of historic development, and never its starting point. For man, by origin, the cousin, if not the direct descendant, of the gorilla, started out from the dark night of animal instinct in order to arrive at the broad daylight of reason. This fully accounts for his past absurdities and partly consoles us for his present errors.

The Character of the Historic Development of Humanity. The entire historic development of man is simply a process of progressive removal from pure animality by way of creating his humanity. Hence it follows that the antiquity of an idea, far from proving anything in favor of it, should on the contrary arouse our suspicions. As to the universality of a fallacy, it proves only one thing: the identity of human nature at all times and in every climate.[2]

The Origin of Man. Organic life, having begun with the simplest hardly organized cell, and having led it through the whole range of transformation—from the organization of plant life to that of animal life—has finally made a man out of it.[3]

Our first ancestors, our Adams and Eves, were, if not gorillas, very near relatives of theirs; omnivorous, intelligent, and ferocious beasts, endowed in a higher degree than the animals of any other species with two precious faculties: the thinking faculty and the urge to rebel.

Thought and Rebellion. These two faculties, combining their progressive action throughout the history of mankind, represent in themselves the negative moment,* aspect, or power in the positive development of human animality, and consequently create all which constitutes humanity in man.[4]

Idealists of all schools, aristocrats, and bourgeois, theologians and metaphysicians, politicians and moralists, clergymen, philosophers, and poets—

---

* The term "moment" is used here as a synonym for the term "factor," as in the expression, "the psychological moment." — James Guillaume.

not forgetting the liberal economists, zealous worshipers of the ideal, as we know—are greatly offended when told that man, with all his magnificent intelligence, his sublime ideas, and his boundless aspirations, is—like all else existing in the world—nothing but matter, only a product of vile matter.[5]

Man, like everything else in Nature, is an entirely material being. The mind, the thinking faculty, the power to receive and reflect different external and internal sensations, to bring them back to memory after they have passed away and to reproduce them by the power of imagination, to compare and distinguish them from one another, to abstract common determinations and thus to create general or abstract concepts, and finally the ability to form ideas by grouping and combining concepts in accordance with various methods—in a word, intelligence, the sole creator of our whole ideal world—is a property of the animal body and especially of the altogether material mechanism of the brain.[6]

The Material Source of the Moral and Intellectual Acts of Man. What we call intelligence, imagination, memory, feeling, sensation, and will, are to us but the various properties, functions, and activities of the human body.[7]

Science has established that all the intellectual and moral acts which distinguish man from the other animal species, such as thought, the manifestations of human intelligence and conscious will, have as their only source the purely material, although doubtless highly perfect, organization of man, without the shadow of intervention by any spiritual or extra-material agency. In short, they are the products resulting from a combination of the diverse, purely physiological functions of the brain.

This discovery is of immense importance from the point of view of science as well as that of life. . . . There are no more gaps of discontinuity between the natural and the human worlds. But just as the organic world, which, being the continuous and direct development of the non-organic world, differs from the latter by the introduction of an active new element—*organic matter* (produced not by the intervention of some extra-material cause—but by the combinations of the same non-organic matter, hitherto unknown to us, and producing in turn, upon the basis and under the conditions of the non-organic world, of which it is the highest result, all the richness of plant and animal life)—in the same way the human world, being the direct continuation of the organic world, is essentially distinguished from the latter by the new element—*thought*. And that new element is produced by the purely physiological activity of the brain and produces at the same time within this material world and under both organic and inorganic conditions, of which it is the final recapitulation, all that we call the intellectual and moral, political and social, development of man—the history of humanity.[8]

The Cardinal Points of Man's Existence. The cardinal points of the most refined human existence, as well as of the most torpid animal existence, will always remain the same: to be born, to develop and grow; to work in order to eat and drink, in order to have shelter and defend oneself, in order to maintain one's individual existence in the social equilibrium of his own species; to love, reproduce and then to die. . . .

Nature Knows of No Qualitative Differences. For man we have to add to these points only one new element—thought and understanding—a faculty and a need which doubtless are already found in a lesser but quite perceptible degree in those animal species which by their organization stand nearest to man; for it seems that Nature knows of no absolute qualitative differences, and that all such differences are in the last analysis reduced to differences in quantity, which, however, only in man attain such commanding and overwhelming power that they gradually transform all his life.

Wrong Conclusions from the Fact of the Animal Descent of Man. As it has been well observed by one of the greatest thinkers of our age, Ludwig Feuerbach, man does everything the animals do, only he does it in a more and more *humane way*. Therein lies all the difference, but it is an enormous difference.[9]

In this connection it will not be amiss to repeat the above to many of the partisans of modern naturalism or materialism, who, because man in our days has discovered his full and complete kinship with all the other animal species and his immediate and direct descent from the earth—and also because man has renounced the absurd and vain boastings of spirituality which, under the pretext of granting him absolute liberty, condemned him in fact to perpetual slavery—imagine that this gives them the right to shed all respect for man. Such people may be compared to lackeys, who, having found out the plebeian origin of one eliciting respect by his natural dignity, believe themselves entitled to treat him as their equal, for the simple reason that they cannot conceive of any other dignity but the one produced by aristocratic birth. Others are so happy over the discovery of man's kinship with the gorilla that they would gladly retain him in the animal state, and they refuse to understand that man's whole historic mission, his dignity and liberty, consist in getting further and further away from that state.[10]

The Historic World. Yes, man does everything the animals do, only he does it in a more and more *humane* way. Therein lies all the difference, but it is an enormous difference. It embraces all civilization, with all the marvels of industry, science, and the arts; with all the developments of humanity—religious, esthetic, philosophic, political, economic, and social—in a word, the whole domain of history. Man creates this historic world by the exercise of an active power which is found in every living being, which constitutes the essence of all organic life, and which tends to assimilate and transform the external world in accordance with everyone's needs. The active force is of course instinctive and inevitable, and precedes any thought, but when illumined by man's reason and determined by his conscious will, it becomes transformed within man and for man into intelligent and free labor.[11]

Labor Is a Necessity.   All animals must work in order to live. All of them, according to their needs, their understanding, and their strength, take part, without noticing or being aware of it, in this slow work of transforming the surface of the earth into a place more favorable to animal life. But this work becomes properly human only when it begins to satisfy, not merely the fixed and inevitably circumscribed needs of animal life, but also those of the thinking and speaking social being who endeavors to win and realize his freedom to the full.[12]

Slavery in Nature.   The accomplishment of this immense, boundless task is not only effected by man's intellectual and moral development, but also by the process of material emancipation. Man becomes man in reality, he conquers the possibility of development and inner perfection provided only that he breaks, to some extent at least, the slave-chains which Nature fastened upon its children. Those chains are hunger, privation of all sorts, physical pain, the influence of climate and seasons, and in general, the thousands of conditions of animal life which keep the human being in almost absolute dependence upon his immediate environment; the constant dangers which in the guise of natural phenomena threaten him on all sides; the perpetual fear which lurks in the depths of all animal existence and which dominates the natural and savage individual to such an extent that he finds within himself no power of struggle or resistance; in other words, not a single element of the most absolute slavery is lacking.[13]

Fear Compels Struggle.   The perpetual fear which he feels, and which underlies every animal's existence, form also, as I shall be able to show later, the first basis of every religion. It is this fear that makes it necessary for the animal to struggle throughout its life against dangers threatening it from the outside; and to maintain its own existence—individual and social—at the expense of everything surrounding it. . . .

Work Is the Highest Law of Life.   Every animal works; it lives only by working. Man as a living being, is not exempt from this necessity, which is the supreme law of life. He must work in order to maintain his existence, in order to develop in the fulness of his being. There exists, however, an enormous difference between the work of man and the work of animals of all species. The work of animals is stagnant, because their intelligence is stagnant; on the contrary, man's work is progressive, his intelligence being highly progressive in character.

The Superiority of Man.   Nothing proves better the decisive inferiority of all animal species, compared to man, than the incontestable fact that the methods and results of work, individual and collective, of the many other animal species,—while frequently being so ingenious as to give the impression of being guided and effected by scientifically trained intelligence,—do not change and hardly improve at all. Ants, bees, beavers, and other animals which live in societies do now precisely the same thing which they were doing 3,000 years ago, showing that there is nothing progressive about their intelligence. Today they are just as skilled and just as stupid as they were thirty or forty centuries ago.

Progress in the Animal World.   There is certainly a progression in the animal world. But it is the species themselves, the families, and even the classes, that undergo slow transformations, driven along by the struggle for existence—the supreme law of the animal world, by virtue of which intelligent and energetic organizations force out inferior species that show themselves incapable of holding their own in the constant struggle. In this respect —and only in this one—there is movement and progress in the animal world. But within the species themselves, within the families and classes of animals, such movement and progress are absent or nearly absent.[14]

Character of Man's Work.   Man's work, from the point of view of methods as well as of results, is just as capable of progressive development and improvement as his intelligence. Man builds his world by combining his neuro-cerebral energy with his muscular work, his scientifically trained mind with physical power, and by applying his progressive thought to work, which, being at first exclusively animal, instinctive, blind, and almost mechanical, becomes more and more rational as time goes on.

In order to visualize this vast ground which man has covered in the course of his historic development, one must compare the huts of the savages with the beautiful palaces of Paris which the brutal Prussians thought themselves destined by Providence to destroy, and also compare the pitiful armaments of primitive populations with the terrible machines of destruction which came as the last word of German civilization.[15]

CHAPTER 7 *Man as Conqueror of Nature*

What all the other animal species, taken together, could not accomplish, was done by man. He actually transformed the greater part of the earth, making it into a habitable place fit for human civilization. He overcame and mastered Nature. He turned this enemy, the first terrible despot, into a useful servant, or at least into an ally as powerful as it is faithful.

What Does It Mean to Conquer Nature?   It is necessary, however, to have some idea about the true meaning of the expression: *To conquer Nature or master Nature. . . .* The action of Man upon Nature, like any other action in the world, is inevitably determined by the laws of Nature. It is, without doubt, the direct continuation of the mechanical, physical, and chemical action of all inorganic, complex, and elementary entities. It is the most direct continuation of the action of plants upon their natural environment and of the more and more developed and conscious action of all animal species. It is indeed nothing but animal action, governed by progressive intelligence and science, both of which are a new mode of transformation of matter in man; hence it follows that when man acts upon Nature, it is in reality the case of Nature working upon itself. And one can see clearly that no rebellion against Nature is possible.[1]

Man and the Laws of Nature. Therefore man will never be able to combat Nature; he cannot conquer nor master it. When man undertakes and commits act which seemingly militate against Nature, he once more obeys the laws of that very same nature. Nothing can free him from their domination; he is their unconditional slave. But this indeed is no slavery at all, inasmuch as every kind of slavery presupposes two beings existing side by side and one of them subject to the other. Man being a part of Nature and not outside of it therefore cannot be its slave.[2]

Yet still, in the heart of Nature, there exists a slavery from which man must free himself if he does not want to renounce his humanity; this is the natural world which envelops him and which is usually called *external Nature.* It is the sum total of things, phenomena, and living beings which envelop and keep on tormenting man, without and outside of which he could not exist for even one solitary moment, but which nevertheless seem to be plotting against him so that every moment of his life he is forced to fight for his existence. Man cannot escape from this external world, for it is only in this world that he can live and draw his sustenance, but at the same time he has to safeguard himself against it, for it always seems intent upon devouring him.[3]

What then is the meaning of the expression: *To combat, to master Nature?* Here we have an everlasting misunderstanding, which is due to the two-fold meaning given to the term *Nature.* On the one hand Nature is regarded as the universal totality of things and beings as well as of natural laws; against Nature thus conceived, as I have already pointed out, no struggle of any kind is possible, for this kind of Nature envelops and comprises everything; it is the absolute, all-powerful being. On the other hand, by *Nature* is understood the more or less limited totality of phenomena, things, and beings which envelop man; in short, his external world. Against this external Nature, struggle is not only possible but inevitable, being forced by universal Nature upon everything that lives or exists.

For, as I have already pointed out, everything that exists and every living being carries within itself the two-fold law of Nature: 1. No existence is possible outside of one's natural environment and its external world; 2. In that external world only that can maintain itself which exists and lives at the expense of that world and is in constant struggle against it.

The Necessity of Struggle Against External Nature. Man, endowed with faculties and attributes which universal Nature bestowed upon him can and should conquer and master this external world. He, on his part, must subdue it and wrest from it his freedom and humanity.[4]

Long before the beginnings of civilization and history, during a far distant period which may have lasted many thousands of years, man was nothing but a wild animal among many other wild animals—a gorilla, perhaps, or a close relation to it. A carniverous or—which is more likely—an omnivorous animal, he was no doubt more voracious, savage, and fierce than his cousins of other species. Like the latter he worked and waged a destructive struggle.

The Ideal State: What Brought Man out of the Brute Paradise? This was the state of innocence, glorified by all kinds of religions—the ideal state so much extolled by Jean Jacques Rousseau. What forced him out of this animal paradise? It was his progressive intelligence, naturally, necessarily, and gradually applied to his animal work. . . . Man's intelligence develops and progresses only through knowledge of real things and facts; only through thoughtful observation and an ever more and more exact and painstaking examination of the relations and the regular sequences of the phenomena of Nature, and of the various stages of their development,—in short, of their inherent laws.

Knowledge of Natural Laws Furthers Human Aims. Once man acquires knowledge of these laws governing all beings, himself included, he learns to foresee certain phenomena enabling him to forestall their effects or to safeguard himself against their unwelcome and harmful consequences. Besides, this knowledge of the laws governing the development of the phenomena of Nature applied to his muscular work, which at first is purely instinctive and animal in its character, enables him in the long run to derive benefit from those natural things and phenomena, the totality of which constitutes the eternal world, the same world which was so hostile at first, but which, owing to science, ends up by contributing powerfully toward the realization of man's aims.[5]

Man Slow to Utilize Fire. Many centuries passed before man, who was just as wild and dull-witted as the apes, learned the art, now so rudimentary, trivial, and at the same time so valuable, of making fire and using it for his own needs. . . . Those extremely simple arts, which today constitute the domestic economy of the least civilized peoples, involved immense inventive efforts on the part of the earliest generations. That accounts for the desperately slow tempo of man's development during the pre-historic period, compared with his rapid development in our days.

Knowledge Is the Weapon of Victory. It was in this manner that man transformed and continues to transform his environment, external Nature, that he conquers and masters it. Did this come as a result of man's revolt against the laws of universal Nature, which embraces all that exists and which also constitute's man's nature? On the contrary. It is through the knowledge and the most attentive and exact observation of this law, that man succeeds not only in freeing himself from the yoke of external Nature, but likewise in at least partly subduing it.

But man does not content himself alone with that. Just as the human mind is capable of making an abstraction out of its own body and personality, and treating it as an external object, so does man, who is constantly driven on by an inner urge inherent in his being, apply the same procedure, the same method, in order to modify, correct, and perfect his own nature. This is a natural inner yoke which man must also learn to shake off.

At first this yoke appears to him in the form of his own weakness, imperfection, or personal infirmities—bodily as well as intellectual and moral infirmities—and then it appears in the most general form of his brutality or animality contrasted with his human nature, which progressively grows within him as his social environment develops.[6]

Battling Inner Slavery.   Man has no other means of struggling against this inner slavery except through the science of the natural laws governing his individual and collective development and the application of that science to his individual training (by means of hygiene, physical exercise, exercising of his affections, mind, and will, and likewise by means of a rational education), as well as to the gradual change of the social order.

Universal Nature Is Not Hostile to Man.   Being the ultimate product of Nature on this earth, man, through his individual and social development, continues, so to speak, the work, creation, movement, and life of Nature. His most intelligent and abstract thoughts and actions, which as such are far removed from what is usually called Nature, are in reality only Nature's new creations and manifestations. Man's relations to this universal Nature cannot be external, cannot be those of slavery or of struggle; he carries this Nature within himself and is nothing outside of it. But in studying its laws, in identifying himself in some measure with them, in transforming them by a psychological process of his own brain into ideas and human convictions—he frees himself from the triple yoke imposed upon him, first by external Nature, then by his inner individual nature, and finally, by society, of which he is a product.[7]

No Revolt Is Possible Against Universal Nature.   It seems to me quite evident from what has already been said that no revolt is possible on the part of man against what I call universal causality or universal Nature; the latter envelops and pervades man; it is within and outside of him, and it constitutes his whole being. In revolting against this universal Nature, he would revolt against himself. It is evident that man cannot even conceive the slightest urge or need for such a revolt; since he does not exist apart from Universal Nature, since he carries it within himself and since at every moment of his life he finds himself wholly identical with it, he cannot consider or feel himself a slave of this Nature.

On the contrary, it is only by studying and by making use, by means of his thought, of the external laws of this Nature—laws which manifest themselves equally in everything constituting his external world as well as his own individual development (bodily, intellectual, and moral)—that he succeeds in gradually shaking off the yoke of external Nature, of his own natural imperfections, and as we shall see further on, the yoke of an authoritarian social organization.

The Dichotomy of Spirit and Matter. But how then could there arise in man's mind the historic thought of separation of spirit and matter? How could man ever conceive this impotent, ridiculous, but at the same time historic attempt to revolt against Nature? This thought and attempt occurred simultaneously with the historic conception of the idea of God, of which in effect they are the necessary corollary. Man at first understood by the word *Nature* only what we call external Nature, his own body included. What we call universal Nature he called "God"; hence the laws of Nature appeared not as inherent laws but as manifestations of the Divine Will, God's commandments imposed from above upon Nature as well as upon man. In line with this, man, siding with God, whom he himself created in opposition to Nature and his own being, declared himself in revolt against Nature, and laid the foundation for his own political and social slavery.

Such has been the historic work of all the religious cults and dogmas.[8]

CHAPTER 8 *Mind and Will*

Man's Life Is the Continuation of Animal Life; Intelligence Is a Quantitative but Not a Qualitative Difference. The individual as well as the social life of man was in the beginning nothing but the immediate continuation of animal life—complicated by a new element: the faculty of thinking and speaking.

Man is not the only intelligent animal on earth. Far from it. Comparative psychology proves that there is no animal which is altogether devoid of intelligence, and that the closer a species approaches man in its organization and especially in the structure of its brain, the higher it stands in the development of its intelligence. But only in man does intelligence reach the high stage of development which can properly be called *the* thinking faculty; that is, the power to compare, separate, and combine the representations of external and internal objects given to us by our senses; to form groups of such representations; and then again to compare and combine those groups, which are not real entities nor representations of objects perceived by our senses, but only *abstract notions* formed and classified by the work of our mind, and which, retained by our memory—another faculty of our brain— become the starting point or basis for those conclusions which we call *ideas*.

Only Man Is Endowed with the Power of Speech. All these functions of our brain would be impossible if man were not endowed with another faculty, complementing the thinking faculty and being inseparable from it: the faculty to incorporate, so to speak, and to identify by external signs all the operations of the mind, the material movements of the brain, up to their most subtle, most complicated variations and modifications; in short, if man were not endowed with the *power of speech*. All other animals have a lan- guage—who doubts that? But since their intelligence never rises above material representations, or, what is more—above the most elementary com- parison and combination of those representations—their language, lacking organization and incapable of development, can express only material sen- sations and notions but never ideas.[1]

From these ideas man deduces conclusions or necessary logical applica- tions. We meet people, alas, quite often, who have not yet reached the full possession of this faculty, but we never saw or heard any member of an inferior species exercising this faculty, unless we are given the instance of Balaam's ass, or of other such animals recommended by various religions to our faith and esteem. Thus we can say, without fear of being refuted, that of all the animals living upon this earth only man is able to think.

The Faculty of Abstraction. Only man is endowed with this power of abstraction, no doubt developed and fortified within the human species by age-long exercise. By inwardly and gradually elevating man above the ob- jects surrounding him, above all that which is called the external world, and even above himself as an individual, this faculty enables man to conceive, to create the idea of the totality of existences, of the Universe, of Infinity or the Absolute—an idea altogether abstract and, if you please, devoid of any content, but nevertheless an all-powerful idea, and the instrumental cause of all the subsequent conquests of man. For it is this idea only that forces him out of the sham beatitudes and the stupid innocence of the animal paradise, in order to lead him to the triumphs and the infinite torments of a bound- less development.

The Germ of Analysis and Scientific Experiments. Owing to this fac- ulty of abstraction, man, by rising above the immediate pressure exercised by all external objects upon every individual, can compare one object with the others and observe their relations. Here is the beginning *of analysis and of experimental science*. And owing to this same faculty, man undergoes a process of inner bifurcation, rising above his own drives, instincts, and urges, in so far as these are of a passing and particular nature. This enables him to compare his inner drives just as he compares external objects and movements, and to side with some against others in accordance with the (social) ideal crystalizing within him. Here we already have the awakening of *conscience* and of what we call *will*.[2]

The Human World Begins.　With the first awakening of thought manifested in speech begins the exclusively human world, the world of abstractions. Owing to this faculty of abstraction, as we already have said, man, born and produced of Nature, creates for himself, in the midst of and under the conditions of this same Nature, a second existence which conforms with and is progressive in the same way as his ideal.

The Dialectics of Human Development.　Whatever lives, we add for greater clarity, tends to realize itself in the fullness of its being. Man, at the same time both a thinking and a living entity, must first of all know himself in order to attain full self-realization. This is the cause of the vast lag which we observe in his development and by reason of which many hundreds of centuries were necessary for man to arrive at the present state of society in the most civilized countries—a state that is still far behind the ideal toward which we are heading. Man had to exhaust all the stupidities and all possible adversities in order to be able to realize the modicum of reason and justice which now prevails in the world.

The last phase and the supreme goal of all human development is *liberty*. Jean Jacques Rousseau and his disciples were wrong in seeking this liberty in the beginnings of history when man, still totally lacking any self-knowledge and therefore quite incapable of working out any kind of contract, was suffering under the yoke of that inevitability of natural life to which all animals are subject.

Nature and Human Freedom.　Man could free himself from this yoke, in a certain sense, only by the gradual use of his reason, which, although developing very slowly, discerned little by little the laws governing the external world as well as those which are inherent in our own nature, and appropriated them, so to say, by transforming them into ideas—almost spontaneous creations of our own brains. While continuing to obey those laws man in reality simply obeyed his own thoughts.

In respect to Nature this is for man the only possible dignity and freedom. There will never be any other freedom; for natural laws are immutable and inevitable; they are the very basis of all existence, and constitute our own being, so that no one can rebel against them without immediately arriving at the absurd or without causing his own destruction. But in recognizing and assimilating them with his own mind, man rises above the immediate pressure of his external world, and then, becoming in turn a creator, henceforth obeying only his own ideas, he more or less transforms the latter in accordance with his progressive needs, impressing upon it to some extent the image of his own humanity.

Universal Conation and the Elan Vitale.　Thus what we call the human world has no other immediate creator but man himself, who produces it by overcoming step by step the external world and his own bestiality, thus gaining for himself his liberty and human dignity. He conquers them, impelled by a force which is independent of him, an irresistible force inherent in all living beings. This force is the universal current of life, the same one which we call universal causality, Nature, which manifests itself in all living beings, plants or animals, in the urge of every individual to realize for himself the conditions necessary for the life of its species—that is, to satisfy his needs.

Free Will.   This urge, this essential and supreme manifestation of life, constitutes the basis of what we call *will*. Inevitable and irresistible in all the animals, the most civilized man included, instinctive (one might almost say mechanical) in the lower organisms, more intelligent in the higher species, it reaches full awareness only in man, who, owing to his intelligence (which raises him above instinctive drives and enables him to compare, criticize, and regulate his own needs), is the only one among all the animals on earth possessing conscious self-determination—*a free will.*

Freedom of Will Is Only Relative.   It stands to reason that this freedom of human will in the face of the universal life current or this absolute causality, in which every will is, so to speak, only a streamlet, has no other meaning but the one given to it by reflection, inasmuch as it is opposed to mechanical action or even instinct. Man apprehends and is clearly aware of natural necessities which, being reflected in his brain, are reborn through a little known physiological process as the logical succession of his own thoughts. This comprehension in the midst of his absolute and unbroken dependence gives him the feeling of self-determination, of conscious, spontaneous will and liberty.

Natural Drives Are Sublimated but Not Suppressed by Man.   Short of suicide—partial or total—no man can free himself from his natural urges, but he can regulate and modify them by striving more and more to make them conform to what at different epochs of intellectual and moral development he calls the just and beautiful.[3]

Freedom of Will Is Qualified but Not Unconditional.   Since every man at his birth and during the whole course of his development throughout his life, is nothing else but the result of a countless number of actions, circumstances, and conditions, material and social, which continue shaping him as long as he lives, where could he—a small, transient, and hardly perceptible link in the universal concatenation of all past, present, and future beings—get the power to break by an act of will this eternal and all-powerful solidarity, this absolute and universal entity which has real existence but which no human imagination can ever hope to comprehend?

Let us recognize once for all that against this universal Nature, our mother who shapes us, brings us up, feeds us, surrounds, and permeates us to the marrow of our bones, to the deepest recesses of our intellectual and moral being, and which end by smothering us in her maternal embraces—

that against this universal Nature there can be neither independence nor revolt.

Rational Liberty: The Only Possible Liberty. True, man, with the aid of knowledge and by the thoughtful application of the laws of Nature, gradually emancipates himself, but not from the universal yoke which he bears, together with all the living beings and the existing things that come into and disappear in this world. Man only frees himself from the brutal pressure exercised upon him by his *own* external world—material and social—which includes all the things and all the men surrounding him. He rules over things through science and work; as to the arbitrary yoke imposed by men, he throws it off through revolution.

Such is the only rational meaning of the word *liberty*: that is, the rule over external things, based upon the respectful observation of the laws of Nature. It is independence from the pretensions and despotic acts of men; it is science, work, political revolt, and, along with all that, it is finally the well thought-out and free organization of the social environment in conformity with the natural laws inherent in every human society. The first and last condition of this liberty rests then in absolute submission to the omnipotence of Nature, and the observation and the most rigid application of its laws.[4]

Like Mind, Will Is a Function of Matter. Like intelligence, will then is not a mystic, immortal, and divine spark which was miraculously dropped down from Heaven to earth to give life to pieces of flesh, to lifeless bodies. It is the product of organized and living flesh, the product of the animal organism. Man's organism is the most perfect of all organisms, and, consequently, man's will and intelligence are relatively the most perfect and above all the most capable of ever greater progress and perfection.

Neural and Muscular Power. Will, like intelligence, is a neural faculty of the animal organism and has the brain as its special organ. . . . Muscular or physical force and neural force, or the power of will and intelligence, have this in common: first, that every one of them depends upon the organization of the animal which the latter received at birth and which in consequence is the product of a multitude of circumstances and causes not only lying outside of this animal organization but preceding it; and second, that all are capable of development with the aid of exercise and training, which once more goes to prove that they are the product of external causes and actions.

It is clear that being in respect to their nature and their intensity simply the effects of causes that are altogether independent of them, these forces themselves have only relative independence in the midst of that universal causality which constitutes and embraces the worlds. What is muscular force? It is a material force of certain intensity generated within the animal by the concurrence of influences or antecedent causes and which at a given moment enables the animal to oppose to the pressure of external forces not absolute but a somewhat relative resistance.

Will Is Determined by Structure of Organism. The same holds true about the moral force which we call the power of will. All animal species are endowed with this power in various degrees, and this difference is first of all determined by the particular nature of their organism. Among all the animals of this earth the human species is endowed with it to the highest extent. But even within this very species not all individuals receive at their birth an equal volitional disposition, the greater or lesser will-capacity being determined beforehand by the relative health and normal development of one's body, and above all by a more or less fortunate brain structure. Here then, at the very beginning, we have a difference for which man is in no way responsible. Is it my fault that Nature endowed me with an inferior will-capacity? The most rabid theologians and metaphysicians will not dare say that what they call souls—that is, the sum total of affective, intellectual, and volitional faculties which everyone receives at birth—are all equal.

The Role of Exercise in the Training of the Will. True, the volitional faculty, as well as the other faculties of man, can be developed by education and appropriate exercises. Those exercises accustom children gradually to refrain from manifesting immediately every slight impression, and to control more or less the reflex movements of their muscles when stimulated by internal and external sensations transmitted by their nerves.

At a later stage, when a certain degree of the power of reflection is developed within the child by an education suitable to his character, the same exercise, becoming in turn more and more conscious in character and calling to its aid the merging intelligence of the child and basing itself to a certain extent upon the violitional power developing within him—trains the child to repress the immediate expression of its feelings and desires and to subject all the voluntary movements of the body, as well as that which is called its soul, its very thought, its words and acts, to a dominant aim, *whether good or bad.*

Is Man Responsible for His Upbringing? Man's will, thus developed and trained, is evidently nothing else but the product of influences lying outside of him and, reacting upon the will, they determine and shape it independently of his own resolves. Can a man be held responsible for the upbringing, bad or good, adequate or inadequate, which he gets? . . .

Up to a certain point man can become his own educator, his own instructor as well as creator. But it is to be seen that what he acquires is only a relative independence and that in no way is he released from the inevitable dependence, or the absolute solidarity by which he, as a living being, is irrevocably chained to the natural and social world.[5]

CHAPTER 9 *Man Subject*
To Universal Inevitability

Animal or Human Will Is Not the Creative Motive Power. It having been proven that animal will, human will included, is an altogether formal power, capable, as we shall see further, of modifying to a certain point, through the knowledge of natural laws and by strictly submitting its actions to those laws, the relations between man and the things surrounding him as well as the relations between the things themselves (but not capable of producing or creating the essence of animal life); it having been proven that the altogether relative power of this will, once put up against the only existing absolute power of universal causality would forthwith appear as absolute impotence or as a relative cause of new relative effects determined and produced by the very same causality—it becomes evident that it is not in the animal will but in the universal and inevitable solidarity of things and beings that we have to look for the mighty motive power which creates the animal and human world.

The Universal Motive Power Is Blind and Unconscious. This motive power we call neither intelligence nor will. For in fact it has not and cannot have any self-consciousness, determination, or resolution of its own. It is not the indivisible, substantial, and single being as represented by the metaphysicians, but the product and, as I have said, a *result* eternally reproduced by all the transformations of beings and things within the Universe. In a word, it is not an idea but a universal fact, beyond which it is impossible to conceive anything. And this fact is not at all an immutable being, but is, on the contrary, perpetual movement, manifesting and forming itself by an infinity of relative action and reaction—mechanical, physical, chemical, geologic, and those of the plant, animal, and human worlds. As the resultant of that combination of relative and countless movements, this universal motive power is all-powerful just as it is inevitable, blind, and unconscious.

It creates worlds and is at the same time their product. In every domain of earthly nature it manifests itself through laws or particular forms of development. In the inorganic world, in the geologic formation of our sphere, it presents itself as the incessant action and reaction of mechanical, physical, and chemical laws which seemingly can be reduced to one basic law: the law of gravitation and movement, or rather of material attraction, all other laws being only its various manifestations and transformations. Those laws, as I have already observed, are general in the sense that they encompass all phenomena produced upon the earth, governing the relations and the development of organic, vegetable, animal, and social life as well as the inorganic totality of things.

The Law of Nutrition, Formulated by Auguste Comte. In the organic world the same universal motive power manifests itself through a new law based upon the sum total of the general laws, which doubtless is but a new transformation, the secret of which has escaped us until now, but which is a particular law in the sense that it manifests itself only in living beings: plants, animals, and man. This is the law of nutrition, which, using the expression of Auguste Comte, consists: "1. In the inner *absorption* of nutritive materials drawn from the ambient system and their gradual assimilation. 2. In the outward *exhalation* of molecules, which from that moment become foreign to the organism and necessarily disintegrate in the accomplishment of nutrition."*

This law is particular in the sense that it is not applied to the inorganic world, but *it is general and fundamental for all living beings*. The problem of nourishment, *the great problem of social economy*, is the real basis of all the subsequent developments of humanity.

Sensibility and Irritability—The Specificae of the Animal World. In the animal world itself the same universal motive power reproduces this generic law of nutrition in a new and peculiar form, by combining it with two properties which distinguish animals from plants: the properties of *sensibility and irritability*. Those faculties are evidently material, and the so-called ideal faculties—the feeling called moral in order to differentiate it from physical sensation, as well as the faculties of will and intelligence—are but their higher expression or their ultimate transformation. Those two properties—sensibility and irritability—are found only among animals. Combined with the law of nutrition, which is common to animals as well as to plants, those properties constitute the particular generic law of all the animal world.[1]

The Genesis of Animal Habits. The various functions which we call animal faculties are not optional in the sense that the animal may or may not exercise them. All faculties are essential properties, necessities inherent in the animal organization. The different species, families, and classes of animals differ among themselves either by the total absence of some faculties or by the overdevelopment of some of those faculties at the expense of the others.

Even within the animal species, families, and classes, individuals are not equally successful. The perfect specimen is the one in which all the characteristic organs of the order to which the individual belongs are harmoniously developed. The lack or the weakness of one of those organs constitutes a defect, and when the organ is of an essential kind, it may lead to

---

* Auguste Comte, *Cours de Philosophie Positive*. Tome III; p. 464 (Bakunin's footnote.)

the individual becoming a monster. Monstrosity or perfection, excellence or defect—all that is given to the individual by Nature and is received by him at his birth.

But once a faculty exists, *it has to be exercised*, and up to the time when the animal has arrived at a stage of natural decline, it necessarily tends to develop and strengthen this faculty by repeated exercise, which creates habit —the basis of all animal development. And the more it is exercised and develops, the more does it become an irresistible force within the animal, a force to be obeyed implicitly.

The Animal Is Compelled to Exercise Its Faculties. It happens at times that a malady or external circumstances more powerful than this natural tendency of the individual, hinder the exercise and the development of one or several faculties. In that case respective organs become atrophied and the whole organism is stricken with suffering in the measure of the importance of these faculties and their corresponding organs. The individual may die from it, but in so far as he lives, in so far as he still has other faculties left, he must exercise them under the pain of death. The individual therefore is not the master of those faculties, but their involuntary agent, their slave.

. . . Being a living organism, endowed with the two-fold property of sensibility and irritability, and as such capable of experiencing pain as well as pleasure, every animal, man included, is forced by its own nature to eat, drink, and to move about. This it has to do in order to obtain nourishment, as well as in response to the supreme need of its muscles. In order to *maintain its existence, the organism must protect itself against anything menacing its health,* its nourishment, and all the conditions of its life. It must *love, mate, and procreate.* It must reflect, in the measure of its intellectual capacity, on the conditions for the preservation of its own existence. It *must want* all these conditions for itself. And directed by a sort of prevision based upon experience, of which no animal is totally devoid, it is *forced to work,* in the measure of its intelligence and muscular force, in order to provide for the more or less distant future.

Animal Drives Reach Stage of Self-Consciousness in Man. Inevitable and irresistible in all animals, the most civilized man not excepted, this imperious and fundamental tendency of life constitutes the very basis of all animal and human passions. It is instinctive, one might say mechanical, in the lowest organizations, it is more conscious in the higher species, and it reaches the stage of full self-consciousness only in man, the latter being endowed with the precious faculty of combining, grouping, and fully expressing his thoughts. Man is the only one capable of abstracting himself, in his thought, from the external world and even from his own inner world, and of rising to the universality of things and beings. Being able, from the heights of this abstraction, to view himself as an object of his own thought, he can compare, criticize, order, and subordinate his own needs, without overstepping the vital conditions of his own existence. All that permits him, within very narrow limits of course, and without being able to change anything in the universal and inevitable flow of causes and effects, to determine by *abstract reflection* his own acts, which gives him, in relation to Nature, the false appearance of spontaneity and absolute independence.[2]

What Sort of Free Will Does Man Possess? Does man really possess free will? Yes and no, depending upon the construction put upon this expression. If by free will is meant free *arbitrary* will, that is to say, the presumed faculty of the human individual to determine himself freely and independently of any external influence; if, as it is held by all religious and metaphysical systems, by this pretended free will man is to be removed from the principle of universal causality which determines the existence of everything and which renders everyone dependent upon all the others—we can do nothing else but reject such freedom as nonsense, since no one can exist outside of this universal causality.[3]

Statistics as a Science Are Possible Only on the Basis of Social Determinism. Socialism, based upon positive science, rejects absolutely the doctrine of "free will." It recognizes that all the so-called vices and virtues of men are only the product of the combined action of Nature and society. Nature, by the power of ethnographic, physiological, and pathological influences, produces the faculties and tendencies which are called natural, while the social organization develops them, restrains them, or warps their development. All men, with no exceptions, at every moment of their lives are what Nature and society have made them.

Only this natural and social necessity makes possible the rise of statistics as a science. This science does not content itself with verifying and enumerating social facts, but in addition it strives to explain the connection and the correlation of those facts in the organization of society. Criminal statistics, for instance, establish the fact that in one and the same country, in one and the same city, during a period of ten, twenty, or thirty years, one and the same crime or misdemeanor is repeated every year in almost the same proportion; that is, provided no political or social crisis has changed the attitude of society there. What is even more remarkable is that the methods used in committing crimes also are repeated from year to year with the same frequency. For instance, the number of poison murders and of knifings or shootings as well as the number of suicides committed in a certain way are almost always the same. This led Quetelet to make the following memorable statement: "Society prepares the crimes while individuals merely carry them out."

The Idea of Free Will Leads to Its Corollary, the Idea of Providence. This periodic repetition of the same facts would be impossible if the intellectual and moral proclivities of men, as well as their acts, depended upon their "free will." The term "free will" either has no meaning at all or it signifies that the individual makes spontaneous and self-determined decisions, wholly apart from any outside influence of the natural or social order. But if that were so, if men depended only upon themselves, the world would be ruled by chaos which would preclude any solidarity among people. Millions of free wills, independent of each other, would tend toward mutual destruction, and no doubt they would succeed in achieving it were it not for the despotic will of divine Providence which "guides them while they hustle and bustle," and in abasing them all at the same time, it establishes order in the midst of human confusion.

The Practical Implications of the Idea of Divine Providence. That is why all the protagonists of the doctrine of free will are compelled by logic to recognize the existence and action of divine Providence. This is the basis of all theological and metaphysical doctrines. It is a magnificent system which for a long time satisfied the human conscience, and, one must admit, from the point of view of abstract thinking or poetical and religious fantasy, it does impress one with its harmony and grandeur. But, unfortunately, the counterpart of this system grounded in historic reality has always been horrifying, and the system itself fails to stand the test of scientific criticism.

Indeed, we know that while Divine Right reigned upon the earth, the great majority of people were subjected to brutal, merciless exploitation, and were tormented, oppressed, and slaughtered. We know that up to now the masses of people have been kept in thralldom in the name of religious and metaphysical divinity. And it could not be otherwise, for if the world —Nature as well as human society—were governed by a divine will, there could be no place in it for human freedom. Man's will is necessarily weak and impotent before the will of God. Thus when we try to defend the metaphysical, abstract, or imaginary freedom of men, the free will, we end up by denying real freedom. Before God, the Omnipotent and Omnipresent, man is only a slave. And since man's freedom is destroyed by divine Providence, there remains only privilege, that is, special rights vouchsafed by Divine Grace to certain individuals, to a certain hierarchy, dynasty, or class.[4]

Science Rejects Free Will. That accumulated, co-ordinated, and assimilated experience which we call science proves that "free will" is an untenable fiction running counter to the nature of things; what we call the will is only the manifestation of a certain kind of neural activity, just as our physical power is the result of the activity of our muscles. Consequently, both are equally the products of natural and social life, that is, of the physical and social conditions amid which every man is born and grows up.[5]

Will and Intelligence Are Only Relatively Independent. Thus conceived and explained, man's will and intelligence can no longer be considered an absolutely autonomous power, independent of the material world and capable, in conceiving thoughts and spontaneous acts, of breaking the inevitable chain of causes and effects which constitutes the universal solidarity of the worlds. The apparent *independence* of will and intelligence is *largely relative,* for like the muscular force of man, these forces or nervous capacities are engendered in every individual by the concurrence of circumstances, influences, and external actions—material and social—which are absolutely independent of his thought and his will. And just as we have had to reject the possibility of what the metaphysicians call spontaneous ideas, we have to reject the spontaneous acts of the will, the *arbitrary freedom of will* and the moral responsibility of man, in the *theological, metaphysical, and juridical senses of the word.*[6]

Moral Responsibility with Man and Animals. No one speaks of the free will of animals. Everyone agrees that animals, at every instant of their lives and in every act of theirs, are governed by causes that are independent of their thought and will. Everyone agrees that animals inevitably follow the impulses received from the external world as well as from their inner nature; in a word, that there is no possibility of their ideas and spontaneous acts of their will disrupting the universal flow of life, and that, consequently, they can bear no responsibility, either juridical or moral. And yet all animals are unquestionably endowed with will and intelligence. Between the corresponding faculties of animals and man there is only a quantitative difference, a difference of degree. Then why do we declare man absolutely responsible and the animal absolutely devoid of responsibility?

I believe that the error consists not in this idea of responsibility, which exists in a very real manner, not only in men but in animals also, although in a different degree. It consists in the *absolute sense* which our human vanity, backed up by a theological or metaphysical aberration, imparts to human responsibility. The whole error is contained in this word *absolute.* Man is not *absolutely* responsible and animals are not *absolutely* irresponsible. The responsibility of the one as well as that of the other is *relative* to the degree of reflection of which any one of them is capable.

Responsibility Exists, but It Is Relative. We can accept it as a general axiom that nothing exists or ever can be produced in the human world which does not exist in the animal world, in the embryonic state at least, humanity being simply the latest development of animality upon earth. It follows then that if there is no animal responsibility, there cannot be responsibility on the part of man, the latter being subject to the absolute impotence of Nature as much as the most imperfect animal on earth; from the absolute point of view animal and man are equally irresponsible.

But relative responsibility certainly exists in the animal world in various degrees. Imperceptible in the lower species, it becomes quite pronounced in animals endowed with a superior organization. Beasts bring up their progeny, and they develop in the latter, in their own manner, intelligence; that is, the comprehension or knowledge of things—and will; that is, the faculty, the inner force, which enables us to control our instinctive movements. And they even punish with parental tenderness the disobedience of their little ones. So even with animals there is the beginning of moral responsibility.

Man's Will Is Determined at Every Moment. We have seen that man is not responsible in respect to intellectual capacities received at birth nor in respect to the upbringing—bad or good—which he received before the age of manhood or at least before the age of puberty. But then we arrive at a point where man becomes aware of himself, when, endowed with the intellectual and moral qualities already inculcated through the education received from the outside, he becomes to some extent his own creator, evidently being able himself to develop, expand, and strengthen his will and intelligence. Is a man to be held accountable if he fails to make use of this inner possibility?

But how can he be held accountable? It is evident that at the moment when he finds himself capable or morally obligated to make this resolution to work upon himself, he has not yet launched upon this spontaneous, inner work which will make him to some degree his own creator; at that moment he is nothing else but the product of external influences which led him to that point. Hence, the resolution which he is about to make will depend not upon the power of the self-acquired will and thought—inasmuch as his own work has not yet started—but upon that which Nature and his education has already given him and which is independent of his own resolutions. The resolution—whether good or bad—which he is about to make, will be the effect or immediate product of Nature and his education, for which he is not responsible. So it follows that such a resolution does not in any way imply responsibility on the part of the individual making it.

Universal Inevitability Rules Human Will. It is evident that the idea of human responsibility, an altogether relative idea, cannot be applied to man taken in isolation and considered as an individual in a state of nature, detached from the collective development of society. Viewed as such in the presence of that universal causality, in the midst of which all that which exists is at the same time the cause and effect, the creator and the creature, every man appears to us at every moment of his life as a being who is absolutely determined and incapable of breaking or even interrupting the universal flow of life, and consequently is divested of all juridical responsibility. With all the self-consciousness produced within him by the mirage of a sham spontaneity, and notwithstanding his will and intelligence—which are the indispensable conditions for building up his liberty against the external world, including the men which surround him—man, like all the animals on this earth, remains nevertheless in absolute subjection to the universal inevitability governing the world.[7]

CHAPTER 10 *Religion in Man's Life*

The Genesis of Faith in God Should Be the Object of Rational Study.
To people who think logically and whose minds function on the level of
modern science, this unity of the Universe and Being has become a well
established fact. One must, however, recognize that this fact which is so
simple and self-evident that anything opposed to it appears absurd to us,
finds itself in flagrant contradiction to the universal consciousness of humanity. The latter, manifesting itself in the course of history in widely
diverse forms, has always unanimously recognized the existence of two
distinct worlds: the spiritual and material world, and the divine and real
world. Beginning with the crass fetichists who worshipped in the world
surrounding them the action of a supernatural power embodied in some
material object, all peoples have believed and still believe in the existence of
some kind of divinity.

This overwhelming unanimity, in the opinion of many people, carries
more weight than the proofs of science; and if the logic of a small number
of consistent but isolated thinkers contradicts this universal assent, the worse
—these people declare—for this logic.

Thus the antiquity and universality of the belief in God have become,
contrary to all science and logic, irrefutable proofs of the existence of God.
But why should it be so? Until the age of Copernicus and Galileo the whole
world, with the exception of the Pythagoreans, believed that the sun revolved around the earth. Did the universality of such a belief prove the
validity of its assumptions? Beginning with the origin of historic society
down to our own period, a small conquering minority has been and still is
exploiting the forced labor of the masses of workers—slaves or wage-earners.
Does it follow that the exploitation of the labor of someone else by parasites is not an iniquity, robbery, and theft? Here are two examples which
show that the arguments of our Deists are utterly worthless.

And, indeed, there is nothing more universal, more ancient, than absurdity; it is truth, on the contrary, that is relatively much younger, always
being the result, the product, of historic development, and never its starting point. For man, by origin the cousin, if not the direct descendant of
the gorilla, started out with the dark night of animal instinct in order to
arrive at the broad daylight of reason. This fully accounts for his past absurdities and partly consoles us for his present errors. Man's whole historic
development is simply a process of progressive removal from pure animality
through the creation of his humanity.

Hence it follows that the antiquity of an idea, far from proving anything in favor of it, should on the contrary arouse our suspicions. As to the universality of a fallacy, it proves only one thing: the identity of human nature at all times and in every climate. And since all peoples have at all times believed in and still believe in God, we must conclude, without letting ourselves be taken in by this questionable concept, which to our mind cannot prevail against logic nor science, that the idea of divinity, which no doubt we ourselves produced, is a necessary error in the development of humanity. We must ask ourselves how and why it came into existence, and why it is still necessary for the great majority of the human species.[1]

Study of Origin of Religion as Important as Critical Analysis of It. Not until we account to ourselves for the manner in which the idea of the supernatural or divine world came into existence, and necessarily had to make its appearance in the natural development of the human mind and human society, not until that time, strong as may be our scientific conviction as to the absurdity of this idea, shall we ever be able to destroy it in the opinion of the majority. And without this knowledge we shall never be able to attack it in the depths of the human being where it took root. Condemned to a fruitless and endless struggle, we would forever have to content ourselves with fighting it solely on the surface, in its countless manifestations, the absurdity of which is no sooner beaten down by the blows of common sense than it will reappear in a new and no less nonsensical form. While the root of the belief in God remains intact, it will never fail to bring forth new offshoots. Thus, for instance, in certain circles of civilized society, spiritualism tends to establish itself upon the ruins of Christianity.[2]

How Could the Idea of Dualism Ever Arise? More than ever are we convinced of the urgent necessity of solving the following question:

Since man forms one whole with Nature and is but the material product of an indefinite quantity of exclusively material causes, how did this duality—the assumed existence of two opposite worlds, one spiritual, the other material, one divine, the other natural—ever come into existence, become established, and take such deep roots in human consciousness?[3]

The Spring Source of Religion. The incessant action and reaction of the whole upon every single point, and the reciprocal action of every single point upon the whole, constitutes, as we have already said, the life, the supreme and generic law, and the totality of worlds which always produces and is produced at the same time. Everlastingly active and all-powerful, this universal solidarity, this mutual causality, which henceforth we shall designate by the term *Nature*, created among the countless number of other worlds our earth, with its hierarchy of beings, from the minerals up to man. It constantly reproduces those beings, develops them, feeds and preserves them, and when their time comes, or frequently before their time arrives, it destroys, or rather transforms, them into other beings. It is then the almighty power against which no independence or autonomy is possible; it is the supreme being which embraces and permeates by its irresistible action the existence of all beings. Among living beings there is not one that does not carry within himself in a more or less developed form the feeling or the perception of this supreme influence and of this absolute dependence.[4]

The Essence of Religion Is the Feeling of Absolute Dependence Upon Eternal Nature. Religion, like all other human things, as one can see, has its primary source in animal life. It is impossible to say that any animal, apart from man, has anything approaching definite religion, for even the crudest religion presupposes a degree of reflection to which no animal except man has yet risen. But it is likewise impossible to deny that the existence of all the animals, with no exceptions, reveals all the constitutive elements, the materials, so to speak, of religion, excepting of course that ideal aspect —thought—which sooner or later will destroy it. And, indeed, what is the real substance of all religion? It is precisely this feeling of the absolute dependence of the ephemeral individual upon eternal and all-powerful Nature.

Instinctive Fear Is the Beginning of Religion. It is difficult for us to observe this feeling and analyze all of its manifestations in the animals of the lower species. We can say, however, that the instinct of self-preservation, which is found in even the relatively poorest animal organizations, is a sort of common wisdom engendered in everyone under the influence of a feeling which, as we have stated, is an effect religious in its nature. In animals endowed with a more complete organization and which are nearer to man, this feeling is manifested in a manner more perceptible to us, in the instinctive and panic fear, for example, which seizes them at the approach of some great natural catastrophe such as earth tremors, forest fires, or great storms. In general, one may say, fear is one of the predominant feelings in animal life.

All animals living at large are shy, which proves that they live in a state of incessant, instinctive fear, so that they are always obsessed with the feeling of danger; that is to say, they are aware to some extent of an all-powerful influence which always and everywhere pursues, permeates, and encompasses them. This dread—the theologians would say the dread of God—is the beginning of the wisdom, i.e., of religion. But with animals it does not become religion because they lack the power of reflection which dictates the feeling, determines its object, and transmutes it into consciousness, into thought. Thus there is reason in this claim of man being religious by nature: he is religious like other animals, but only he, upon this earth, *is conscious of his religion.*

Fear the First Object of Nascent Reflective Thought. Religion is said to be the first awakening of reason; yes, but in the form of unreason. Religion, as we observed just now, begins with fear. And indeed, man, awakening with the first rays of the inward sun which we call self-consciousness, and emerging slowly, step by step, from the somnambulistic half-dream, from the entirely instinctive existence which he led while still in the state of pure innocence, that is, in the animal state—in addition, having been born like all animals, with fear of the external world, which, it is true, produced and nourishes him, but which at the same time oppresses, crushes, and threatens to swallow him at every moment—man was bound to make this very fear the first object of his nascent reflective thought.

It can be assumed that with primitive man, at the first awakening of his intelligence, this instinctive dread must have been stronger than with the animals of other species. First, because he was born worse equipped for the struggle than other animals, and because his childhood lasts much longer. And also because that very faculty of reflective thought, just emerging into the open and not yet reaching a degree of sufficient maturity and power to discern and make use of external objects, was bound to wrench man away from the union and instinctive harmony with Nature in which —like his cousin, the gorilla—he had found himself prior to the awakening of his thought. Thus the power of reflection isolated him in the midst of this Nature which, having become alien to him, was bound to appear through the prism of his imagination, stimulated and enlarged by the effect of this incipient reflection, as a somber and mysterious power, infinitely more hostile and menacing than in reality.

The Pattern of Religious Sensations Among Primitive Peoples. It is exceedingly difficult, if not altogether impossible, to render to ourselves an exact account of the first religious sensations and imaginings of savages. In their details, they probably were just as diverse as the character of the various primitive tribes who experienced them, and as diverse as the climate, the habitat, and all the other circumstances in which they were developed. But since, after all, those sensations and fancies were human in character, they were bound, notwithstanding this great diversity of details, to have a few simple general points in common, which we shall attempt to determine. Whatever the origin of various human groups and of the separation of human races on this earth; whether all men had one Adam (a gorilla or the cousin of a gorilla) as ancestor, or whether they sprang from several such ancestors created by Nature at different points and in different epochs quite independently of one another, the faculty which properly constitutes and creates the humanity of all men—reflection, the power of abstraction, reason, thought, in a word, the faculty of conceiving ideas (and the laws which determine the manifestation of this faculty)—remain identical at all times and places. Everywhere and always they remain the same, so that no human development can run counter to these laws. This gives us the right to believe that the principal phases observed in the first religious development of one people are certain to reproduce themselves in the development of all other populations of the earth.

Fetichism, the First Religion, Is a Religion of Fear. Judging by the unanimous reports of travelers who for centuries had been visiting the oceanic isles, or of those who in our day have penetrated the interior of Africa, *fetichism* must have been the first religion, the religion of all savage peoples, who are the least removed from the state of nature. But fetichism is simply *a religion of fear*. It is the first human expression of that sensation of absolute dependence, mingled with instinctive terror, which we find at the bottom of all animal life, and which, as we have said, constitutes the religious relation with all-powerful Nature of the individual of even the lowest species.

Who does not know of the influence exercised and the impression produced upon all living beings, not even excepting plants, by the great and regular phenomena of Nature: such as the rising and setting of the sun, moonlight, the recurrence of the seasons, the succession of cold and heat, the particular and constant action of the ocean, of mountains, deserts, or natural catastrophes such as tempests, eclipses, and earthquakes, and also the varied and mutually destructive relations of animals among themselves and with the plant species? All these constitute for every animal a totality of conditions of existence, a specific character and nature of its own, and we are almost tempted to say—a particular cult—for in all animals, in all living beings, one can find a sort of Nature worship, compounded of fear and joy, hope and anxiety, and in point of feeling greatly resembling human religion. Even invocation and prayer are not lacking.

The Difference between the Religious Feeling of Man and Animal. Consider the tame dog imploring his master for a caress or look; isn't he the image of a man kneeling before his God? Doesn't that dog transfer, with his imagination and even with the rudiments of thought developed within him by experience, the omnipotence of Nature besetting him to his master, just as man transfers it to God? What is the difference between the religious feeling of man and dog? It is not reflection as such, it is the degree of reflection, or rather the ability to establish and conceive it as an abstract thought, to generalize it by designating it with a name, human speech having the particular characteristic that it expresses only a concept, an abstract generality, being incapable of naming the real things which act immediately upon our senses.

And since speech and thought are two distinct but inseparable forms of one and the same act of human reflection, the latter, by establishing the object or terror and animal worship or of man's first natural cult, universalizes it, transforms it into an abstract entity, and seeks to designate it by a name. The object really worshiped by any individual always remains the same: it is *this* stone, *this* piece of wood; but from the moment that it is named by a word, it becomes an object or an abstract notion, *a* piece of wood or *a* stone in general. Thus with the first awakening of thought manifested by speech begins the exclusively human world, the world of abstractions.

The First Stirrings of the Faculty of Abstraction. Owing to this faculty of abstraction, as we have already said, man, born in and produced by Nature, creates for himself, under the conditions of that Nature, a second existence conforming to his ideal and like himself capable of progressive development.[5] This faculty of abstraction, the source of all of our knowledge and ideas, is likewise the only cause of all human emancipations.

But the first awakening of that faculty, which is nothing else but reason, does not immediately produce freedom. When it begins to work within man, slowly disengaging itself from the swaddling clothes of its animal instincts, it first manifests itself not in the form of *reasoned reflection* which recognizes its own activity and is consciously aware of it, but in the form of *imaginative reflection*, or of unreason. As such it gradually delivers man from the natural slavery besetting him in his cradle, only to plunge him into immediate subjection to a new, thousandfold harsher, and more terrible slavery—the slavery of religion.

Is Fetichism a Step Backward, Compared with the Inchoate Religious Feelings of Animals?. It is this imaginative reflection of man which transforms the natural cult, elements and traces of which we have noted among all animals, into a human cult, in its most elementary form—that of fetichism. We have pointed out the example of animals instinctively worshiping the great phenomena of Nature which actually exert upon their lives an immediate and powerful influence, but we have never heard of animals worshiping an inoffensive piece of wood, a dish-cloth, a bone, or a stone, whereas we find that practice in the primitive religion of savages and even in Catholicism. How can one account for this to all appearances strange anomaly which, in respect to sound sense and the feeling of reality, shows man as being quite inferior to the most primitive animals?

Imaginative Reflection the Spring Source of Fetichistic Religions. This absurdity is the product of the imaginative reflection of the savage. Not only does he feel the almighty power of Nature as other animals do, but he makes it the object of constant reflection, he establishes and generalizes it by giving it some kind of a name, he makes it the focal center of his infantile fancies. Still unable to embrace with his paltry thought the universe, or our terrestrial sphere, or even the confined environment in which he lives, he seeks everywhere the whereabouts of this almighty power, of which the feeling, already reflected in his consciousness, continually besets him. And by the play of his ignorant fantasy, the workings of which would now be difficult to explain, he attaches this almighty power to this or that piece of wood, rag, or stone. . . . That is pure fetichism, the most religious, that is to say, the most absurd religion of all.

The Sorcery Cult. Following fetichism, or sometimes existing alongside of it, comes the sorcery cult. This cult, if not much more rational, is more natural than pure fetichism. It surprises us less than the latter because we are more used to it, being still surrounded by sorcerers: spiritualists, mediums, clairvoyants with their hypnotizers, and even priests of the Roman Catholic and the Greek Orthodox churches who pretend to have the power of compelling God, with the aid of a few mysterious formulas, to enter into ["holy"] water or to become trans-substantiated into bread and wine—are not all these subduers of divinity, which readily submits to their enchantments, also sorcerers of a kind? True, their divinity, the product of a development lasting several thousands of years, is much more complex than the divinity of primitive sorcery, whose only object is the idea of almighty power, already established by the imagination but still indeterminate in its connotation, whether of the moral or intellectual order.

The distinction of good and bad, just and unjust, is still unknown. One is still in the dark as to what this divinity loves and hates, what it wants or does not want; it is neither good nor bad, it is just almighty power and nothing else but that. However, the character of the divinity begins to take on some outline: it is egoistical and vain, it loves flattery, genuflections, the humiliation and immolation of human beings, their adoration and sacrifices—and it cruelly persecutes and punishes those who don't want to submit to its will: the rebels, the haughty ones, the impious. This, as is known, is the basic feature of divine nature in all the past and present gods created by human unreason. Did there ever exist in the world a being more atrociously jealous, vain, bloody, and egoistic than the Jewish Jehovah or God, the Father of the Christians?

The Idea of God Becomes Separated from the Sorcerer. In the cult of primitive sorcery, the divinity—or this indeterminate almighty power—appears at first as inseparable from the person of the sorcerer: he is God himself, like the fetich. But after a certain time, the role of the supernatural man, the man-God, becomes no longer tenable for the real man—especially for the savage, who has not yet found any means of refuge from the indiscreet questions of his believers. The sound sense, the practical spirit of the savage, which continues to develop parallel with his religious imagination, ends up by showing the impossibility of any man who is subject to human frailties and infirmities being a god. To him the sorcerer remains supernatural, but only for an instant, when the latter is possessed. Possessed by whom? By the almighty power, by God. . . .

The Next Phase: Worship of Natural Phenomena as God. Hence the divinity is usually found outside of the sorcerer. But where is it to be sought? The fetich, the God-thing, is already obsolete, and the sorcerer, the man-God, also is being lived down as a definite stage of religious experience. At a stage already advanced, developed, and enriched with the experience and tradition of several centuries, man now seeks divinity far away from him but still in the realm of things that have real existence: in the sun, in the moon, in the stars, religious thought begins to embrace the universe.

Pantheism: Seeking the Invisible Soul of the Universe. Man could reach this point only after many centuries had passed. His faculty of abstraction, his already developed reason, became stronger and more experienced through the practical knowledge of things surrounding him, and by observation of their relations or mutual causality, while the periodical recurrence of natural phenomena gave him the first notion of certain laws of Nature.

Man begins to work up an interest in the totality of phenomena and their causes. At the same time he begins to know himself and, owing to this power of abstraction which enables him to rise in his thought above his own being and to make it an object of his own reflection, he begins to separate his material and living being from his thinking being, his external self from his inner self, his body from his soul. But once this distinction is made and established in his thought, he naturally transfers it to his God, and he begins to seek the invisible soul of this universe of appearance. It was in this manner that the pantheism of the Hindus was bound to come into existence.

The Pure Idea of God.   We must dwell upon this point, for it is here that religion, in the full sense of the word, begins, and with it—real theology and metaphysics. Until then the religious imagination of man, obsessed with the fixed idea of an almighty power, proceeded along its natural course, seeking, by the way of experimental investigation, the source and the cause of this almighty power,—at first in the nearest objects; in the fetiches, then in the sorcerers, still later in the great natural phenomena, and finally in the stars—but always attaching it to some visible and real object, far removed though it might be from him.

But now he supposes the existence of a spiritual God, an invisible, extra-mundane God. On the other hand, until now all his gods were limited and particular beings, holding their places among other non-divine beings who were not endowed with the almighty power but who nevertheless had real existence. But now he posits for the first time a universal divinity: a Being of Beings, the substance and creator of all the confined and particular beings—the universal soul of the whole universe, the great All. Here then begins the true God and with him—true religion.

Unity Is Not Found in Reality but Is Created by Man's Mind.   We should now examine the process by which man arrived at this result, in order to establish, in its historic origin, the true nature of divinity.

The whole question reduces itself to the following: How did the representation of the universe and the idea of its unity ever originate with man? Let us begin by stating that the representation of the universe cannot exist for the animal, for unlike all the real objects which surround him—great or small, far or near—this representation is not given as an immediate perception to our senses. It is an abstract being, and therefore it can exist only through the abstract faculty—that is, for man only.

Let us see then how it is formed within man. Man sees himself surrounded by external objects; he himself, inasmuch as he is a living being, is an object of his own thought. All these objects which he slowly and gradually learns to discern are interlinked by mutual, unvarying relations which he also will learn to comprehend to a greater or lesser extent; and still, notwithstanding these relations which bring them together without merging them into one, those objects remain apart from one another.

Thus the external world presents to man only a diversity of countless objects, actions, separate and distinct relations, without the slightest semblance of unity: it is an endless juxtaposition, but it is not a totality. Whence comes unity? It lies in man's thought. Man's intelligence is endowed with an abstract faculty which enables him, after he has slowly gone over and examined separately, one after the other, a number of objects to comprehend them instantaneously in a single representation, to unite them in a single act of thought. Thus it is man's thought which creates unity and transfers it to the diversity of the external world.

God Is the Highest Abstraction. It follows that this unity is not a concrete and real being, but an abstract being, produced only by the abstracting faculty of man. We say *abstracting* because, in order to unite so many different objects in a single representation, our thought must abstract all their differences—that is, their separate and real existence—and to retain only what they have in common. It follows that the greater the number of objects comprehended by this conceptual unity, the more extensive its sweep—which constitutes its positive determination—the more abstract it becomes and the more it is stripped of reality.

Life with all its exuberance and transitory magnificence is to be found below, in diversity—death with its eternal and sublime monotony is high above, in unity. Try to rise higher and higher through this power of abstraction, to go beyond this terrestrial world, embrace in one single thought the solar world, imagine this sublime unity: what would remain to fill it up? The savage would find it difficult to answer such a question, but we shall answer it for him: there would remain matter with what we call the power of abstraction, matter in motion with its various phenomena such as light, heat, electricity, and magnetism, which are, as it has been proven, different manifestations of one and the same thing.

But if, through the power of this boundless faculty of abstraction, which knows no limit, you rise still higher, above the solar world, and you unite in your thought not only the millions of suns which we see shining in the firmament, but also the myriads of invisible solar systems the existence of which we infer by our thought, by the same reason which, knowing no limits to the working of its abstracting faculty, refuses to believe that the universe (that is to say, the totality of all the existing worlds) may have a limit or an end—and then abstracting from it, by the same thought, the particular existence of every one of the existing worlds, when you try to visualize the unity of this infinite universe, what remains to determine it and fill it up? Only one word, one abstraction: *the Indeterminate Being*—that is, immobility, the void, absolute nothingness; God.

God is then the absolute abstraction, the product of human thought itself, which, like the power of abstraction, has passed beyond all the known beings, all the existing worlds, and, having divested itself by this act from all real content, having arrived at nothing else but the absolute world, it poses before itself, without, however, recognizing itself in this sublime nudity, as *the One and Only Supreme Being*.[6]

CHAPTER 11 *Man Had to Look for God Within Himself*

God's Attributes. In all the religions which divide the world among themselves and which have a more or less developed theology—except Buddhism, the strange doctrine of which, completely misunderstood by its hundreds of millions of followers, established a religion without God—in all the systems of metaphysics, God appears to us above all as a supreme being, eternally pre-existent and pre-determining, containing in himself the thought and the generating will anterior to all existence: the source and eternal cause of all creation, immutable and always equal to himself in the universal movement of created worlds. As we have already seen, this God is not found in the real universe, at least not in that portion of it which lies within the reach of man's knowledge. Not having been able to find God outside of himself, man had to look for him within himself. How did he look for him? By disregarding all living and real things, all visible and known worlds.

But we have seen that at the end of this fruitless journey, man's abstracting faculty or action finds only a single object: itself, divested of all content and deprived of all movement; it finds itself as an abstraction, as an absolutely immovable and absolutely empty being. We would say: absolute non-Being. But religious fantasy says: the Supreme Being—God.

Man Found God and Became Its Creature. Besides, as we have observed earlier, it was led to this abstraction by taking the example of the difference or even the opposition which reflection, already developed to this point, begins to establish between the external man—his body—and his inner world, comprising his thought and will—the human soul. Not being aware, of course, that the latter is nothing but the product and the last, always renewed, expression of man's organism; seeing, on the contrary, that in daily life the body seems always to obey the suggestions of thought and will, and therefore assuming that the soul is, if not the creator, at least the master of the body, (which therefore has no other mission than that of ministering to it and giving it outward expression)—the religious man, from the moment that, owing to his faculty of abstraction, he arrived, in the manner we have just described, at the conception of a universal and supreme being, which is no other thing than this power of abstraction positing itself as its own object, made of it the soul of the whole universe: God.

The Created Thing Becomes the Creator. Thus the true God—the universal, external, immutable God created by the two-fold action of religious imagination and man's abstractive faculty—was posited for the first time in history. But from the moment that God became known and established, man, forgetting or rather not being aware of the action of his own brain which created this God, and not being able to recognize himself any longer in his own creation—the universal abstraction—began to worship it. Thus the respective roles of man and God underwent a change: the thing created became the presumed and true creator, and man took his place among other miserable creatures, as one of them, though hardly more privileged than the rest.

The Logical Implications of the Recognition of God. Once God has been posited, the subsequent progressive development of various theologies can be explained naturally as the reflection of the development of humanity in history. For as soon as the idea of a supernatural and supreme being had got hold of man's imagination and established itself as his religious conviction—to the extent that the reality of this being appeared to him more certain than that of real things to be seen and touched with his hands—it began to appear natural to him that this idea should become the principal basis of all human experience, and that it should modify, permeate, and dominate it absolutely.

Immediately the Supreme Being appeared to him as the absolute master, as thought, will, the source of everything—as the creator and regulator of all things. Nothing could rival him, and everything had to vanish in his presence since the truth of everything resided in him alone, and every particular being, man included, powerful as it might appear, could exist henceforth only with God's sanction. All that, however, is entirely logical, for otherwise God would not be the Supreme, All-Powerful, Absolute Being; that is to say, he could not exist at all.

God Is a Robber. Henceforth, as a natural consequence, man attributed to God all the qualities, forces, and virtues which he gradually discovered in himself or in his surroundings. We have seen that God, posited as a supreme being, is simply an absolute abstraction, devoid of all reality, content, and determination, and that he is naked and null like nothingness itself. And as such he fills and enriches himself with all the realities of the existing world, and though only its abstraction he appears to the religious fantasy as its Lord and Master. Hence it follows that God is the absolute despoiler and that since anthropomorphism is the very essence of all religion, Heaven—the habitation of the immortal gods—is nothing but a crooked mirror which sends back to the believing man his own image in a reversed and swollen form.

Religion Distorts Natural Trends. But the action of religion consists not only in that it takes away from the earth its richness and natural powers, and from man his faculties and virtues in the measure that he discovers them in his historic development, in order to transfer them to Heaven and transmute them into so many divine beings or attributes. In effecting this transformation, religion radically changes the nature of those powers and qualities, and it falsifies and corrupts them, giving them a direction that is diametrically opposed to their original trend.

Divine Love and Justice Become Scourges of Humanity. Thus man's reason, the only organ which he possesses for the discernment of truth, in becoming divine reason, ceases to be intelligible and imposes itself upon believers as a revelation of the absurd. It is thus that respect for Heaven is translated into contempt for the earth, and adoration of divinity into disparagement of humanity. Man's love, the immense natural solidarity which interlinks all individuals, all peoples, and, rendering the happiness and liberty of everyone dependent upon the liberty and happiness of others, must unite all of them sooner or later, in spite of differences of race and color, into one brotherly commune—this love, transmuted into divine love and religious charity, forthwith becomes the scourge of humanity. All the blood shed in the name of religion from the beginning of history, and the millions of human victims immolated for the greater glory of God, bear witness to it. . . .

And finally, justice itself, the future mother of equality, once carried over by religious fantasy into celestial regions and transformed into divine justice, immediately comes back to the earth in the theological form of divine grace, and always and everywhere siding with the strongest, it sows among men only violence, privileges, monopolies, and all the monstrous inequalities consecrated by historic right.

The Historic Necessity of Religion. We do not pretend therewith to deny the historic necessity of religion, nor do we affirm that it has been an absolute evil in history. If it is such an evil, it was, and unfortunately still is, an inevitable evil for the vast ignorant majority of humanity, being just as inevitable as errors and divagations were in the development of all human faculties. Religion, as we have said, is the first awakening of man's reason in the form of divine unreason; it is the first gleam of human truth through the divine veil of falsehood; the first manifestation of human morality, of justice and right through the historic iniquities of divine grace; and, finally, it is the apprenticeship of liberty under the humiliating and painful yoke of divinity, a yoke which in the long run will have to be broken in order to conquer in fact the reasonable reason, the true truth, the full justice, and real liberty.

Religion the First Step Toward Humanity.   In religion, man the animal, in emerging from bestiality, makes the first step toward humanity; but so long as he remains religious he will never attain his aim, for every religion condemns him to absurdity, and, misdirecting his steps, makes him seek the divine instead of the human. Through religion, peoples who have scarcely freed themselves from natural slavery, in which other animal species are deeply sunk, forthwith relapse into a new slavery, into bondage to strong men and castes privileged by divine election.[1]

All the religions with their gods were never anything else but the creation of the credulous fantasy of men who had not yet reached the level of pure reflection and free thought based upon science. Consequently, the religious Heaven was nothing but a mirage in which man, exalted by faith, so long ago encountered his own image, one, however, that was enlarged and reversed—that is, *deified.*

The history of religions, of the grandeur and decline of the gods succeeding one another, is therefore nothing but the history of the development of the collective intelligence and consciousness of mankind. In the measure that they discovered in themselves or in external Nature a power, a capacity, or any kind of quality, they attributed these to their gods, after exaggerating and enlarging them beyond measure, as children do, by an act of religious fantasy. Thus, owing to this modesty and generosity of men, Heaven waxed rich with the spoils of earth, and, by a natural consequence, the richer Heaven grew, the more wretched humanity became. Once installed, God was naturally proclaimed the master, the source, and disposer of all things, the real world was nothing but his reflection, and man, his unconscious creator, bowed down before him, avowing himself God's creature and slave.

Christianity Is the Absolute and Final Religion.   Christianity is precisely the religion *par excellence,* because it exhibits and manifests the very nature and essence of every religion, which are: systematic, absolute impoverishment, enslavement, and abasement of humanity for the benefit of divinity—the supreme principle not only of every religion but of all metaphysics, and of the deistic and the pantheistic schools alike. God being everything, the real world and man are nothing. God being truth, justice, and infinite life, man is falsehood, iniquity, and death. God being master, man is the slave. Incapable of finding for himself the road to truth and justice, he has to receive them as a revelation from above, through intermediaries elected and sent by divine grace.

But whoever says revelation says revealers, prophets, and priests, and these, once recognized as God's representatives on earth, as teachers and leaders of humanity toward eternal life, receive thereby the mission of directing, governing, and commanding it in its earthly existence. All men owe them faith and absolute obedience. Slaves of God, men must also be slaves of the Church and the State, in so far as the latter is consecrated by the Church. Of all the religions that existed and still exist, Christianity was the only one that understood this fact perfectly, and among all the Christian sects it was the Roman Catholic Church that proclaimed and carried it out with rigorous consistency. That is why Christianity is the absolute religion, the final religion, and why the Apostolic and Roman Church is the only consistent, legitimate, and divine church.

With all due deference to all the semi-philosophers, and to all the so-called religious thinkers, we say: *The existence of God implies the abdication of human reason and justice; it is the negation of human liberty and it necessarily ends in both theoretical and practical slavery.*

God Connotes the Negation of Liberty.   And unless we desire slavery, we cannot and should not make the slightest concession to theology, for in this mystical and rigorously consistent alphabet, anyone starting with A must inevitably arrive at Z, and anyone who wants to worship God must renounce his liberty and human dignity.

God exists; hence man is a slave.

Man is intelligent, just, free; hence God does not exist.

We defy anyone to avoid this circle; and now let all choose.[2]

Religion Is Always Allied with Tyranny.   In addition, history shows us that the preachers of all religions, except those of the persecuted churches, were allied with tyranny. And even the persecuted priests, while combating and cursing the powers that persecuted them, were they not at the same time disciplining their own believers and thus laying the ground for a new tyranny? Intellectual slavery, of whatever nature it may be, will always have as a natural result both political and social slavery.

At the present time Christianity, in its various forms, and along with it the doctrinaire and deistic metaphysics which sprang from Christianity and which essentially is nothing but theology in disguise, are without doubt the most formidable obstacles to the emancipation of society. The proof of this is that all the governments, all the statesmen of Europe, who are neither metaphysicians, nor theologians, nor deists, and who at heart believe in neither God nor Devil, passionately and obstinately defend metaphysics as well as religion, and any sort of religion, so long as it teaches, as all of them do in any case, patience, resignation, and submission.

Religion Must Be Combated.   The obstinacy with which the statesmen defend religion proves how necessary it is to combat and overthrow it.

Is it necessary to recall here to what extent religious influences demoralize and corrupt the people? They destroy their reason, the chief instrument of human emancipation, and by filling man's mind with divine absurdities, they reduce the people to imbecility, which is the foundation of slavery. They kill man's working energy, which is his greatest glory and salvation, work being the act by which man becomes a creator, by which he fashions his world; it is the foundation and the condition of human existence and likewise the means whereby man wins at the same time his liberty and his human dignity.

Religion destroys this productive power in people by inculcating disdain for earthly life in comparison with celestial beatitude and indoctrinating the people with the idea that work is a curse or a deserved punishment while idleness is a divine privilege. Religions kill in man the idea of justice, that strict guardian of brotherhood and the supreme condition of peace, ever tipping the balance on the side of the strongest, who are always the privileged objects of divine solitude, grace, and benediction. And, finally, religion destroys in men their humanity, replacing it in their hearts with divine cruelty.

Religions Are Founded on Blood.   All religions are founded on blood, for all, as is known, rest essentially on the idea of sacrifice—that is, on the perpetual immolation of humanity to the insatiable vengeance of divinity. In this bloody mystery man is always the victim, and the priest—a man also, but one privileged by grace—is the divine executioner. That explains why the priests of all religions, the best, the most humane, the gentlest, almost always have at the bottom of their hearts—and if not in their hearts, in their minds and imaginations (and we know the influence exercised by either upon the hearts of men)—something cruel and bloody. And that is why whenever the question of abolishing capital punishment comes up for discussion, the priests—of the Roman Catholic, Russian and Greek Orthodox, and the Protestant churches—are unanimously for preserving this punishment.

Triumph of Humanity Incompatible with Survival of Religion.   The Christian religion, more than any other religion, was founded upon blood, and was historically baptized in it. One can count the millions of victims which this religion of love and forgiveness has sacrificed to the vengeance of its God. Let us recall the tortures which it invented and inflicted upon its victims. And has it now become more gentle and humane? Not at all! Shaken by indifference and skepticism, it has merely become powerless, or rather less powerful, for unfortunately even now it is not altogether deprived of its power to cause harm.

Observe it in the countries where, galvanized by reactionary passions, it gives the outward impression of coming to life again: is not its first motto *vengeance and blood*, and its second *the abdication of human reason*, and slavery its conclusion? While Christianity and the Christian preachers, or any other divine religion for that matter, continue exercising the slightest influence upon the masses of the people, reason, liberty, humanity, and justice will never triumph on the earth. For so long as the masses of the people are sunk in religious superstition, they will always be a pliable instrument in the hands of all despotic powers leagued against the emancipation of humanity.

That is why it is of the utmost importance to free the masses from religious superstition, not only because of our love for them, but for our own sake, in order to save our own liberty and security. This aim, however, can be attained only in two ways: through *rational science* and through the *propaganda of Socialism.*[3]

Only Social Revolution Can Destroy Religion. It is not the propaganda of free thought that will be able to kill religion in the minds of the people. The propaganda of free thought is certainly very useful; it is indispensable as an excellent means of converting individuals of advanced, progressive views. But it will hardly be able to make a breach in the people's ignorance because religion is not only an aberration or a deviation of thought but it still retains its special character of a natural, living, powerful protest on the part of the masses against their narrow and wretched lives. The people go to church as they go to a pot-house, in order to stupefy themselves, to forget their misery, to see themselves in their imagination, for a few minutes at least, free and happy, as happy as others, the well-to-do people. Give them a human existence, and they will never go into a pot-house or a church. And it is only the Social Revolution that can and shall give them such an existence.[4]

CHAPTER 12   *Ethics: Divine or Bourgeois Morality*

The Dialectics of Religion. Religion, as we have said, is the first awakening of human reason in the form of divine unreason. It is the first gleam of human truth through the divine veil of falsehood; the first manifestation of human morality, of justice and right, through the historic iniquities of divine grace. And, finally, it is the apprenticeship of liberty under the humiliating and painful yoke of divinity, a yoke which in the long run will have to be broken in order to conquer in fact reasonable reason, true truth, full justice, and real liberty.

Religion Inaugurates a New Bondage in Place of Natural Slavery. In religion, man—the animal—in emerging from bestiality, makes his first step toward humanity; but so long as he remains religious, he will never attain his aim, for every religion condemns him to absurdity, and, misdirecting his steps, makes him seek the divine instead of the human. Through religion, peoples who have scarcely freed themselves from natural slavery in which other animal species are deeply sunk, forthwith relapse into a new slavery, into bondage to strong men and castes privileged by divine election.

Gods as Founders of States. One of the principal attributes of the immortal Gods consists, as we know, in their acting as legislators for human society, as founders of the State. Man—so nearly all religions maintain—were he left to himself, would be incapable of discerning good from evil, the just from the unjust. Thus it was necessary that the Divinity itself, in one or another manner, should descend upon earth to teach man and establish civil and political order in human society. Whence follows this triumphant conclusion: that all laws and established powers consecrated by Heaven must be obeyed, always and at any price.

Morality Rooted in the Animal Nature of Man. This is very convenient for the rulers but very inconvenient for the governed. And since we belong with the latter, we have a particular interest in closely examining this old tenet, which was instrumental in imposing slavery upon us, in order to find a way of freeing ourselves from its yoke.

The question has now become exceedingly simple: God not having any existence at all, or being only the creation of our abstractive faculty, united in first wedlock with the religious feeling that has come down to us from our animal stage; God being only a universal abstraction, incapable of movement and action of his own: absolute Non-Being, imagined as absolute being and endowed with life only by religious fantasy; absolutely void of all content and enriched only with the realities of earth; rendering back to man that of which he had robbed him only in a denaturalized, corrupted, divine form—God can neither be good nor wicked, neither just nor unjust. He is not capable of desiring, of establishing anything, for in reality he is nothing, and becomes everything only by an act of religious credulity.

The Root of Ideas of Justice and Good. Consequently, if this credulity discovered in God the ideas of justice and good it was only because it had unconsciously endowed him with it; it gave, while it believed itself to be the recipient. But man cannot endow God with those attributes unless he himself possesses them. Where did he find them? In himself, of course. But whatever man has came down to him from his animal stage—his spirit being simply the unfolding of his animal nature. Thus the idea of justice and good, like all other human things, must have had their root in man's very animality.[1]

Basis of Morality Is to Be Found Only in Society. The common and basic error of all the idealists, an error which flows logically from their whole system, is to seek the basis of morality in the isolated individual, whereas it is found—and can only be found—in associated individuals. In order to prove it, we shall begin by doing justice, once and for all, to the isolated or absolute individual of the idealists.

The Solitary Individual is a Fiction. This solitary and abstract individual is just as much of a fiction as is God. Both were created simultaneously by the fantasy of believers or by childish reason, not by reflective, experimental, and critical reason, but at first by the imaginative reason of the people, later developed, explained, and dogmatized by the theological and metaphysical theorists of the idealist school. Both representing abstractions that are devoid of any content and incompatible with any kind of reality, they end in mere nothingness.

I believe I have already proved the immorality of the God-fiction. Now I want to analyze the fiction, immoral as it is absurd, of this absolute and abstract human individual whom the moralists of the idealist school take as the basis of their political and social theories.

The Self-Contradictory Character of the Idea of an Isolated Individual. It will not be very difficult for me to prove that the human individual whom they love and extol is a thoroughly immoral being. It is personified egoism, a being that is pre-eminently anti-social. Since he is endowed with an immortal soul, he is infinite and self-sufficient; consequently, he does not stand in need of anyone, not even God, and all the less of other men. Logically he should not endure, alongside or above him, the existence of an equal or superior individual, immortal and infinite to the same extent or to a larger degree than himself. By right he should be the only man on the earth, and even more than that: he should be able to declare himself the sole being, the whole world. For infinity, when it meets anything outside of itself, meets a limit, is no more infinity, and when two infinities meet, they cancel each other.

The Contradictory Logic of the Self-Sufficient Individual Can Be Overcome Only by the Materialist Point of View. Why do the theologians and metaphysicians, who otherwise have proven themselves subtle logicians, let themselves run into this inconsistency by admitting the existence of many equally immortal men, that is to say, equally infinite, and above them the existence of a God who is immortal and infinite to a still higher degree? They were driven to it by the absolute impossibility of denying the real existence, the mortality as well as the mutual independence of millions of human beings who have lived and still live upon the earth. This is a fact which, much against their will, they cannot deny.

Logically they should have inferred from this fact that souls are not immortal, that by no means do they have a separate existence from their mortal and bodily exterior, and that in limiting themselves and finding themselves in mutual dependence upon one another, in meeting outside of themselves an infinity of diverse objects, human individuals, like everything else existing in this world, are transitory, limited, and finite beings. But in recognizing that, they would have to renounce the very basis of their ideal theories, they would have to raise the banner of pure materialism or experimental and rational science. And they are called upon to do it by the mighty voice of the century.

Idealists Escape From Reality into Contradictions of Metaphysics.
They remain deaf to that voice. Their nature of inspired men, of prophets,
doctrinaires, and priests, and their minds, impelled by the subtle falsehoods
of metaphysics, and accustomed to the twilight of idealistic fancies—rebel
against frank conclusions and the full daylight of simple truth. They have
such a horror of it that they prefer to endure the contradiction which they
themselves have created by this absurd fiction of an immortal soul, or hold
it their duty to seek its solution in a new absurdity—the fiction of God.

From the point of view of theory, God is in reality nothing else but
the last refuge and the supreme expression of all the absurdities and contradictions of idealism. In theology, which represents metaphysics in its
childish and naive stage, God appears as the basis and the first cause of the
absurd, but in metaphysics, in the proper meaning of the word—that is to
say, in a refined and rationalized theology—he, on the contrary, constitutes the last instance and the supreme recourse, in the sense that all the
contradictions which seem to be insoluble in the real world, find their
explanation in God and through God—that is, through an absurdity
enveloped as much as possible in rational appearance.

The Idea of God as the Only Solution of Contradictions. The existence of a personal God and the immortality of the soul are inseparable
fictions; they are two poles of one and the same absolute absurdity, one
evoking the other and vainly seeking in the other its explanation and its
reason for being. Thus, to the evident contradiction between the assumed
infinity of every man and the real fact of the existence of many men, and
therefore an infinite number of beings who find themselves outside of
one another, thereby necessarily limiting one another; between their
mortality and their immortality; between their natural dependence and
absolute independence of one another, the idealists have only one answer:
God. If this answer does not explain anything to you, if it does not satisfy you, the worse it is for you. They have no other explanation to offer.[2]

The Fiction of Individual Morality Is the Negation of All Morality.
The fiction of the immortality of the soul and the fiction of individual
morality, which is its necessary consequence, are the negation of all
morality. And in this respect one has to render justice to the theologians,
who, being more consistent and more logical than the metaphysicians,
boldly deny what in the general acceptance is now called *independent
morality*, declaring with much reason that once the immortality of the
soul and the existence of God are admitted, one also must recognize that
there can be only one single morality, that is, the divine revealed law,
religious morality—the bond existing between the immortal soul and God,
through God's grace. Outside of this irrational, miraculous, and mystic
bond, the only holy and saving bond, and outside of the consequences that
it entails for men, all the other bonds are null and insignificant. Divine
morality is the absolute negation of human morality.

The Egoism of Christian Morality. Divine morality found its perfect expression in the Christian maxim: "Thou shalt love God more than thyself and thou shalt love thy neighbor as much as thyself," which implies the sacrifice of both oneself and one's neighbor to God. One can admit the sacrifice of oneself, this being an obvious act of sheer folly, but the sacrifice of one's fellow-man is from the human point of view absolutely immoral. And why am I forced toward this inhuman sacrifice? For the salvation of my own soul. That is the last word of Christianity.

Thus in order to please God and save my soul, I have to sacrifice my fellow-man. This is absolute egoism. This egoism, by no means destroyed or diminished but only disguised in Catholicism by its forced collective character and the authoritarian, hierarchic, and despotic unity of the Church, appears in all its cynical frankness in Protestantism, which is a sort of religious "Let him save himself who can."

Egoism is the Basis of Idealistic Systems. The metaphysicians in their turn try to mitigate this egoism, which is the inherent and fundamental principle of all idealistic doctrines, by speaking very little—as little as possible—of man's relations with God, while dealing at length with the relations of men to one another. That is not so nice, candid, or logical on their part. For, once the existence of God is admitted, it becomes necessary to recognize the relations of man to God. And one has to recognize that in the face of those relations to the Absolute and Supreme Being, all other relations necessarily take on the character of mere pretense. Either God is no God at all, or his presence absorbs and destroys everything.

The Contradictions in the Metaphysical Theory of Morality. Thus metaphysicians seek morality in the relations of men among themselves, and at the same time they claim that morality is an absolutely individual fact, a divine law written in the heart of every man, independently of his relations with other human individuals. Such is the ineradicable contradiction upon which the moral theory of the idealists is based. Since prior to entering into any relation with society and therefore independently of any influence which society exerts upon me, I already bear within me the moral law inscribed by God himself in my heart,—this moral law must necessarily be strange and indifferent, if not hostile, to my existence in society. It cannot have as its concern my relations with men; it can only determine my relations with God, as it is quite logically affirmed by theology. So far as men are concerned, from the point of view of this law, they are perfect strangers to me. And inasmuch as the moral law is formed and inscribed in my heart apart from my relations with men, it therefore has nothing to do with them.

The Moral Law Is Not an Individual But a Social Fact. But, we are told, this law specifically commands us to love people as ourselves because they are our fellow-creatures, and not to do anything to them which we would not like to have done to ourselves: and in our relations with them to observe equality, justice, and identical morality. To this I shall answer that if it is true that the moral law contains such a commandment, I must hence conclude that it was not created nor inscribed in my heart. For it necessarily presupposes an existence preceding in time my relations with other men, my fellow-creatures, and so it did not create those relations, but, having found them already established, it only regulates them, and is in a certain way their developed manifestation, explanation, and product. It follows that the moral law is not an individual but a social fact, a creation of society.

The Doctrine of Innate Moral Ideas. Were it otherwise, the moral law inscribed in my heart would be an absurdity. It would regulate my relations with beings with whom I have no relations and of whose very existence I am completely unaware.

The metaphysicians have an answer to this. They say that every human individual, when he is born, brings with him this law inscribed by God's hand in his heart, but that this law is at first found in a latent state, in a state of mere potentiality, unrealized or unmanifested for the individual himself, who cannot realize it and who succeeds in deciphering it within himself only by developing in the society of his fellow-creatures; in a word, that he becomes conscious of this law which is inherent in him only through his relations with other men.

The Platonic Soul. This plausible, if not judicious, explanation leads us to the doctrine of innate ideas, feelings, and principles. It is an old familiar doctrine. The human soul, immortal and infinite in its essence, but corporeally determined, limited, weighed down, and so to speak blinded and abased in its real existence, contains all those eternal and divine principles, without, however, being consciously aware of them. Since it is immortal, it necessarily had to be eternal in the past as well as in the future. For if it had a beginning, it is inevitably bound to have an end, and therefore can by no means be immortal. What was its nature, what had it been doing during all the time it had left behind it? Only God knows that.

As for the soul itself, it does not remember, it is clearly ignorant of this alleged previous existence. It is a great mystery, full of crying contradictions, and in order to solve it one has to turn to the supreme contradiction, God himself. At any rate, the soul, without being aware of it, carries within some mysterious portion of its being all these divine principles. But, lost in its earthly body, brutalized by the grossly material conditions of its birth and its existence upon the earth, it is no more capable of conceiving them, or even of bringing them back into its memory. It is as if it had never possessed them at all.

The Soul Is Stirred into Self-Awareness. But here a multitude of human souls, all equally immortal in their essence and all equally brutalized, debased, and materialized by their earthly existence, meet one another as members of human society. At first they recognize one another so little that one materialized soul devours another. Cannibalism, as we know, was the first human practice. Then, continuing to wage their fierce wars, every one of them strives to enslave the others—this is the long period of slavery, which is still far from having drawn to an end.

Neither cannibalism nor slavery reveals any traces of divine principles. But in this incessant struggle of peoples and men against one another which constitutes history and which has resulted in immeasurable sufferings, the souls gradually begin to stir from their torpor, begin to come into their own, recognize themselves, and get an ever deeper knowledge of their intimate being; in addition, roused and provoked by one another, they begin to recollect themselves, at first in a form of presentiment, and then in glimpses, finally grasping ever more clearly the principles which God from time immemorial had traced with his own hand.

Discovery and Dissemination of Divine Truths of Morality. This awakening and recollection take place at first not in the more infinite and immortal souls. That would be absurd since infinity does not admit of any comparative degrees: the soul of the worst idiot is just as infinite and immortal as that of the greatest genius.

It takes place in the less grossly materialized souls, which are therefore the most capable of awakening and recollecting themselves. These are men of genius, inspired by God, men of divine revelation, legislators and prophets. Once these great and saintly men, illumined and inspired by the spirit, without whose aid nothing great or good is done in this world, have discovered within themselves one of those divine truths which every man subconsciously carries within his own soul, it naturally becomes easier for the more grossly materialized souls to make the same discovery within themselves. It is thus that every great truth, all the eternal principles which manifested themselves at first in history as divine revelations, are later reduced to truths which no doubt are divine but which nevertheless everyone can and should find in himself and recognize as the bases of his own infinite essence or his immortal soul.

This explains how a truth, at first revealed by one man, spreads outwardly little by little, makes converts, few in number at the start and usually persecuted, as well as the master himself, by the masses, and by the official representatives of society; and then, spreading more and more because of those persecutions, it ends up by getting hold sooner or later of the collective mind. After having been an exclusively individual truth, it finally is changed into a socially accepted truth; actualized—for good or evil—in the public and private institutions of society, it becomes law.

The Metaphysical Theory of Morality is Old Theology in Disguise. Such is the general theory of the moralists of the metaphysical school. At first sight, as I have already said, it appears to be a quite plausible theory, seemingly successful in reconciling the most disparate things: divine revelation and human reason, immortality and the absolute independence of individuals—with their mortality and their absolute dependence, individualism, and Socialism. But when we examine this theory and its consequences, we can easily see that this is only an apparent reconciliation revealing under the false-face of rationalism and Socialism the old triumph of divine absurdity over human reason, and individual egoism over social solidarity. In the last instance, it leads to the absolute isolation of the individual and consequently to the negation of all morality.

Asocial Character of Metaphysical Morality. What we have to consider here is the moral consequences of this theory. Let us establish first that its morality, notwithstanding its socialistic appearance, is a deeply and exclusively individualistic morality. That having been established, it will not be difficult to prove that, such being its dominant character, it is in fact the negation of all morality.

In this theory the immortal and individual soul of every man, which is infinite and absolutely complete in its essence, and as such not standing in need of anyone else, nor having to enter into any kind of inter-relations in order to find its completion—finds itself at first imprisoned and as if annihilated in the mortal body. While in this fallen state, the reason for which probably will always remain unknown to us, the human mind being incapable of discovering those reasons which are to be found only in the absolute mystery, in God; reduced to this material state and to absolute dependence upon the external world, the human soul stands in need of society in order to wake up, to bring back to mind the memory of itself, to become aware of itself and of the divine principles which from time immemorial have been lodged in it by God and which constitute its true essence.

Contemplation of Divine Absurdity. Such is the socialistic character and the socialistic aspect of this theory. The relations of men to men and of every human individual to the rest of his kind—in short, social life—appear only as a necessary means of development, as a bridge, and not as a goal. The absolute and final goal of every individual is himself, apart from all the other human individuals—it is himself facing the absolute individuality: God. He needs other men in order to emerge from his state of near-annihilation upon earth, in order to rediscover himself, to grasp again his immortal essence, but once he has found this essence, henceforth finding his source of life in that alone, he turns his back upon other people and sinks into contemplation of the mystical absurdity, into adoration of his God.[3]

CHAPTER 13 *Ethics: Exploitation*
of the Masses

Self-Sufficiency of the Individual. If he [the human individual] still retains some relations with other people, it is not because of an ethical urge, and not because of his love for them, for we love only those whom we need or who need us. But a man who has just rediscovered his infinite and immortal essence, and who is complete in himself, stands in need of no one but God, who, because of the mystery, which only metaphysicians understand, seems to possess an infinity which is more infinite and an immortality which is more immortal than that of men. Henceforth, sustained by divine omniscience and omnipotence, the self-centered and free individual does not feel any more the need of associating with other men. And if he still continues to maintain relations with them, he does it only for two reasons: First, while he is still wrapped up in his mortal body, he has to eat, get clothes and shelter, and defend himself against external Nature as well as against attacks by men; and if he is a civilized man, he stands in need of a certain minimum of material things which give him ease, comfort, and luxury, some of which, unknown to our ancestors, are now considered objects of prime necessity.

Exploitation Is the Logical Consequence of the Idea of Morally Independent Individuals. He could, of course, follow the example of the saints of past centuries and seclude himself in a cave, subsisting upon roots. But this does not appear to be to the taste of modern saints, who no doubt believe that material comfort is necessary for the salvation of the soul. Man thus cannot get along without those things. But those things can be produced only by the collective labor of men; the isolated labor of one man would not be able to produce one millionth part thereof. So it follows that the individual in possession of his immortal soul and his inner liberty independent of society—the modern saint—has *material* need of society, without feeling the slightest need of society from a moral point of view.

But how should we name relations which, being motivated only by material needs, are not sanctioned nor backed up by some moral need? Evidently there is only one name for it: *Exploitation*. And, indeed, in the metaphysical morality and in the bourgeois society which, as we know, is based on this morality, every individual necessarily becomes the *exploiter* of society—that is, of everyone else—and the role of the State, in its various forms, beginning with the theocratic State and absolute monarchy and ending with the most democratic Republic based upon genuine universal suffrage, consists only in regulating and guaranteeing this mutual exploitation.

Guerra Omnium Contra Omnia: The Inevitable Result of Metaphysical Morality. In bourgeois society, based upon metaphysical morality, every individual, through necessity or by the very logic of his position, appears as an exploiter of others, for *materially* he stands in need of everyone else, though *morally* he needs no one. Consequently, everyone escaping social solidarity as a hindrance to the full liberty of his soul, but seeing it as a necessary means to maintain his own body, considers society only from the point of view of personal, material utility, contributing only that which is absolutely necessary, to have not the right but the power to obtain for himself this utility.

Everyone views society from the angle of an exploiter. But when all are exploiters, they necessarily must divide into fortunate and unfortunate exploiters, for every exploitation presupposes the existence of persons exploited. There are actual exploiters and those who can be classed in that category only when taken in the potential sense of this term. The latter constitute the majority of people who simply aspire to become exploiters but are not such in reality, being in fact ceaselessly exploited. Here then is what metaphysical or bourgeois ethics lead to in the realm of social economy: to a ruthless and never-ending war among all individuals, to a furious war in which the majority perishes in order to assure the triumph of and prosperity for a small number of people.

Love For Men Takes Second Place After Love of God. The second reason which may lead an individual who has already arrived at the stage of self-possession to maintain his relations with other people is the desire to please God and to carry out the duty he feels to fulfill the Second Commandment.

The First Commandment enjoins man to love God more than himself; the second, to love men, one's fellow-creatures, as much as oneself, and to do to them, *for the love of God,* all the good which one would like to have done to oneself.

Note these words: *for the love of God.* They express perfectly the character of the only human love possible in metaphysical ethics, which consists precisely in not loving men for their own sake, for their own need, but solely in order to please the sovereign master. This, however, is the way it must be: once metaphysics admits the existence of God and the relations between God and men, it must, like theology, subordinate to them all human relations. The idea of God absorbs and destroys all that which is not God, replacing human and earthly realities with divine fictions.

God Cannot Love His Subjects. In the metaphysical morality, as I have said, the man who has arrived at conscious awareness of his immortal soul and its individual freedom before God and in God, cannot love men, for morally he does not need them any more, and one can only love those who have need of one.

If theologians and metaphysicians are to be believed, the first condition has been fulfilled in the relations of men to God, it being claimed by both that man cannot get along without God. Man then can and should love God, for he needs him so much. As to the second condition—the possibility of loving only the one who feels the need of this love—it has not in the least been realized in the relations of man to God. It would be impious to say that God may feel the need of man's love. For to feel any need whatsoever is to lack something essential to the fullness of being, and it is therefore a manifestation of weakness, an avowal of poverty. God, absolutely complete in himself, cannot feel the need of anyone or anything. Not standing in need of men's love, he cannot love them; and that which is called God's love for men is in reality nothing but absolute overbearing power, similar to and naturally more formidable than the power exercised by the mighty German Emperor toward his subjects.

True Love Can Exist Only Among Equals. True, real love, the expression of a mutual and equally felt need, can exist only among equals. The love of the superior for the inferior is oppression, effacement, contempt, egoism, pride, and vanity triumphant in a feeling of grandeur based upon the humiliation of the other party. And the love of the inferior for the superior is humiliation, the fears and the hopes of a slave who expects from his master either happiness or misfortune.

God's Relation to Man Is a Master-Slave Relation. Such is the character of the so-called love of God for men and of men for God. It is despotism on the part of one and slavery on the part of the other.

What do these words signify: to love men and to do good to them, for the love of God? It means to treat them as God would have them treated. And how does he want them to be treated? Like slaves! God by his nature is forced to treat them in the following manner: Being himself the absolute Master, he is compelled to consider them as absolute slaves; and since he considers them slaves, he cannot treat them otherwise.

There is only one way to emancipate those slaves, and that is self-abdication, self-annihilation, and disappearance on the part of God. But that would be too much to demand from this almighty power. He could sacrifice his only son, as the Gospels tell us, to reconcile the strange love which he bears toward men with his no less peculiar eternal justice. But to abdicate, to commit suicide for the love of men—that he will never do, at least not so long as he is not forced to do it by scientific criticism. So long as the credulous fancy of men suffers his existence, he will be the absolute sovereign, the master of slaves. It is clear then that to treat men according to God can mean nothing else but treat them as slaves.

Man's Love According to God. Man's love in the image of God is love for their slavery. I, the immortal and complete individual by the grace of God, who feel myself free precisely because I am the slave of God, don't need any man to render my happiness and my intellectual and moral existence more complete, but I maintain my relations with them in order to obey God, and in loving them for the sake of the love of God, in treating them pursuant to God's love, I want them to be God's slaves like myself. If it then pleases the Sovereign Lord to choose me for the task of making his holy will prevail upon the earth, I shall know well how to force men to be slaves.

Such is the true character of that which God's sincere worshipers call their love for men. It is not so much devotion on the part of those who love as the forced sacrifice of those who are the objects, or rather the victims, of that love. It is not their emancipation, it is their enslavement for the greater glory of God. And it is thus that divine authority was transformed into human authority and that the Church became the founder of the State.

Rule by the Elect.   According to this theory, all men should serve God in this fashion. But, as we know, many are called, but few are chosen. And besides, if all were capable, of fulfilling it in equal measure, that is to say, if all had arrived at the same degree of intellectual and moral perfection, of saintliness and liberty in God, this service would become superfluous. If it is necessary, it is because the vast majority of human individuals have not yet arrived at that point, from which follows that this still ignorant and profane mass of people has to be loved and treated in accordance with the ways of God—that is to say, to be governed and enslaved by a minority of saints, whom God, in one way or another, never fails himself to choose and to establish in a privileged position enabling them to fulfill this duty.

Everything For the People, Nothing By the People.   The sacramental formula for governing the masses of people—for their own good no doubt, for the salvation of their souls, if not their bodies—used by the saints as well as by the nobles in the theocratic and aristocratic States, and also by the intellectuals and the rich people in the doctrinaire, liberal, and even republican States based upon universal suffrage, is always the same: "*Everything for the people, nothing by the people.*"

Which signifies that saints, nobles, or privileged groups—privileged in point of wealth or in point of possession of scientifically trained minds—are all nearer to the ideal or to God as some say, or to reason, justice, and true liberty as others have it, than the masses of people, and therefore have the holy and noble mission of governing them. Sacrificing their own interests and neglecting their own affairs, they are to devote themselves to the happiness of their *lesser brethren*—the people. Government to them is no pleasure, it is a painful duty. They do not seek to gratify their own ambitions, vanity, or personal cupidity, but only the occasion to sacrifice themselves for the common weal. And that no doubt is why the number of people competing for public offices is so small and why kings, ministers, and large and small officeholders accept power only with reluctant hearts.

To Exploit and to Govern Mean One and the Same Thing. Such are, in a society conceived according to the theory of the metaphysicians, the two different and even opposed kinds of relations which may exist among individuals. The first are those of *exploitation,* and the second are those of *government.* If it is true that to govern means to sacrifice oneself for the good of the governed, this second relation contradicts in fact the first—the one of exploitation.

But let us look more closely into the matter. According to the idealistic theory—theological or metaphysical—those words, *"the good of the masses,"* do not signify their earthly well-being, nor their temporal happiness. What do several decades of earthly life amount to in comparison with eternity! Therefore the masses should be governed not with a view to the crass happiness afforded by material blessings upon the earth, but with a view to their eternal salvation. To complain of material privations and sufferings can even be regarded as a lack of education, once it is proven that a surfeit of material enjoyment blights the immortal soul. But then the contradiction disappears: *to exploit and to govern* mean the same thing, one completing the other and in the long run serving as its means and end.

Exploitation and Government.   Exploitation and Government are two inseparable expressions of that which is called politics, the first furnishing the means with which the process of governing is carried on, and also constituting the necessary base as well as the goal of all government, which in turn guarantees and legalizes the power to exploit. From the beginning of history both have constituted the real life of all States: theocratic, monarchic, aristocratic, and even democratic States. Prior to the Great Revolution toward the end of the eighteenth century, the intimate bond between exploitation and government was disguised by religious, loyalist, knightly fictions; but ever since the brutal hand of the bourgeoisie has torn off these rather transparent veils, ever since the revolutionary whirlwind scattered all the vain fancies behind which the Church, the State, the theocracy, monarchy, and aristocracy were carrying on serenely and for such a long time their historic abominations; ever since the bourgeoisie, tired of being the anvil, in turn became the hammer, and inaugurated the modern State, this inevitable bond has revealed itself as a naked and incontestable truth.[1]

[This bond is fully revealed in the ethics of the bourgeois society in which man's morality is determined] by his ability to acquire property when he is born poor, or to preserve and augment it if he is lucky enough to have come into wealth by inheritance.

The Criterion of Bourgeois Morality.   Morality has for its basis the family. But the family has property for its basis and condition of real existence. It follows that property had to be considered as the condition and the proof of the moral value of man. An intelligent, energetic, and honest individual will never fail to acquire this property, which is the necessary social condition of *respectability* on the part of man and citizen, the manifestation of his manly power, the visible sign of his capacities as well as of his honest dispositions and intentions. The barring of non-acquisitive abilities [from directing social life] is then not only a fact but in principle it is even a perfectly legitimate measure. It is a stimulus for honest and capable individuals and a just punishment for those who, being capable of acquiring property, neglect or disdain doing it.

This negligence, this disdain, can have for its source only laziness, laxness, inconsistency of mind or character. Those are quite dangerous individuals: the greater their abilities, the more are they to be condemned and the more severely are they to be punished. For they carry disorganization and demoralization into society. (Pilate did wrong in hanging Jesus Christ for his religious and political opinions; he should have thrown him into prison as a sluggard and a vagabond.[2])

Bourgeois Morality and the Gospels. Therein lies the deepest essence of the bourgeois conscience, of all bourgeois morality. There is no need to point out here the extent to which this morality contradicts the basic principles of Christianity, which, scorning the blessings of this world, (it is the Gospels that are emphatic in scorning the good things of this world, while the preachers of the Gospels are far from disdaining them) forbids the amassing of earthly treasures, because, as it says, "where thy treasure is there will thy heart be also"; it is the Gospels that bid us to imitate the birds of Heaven, which neither labor nor sow, but which live just the same.

I have always admired the marvelous ability of the Protestants to read the words of the Gospels in their own construction, to transact their business, and at the same time to regard themselves as sincere Christians. We will let that go, however. But examine carefully in all their minute details the bourgeois social relations, social and private, the speeches and acts of the bourgeoisie of all countries—and you will find in all of them the deeply implanted naive and basic conviction that *an honest man, a moral man, is he who knows how to acquire, conserve, and augment property, and that a property-owner is the only one worthy of respect.*

In England two prerequisites are attached to the right to be called *a gentleman:* he must go to church, but most of all he must own property. And the English language has a very forceful, picturesque, and naive expression: *That man is worth so much*—That is to say, five, ten, or perhaps a hundred thousand pounds sterling. What the British (and the Americans) say in their grossly naive manner, the bourgeoisie all over the world have in their thoughts. And the vast majority of the bourgeoisie—in Europe, America, Australia, in all the European colonies scattered throughout the world, is so convinced of this basic view that it never even suspects the deep immorality and inhumanity of such ideas.

The Collective Depravity of the Bourgeoisie. The only thing that speaks in favor of the bourgeoisie is the very naiveté of this depravity. It is a collective depravity imposed as an absolute moral law upon all the individuals belonging to that class, which comprises: priests, the nobility, functionaries, military and civil officers, the Bohemian world of artists and writers, industrialists and salesmen, and even workers who strive to become bourgeois—all those who, in a word, want to succeed individually, and who, tired of being an anvil like the great majority of people, want to become in turn a hammer—everybody, with the exception of the proletariat.

This thought, being universal in its scope, is the great immoral force underlying all the political and social acts of the bourgeoisie, and being the more mischievous and pernicious in its effects because it is regarded as the basis and measure of all morality. This circumstance extenuates, explains, and to some extent legitimizes the fury displayed by the bourgeoisie and the atrocious crimes committed by it against the proletariat in June, 1848. There is no doubt that the bourgeoisie would have shown itself no less furious if in defending property privileges against the Socialist workers, it believed that it was only acting in defense of its own interests, but [in that event] it would not have found within itself the energy, the implacable passion, and the unanimity of rage which was instrumental in bringing about its victory in 1848.

The bourgeoisie found this power within itself because it was deeply convinced that in defending its own interests it was at the same time defending the sacred foundations of morality; because very seriously, much more seriously than they themselves realize, *Property is their God,* their only God, which long ago replaced in their hearts the heavenly God of the Christians. And, like the latter in the days of yore, the bourgeois are capable of suffering martyrdom and death for the sake of this God. The ruthless and desperate war which they wage for the defense of property is not only a war of interests: it is a religious war in the full meaning of the word. And the fury and atrocity of which religious wars are capable are well known to any student of history.

The Theology and Metaphysics of the Religion of Property. Property is a god. This god already has its theology (called State Politics and Juridical Right) and also its morality, the most adequate expression of which is summed up in the phrase: "That man is worth so much."

Property—the god—also has its metaphysics. It is the science of the bourgeois economists. Like any metaphysics it is a sort of twilight, a compromise between truth and falsehood, with the latter benefiting by it. It seeks to give falsehood the appearance of truth and leads truth to falsehood. Political economy seeks to sanctify property by labor and to represent it as the realization, the fruit, of labor. If it succeeds in doing this, it will save property and the bourgeois world. For labor is sacred, and whatever is based upon labor is good, just, moral, human, legitimate.

One's faith, however, must be of a sturdy kind to enable him to swallow this doctrine, for we see the vast majority of workers deprived of all property. And what is more, we know from the avowal of the economists and their own scientific proofs, that in the present economic organization, which they defend so passionately, *the masses will never come to own property;* and that, consequently, their labor does not emancipate and ennoble them, for, notwithstanding all their labor, they are condemned to remain eternally without property—that is, outside of morality and humanity. On the other hand, we see that the richest property owners, and consequently the most worthy, humane, moral, and respectable citizens, are precisely those who work the least or who do not work at all.

The reply to this is that now it is impossible to remain rich, to preserve —and even less so—to increase one's wealth, without working. Then let us agree upon the proper use of the word "work": there is work and work. There is productive labor and there is the labor of exploitation. The first is the labor of the proletariat; the second, that of property-owners. The one who turns to good account the lands cultivated by someone else, simply exploits the labor of someone else. The one who increases the value of his capital, whether in industry or in commerce, exploits some one else's labor. The banks which grow rich as a result of thousands of credit transactions, the Stock Exchange speculators, the share-holders who get large dividends without doing a stitch of work; Napoleon III, who became so rich that he was able to raise to wealth all his protegés; King Wilhelm I, who, proud of his victories, is already preparing to levy billions upon poor France, and who already has become rich and is enriching his soldiers with his plunder —all these people are workers, but what kind of workers! Highway robbers! Thieves and ordinary robbers are "workers" to a much greater extent, for, in order to get rich in their own way, they "work" with their own hands.

It is evident to anyone who does not want to be blind that productive work creates wealth and yields to the producer only poverty, and that it is only non-productive, exploiting labor, that yields property. But since property is morality it follows that *morality, as the bourgeois understands it, consists in exploiting someone else's labor.*[3]

Exploitation and Government Are the Faithful Expression of Metaphysical Idealism. Exploitation is the visible body, and government is the soul of the bourgeois regime. And as we have just seen, both of them in this intimate bond are, from the theoretical and practical point of view, the necessary and faithful expression of metaphysical idealism, the inevitable consequence of this bourgeois doctrine which seeks the liberty and morality of individuals outside of social solidarity. This doctrine has as its aim an exploiting government by a small number of fortunate and elect people, an exploited slavery of a great number, and for all—the negation of any morality and any liberty whatever.[4]

CHAPTER 14 *Ethics: Morality of the State*

The Theory of Social Contract. Man is not only the most individual being on earth—he is also the most social being. It was a great fallacy on the part of Jean Jacques Rousseau to have assumed that primitive society was established by a free contract entered into by savages. But Rousseau was not the only one to uphold such views. The majority of jurists and modern writers, whether of the Kantian school or of other individualist and liberal schools, who do not accept the theological idea of society being founded upon divine right, nor that of the Hegelian school—of society as the more or less mystic realization of objective morality— nor the primitive animal society of the naturalist school—take *nolens volens*, for lack of any other foundation, the *tacit contract*, as their point of departure.

A tacit contract! That is to say, a wordless, and consequently a thoughtless and will-less contract: a revolting nonsense! An absurd fiction, and what is more, a wicked fiction! An unworthy hoax! For it assumes that while I was in a state of not being able to will, to think, to speak, I bound myself and all my descendants—only by virtue of having let myself be victimized without raising any protest—into perpetual slavery.[1]

Lack of Moral Discernment in the State Preceding the Original Social Contract. From the point of view of the system which we are now examining the distinction between good and bad did not exist prior to the conclusion of the social contract. At that time every individual remained isolated in his liberty or in his absolute right, paying no attention to the freedom of others except in those cases wherein such attention was dictated by his weakness or his relative strength—in other words, by his own prudence and interest. At that time egoism, according to the same theory, was the supreme law, the only extant right. The good was determined by success, the bad only by failure, and justice was simply the consecration of the accomplished fact, however horrible, cruel, or infamous it might be— as is the rule in the political morality which now prevails in Europe.

The Social Contract as the Criterion of Good and Bad. The distinction between good and bad, according to this system, began only with the conclusion of the social contract. All that which had been recognized as constituting the general interest was declared to be the good, and everything contrary to it, the bad. Members of society who entered into this compact, having become citizens, having bound themselves by solemn obligations, assumed thereby the duty of subordinating their private interests to the common weal, to the inseparable interest of all. They also divorced their individual rights from public rights, the only representative of which—the State—was thereby invested with the power to suppress all the revolts of individual egoism, having, however, the duty of protecting every one of its members in the exercise of his rights in so far as they did not run counter to the general rights of the community.

The State Formed by the Social Contract Is the Modern Atheistic State. Now we are going to examine the nature of the relations which the State, thus constituted, is bound to enter into with other similar States, and also its relations to the population which it governs. Such an analysis appears to us to be the more interesting and useful inasmuch as the State, as defined here, is precisely the modern State in so far as it is divorced from the religious idea: it is the lay State or the atheist State proclaimed by modern writers.

Let us then see wherein this morality consists. The modern State, as we have said, has freed itself from the yoke of the Church and consequently has shaken off the yoke of universal or cosmopolitan morality of the Christian religion, but it has not yet become permeated with the humanitarian idea or ethics—which it cannot do without destroying itself, for in its detached existence and isolated concentration the State is much too narrow to embrace, to contain the interests and consequently the morality of, humanity as a whole.

Ethics Identified with State Interests. Modern States have arrived precisely at that point. Christianity serves them only as a pretext and a phrase, only as a means to fool the simpletons, for the aims pursued by them have nothing in common with religious goals. And the eminent statesmen of our times—the Palmerstons, the Muravievs, the Cavours, the Bismarcks, the Napoleons, would laugh a great deal if their openly professed religious convictions were taken seriously. They would laugh even more if anyone attributed to them humanitarian sentiments, considerations, and intentions, which they have always treated publicly as mere silliness. Then what constitutes their morality? Only State interests. From this point of view, which, with very few exceptions, has been the point of view of statesmen, of *strong men* of all times and all countries, all that is instrumental in conserving, exalting, and consolidating the power of the State is good—sacrilegious though it might be from a religious point of view and revolting as it might appear from the point of view of human morality—and vice versa, whatever militates against the interests of the State is bad, even if it be in other respects the most holy and humanely just thing. Such is the true morality and secular practice of all States.

The Collective Egoism of Particular Associations Raised into Ethical Categories. Such also is the morality of the State founded upon the theory of social contract. According to this system, the good and the just, since they begin only with the social contract, are in fact nothing but the content and the end-purpose of the contract—that is to say, *the common interest and the public right of all individuals who formed this contract, with the exception of those who remained outside of it.* Consequently, by good in this system is meant only the greatest satisfaction given to the collective egoism of a particular and limited association, which, being founded upon the partial sacrifice of the individual egoism of every one of its members, excludes from its midst, as strangers and natural enemies, the vast majority of the human species whether or not it is formed into similar associations.

Morality Is Co-Extensive Only With the Boundaries of Particular States. The existence of a single limited State necessarily presupposes the existence, and if necessary provokes the formation, of several States, it being quite natural that the individuals who find themselves outside of this State and who are menaced by it in their existence and liberty, should in turn league themselves against it. Here then we have humanity broken up into an indefinite number of States which are foreign, hostile, and menacing toward one another.

There is no common right, and no social contract among them, for if such a contract and right existed, the various States would cease to be absolutely independent of one another, becoming federated members of one great State. Unless this great State embraces humanity as a whole, it will necessarily have against it the hostility of other great States, federated internally. Thus war would always be the supreme law and the inherent necessity of the very existence of humanity.

Jungle Law Governs Interrelations of States. Every State, whether it is of a federative or a non-federative character, must seek, under the penalty of utter ruin, to become the most powerful of States. It has to devour others in order not to be devoured in turn, to conquer in order not to be conquered, to enslave in order not to be enslaved—for two similar and at the same time alien powers, cannot co-exist without destroying each other.

The Universal Solidarity of Humanity Disrupted by the State. *The State then is the most flagrant negation, the most cynical and complete negation of humanity.* It rends apart the universal solidarity of all men upon earth, and it unites some of them only in order to destroy, conquer, and enslave all the rest. It takes under its protection only its own citizens, and it recognizes human right, humanity, and civilization only within the confines of its own boundaries. And since it does not recognize any right outside of its own confines, it quite logically arrogates to itself the right to treat with the most ferocious inhumanity all the foreign populations whom it can pillage, exterminate, or subordinate to its will. If it displays generosity or humanity toward them, it does it in no case out of any sense of duty: and that is because it has no duty but to itself, and toward those of its members who formed it by an act of free agreement, who continue constituting it on the same free basis, or, as it happens in the long run, have become its subjects.

Since international law does not exist, and since it never can exist in a serious and real manner without undermining the very foundations of the principle of absolute State sovereignty, the State cannot have any duties toward foreign populations. If then it treats humanely a conquered people, if it does not go to the full length in pillaging and exterminating it, and does not reduce it to the last degree of slavery, it does so perhaps because of considerations of political expediency and prudence, or even because of pure magnanimity, but never because of duty—for it has an absolute right to dispose of them in any way it deems fit.

Patriotism Runs Counter to Ordinary Human Morality. This flagrant negation of humanity, which constitutes the very essence of the State, is from the point of view of the latter the supreme duty and the greatest virtue: it is called *patriotism* and it constitutes the *transcendent morality* of the State. We call it the transcendent morality because ordinarily it transcends the level of human morality and justice, whether private or common, and thereby it often sets itself in sharp contradiction to them. Thus, for instance, to offend, oppress, rob, plunder, assassinate, or enslave one's fellow-man is, to the ordinary morality of man, to commit a serious crime.

In public life, on the contrary, from the point of view of patriotism, when it is done for the greater glory of the State in order to conserve or to enlarge its power, all that becomes a duty and a virtue. And this duty, this virtue, are obligatory upon every patriotic citizen. Everyone is expected to discharge those duties not only in respect to strangers but in respect to his fellow-citizens, members and subjects of the same State, whenever the welfare of the State demands it from him.[2]

The Supreme Law of the State. The supreme law of the State is self-preservation at any cost. And since all States, ever since they came to exist upon the earth, have been condemned to perpetual struggle—a struggle against their own populations, whom they oppress and ruin, a struggle against all foreign States, every one of which can be strong only if the others are weak—and since the States cannot hold their own in this struggle unless they constantly keep on augmenting their power against their own subjects as well as against the neighbor States—it follows that the supreme law of the State is the augmentation of its power to the detriment of internal liberty and external justice.[3]

The State Aims to Take the Place of Humanity. Such is in its stark reality the sole morality, the sole aim of the State. It worships God himself only because he is its own exclusive God, the sanction of its power and of that which it calls its right, that is, the right to exist at any cost and always to expand at the cost of other States. Whatever serves to promote this end is worth while, legitimate, and virtuous. Whatever harms it is criminal. The morality of the State then is the reversal of human justice and human morality.

This transcendent, super-human, and therefore anti-human morality of States is not only the result of the corruption of men who are charged with carrying on State functions. One might say with greater right that corruption of men is the natural and necessary sequel of the State institution. This morality is only the development of the fundamental principle of the State, the inevitable expression of its inherent necessity. The State is nothing else but the negation of humanity; it is a limited collectivity which aims to take the place of humanity and which wants to impose itself upon the latter as a supreme goal, while everything else is to submit and minister to it.

The Idea of Humanity, Absent in Ancient Times, Has Become a Power in Our Present Life. That was natural and easily understood in ancient times when the very idea of humanity was unknown, and when every people worshiped its exclusively national gods, who gave it the right of life and death over all other nations. Human right existed only in relation to the citizens of the State. Whatever remained outside of the State was doomed to pillage, massacre, and slavery.

Now things have changed. The idea of humanity becomes more and more of a power in the civilized world, and, owing to the expansion and increasing speed of means of communication, and also owing to the influence, still more material than moral, of civilization upon barbarous peoples, this idea of humanity begins to take hold even of the minds of uncivilized nations. This idea is the invisible power of our century, with which the present powers—the States—must reckon. They cannot submit to it of their own free will because such submission on their part would be equivalent to suicide, since the triumph of humanity can be realized only through the destruction of the States. But the States can no longer deny this idea nor openly rebel against it, for having now grown too strong, it may finally destroy them.

The State Has to Recognize in Its Own Hypocritical Manner the Powerful Sentiment of Humanity. In the face of this painful alternative there remains only one way out: and that is hypocrisy. The States pay their outward respects to this idea of humanity; they speak and apparently act only in the name of it, but they violate it every day. This, however, should not be held against the States. They cannot act otherwise, their position having become such that they can hold their own only by lying. Diplomacy has no other mission.

Therefore what do we see? Every time a State wants to declare war upon another State, it starts off by launching a manifesto addressed not only to its own subjects but to the whole world. In this manifesto it declares that right and justice are on its side, and it endeavors to prove that it is actuated only by love of peace and humanity and that, imbued with generous and peaceful sentiments, it suffered for a long time in silence until the mounting iniquity of its enemy forced it to bare its sword. At the same time it vows that, disdainful of all material conquest and not seeking any increase in territory, it will put an end to this war as soon as justice is reestablished. And its antagonist answers with a similar manifesto, in which naturally right, justice, humanity, and all the generous sentiments are to be found respectively on its side.

Those mutually opposed manifestoes are written with the same eloquence, they breathe the same virtuous indignation, and one is just as sincere as the other; that is to say, both of them are equally brazen in their lies, and it is only fools who are deceived by them. Sensible persons, all those who have had some political experience, do not even take the trouble of reading such manifestoes. On the contrary, they seek to uncover the interests driving both adversaries into this war, and to weigh the respective power of each of them in order to guess the outcome of the struggle. Which only goes to prove that moral issues are not at stake in such wars.

Perpetual War Is the Price of the State's Existence. The rights of peoples, as well as the treaties regulating the relations of States, lack any moral sanction. In every definite historic epoch they are the material expression of the equilibrium resulting from the mutual antagonism of States. So long as States exist, there will be no peace. There will be only more or less prolonged respites, armistices concluded by the perpetually belligerent States; but as soon as a State feels sufficiently strong to destroy this equilibrium to its advantage, it will never fail to do so. The history of humanity fully bears out this point.[4]

Crimes Are the Moral Climate of the States. This explains to us why ever since history began, that is, ever since States came into existence, the political world has always been and still continues to be the stage for high knavery and unsurpassed brigandage—brigandage and knavery which are held in high honor, since they are ordained by patriotism, transcendent morality, and by the supreme interest of the State. This explains to us why all the history of ancient and modern States is nothing more than a series of revolting crimes; why present and past kings and ministers of all times and of all countries—statesmen, diplomats, bureaucrats, and warriors—if judged from the point of view of simple morality and human justice, deserve a thousand times the gallows or penal servitude.

For there is no terror, cruelty, sacrilege, perjury, imposture, infamous transaction, cynical theft, brazen robbery, or foul treason which has not been committed and all are still being committed daily by representatives of the State, with no other excuse than this elastic, at times so convenient and terrible phrase *reason of State*. A terrible phrase indeed! For it has corrupted and dishonored more people in official circles and in the governing classes of society than Christianity itself. As soon as it is uttered everything becomes silent and drops out of sight: honesty, honor, justice, right, pity itself vanishes and with it logic and sound sense; black becomes white and white becomes black, the horrible becomes humane, and the most dastardly felonies and most atrocious crimes become meritorious acts.[5]

Crime—the Privilege of the State. What is permitted to the State is forbidden to the individual. Such is the maxim of all governments. Machiavelli said it, and history as well as the practice of all contemporary governments bear him out on that point. Crime is the necessary condition of the very existence of the State, and it therefore constitutes its exclusive monopoly, from which it follows that the individual who dares commit a crime is guilty in a two-fold sense: first, he is guilty against human conscience, and, above all, he is guilty against the State in arrogating to himself one of its most precious privileges.[6]

State Morality According to Machiavelli. The great Italian political philosopher, Machiavelli, was the first who gave currency to this phrase (*reason of State*), or at least he gave it its true meaning and the immense popularity which it has enjoyed ever since in governmental circles. Realistic and positive thinker that he was, he came to understand—and he was the first one in this respect—that the great and powerful States could be founded and maintained only by crime—by many great crimes—and by a thorough contempt for anything called honesty.

He wrote, explained, and argued his case with terrible frankness. And since the idea of humanity was wholly ignored in his time; since the idea of fraternity—not human, but religious—preached by the Catholic Church had been, as it always is, nothing but a ghastly irony belied at every instant by the acts of the Church itself; since in his time no one believed that there was such a thing as popular rights—the people having been considered an inert and inept mass, a sort of cannon-fodder for the State, to be taxed, impressed into forced labor and kept in a state of eternal obedience,—in view of all this Machiavelli arrived quite logically at the idea that the State was the supreme goal of human existence, that it had to be served at any cost, and that since the interest of the State stood above everything else, a good patriot should not recoil from any crime in order to serve the State.

Machiavelli counsels recourse to crime, urges it, and makes it the *sine qua non* of political intelligence as well as of true patriotism. Whether the State is called monarchy or republic, crime will always be necessary to maintain and assure its triumph. This crime will no doubt change its direction and object, but its nature will remain the same. It will always be the forced and abiding violation of justice and of honesty—for the good of the State.

Wherein Machiavelli Was Wrong. Yes, Machiavelli was right: we cannot doubt it now that we have the experience of three and a half centuries added to his own experience. Yes, History tells us that while small States are virtuous because of their feebleness, powerful States sustain themselves only through crime. But our conclusion will differ radically from that of Machiavelli, and the reason thereof is quite simple: we are the sons of the Revolution and we have inherited from it the Religion of Humanity which we have to found upon the ruins of the Religion of Divinity. We believe in the rights of man, in the dignity and necessary emancipation of the human species. We believe in human liberty and human fraternity based upon human justice.[7]

Patriotism Deciphered. We have already seen that by excluding the vast majority of humanity from its midst, by placing it outside of the obligations and reciprocal duties of morality, of justice, and of right, the State denies humanity with this high-sounding word, *Patriotism,* and imposes injustice and cruelty upon all of its subjects as their supreme duty.[8]

Man's Original Wickedness—the Theoretical Premise of the State. Every State, like every theology, assumes that man is essentially wicked and bad. In the State which we are going to examine now, *the good,* as we have already seen, begins with the conclusion of the social contract, and therefore is only the product of this contract—its very content. It is not the product of liberty. On the contrary, so long as men remain isolated in their absolute individuality, enjoying all their natural liberty, recognizing no limits to this liberty but those imposed by fact and not by right, they follow only one law—the law of natural egoism.

They insult, maltreat, rob, murder, and devour one another, everyone according to the measure of his intelligence, of his cunning, and of his material forces, as is now being done by the States. Hence human liberty produces not good but evil, man being *bad* by nature. How did he become bad? That is for theology to explain. The fact is that the State, when it came into existence, found man already in that state and it set for itself the task of making him good; that is to say, of transforming the natural man into a citizen.

One might say to this that inasmuch as the State is the product of a contract freely concluded by men and since good is the product of the State, it follows that it is the product of liberty. This, however, would be an utterly wrong conclusion. The State, even according to this theory, is not the product of liberty, but, on the contrary, the product of the voluntary negation and sacrifice of liberty. Natural men, absolutely free from the point of view of *right,* but *in fact* exposed to all the dangers which at every instant of their lives menace their security, in order to assure and safeguard the latter sacrifice, abdicate a greater or lesser portion of their liberty, and inasmuch as they sacrifice it for the sake of their security, in so far as they become citizens, they also become the *slaves of the State.* Therefore we have the right to affirm that from the point of view of the State the good *arises not from liberty, but, on the contrary, from the negation of liberty.*

Theology and Politics. Is it not remarkable, this similitude between theology (the science of the Church) and politics (the theory of the State), this convergence of two apparently contrary orders of thoughts and facts upon one and the same conviction: that of the necessity of sacrificing human liberty in order to make men into moral beings and transform them into saints, according to some, and virtuous citizens, according to others? As for us, we are hardly surprised at it, for we are convinced that politics and theology are both closely related, stemming from the same origin and pursuing the same aim under two different names; we are convinced that every State is a terrestrial Church, just as every Church with its Heaven —the abode of the blessed and the immortal gods—is nothing but a celestial State.

The Similarity of the Ethical Premises of Theology and Politics. The State then, like the Church, starts with this fundamental assumption that all men are essentially bad and that when left to their natural liberty they will tear one another apart and will offer the spectacle of the most frightful anarchy wherein the strongest will kill or exploit the weaker ones. And is not this just the contrary of what is now taking place in our exemplary States?

Likewise the State posits as a principle the following tenet: In order to establish public order it is necessary to have a superior authority; in order to guide men and repress their wicked passions, it is necessary to have a leader, and also to impose a curb upon the people, but this authority must be vested in a man of virtuous genius,* a legislator for his people, like Moses, Lycurgus, or Solon—and that leader and that curb will embody the wisdom and the repressive power of the State.[9]

Society not a Product of a Contract. The State is a transitory historic form, a passing form of society—like the Church, of which it is a younger brother—but it lacks the necessary and immutable character of society which is anterior to all development of humanity and which, partaking fully of the almighty power of natural laws, acts, and manifestations, constitutes the very basis of human existence. Man is born into society just as an ant is born into its ant-hill or a bee into its hive; man is born into society from the very moment that he takes his first step toward humanity, from the moment that he becomes a human being, that is, a being possessing to a greater or lesser extent the power of thought and speech. Man does not choose society; on the contrary, he is the product of the latter, and he is just as inevitably subject to the natural laws governing his essential development as to all the other natural laws which he must obey.

Revolt Against Society Inconceivable. Society antedates and at the same time survives every human individual, being in this respect like Nature itself. It is eternal like Nature, or rather, having been born upon our earth, it will last as long as the earth. A radical revolt against society would therefore be just as impossible for man as a revolt against Nature, human society being nothing else but the last great manifestation or creation of Nature upon this earth. And an individual who would want to rebel against society that is, against Nature in general and his own nature in particular—would place himself beyond the pale of real existence, would plunge into nothingness, into an absolute void, into lifeless abstraction, into God.

So it follows that it is just as impossible to ask whether society is good or evil as it is to ask whether Nature—the universal, material, real, absolute,

---

* The ideal of Mazzini. (Bakunin's footnote.)

sole, and supreme being—is good or evil. It is much more than that: it is an immense, positive, and primitive fact, having had existence prior to all consciousness, to all ideas, to all intellectual and moral discernment; it is the very basis, it is the world in which, inevitably and at a much later stage, there began to develop that which we call good and evil.

The State a Historically Necessary Evil. It is not so with the State. And I do not hesitate to say that the State is an evil but a historically necessary evil, as necessary in the past as its complete extinction will be necessary sooner or later, just as necessary as primitive bestiality and theological divagations were necessary in the past. The State is not society; it is only one of its historical forms, as brutal as it is abstract in character. Historically, it arose in all countries out of the marriage of violence, rapine, and pillage—in a word, of war and conquest—with the Gods created in succession by the theological fancies of the nations. From its very beginning it has been—and still remains—the divine sanction of brutal force and triumphant iniquity. Even in the most democratic countries, like the United States of America and Switzerland, it is simply the consecration of the privileges of some minority and the actual enslavement of the vast majority.

Revolt Against the State. Revolt against the State is much easier because there is something in the nature of the State which provokes rebellion. The State is authority, it is force, it is the ostentatious display of and infatuation with power. It does not seek to ingratiate itself, to win over, to convert. Every time it intervenes, it does so with particularly bad grace. For by its very nature it cannot persuade but must impose and exert force. However hard it may try to disguise this nature, it will still remain the legal violator of man's will and the permanent denial of his liberty.

Morality Presupposes Freedom. And even when the State enjoins something good, it undoes and spoils it precisely because the latter comes in the form of a command, and because every command provokes and arouses the legitimate revolt of freedom; and also because, from the point of view of true morality, of human and not divine morality, the good which is done by command from above ceases to be good and thereby becomes evil. Liberty, morality, and the humane dignity of man consist precisely in that man does good not because he is ordered to do so, but because he conceives it, wants it, and loves it.[10]

CHAPTER 15   *Ethics: Truly Human or Anarchist Morality*

Socialism and Materialism Lead to a Truly Human Morality. Having shown how idealism, starting with the absurd ideas of God, immortality of the soul, the *original* freedom of individuals, and their morality independent of society, inevitably arrives at the consecration of slavery and immorality, I now have to show how real science, materialism and socialism—the second term being but the true and complete development of the first, precisely because they take as their starting point the material nature and the natural and primitive slavery of men, and because they bind themselves to seek the emancipation of men not outside but within society, not against it but by means of it—are bound to end in the establishment of the greatest freedom of individuals and the highest human morality.[1]

The Instinct for Individual Self-Preservation and for Preservation of Species. The elements of what we call morality are already found in the animal world. In all the animal species, with no exception, but with a great difference in development, we find two opposed instincts: the instinct for preservation of the individual and the instinct for preservation of the species; or, speaking in human terms, *the egoistic and the social instincts*. From the point of view of science, as well as from the point of view of Nature itself, those two instincts are equally natural and hence equally legitimate, and, what is even more important, they are equally necessary in the natural economy of beings. The individual instinct is in itself the basic condition for the preservation of the species, for if the individuals did not defend themselves with all their power against all the privations and against all the external pressures constantly menacing their existence, the species itself, which only lives in and through the individuals, would not be able to maintain its existence. But if those two drives are to be judged only from the absolute point of view of the exclusive interest of the species, one may say that social instinct is good, and individual instinct, inasmuch as it is opposed to it, is bad.

The Unbalanced Development of Those Instincts in the Animal World and Among Higher Insects. With the ants and bees it is virtue that predominates, for in both of them social instinct appears to over-ride individual instinct. It is altogether different among wild beasts, and in general one may say that in the animal world egoism is the predominant instinct. Here the instinct of the species, on the contrary, awakens only during short intervals and lasts only so long as it is necessary for the procreation and education of the family.

Egoism and Sociability Are Paramount in Man. It is altogether different with man. It seems, and this has provided one of the pillars of his great superiority over other animal species, that both these opposed instincts —egoism and sociability—are much more powerful and much less distinct from each other in man than among all the other animals. He is more ferocious in his egoism than the wildest beasts and at the same time he is more sociable than ants and bees.[2]

Humanity Is Present Even in the Lowest Character. All human morality, every collective and individual morality, rests basically upon *human respect*. What do we mean by human respect? It is recognition of humanity, of human right and of human dignity in every man of whatever race, color, and degree of intellectual and even moral development he may be. But if a man is stupid, wicked, contemptible, can I respect him? If that were the case, no doubt I would find it impossible to respect his villainy, his stupidity, and brutality; they would make me feel disgusted and indignant; and if necessary I would take most energetic measures against them, not even stopping at killing such a man if no other means were left to defend my life against him, my rights, or whatever I respect or is dear to me. But in the midst of the most energetic and fierce—and if necessary even mortal —struggle against him, I would have to respect his human nature.

Regeneration of Character Possible with Change of Social Conditions. Only at the price of showing such respect can I retain my own human dignity. But if he himself does not recognize this dignity in others, can we recognize the same in himself? If he is a kind of ferocious animal, or even worse, as it sometimes happens, would it not be to indulge in fictions if we acknowledged human nature in him? Not at all! For whatever depths his intellectual and moral degradation may reach at any particular moment, unless he is congenitally insane or an idiot—in which case he should be treated not as a criminal but as a sick person—and if he is in full possession of the sense and intelligence allotted to him by Nature, then his human character, amid the most monstrous deviations, still exists in him, in a very real manner, *as a possibility, always present with him so long as he lives, that somehow he may become aware of his humanity if only a radical change is effected in the social conditions which made him what he is.*

Social Environment the Determining Factor. Take the most intelligent ape possessing the finest character, put it under the best, most humane conditions—and you will never succeed in making a man out of it. Take the most hardened criminal or a man of the poorest mind, and, provided neither one of them suffers from some organic *lesion* which may bring about either idiocy or incurable madness of the other—you will soon come to recognize that if one has become a criminal and the other has not yet developed to the conscious awareness of his humanity and human duties, *the fault lies not with them nor with their nature, but with the social environment in which they were born and have been developing.*

Free Will Is Denied. Here we come to touch upon the most important point of the social question or the science of man in general. We already have declared repeatedly that we *absolutely deny the existence of free will*, in the meaning given to it by theology, metaphysics, and jurisprudence; that is, in the sense of a spontaneous self-determination of the individual will of man, independent of all natural and social influences.

Intellectual and Moral Capacities Are the Expression of Bodily Structure. We deny the existence of a soul, *of a moral entity having existence separate from the body*. On the contrary, we affirm *that just as the body of the individual, with all of its instinctive faculties and predispositions, is nothing but the result of all the general and particular causes that have determined its particular organization, so, what we improperly call the soul—his intellectual and moral capacities—is the direct product or rather the natural immediate expression of this very organization, and especially of the degree of organic development reached by the brain as a result of the concurrence of the totality of causes independent of his will.*

Individuality Fully Determined by the Sum Total of Preceding Causes. Every individual, even the most insignificant one, is the product of centuries of development: the history of causes working toward the formation of such an individual has no beginning. If we possessed the gift, which no one ever has had and no one ever will have, of apprehending and embracing the infinite diversity of transformations of matter or of being that have inevitably succeeded one another from the emergence of our terrestrial globe until the birth of this particular individual, we might be able to say with mathematical precision, without ever knowing that individual, what his organic nature is, and to determine to the minutest detail the measure and character of his intellectual and moral faculties—in a word, his *soul*, as it was in the first hour of his birth.

We have no possibility of analyzing and embracing all these successive transformations, but we can say without fear of being mistaken that *every human individual from the moment of his birth is entirely the product of historic development, that is, of the physiological and social development of his race, of his people, of his caste (if there are castes in his country), of his family, his ancestors, and the individual natures of his father and mother, who have directly transmitted to him by way of physiological heritage, as the natural point of departure for him, and as the determination of his individual nature, all the inevitable consequences of their own previous existence, material as well as moral, individual as well as social, including their thoughts, their feelings, and their acts, including the various vicissitudes of their lives, and the great or small events in which they took part, and likewise including the immense diversity of accidents to which they were subject, along with all that they themselves had inherited in the same way from their own parents.*

Differences Are Determined. There is no need to mention again (for no one disputes it), that differences among races, peoples, and even among classes and families, are determined by geographic, ethnographic, physiological, and economic causes (the economic cause comprises two important points: the question of occupation—the collective division of labor in society and the distribution of wealth—and the question of nourishment, in respect to quantity as well as quality), and also historic, religious, philosophic, juridical, political, and social causes; and that all these causes, combined in a manner differing for every race, every nation, and, more often, for every province and every commune, for every class and every family, impart to everyone his or her own specific physiognomy; that is, a different physiological type, a sum of particular predispositions and capacities—independently of the will of the individuals, who are made up of them and who are altogether their products.

Thus every human individual, at the moment of his birth, is the material, organic derivative of all that infinite diversity of causes which produced him in their combination. His soul—that is, his organic predisposition toward the development of feelings, ideas, and will—is nothing but a product. It is completely determined by the individual physiological quality of his neuro-cerebral system which, like the other parts of his body, absolutely depends upon the more or less fortuitous combination of causes. It mainly constitutes what we call the *particular, original nature of the individual*.

Development Brings out the Implicit Individual Differences. There are as many different natures as there are individuals. Individual differences manifest themselves the clearer as they develop; or rather, they not only manifest themselves with greater power, they actually become greater as the individuals develop, for the external things and circumstances, the thousand elusive causes that influence the development of individuals, are in themselves extremely diverse in character. As a result, we find that the farther an individual advances in life, the more his individual nature becomes delineated, the more he stands out from other individuals by reason of his virtues as well as of his faults.

The Uniqueness of the Individual. To what point is the particular nature or the soul of the individual—that is, the individual particularities of the neuro-cerebral apparatus—developed in new-born infants? The proper answer to this question can be given only by physiologists. We know only that all these particularities must necessarily be hereditary, in the sense that we have tried to explain. That is, they are determined by an infinity of the most diverse and most disparate causes: material and moral, mechanical and physical, organic and spiritual, historical, geographical, economic, and social, great and small, permanent and casual, immediate and far removed in space and time, and *the sum total of which is combined in a single living being and is individualized, for the first and last time, in the current of universal transformations, in this child only, who, in the* *individual acceptance of this word, never had and never will have an exact duplicate.*

It remains now to find out to what point and in which sense this individual nature is really determined at the moment the child leaves its mother's womb. Is that determination only material, or spiritual and moral at the same time, at least in its tendency and natural capacity or its instinctive predisposition? Is the child born intelligent or foolish, good or bad, endowed with will or deprived of it, predisposed to develop along the lines of some particular talent? Can the child inherit the character, habits, and defects, or the intellectual and moral qualities of its parents and ancestors?

Are There Innate Moral Characteristics?   What interests us above all in this question is to know whether *moral attributes*—goodness or wickedness, courage or cowardice, strong or weak character, generosity or avarice, egoism or love for one's fellowman, and other positive or negative characteristics of this kind—whether, like intellectual faculties, they can be physiologically inherited from parents or ancestors; or again, whether quite independently of all heredity, they can be formed by the effect of some accidental cause, known or unknown, working in the child while it is still in its mother's womb? In a word, does the child, when it is born, bring into the world *any moral predispositions?*

The Idea of Innate Moral Propensities Leads to the Discredited Phrenological Theory.   We do not think so. The better to deal with this problem we shall first note here that, if we admitted the existence of innate moral qualities, we would have to assume that that they are interlinked in the newborn infant with some physiological, wholly material particularity of its own organism: upon coming out of the womb of his mother, the child has neither soul nor mind, nor feelings, nor even instincts; it is born into all these. It is therefore only a physical being, and its faculties and qualities, if it has them at all, are only anatomic or physiological.

Thus, for a child to be born good, generous, devoted, courageous, or wicked, avaricious, egoistical, and cowardly, it would be necessary that each one of those virtues or defects should correspond to the specific material and, so to speak, local particularities of his organism, and especially of his brain. Such an assumption would lead us to the system of Gall, who believed that he had found, for every quality and every defect, corresponding bumps and cavities upon the cranium. His theory, as we know, has been unanimously rejected by modern physiologists.

The Logical Implications of the Idea of Innate Moral Propensities. But if it were a well-grounded theory, what would be its implications? Once we assumed that defects and vices as well as good qualities are innate, then we would have to ascertain whether they could or could not be overcome by education. In the first case, the responsibility for all the crimes committed by men would fall back upon the society which failed to give them a proper upbringing, and not upon the individuals themselves, who, on the contrary, could be considered only as victims of this lack of foresight on the part of society. In the second case, innate predispositions being recognized as inevitable and incorrigible, no other way would be left for society but to do away with all individuals who are afflicted with some natural or innate vice. But in order not to fall into the horrible vice of hypocrisy, society should then recognize thereby that it would be doing so solely in the interests of self-preservation, and not of justice.

Only the Positive Has Real Existence. There is another consideration which may help us to clarify this question: in the intellectual and moral as well as in the physical world, only the positive has existence; the negative does not exist, it does not constitute a being in itself, it is only a more or less considerable diminution of the positive. Thus cold is not a different property from heat; it is only a relative absence, a very great diminution of heat. The same is true of darkness, which is but light attenuated to the extreme. Absolute cold and darkness do not exist.

In the intellectual world, stupidity is but weakness of mind; and in the moral world malevolence, cupidity, and cowardice are only benevolence, generosity, and courage reduced not to zero but to a very small quantity. Yet small as it is, it is still a positive quantity, which, with the aid of education, can be developed, strengthened, and augmented in a positive sense. But that would be impossible if vices or negative qualities themselves were positive things, in which case they would have to be eradicated and not developed, for their development could proceed only in a negative direction.

Physiology Versus the Idea of Innate Qualities. Finally, without allowing ourselves to prejudge these serious physiological questions, about which we admit our complete ignorance, let us add the following consideration, on the strength of the unanimous opinion of the authorities of modern physiological science. It seems to have been proved and established that in the human organism there are no separate regions and organs for instinctive, sensory, moral, and intellectual faculties, and that all these faculties are developed *in one and the same part of the brain* by means *of the same nervous mechanism.*

Hence it would seem clearly to follow that there can be no question of various moral or immoral predispositions inevitably determining in the organization of an infant particular qualities or hereditary and innate vices, and that *moral innateness* does not differ in any manner from *intellectual innateness,* both reducing themselves to the more or less high degree of perfection attained in general by the development of the brain.[3]

Moral Characteristics Are Transmitted Not by Heredity but by Social Tradition and Education. Thus the general scientific opinion seems to agree that there are no *special organs* in the brain corresponding to diverse intellectual qualities, nor to the various moral characteristics—affections and passions, good or bad. Consequently, qualities or defects cannot be inherited or be innate; as we have already said, in the new-born child this heredity and innateness can be only material and physiological. Wherein then consists the progressive, historically transmissible improvement of the brain, in respect to the intellectual as well as the moral faculties?

Only in the harmonious development of the whole cerebral and neural system, that is, in the faithful, refined, vivid character of the nervous impressions, as well as in the capacity of the brain to transform those impressions into feelings and ideas, and to combine, encompass, and permanently retain in one's mind the widest associations of feelings and ideas.

The associations of feelings and ideas, the development and successive transformations of which constitute the intellectual and moral aspect of the history of humanity, do not bring about in the human brain the formation of new organs corresponding to every separate association, and consequently cannot be transmitted to individuals by way of physiological heredity. What is physiologically inherited is the more and more strengthened, enlarged, and perfected aptitude to conceive and create new associations.

But the associations themselves and the complex ideas represented by them, such as the ideas of God, fatherland, and morality, since they cannot be innate, are transmitted to individuals only through *social traditions and education*. They get hold of the child from the first day of its birth, and inasmuch as they have already become embodied in the surrounding life, in the material and moral details of the social world into which the child has been born, they penetrate in a thousand different ways, first the childish consciousness, and then the adolescent and juvenile consciousness, as it comes to life, grows, and is shaped by their all-powerful influences.[4]

CHAPTER 16 *Ethics: Man Wholly the Product of Environment*

Taking education in the broadest sense of the word, and understanding by it not only the inculcation of moral maxims, but above all the examples given to the child by the persons surrounding him, and the influence of everything he hears and sees; understanding by the term *education* not only the cultivation of the child's mind but also the development of his body through nourishment, hygiene, and physical exercise, we can say, fully convinced that no one will seriously dispute this opinion, that every child, youth, adult, and even the most mature man, is wholly the product of the environment that nourished and raised him—an inevitable, involuntary, and consequently irresponsible product.

He enters life without a soul, without a conscience, without the shadow of an idea or any feeling, but with a human organism whose individual nature is determined by an infinite number of circumstances and conditions preceding the emergence of his will, and which in turn determines his greater or smaller capacity to acquire and assimilate the feelings, ideas, and associations worked out by centuries of development and transmitted to everyone *as a social heritage* by the education which he receives. Good or bad, this education is imposed upon man—and he is in no way responsible for it. It shapes him, in so far as his individual nature allows, in its own image, so that a man thinks, feels, and desires whatever the people around him feel, think, and desire.

Natural Differences Are Not Denied.   But then, we may be asked, how can one account for the fact that education which is completely identical, in appearance at least, often yields widely diverse results in point of development of character, heart, and mind? But, to begin with, do not natures themselves differ at birth? This natural and innate difference, small as it may be, is nevertheless positive and real: difference in temperament, in vital energy, in the predominance of one sense or one group of organic functions over others, difference in vivacity and natural capacities.

We have tried to prove that vices as well as moral qualities—facts of individual and social consciousness—cannot be physically inherited, and that man cannot be physiologically predetermined toward evil, nor irrevocably rendered incapable of good. But we have never meant to deny that individual natures differ widely among themselves, that some of them are endowed to a greater extent than others with a capacity for a full human development. True, we believe that these natural differences are now quite exaggerated and that most of them should be attributed not to Nature but to the different education which has been allotted to each individual.

Physiological Psychology and Pedagogy Are Still in a State of Infancy. In order to decide this question, it is necessary that the two sciences which are called upon to solve it—physiological psychology, or the science of the brain, and pedagogy, the science of education or of the social development of the brain—should emerge from the infantile state in which both of them still are. But once the physiological differences of individuals, of whatever degree they may be, are admitted, it clearly follows that a system of education, excellent in itself as an abstract system, may be good for one but bad for another.

Physiological Heredity Is Not Altogether Denied. It may be argued that however imperfect education may be, it alone cannot explain the undeniable fact that in families which are the most lacking in moral sense we often encounter individuals who strike us because of the nobility of their instincts and feelings. And, on the contrary, we very often meet, in families highly developed in a moral and•intellectual sense, individuals base in heart and intellect.

But this is only an apparent contradiction. In reality, although we have stated that in most cases man is almost entirely the product of the social conditions among which he is formed, and although we have assigned a comparatively small part to the influence of the physiological heredity of the natural qualities received at birth, we have not altogether denied such a part. We have even recognized that in some exceptional cases, in men of genius or of great talent for example, as well as idiots or highly perverse natures, this influence of natural determination upon the development of the individual—a determination as inevitable as the influence of education and society—may be great.

The last word on these questions belongs to the physiology of the brain; but this science has not yet arrived at a point enabling it to solve them even approximately. The only thing we can affirm now with certitude is that all such questions gravitate between two fatalisms—the natural, organic, physiologically hereditary fatalism, and the fatalism of heritage, social tradition, education, and the civic, social, and economic organization of every country. In neither of these two fatalisms is there room for free will.

Accidental and Intangible Factors Making for Particular Developments. But apart from the natural, positive, or negative determination of the individual, which may place him in contradiction to the spirit reigning in his whole family, there may exist in each separate case other hidden causes that in most cases remain unknown, but which nevertheless have to be taken into account. The concurrence of special circumstances, an unforeseen event, an accident insignificant in itself, the chance meeting of some particular person, and sometimes a book falling into the hands of an individual at just the right moment—all that which in a child, in an adolescent, or in a young man, when his imagination is in a state of ferment and when it is still open to the impressions of life, may produce a radical revolution toward good or bad.

To this must be added the elasticity proper to all young natures, especially when they are endowed with a certain natural energy which makes them revolt against too authoritarian and despotically persistent influences, and owing to which even an excess of evil may sometimes produce good.

When Good Results in Evil. Can an excess of goodness, or what goes by the name of good, produce evil? Yes, when it is imposed as a despotic, absolute law—religious, philosophical in a doctrinaire way, political, juridical, social, or as the patriarchal law of the family—in a word, when the good, or what appears to be good, is imposed upon the individual as a negation of freedom, and is not the product of his freedom. But in such a case the revolt against good thus imposed is not only natural but also legitimate; such rebellion, far from being evil, is, on the contrary, good; for there is nothing good outside of freedom, and freedom is the absolute source and condition of all good that is truly worthy of that name: for good is nothing else but freedom.[1]

Socialism Is Based on Determinism. Socialism, being founded upon positive science, absolutely rejects the doctrine of *"free will."* It recognizes that whatever is called human vice and virtue is absolutely the product of the combined action of Nature and society. Nature, through its ethnographical, physiological, and pathological action, creates faculties and dispositions which are called natural, and the organization of society develops them, or on the other hand halts or falsifies their development. All individuals, with no exception, are at every moment of their lives what Nature and society have made them.

Improvement of Man's Morality Is Conditioned by Moralization of Social Environment. Hence it clearly follows that to make men moral it is necessary to make their social environment moral. And that can be done in only one way: by assuring the triumph of justice, that is, the complete liberty of everyone in the most perfect equality for all. Inequality of conditions and rights, and the resulting lack of liberty for all, is the great collective iniquity begetting all individual iniquities. Suppress this source of iniquities and all the rest will vanish along with it.

A Moral Environment Will Be Created by Revolution. In view of the lack of enthusiasm shown by men of privilege for moral improvement —or what is the same thing, for equalizing their rights with others—we fear that the triumph of justice can be effected only through a social revolution.

Three things are necessary for men to become moral, that is, complete men in the full meaning of the word: birth under hygienic conditions; a rational and integral education accompanied by an upbringing based upon respect for work, reason, equality, and liberty: and a social environment wherein the human individual, enjoying full liberty, will be equal, in fact and by right, to all others.

Does such an environment exist? It does not. It follows then that it has to be created.[2]

Human Justice Versus Legal Justice. When we speak of justice we mean not the justice contained in the legal codes and in Roman jurisprudence, based largely upon deeds of violence achieved by force, violence consecrated by time and by the benedictions of some church—Christian or pagan— and as such accepted as the absolute principles from which all law is to be deduced by a process of logical reasoning. We speak of justice that is based solely upon human conscience, the justice found in the conscience of every man, and even in that of children, and which can be expressed only in the words *equal rights*.

This universal justice, which, owing to conquests by force and influences of religion, has never yet prevailed in the political, juridical, or economic world, is to serve as the basis of the new world. Without this justice, there can be neither liberty nor republic nor prosperity nor peace. It must, then, govern all our decisions, so that we may work together effectively for the establishment of peace.

Moral Law in Action.   What we ask is the proclaiming anew of the great principle of the French Revolution: that every man should have the material and moral means to develop his whole humanity, a principle which must be translated into the following problem:

To organize society in such a manner that every individual, man or woman, should, at birth, find almost equal means for the development of his or her various faculties and the full utilization of his or her work. To organize society in such a fashion that exploitation of the labor of others should be made impossible and that every individual should be enabled to enjoy the social wealth, which in reality is produced only by collective labor—only in so far as he contributes directly toward the creation of this wealth.[3]

The Moral Law Emanates From Human Nature.   *The moral law*, the existence of which we, materialists and atheists, recognize in a more real manner than the idealists of any school, is indeed an actual law, which will triumph over all the conspiracies of all the idealists of the world, because it emanates from the very nature of human society, the root basis of which is to be sought not in God but in animality.[4]

The primitive, natural man becomes a free man, becomes humanized, and rises to the status of a moral being,—in a word, he becomes conscious of, and realizes within himself and for himself, his own human form and his rights—only to the degree that he becomes aware of this form and these rights in all his fellow-beings. It follows that in the interests of his own humanity, his own morality and personal freedom, man must aspire toward the freedom, morality, and humanity of all other men.[5]

Freedom Is Not the Negation of Solidarity.   Social solidarity is the first human law; freedom is the second law. Both laws interpenetrate each other and, being inseparable, constitute the essence of humanity. Thus freedom is not the negation of solidarity; on the contrary, it represents the development and, so to speak, the humanizing of it.[6]

Thus respect for the freedom of someone else constitutes the highest duty of men. The only virtue is to love this freedom and serve it. This is the basis of all morality, and there is no other basis.

Since freedom is the result and the clearest expression of solidarity, that is, of mutuality of interests, it can be realized only under conditions of equality. Political equality can be based only upon economic and social equality. And justice is precisely the realization of freedom through such equality.[7]

[What has been said above enables us to draw a clear line of demarcation between the bases of divine and state morality on the one hand, and human morality on the other.]

Wherein Divine Morality Differs From Human Morality. Divine morality is based upon two immoral principles: respect for authority and contempt for humanity. Human morality, on the contrary, is based only upon contempt for authority and respect for liberty and humanity. Divine morality considers work a degradation and a punishment; human morality sees in work the supreme condition of human happiness and dignity. Divine morality leads inevitably to a policy which recognizes only the rights of those who, owing to their privileged position, can live without working. Human morality accords such rights only to those who live by working; it recognizes that only by working does man reach the stature of man.[8]

CHAPTER 17　*Society and the Individual*

Society Is the Basis of Human Existence. Society, preceding in time any development of humanity and fully partaking of the almighty power of natural laws, actions, and manifestations, constitutes the very essence of human existence. Man is born into society, just as an ant is born into an ant-hill or a bee into its hive; man is born into society from the very moment that he becomes a human being, that is, a being possessing to a greater or lesser extent the power of speech and thought. Man does not choose society; on the contrary, he is the product of the latter, and he is just as inevitably subjected to natural laws governing his necessary development as to all other natural laws which he must obey. Society antedates and at the same time survives every human individual, being in this respect like Nature itself; it is eternal like Nature, or rather, having been born upon this earth, it will last as long as our earth itself.

Revolt Against Society Is Inconceivable. A radical revolt by man against society would therefore be just as impossible as a revolt against Nature, human society being nothing else but the last great manifestation or creation of Nature upon this earth. And an individual who would want to rebel against society, that is, against Nature in general and his own nature in particular, would place himself beyond the pale of real existence, would plunge into nothingness, into an absolute void, into lifeless abstraction, into God. It follows that it is just as impossible to ask whether society is good or evil as it is to ask whether Nature—the universal, material, real, absolute, sole, and supreme being—is good or evil. It is much more than that: it is an immense, overwhelming fact, a positive and primitive fact, having existence prior to all consciousness, to all ideas, to all intellectual and moral discernment. It is the very basis, it is the world in which inevitably, and at a much later stage, there begins to develop what we call good and evil.[1]

There Is No Humanity Outside of Society. During a very long period, lasting thousands of years, our species roamed the earth in isolated herds. That was before, together with the first emergence of speech and the first gleam of thought, there awakened within the social and animal environment of one of those human herds, the first self-conscious or free individuality. Apart from society, man would never cease to be a speechless and an unreasoning animal, a thousand times poorer and more dependent upon external Nature than most of the quadrupeds, above which he now towers so proudly.

Even the most wretched individual of our present society could not exist and develop without the cumulative social efforts of countless generations. Thus the individual, his freedom and reason, are the products of society, and not *vice versa*: society is not the product of individuals comprising it; and the higher, the more fully the individual is developed, the greater his freedom—and the more he is the product of society, the more does he receive from society and the greater his debt to it.

Society Is Acted Upon By Individuals. Society in turn is indebted to individuals. One might even say that there is not an individual, inferior though he may be by nature and illfavored by life and upbringing, who does not in turn influence society, be it even to the smallest extent, by his feeble labor, his even more feeble intellectual and moral development, and his attitudes and actions even though they may be almost unnoticed. It stands to reason, of course, that he himself does not even suspect and does not will this influence exerted by him upon the society which produced him.

Individuals Are the Instrumentalities of Social Development. For the real life of society, at every instant of its existence, is nothing but the sum total of all the lives, developments, relations, and actions of all the individuals comprising it. But these individuals got together and united not arbitrarily, not with a compact, but independently of their will and consciousness. They are not only brought together and combined into one, but are begotten, in the material, intellectual, and moral life they express and embody in actuality. Therefore the action of those individuals—the conscious, and in most cases, unconscious action—upon society, which begot them, is in reality a case of society acting upon itself by means of the individuals comprising it. The latter are the instrumentalities of social development begotten and promoted by society.

Man Is Not Born a Free and Socially Independent Individual. Man does not create society but is born into it. He is born not free, but in fetters, as the product of a particular social environment created by a long series of past influences, developments, and historic facts. He bears the stamp of the region, climate, ethnic type, and class to which he belongs, the economic and political conditions of social life, and finally, of the locality, the city or village, the house, family, and circle of people into which he was born.

All that determines his character and nature, gives him a definite language, and imposes upon him, with no chance of resistance on his part, a ready-made world of thoughts, habits, feelings, and mental vistas, and places him, before consciousness awakens in him, in a rigorously determined relationship to the surrounding social world. He becomes organically a member of a certain society, and fettered, inwardly and outwardly, permeated to the end of his days with its beliefs, prejudices, passions, and habits, he is but the most unconscious and faithful reflection of this society.

Freedom Is Generated at a Later Stage of Individual Revolt. Therefore every man is born and, in the very first years of his life, remains the slave of society; and perhaps, not even a slave—because in order to be a slave one has to be aware of his state of slavery—but rather an unconscious and an involuntary offshoot of that society.[2]

Social environment, and public opinion, which always express the material and political opinion of that environment, weigh down heavily upon free thought, and it takes a great deal of power of thought, and even more of anti-social interest and passion, to withstand that heavy oppression. Society itself, by its positive and negative action, generates free thought in man, and in turn, it is society which often crushes it.

Man is so much of a social animal that it is impossible to think of him apart from society.[3]

The Idealists' Point of View. The point of view of the idealists is altogether different. In their system man is first produced as an immortal and free being and ends up by becoming a slave. As a free and immortal being, infinite and complete in himself, he does not stand in need of society. From which follows that if man does enter society he does it because of the original fall, or because he forgets and loses the consciousness of his immortality and freedom.[4]

Individual freedom, according to them, is not the creation, the historic product of society. They maintain that this freedom is prior to all society and that every man, at his birth, brings with him his immortal soul as a divine gift. Hence it follows that man is complete in himself, a whole being, and is in any way absolute only when he is outside of society. Being free prior to and apart from society, he necessarily joins in forming this society by a voluntary act, by a sort of contract—whether instinctive and tacit, or deliberated upon and formal. In a word, in this theory, it is not the individuals who are created by society, but on the contrary, it is they who create it, driven by some external necessity such as work or war.

The State Takes the Place of Society in the Idealistic Theory. One can see that in this theory, society, in the proper meaning of the word, does not exist. The natural, human society, the real starting point of all human civilization, the only environment in which the freedom and individuality of men can arise and develop is altogether foreign to this theory. On the one hand it recognizes only individuals, existing for themselves and free in themselves, and on the other, this conventional society, the State, formed arbitrarily by these individuals and based upon a contract—whether formal or tacit. (They know very well that no historic State ever had any kind of contract for its basis, and that all States were founded by violence, by conquest. But this fiction of free contract as the foundation of the State is quite necessary for them, and without further ceremony they make full use of it.)

The Asocial Character of Christian Saints; Their Lives the Acme of Idealistic Individualism. The human individuals whose mass, united by a convention, forms the State, would appear in this theory as beings altogether singular and full of contradictions. Endowed with an immortal soul and with freedom or free will which is inherent in them, they are on the one hand infinite and absolute beings and as such complete in themselves and for themselves, self-sufficient and needing no one else, not even God, for being immortal and infinite they are themselves gods. On the other hand, they are beings who are very brutal, feeble, imperfect, limited, and absolutely dependent upon external Nature, which sustains, envelops, and finally carries them off to their graves.

Regarded from the first point of view, they need society so little that the latter appears actually to be a hindrance to the fullness of their being, to their perfect liberty. Thus we have seen in the first centuries of Christianity that holy and steadfast men who had taken in earnest the immortality of the soul and the salvation of their own souls broke their social ties, and, shunning all commerce with human beings, sought in solitude perfection, virtue, God. With much reason and logical consistency they came to regard society as a source of corruption and the absolute isolation of the soul as the condition on which all virtues depend.

If they sometimes emerged from their solitude, this was not because they felt the need of society but because of generosity, Christian charity, felt by them in regard to the rest of the people who, still continuing to be corrupted in the social environment, needed their counsel, their prayers, and their guidance. It was always to save others and never to save themselves, nor to attain greater self-perfection. On the contrary, they risked losing their own souls by re-entering society, from which they had escaped in horror, deeming it the school of all corruption, and as soon as their holy work was completed, they would return as quickly as they could to their desert in order to perfect themselves again by incessant contemplation of their individual beings, their solitary souls, alone in the presence of God.

An Immortal Soul Must Be the Soul of an Absolute Being. This is an example to be followed by all those who still believe in the immortality of the soul, in innate freedom or free will, if only they want to save their souls and worthily prepare themselves for eternal life. I repeat: the saintly anchorites who, because of their self-imposed isolation, ended in complete imbecility, were entirely logical. Once the soul is immortal, that is, infinite in its essence, it should therefore be self-sufficient. It is only transitory, limited, and finite beings that can complete one another; the infinite does not have to complete itself.

In meeting another being which is not itself, it feels itself confined by it and therefore it has to shun and ignore whatever is not itself. Strictly speaking, as I have said, the immortal soul should be able to get along without God himself. A being that is infinite in itself cannot recognize alongside of it another being equal to it, and even less so—a being which is superior and above it. For every other infinite being would limit it and consequently make it a fine and determined being.

In recognizing a being as infinite as itself and outside of itself, the immortal soul would thus necessarily recognize itself as a finite being. For infinity must embrace everything and leave nothing outside of itself. It stands to reason that an infinite being cannot and should not recognize an infinite being which is superior to it. Infinity does not admit anything relative or comparative: the terms *infinite superiority* and *infinite inferiority* are absurd in their implication.

The Idea of God and That of Immortality of Soul Are Mutually Contradictory. God is precisely an absurdity. Theology, which has the privilege of being absurd and which believes in things precisely because those things are absurd, places above immortal and consequently infinite human souls, the supreme absolute infinity: God. But by way of offsetting this infinity it creates the fiction of Satan, who represents precisely the revolt of an infinite being against the existence of an absolute infinity, a revolt against God. And just as Satan revolted against the infinite superiority of God, the holy recluses of Christianity, too humble to revolt against God, rebelled against the equal infinity of men, rebelled against society.

The Logic of Personal Salvation. They declared with much reason that they did not need society in order to be saved: and since they were by a strange fatality [here follows an illegible word in Bakunin's manuscript] degraded infinities—the society of God, and self-contemplation in the presence of that absolute infinity, were quite sufficient for them.

I repeat again: their example is one to be followed by all those who believe in the immortality of the soul. From their point of view society cannot offer them anything but certain perdition. And in effect what does it give to men? First, material wealth, which can be produced in sufficient amount only by collective labor. But to one who believes in eternal existence, wealth can be only an object of contempt. For did not Jesus Christ say to his disciples: "Lay not up for yourself treasures upon the earth, for where thy treasure is there will thy heart be also," and "It is easier for a great rope (or a camel in another version) to pass through a needle's eye than for a rich man to enter the kingdom of God"? (I can very well picture to myself the expression upon the faces of the pious and wealthy bourgeois Protestants of England, America, Germany, and Switzerland, as they read those Gospel sentences which are so decisive and disagreeable with regard to them.)

Production of Wealth Is Necessarily a Social Act and Is Incompatible With Personal Salvation. Jesus Christ was right: the lust for material riches and the salvation of the immortal soul are absolutely incompatible, and if one believes in the immortality of the soul, is it not better to renounce the comfort and luxury afforded by society and subsist upon roots, as was done by the saintly hermits in saving their souls for eternity, than to lose one's soul as the price of a dozen years of material pleasures? This calculation is so simple, so evidently just, that we are compelled to think that the pious and rich bourgeois, the bankers, industrialists, and merchants who do such wonderful business by means so well known to us, and who still keep on repeating the sayings of the Gospels, count in no wise upon immortality of soul for themselves, generously abandoning it to the proletariat, while humbly reserving for themselves those miserable material goods which they amass upon this earth.

Culture and Civilized Values Are Incompatible With the Idea of Immortality of the Soul. Apart from material blessings, what else does society give to men? Carnal, human, earthly affections, civilization, and culture of the mind, all of which loom so vastly from the human, transitory, and terrestrial point of view, but which are a mere zero in the face of eternity, immortality, and God. And is not the greatest human wisdom but mere folly before God?

There is a legend of the Eastern Church which tells of two saintly hermits who voluntarily imprisoned themselves for several decades on a desert island, and having isolated themselves from each other and passing their days and nights in contemplation and prayer, finally arrived at a point where both nearly lost the power of speech. Of their old vocabulary they retained only three or four words, all of which, taken together, did not make any sense, but which nevertheless expressed before God the most sublime aspirations of their souls. Of course they lived naturally on roots like herbivorous animals. From the human point of view those two men were imbeciles or madmen, but from the divine point of view, from the point of view of the belief in the immortality of the soul, they showed themselves to be more profound calculators than Galileo and Newton. For they sacrificed a few decades of earthly prosperity and the spirit of this world in order to gain eternal beatitude and the divine spirit.

Society as a Result of Man's Original Fall. It is clear then that man, in so far as he is endowed with an immortal soul, with infinity and liberty inherent in this soul, is pre-eminently an anti-social being. And had he always been wise, if, exclusively preoccupied with his eternity, he had had the intelligence to turn his back upon all the good things, affections, and vanities of this earth, he never would have emerged from the state of divine innocence or imbecility and never would have had to form a society.

In a word, had Adam and Eve never tasted the fruit of the tree of knowledge, we would still be living like beasts in the earthly paradise which God assigned to them for their habitation. But as soon as men wanted to know, to become civilized, humanized, to think, speak, and enjoy material blessings, they necessarily had to emerge from their solitude and organize themselves into a society. For just as they are *inwardly* infinite, immortal, and free, so are they *externally* limited, moral, feeble, and dependent upon the external world.[5]

A contradictory being, inwardly infinite as the spirit, but outwardly dependent, defective, and material, man is compelled to combine with others into a society, not for the needs of his soul, but in order to preserve his body. Society then is formed by a sort of sacrifice of the interests and the independence of the soul to the contemptible needs of the body. It is a veritable fall and enslavement for the individual who is inwardly free and immortal; it is at least a partial renunciation of his primitive liberty.

The Stock Theory of Individual Renunciation of Liberty for the Sake of Forming a Society. We all know the sacramental phrase which in the jargon of all the partisans of the State and juridical right expresses this fall and this sacrifice, this first fateful step toward human enslavement. The individual enjoying complete liberty in his natural state, that is, before he has become a member of any society, sacrifices a part of this freedom when entering society in order that the latter guarantee to him the remaining liberty. When an explanation of this phrase is requested, the usual rejoinder is another phrase of that kind: "The freedom of every human individual should be limited only by the liberty of all other individuals."

In appearance nothing is more just. But this theory, however, contains in embryo the whole theory of despotism. In conformity with the basic idea of idealists of all schools and contrary to all the real facts, the human individual is presented as an absolutely free individual in so far, and only in so far, as he remains outside of society. Hence it follows that society, viewed and conceived only as a juridical and a political society—that is, as a State—is the negation of liberty. Here then is the result of idealism; as one can see, it is altogether contrary to the deductions of materialism which, in agreement with that which is taking place in the real world, makes individual human freedom emerge from society as the necessary consequence of the collective development of humanity.[6]

CHAPTER 18 *Individuals Are Strictly Determined*

Considered from the point of view of their earthly existence—that is, not their fictitious but their real existence—human beings in the mass present such a degrading spectacle, appearing to be so hopelessly lacking in initiative, power of will, and mind, that it takes a great deal of the capacity for self-delusion to be able to find in them an immortal soul and the shadow of any free will whatever. To us they appear as beings that are absolutely and inevitably determined; determined above all by external Nature, by the physical relief of the country surrounding them, and by all the material conditions of their existence. They are determined by countless relations of political, religious, and social character, by customs, usages, laws, by a world of prejudices or thoughts slowly evolved during past centuries; by all that they find at birth already present in society, which they do not create but of which they are first of all products and afterward instruments. Among a thousand people one can hardly find a single person of whom it can be said, from a relative and not an absolute point of view, that he wills and thinks independently.

The Majority Think and Will According to Given Social Patterns. The great majority of human individuals, not only among the *ignorant masses* but among the civilized and privileged classes as well, do not will and do not think any differently from what the world around them wills and thinks. No doubt they believe that they do their own thinking and willing, but in reality they only reproduce slavishly, by rote, with insignificant and scarcely perceptible modifications, the thoughts and wishes of other people. This slavishness, this routine, the never-failing source of commonplaces, this lack of rebellion in the will and the lack of initiative in the thoughts of individuals, are the principal causes of the dismaying slowness of the historic development of humanity. To us materialists and realists, who believe in neither the immortality of the soul nor in free will, this slowness, distressing as it may be, appears only as a natural fact.

Man Is a Social Animal. Emerging from the condition of the gorilla, man arrives only with difficulty at the awareness of his humanity and the realization of his liberty. In the beginning he has neither liberty nor the awareness thereof; he comes into the world as a ferocious beast and as a slave, and he becomes humanized and progressively emancipated only in the midst of society, which necessarily precedes the emergence of man's thought, speech, and will. Man can attain that only through the collective efforts of all the past and present members of this society, which therefore is the natural basis and starting point of his human existence.

Hence it follows that man realizes his individual freedom only by rounding out his personality with the aid of other individuals belonging to the same social environment; he can achieve that only by dint of labor and the collective power of society, without which man would no doubt remain the most stupid and most miserable of all wild animals living upon this earth. According to the materialist system, which is the only natural and logical system, society, far from limiting and decreasing, creates the freedom of the individual, creates, on the contrary, this freedom. Society is the root, the tree of freedom, and liberty is its fruit. Consequently, in every epoch man has to seek his liberty not at the beginning but at the end of history, and one may say that the real and complete emancipation of every individual is the true, great objective, the supreme purpose of history.[1]

Rousseau's Fallacy. It was a great fallacy on the part of Jean Jacques Rousseau to have assumed that primitive society was established by a free contract entered into by savages. But Rousseau was not the only one to uphold such views. Most of the jurists and modern writers, whether of the Kantian or the other individualist and liberal schools, who, since they do not accept the theological idea of society being founded upon divine right, nor that of the Hegelian school (of society being determined as the more or less mystic realization of objective morality), nor the primitive animal society of the naturalist school, take *nolens volens*—lacking any other foundation—the tacit contract, as their point of departure.

A tacit contract! That it to say, a wordless and consequently a thoughtless and will-less contract! A revolting nonsense! An absurd fiction, and what is more—a wicked fiction! An unworthy hoax! For it presupposes that while I was in the state of not being able to will, to think, to speak, I bound myself and my descendants—simply by reason of having let myself be victimized without raising any protest—into perpetual slavery.

Absolute Domination by the State Implied by the Social Contract Theory. The consequences of the *social contract* are in effect disastrous, for they lead to absolute domination by the State. And still, the principle itself, taken as a starting point, seemed extremely liberal in character. Prior to forming this contract, the individuals are supposed to have enjoyed unbounded liberty, for, according to this theory, the natural man, the savage, is in possession of complete freedom. We already have expressed our opinion about this natural liberty, which is simply the absolute dependence of the man-gorilla upon the permanent and besetting influences of the external world. But let us assume, however, that man was really free at the starting point of his historic development; why then was society formed? In order to assure, we are told, his security against all possible invasions of this external world, including invasions by other men—either combined into an association or as isolated individuals—but who do not belong to this newly formed society.

Society as the Result of Limitation of Liberty. So here then we see those primitive men, absolutely free, every one of them by himself and for himself, enjoying this unlimited freedom so long as they do not meet one another, so long as every one of them is immersed in the state of absolute individual isolation. The freedom of one man does not stand in need of the freedom of any other man; on the contrary, every one of those individual liberties is self-sufficient and exists by itself, so that it necessarily appears as the negation of the freedom of all the others, and all of them meeting together, are bound to limit and detract from one another, are bound to contradict, to destroy one another. . . .

In order not to carry out this mutual destruction to the bitter end, they enter into a *contract*—tacit or formal—by which they abandon some of those liberties, so as to assure for themselves the remainder. This contract becomes the foundation of society or rather of the State; for, it is to be noted, that under this theory there is no room for society; it is only the State that has existence, or rather, society, according to this theory, is altogether absorbed by the State.

Social Laws Should Not Be Confounded with Juridical and Political Laws. Society is the natural mode of existence of the human collective, and is independent of any contract. It is governed by customs or traditional usages and never by laws. It progresses slowly through the moving power of individual initiative, but not because of the thought or will of the legislator. There are many laws which govern society without the latter being aware of their presence, but those are natural laws, inherent in the social body, just as physical laws are inherent in material bodies. The greater part of those laws still remain unknown, and yet they have been governing human society ever since its birth, independently of the thought and will of men comprising such society. Those laws therefore should not be confounded with the political and juridical laws which, promulgated by some legislative power, are deemed to be, according to the social contract theory, logical deductions from the first compact knowingly formulated by men.

The Negation of Society Is the Meeting Point of the Absolutist and Liberal Theories of the State. The State is not a direct product of Nature; it does not precede, as society does, the awakening of thought in man,

—and later we shall try to show how *religious consciousness created the State in the midst of a natural society.* According to liberal political writers, the first State was created by man's free and conscious will; but according to the absolutists, the State is a divine creation. In both cases it dominates society and tends to absorb it altogether.

In the second case [the absolutist] this absorption is quite self-explanatory: a divine institution must necessarily devour all natural organizations. What is more curious in this case is that the individualistic school, with its free-contract theory, leads to the same result. And, indeed, this school begins by denying the very existence of a natural society antedating the contract, since such a society would presuppose the existence of natural relations among individuals and consequently *a reciprocal limitation of their liberties*—which would be contrary to the absolute liberty enjoyed, according to this theory, prior to the conclusion of the contract, and which would be neither less nor more than this contract itself, existing as a natural fact and preceding the free contract. According to this theory, human society begins only with the conclusion of the contract. But what then is this society? It is the pure and logical realization of the contract with all of its implied tendencies and legislative and practical consequences—it is the State.[2]

The Hypothetical Absolute Freedom of the Pre-Contract Individuals. How ridiculous then are the ideas of the individualists of the Jean Jacques Rousseau school and of the Proudhonian mutualists who conceive society as the result of the free contract of individuals absolutely independent of one another and entering into mutual relations only because of the convention drawn up among them. As if these men had dropped from the skies, bringing with them speech, will, original thought, and as if they were alien to anything of the earth, that is, anything having social origin. Had society consisted of such absolutely independent individuals, there would have been no need, nor even the slightest possibility of them entering into an association; society itself would be non-existent, and those *free individuals*, not being able to live and function upon the earth, would have to wing their way back to their heavenly abode.[3]

Absolute Individual Liberty Is Absolute Non-Being. Nature, as well as human society, which is nothing else but that same Nature—everything that lives, does so under the categorical condition of decisively interfering in the life of someone else. . . .

The worse it is for those who are so ignorant of the natural and social law of human solidarity that they deem possible and even desirable the absolute independence of individuals in regard to one another. To will it is to will the disappearance of society, for all social life is but the continuous mutual interdependence of individuals and masses. All men, even the most intelligent and the strongest, are at every instant of their lives the producers and the products. Freedom itself, the freedom of every man, is the ever-renewed effect of the great mass of physical, intellectual, and moral influences to which this man is subjected by the people surrounding him and the environment in which he was born and in which he passed his whole life.

To wish to escape this influence in the name of some transcendental, divine freedom, some self-sufficient and absolutely egoistical freedom, is to aim toward non-being. It means to forego influencing one's fellow-man, to forego any social action, even the expression of one's thoughts and feelings—that is, again to tend toward absolute non-being. This notorious independence, so greatly extolled by idealists and metaphysicians, and personal freedom thus conceived—is just non-existence, plain and simple. . . .

To do away with this reciprocal influence is tantamount to death. And in demanding the freedom of the masses we do not intend to do away with natural influences to which man is subjected by individuals and groups. All we want is to do away with factitious, legitimized influences, to do away with *privileges* in exerting influence.[4]

Natural and Social Laws Are of the Same Category. Man can never be free with respect to natural and social laws. Laws, which for the greater convenience of science, are divided into two categories, belong in reality to one and the same category, for they all are equally natural laws, necessary laws which constitute the basis and the very condition of all existence, so that no living beings can rebel against them without destroying themselves.

Natural Laws Are Not Political Laws. But it is necessary to distinguish natural laws from authoritarian, arbitrary, political, religious, and civil laws which the privileged classes have created in the course of history, always to enable exploitation of the work of the masses, always with the sole aim of curbing the liberty of the masses—laws which under the pretext of a fictitious morality, have always been the source of the deepest immorality. Thus we have involuntary and inevitable obedience to all laws which constitute, independently of all human will, the very life of Nature and society; but on the other hand, there should be independence (as nearly unconditional as it is possible to attain) on the part of everyone with respect to all claims to dictate to other people, with respect to all human wills (collective as well as individual) tending to impose not their natural influence but their law, their despotism.

Human Personality Grows Only in Society. As to the natural influence which men exercise upon one another it also is one of those conditions of social life against which revolt would be impossible. This influence is the very basis—material, moral, and intellectual—of human solidarity. The human individual, a product of solidarity, that is, of society, while remaining subject to its natural laws, may well react against it when influenced by feelings coming from the outside and especially from an alien society, but the individual cannot leave this particular society without immediately placing himself in another sphere of solidarity and without becoming sub-jected to new influences. For to man, life outside of all society, and out-side of all human influences, a life of absolute isolation, is tantamount to intellectual, moral, and material death. Solidarity is not the product but the mother of individuality, and human personality can be born and can develop only in human society.[5]

Individual and Social Interests Are Not Incompatible. We are told that in reality it will never be possible to obtain the agreement and uni-versal solidarity between individual interests and those of society, the reason being that these interests are contradictory and therefore cannot counterbalance each other or arrive at some mutual understanding. Our reply to this objection is that if up to now those interests have not arrived at a mutual agreement, it is due solely to the State, which has sacrificed the interests of the majority for the benefit of a privileged minority. That is why this famed incompatibility and the struggle of personal interests with the interests of society reduce themselves to lies and trickery, born out of the theological lie which conceived the doctrine of original sin in order to dishonor man and destroy in him the awareness of his own inner worth.[6]

CHAPTER 19 *Philosophy of History*

The Struggle for Existence in Human History. Whoever has studied history even a little cannot fail to notice that, underlying all the religious and theological struggles, however abstract, sublime, and ideal they may have been, there was always some outstanding material interest. All the racial, national, State, and class wars had only one object, and that was domination, which is the necessary condition of and guarantee for the possession and enjoyment of wealth. Human history, considered from this point of view, is simply the continuation of the great struggle for life, which, according to Darwin, constitutes the basic law of the organic world.[1]

Struggle for Existence Is a Universal Law. Considered from this point of view, the natural world presents to us a deadly and bloody picture of a fierce and perpetual struggle, *a struggle for life.* Man is not the only one to wage this struggle: all animals, all living beings—nay, what is more, all existing things—carry within themselves, although in a less apparent manner than man, the germs of their own destruction, and so to speak are their own enemies. The same natural inevitability begets, preserves, and destroys them. Every class of things, every plant and animal species, lives only at the expense of others; one devours the other, so that the natural world can be regarded as a bloody hecatomb, as a grim tragedy incited by hunger. The natural world is the arena of a ceaseless struggle which knows no mercy nor respite. . . .

Is is possible that this inevitable law also exists in the human and social world?[2]

Wars Are Mainly Economic in Their Motivation. Alas! We find cannibalism at the cradle of human civilization, and along with that, and following in point of time, we find wars of extermination, wars among races and nations: wars of conquest, wars to maintain equilibrium, political and religious wars, wars waged in the name of "great ideas" like the one now waged by France with the present Emperor at its head, patriotic wars for greater national unity like those contemplated now on the one hand by the Pan-German Minister of Berlin and on the other hand by the Pan-Slavist Tsar of St. Petersburg.

And what do we find beneath all that, beneath all the hypocritical phrases used in order to give these wars the appearance of humanity and right? Always the same economic phenomenon: *the tendency on the part of some to live and prosper at the expense of others.* All the rest is mere humbug. The ignorant, the naive, and the fools are entrapped by it, but the strong men who direct the destinies of the State know only too well that underlying all those wars there is only one motive: pillage, the seizing of someone else's wealth and the enslavement of someone else's labor.[3] Political idealism is no less pernicious and absurd, no less hypocritical than the idealism of religion, of which it is but a different manifestation, the worldly or earthly application.[4]

Phases of Historic Development. Men, who are pre-eminently carnivorous animals, began their history with cannibalism. Now they aspire toward universal association, toward collective production and collective consumption of wealth.

But between these two extreme points—what a horrible and bloody tragedy! And we are not yet through with this tragedy. Following cannibalism came slavery, then came serfdom, then wage serfdom, which is to be followed by the terrible day of retribution, and later—much later—the era of fraternity. Here are the phases through which the animal struggle for life must pass in its gradual transformation in the course of historic development into a humane organization of life.[5]

It has been well established that human history, like the history of all other animal species, began with war. This war, which did not have and still has not got any other aim but to conquer the means of existence, had various phases of development running parallel to the various phases of civilization—that is, of the development of man's needs and the means to satisfy them.

The Invention of Tools Marks the First Phase of Civilization. At the beginning man, who was an omnivorous animal, subsisted like many other animals on fruits and plants, and by hunting and fishing. During many centuries man no doubt hunted and fished just as the beasts are still doing, without the aid of any other instruments but those with which he was endowed by Nature. The first time he made use of the crudest weapon, a simple stick or a stone. Therewith he performed an act of thinking and asserted himself, no doubt without suspecting it, as a thinking animal, *as a man*. For even the most primitive weapon had to be adapted to the projected aim, and this presupposes a certain amount of mental calculation, which essentially distinguishes the man-animal from all the other animals. Owing to this faculty of reflecting, thinking, inventing, man perfected his weapons, very slowly, it is true, in the course of many centuries, and thereby was transformed into a hunter or an armed ferocious beast.

Multiplying of Animal Species Is Always in Direct Proportion to the Means of Subsistence. Having arrived at the first stage of civilization, the small human groups found it much easier to obtain their food by killing off living beings, including other men, who also were used as food, than did animals which lacked instruments for hunting or carrying on of wars. And *since the multiplying of animal species is always in direct proportion to the means of subsistence*, it is evident that men were bound to multiply more rapidly than the animals of other species, and that finally the time was bound to arrive when uncultivated Nature was not capable any more of sustaining all the people.

Cattle Breeding the Next Phase of Civilization. If human reason were not progressive by its nature; if it did not develop to an ever greater extent, resting on one hand upon tradition, which preserves for the benefit of future generations all the knowledge acquired by past generations, and on the other hand expanding in scope as a result of the power of speech, which is inseparable from the faculty of thought; if it were not endowed with the unlimited faculty of inventing new processes to defend human existence against all natural forces that are hostile to it—this insufficiency of Nature necessarily would have put a limit on the propagation of the human species.

But owing to that precious faculty which permits him to know, think, and understand, man is able to overcome this natural limit which curbs the development of all other animal species. When natural sources became exhausted he created new artificial sources. Profiting not by physical force but by superior intelligence, he went beyond killing for immediate consumption, and began to subdue, tame, and break in some wild beasts in order to make them serve his ends. Thus in the course of many centuries groups of hunters became transformed into groups of herdsmen.

Cattle Breeding Superseded by Agriculture. This new source of subsistence helped to increase even more the human species, which in turn placed before the human race the necessity of inventing ever new means of subsistence. The exploitation of animals was not sufficient any more and so men began to cultivate land. Nomadic peoples and herdsmen were transformed in the course of many more centuries into agricultural people.

It was at this stage of history that slavery in the proper sense of the word began. Men, who were savages in the full sense of that word, began at first by devouring the enemies who had been killed or made prisoners. But when they realized the advantages obtained by making use of dumb animals instead of killing them, they likewise were led to see the advantage accruing from making the same use of man, the most intelligent of all animals. So the vanquished enemy was not devoured any longer, but instead became a slave, forced to work in order to maintain his master.

Slavery Makes Its Appearance With the Agricultural Phase of Civilization. The work of the pastoral peoples is so simple and easy that it hardly requires the work of slaves. That is why we see that with the nomadic and pastoral tribes the number of slaves was quite limited, if they were not altogether absent. It is different with agricultural and settled peoples. Agriculture demands assiduous, painful, day-to-day labor. And the free man of the forests and plains, the hunter or cattle-breeder, takes to agriculture with a great deal of repugnance. That is why, as we see it now, for example, with the savage peoples of America, it was upon the weaker sex, the women, that the heaviest burdens and the most distasteful domestic work were thrown. Men knew of no other occupation but hunting and war-making, which even in our own times are still considered the most noble callings, and, holding in disdain all other occupations, they lazily smoked their pipes while their unfortunate women, those natural slaves of the barbarous man, succumbed under the burden of their daily toil.

Another forward step is made in civilization—and the slave takes the part of the woman. A beast of burden, endowed with intelligence, forced to bear the whole load of physical labor, he creates leisure for the ruling class and makes possible his master's intellectual and moral development.[6]

The Goals of Human History. The human species, having started out with animal existence, tends steadfastly toward the realization of humanity upon the earth. . . . And history itself set us this vast and sacred task of transforming the millions of wage-slaves into a human, free society based upon equal rights for all.[7]

The Three Constituent Elements of Human History. Man emancipated himself through his own efforts; he separated himself from animality and constituted himself a man; he began his distinctively human history and development by an act of disobedience and knowledge—that is, by *rebellion* and by *thought*.

Three elements, or if you like, three fundamental principles, constitute the essential conditions of all human development, collective or individual, in history: 1. *human animality;* 2. *thought;* and 3. *rebellion.* To the first properly corresponds *social* and *private economy;* to the second, *science;* and to the third, *liberty.*[8]

What Is Meant By Historic Elements. By historic elements I mean the general conditions of any real development whatever—for example, in this case, the conquest of the world by the Romans and the meeting of the God of the Jews with the ideal of divinity of the Greeks. To impregnate the historical elements, to cause them to run through a series of new historic transformations, a living spontaneous fact was needed, without which they might have remained many centuries longer in a state of unproductive elements. This fact was not lacking in Christianity; it was the propaganda, martyrdom, and death of Jesus Christ.[9]

History Is the Revolutionary Negation of the Past. But from the moment that this animal origin of man is accepted, everything is explained. History then appears to us as the revolutionary negation of the past, now slow, apathetic, sluggish, now passionate and powerful. It consists precisely in the progressive denial of the primitive animality of man through the development of his humanity. Man, a wild beast, cousin of the gorilla, has emerged from the profound darkness of animal instinct into the light of the mind, which explains in a wholly natural way all his past mistakes and partly consoles us for his present errors.[10]

The Dialectics of Idealism and Materialism. Every development implies the negation of its starting point. The basis or starting point, according to the materialistic school, being material, the negation must necessarily be ideal. Starting from the totality of the real world, or from what is abstractly called matter, it logically arrives at the real idealization—that is, at the humanization, at the full and complete emancipation—of society. On the contrary, and for the same reason, the basis and starting point of the idealistic school being ideal, it necessarily arrives at the materialization of society, at the organization of brutal despotism and an iniquitous and ignoble exploitation, in the form of Church and State. The historic development of man, according to the materialistic school, is a progressive ascension; in the idealistic system it can be nothing but a continuous fall.

Whatever human question we may want to consider, we always find the same essential contradiction between the two schools. Thus materialism starts from animality to establish humanity; idealism starts with divinity to establish slavery and condemn the masses to perpetual animality. Materialism denies free will and ends in the establishment of liberty; idealism, in the name of human dignity, proclaims free will, and, on the ruins of every liberty, founds authority. Materialism rejects the principle of authority, because it rightly considers it the corollary of animality, and because, on the contrary, the triumph of humanity, which is the object and chief significance of history, can be realized only through liberty. In a word, whatever question we may take up, we will always find the idealists in the very act of practical materialism, while we see the materialists pursuing and realizing the most grandly ideal aspirations and thoughts.

Matter in the Idealist Conception. History, in the system of the idealists, can be nothing but a continuous fall. They begin with a terrible fall, from which they can never recover—by a somersault from the sublime regions of the pure and absolute idea into matter. And into what kind of matter! Not into matter that is eternally active and mobile, full of properties and forces, life and intelligence, as we see it in the real world—but into abstract matter, impoverished and reduced to absolute through the regular looting by those Prussians of thought, that is, the theologians and metaphysicians, who have stripped it of everything to give it to their emperor—to their God; into the matter which, deprived of all action and movement of its own, represents, in opposition to the divine idea, nothing but absolute stupidity, impenetrability, inertness, and immobility.[11]

Humanistic Values in History.   Science knows that respect for man is the supreme law of humanity, and that the great, the real goal of history, its only legitimate objective, is the humanization and emancipation, the real liberty, the prosperity and happiness of each individual living in society. For, in the final analysis, if we would not fall back into the liberty-destroying fiction of the public weal represented by the State, a fiction always founded on the systematic immolation of the great masses of people, we must clearly recognize that collective liberty and prosperity exist only in so far as they represent the sum of individual liberties and prosperities.[12]

Man emerged from animal slavery, and passing through divine slavery, a transitory period between his animality and his humanity, he is now marching on to the conquest and realization of human liberty. Whence it follows that the antiquity of a belief, of an idea, far from proving anything in its favor, ought, on the contrary, to make it suspect. For behind us is our animality and before us our humanity, and the light of humanity—the only light that can warm and enlighten us, the only thing that can emancipate us, and give us dignity, freedom, and happiness, that can make us realize fraternity among us—is never at the beginning, but in relation to the epoch in which we live, always at the end of history. Let us then never look backward, let us look ever forward; for forward is our sunlight and salvation. If it is permissible, and even useful and necessary, to turn back to study our past, it is only in order to establish what we have been and must no longer be, what we have believed and thought and must no longer believe or think, what we have done and must do nevermore.[13]

The Uneven Course of Human Progress.   So long as a people has not fallen into a state of decadence there is always progress in this salutary tradition—this sole teacher of the masses. But one cannot say that this progress is the same in every epoch of the history of a people. On the contrary, it proceeds by leaps and bounds. At times it is very rapid, very sensitive, and far-reaching; at other times it slows down or stops altogether, and then again it even seems to go backward. What accounts for all that?

This evidently depends upon the character of events in a given historic epoch. There are events which electrify people and push them ahead; other events have such a deplorable, disheartening, and depressing effect upon the people's state of mind as very often to crush, lead astray, or at times altogether pervert them. In general one can observe in the historic development of people two inverse movements which I shall permit myself to compare to the ebb and flow of the oceanic tides.

Humanity Has Meaning Only in the Light of Its Basic Humanistic Drives. In certain epochs, which ordinarily are the precursors of great historic events, great triumphs of humanity, everything appears to proceed at an accelerated rate, everything exhales vigor and power; minds, hearts, and wills seem to act in unison as they reach out toward the conquest of new horizons. It seems then as if an electric current were set running throughout all society, uniting individuals the furthest removed from one another in one and the same feeling, and the most disparate minds in a single thought, and imprinting on all the same will.

At such a time everyone is full of confidence and courage, because he is carried away by the feeling which animates everybody. Without getting away from modern history, we can point to the end of the eighteenth century, the eve of the Great [French] Revolution, as being one of those epochs. Such also was, although to a considerably lesser degree, the character of the years preceding the Revolution of 1848. And finally, such, I believe, is the character of our own epoch, which seems to presage events that perhaps will transcend those of 1789 and 1793. And is it not true that all we see and feel in those grand and mighty epochs can be compared to the spring-tides of the ocean?

The Ebbing of the Great Creative Tides of Human History. But there are other epochs, gloomy, disheartening, and fateful, when everything breathes decadence, prostration, and death, and which present a veritable eclipse of the public and private mind. Those are the ebb tides which always follow great historic catastrophes. Such was the epoch of the First Empire and that of the Restoration. Such were the nineteen or twenty years following the catastrophe of June, 1848. Such will be, to an even more terrible extent, the twenty or thirty years which will follow the conquest of France by the armies of Prussian despotism, that is, if the workers, if the French people, prove cowardly enough to give up France.[14]

History Is the Gradual Unfoldment of Humanity. One can clearly conceive the gradual development of the material world, as well as of organic life and of the historically progressive intelligence of man, individually or socially. It is an altogether natural movement, from the simple to the complex, from the lower to the higher, from the inferior to the superior; a movement in conformity with all of our daily experiences, and consequently in conformity also with our natural logic, with the distinctive laws of our mind, which, being formed and developed only through the aid of these same experiences are, so to speak, only its mental, cerebral reproduction or its recapitulation in thought.[15]

PART II

Criticism of Existing Society

*Property Could Arise
Only in the State*

The doctrinaire philosophers, as well as the jurists and economists, always assume that property came into existence before the rise of the State, whereas it is clear that the juridical idea of property, as well as family law, could arise historically only in the State, the first inevitable act of which was the establishment of this law and of property.[1]

Property is a god. This god already has its theology (which is called State politics and juridical right) and also its morality, the most adequate expression of which is summed up in the phrase: "This man is worth so much."

The Theology and Metaphysics of Property. The property god also has its metaphysics. It is the science of the bourgeois economists. Like any metaphysics it is a sort of twilight, a compromise between truth and falsehood, with the latter benefiting by it. It seeks to give falsehood the appearance of truth and leads truth to falsehood. Political economy seeks to sanctify property through labor and to represent it as the realization, the fruit, of labor. If it succeeds in doing this, it will save property and the bourgeois world. For labor is sacred, and whatever is based upon labor, is good, just, moral, human, legitimate. One's faith, however, must be of the sturdy kind to enable him to swallow this doctrine, for we see the vast majority of workers deprived of all property; and what is more, we have the avowed statements of the economists and their own scientific proofs to the effect that under the present economic organization, which they defend so passionately, the masses *will never come to own property;* that, consequently, their labor does not emancipate and ennoble them, for, all their labor notwithstanding, they are condemned to remain eternally without property—that is, outside of morality and humanity.

Only Non-Productive Labor Yields Property.   On the other hand, we see that the richest property owners, and consequently the most worthy, humane, moral, and respectable citizens, are precisely those who work the least or who do not work at all. To that the answer is made that nowadays it is impossible to remain rich—to preserve, and even less so, to increase one's wealth—without working. Well, let us then agree upon the proper use of the term *work*: there is work and work. There is productive labor and there is the labor of exploitation.

The first is the labor of the proletariat; the second that of property owners. He who turns to good account lands cultivated by someone else, simply exploits someone else's labor. And he who increases the value of his capital, whether in industry or in commerce, exploits the labor of others. The banks which grow rich as a result of thousands of credit transactions, the Stock Exchange speculators, the shareholders who get large dividends without raising a finger; Napoleon III, who became so rich that he was able to raise to wealth all his protégés; King William I, who, proud of his victories, is preparing to levy billions upon poor unfortunate France, and who already has become rich and is enriching his soldiers with this plunder—all those people are workers, but what kind of workers! Highway robbers! Thieves and plain ordinary robbers are "workers" to a much greater extent, for in order to get rich in their own way they have to "work" with their own hands.

It is evident to anyone who is not blind about this matter that productive work creates wealth and yields the producers only misery, and that it is only non-productive, exploiting labor that yields property. But since property is morality, it follows that *morality, as the bourgeois understands it, consists in exploiting someone else's labor.*[2]

Property and Capital Are Labor-Exploiting in Their Essence. Is it necessary to repeat here the irrefutable arguments of Socialism which no bourgeois economist has yet succeeded in disproving? *What is property, what is capital, in their present form?* For the capitalist and the property owner they mean the power and the right, guaranteed by the State, to live without working. And since neither property nor capital produces anything when not fertilized by labor—that means the power and the right to live by exploiting the work of someone else, the right to exploit the work of those who possess neither property nor capital and who thus are forced to sell their productive power to the lucky owners of both.

Property and Capital Are Iniquitous in Their Historic Origin and Parasitic in Their Present Functioning. Note that I have left out of account altogether the following question: In what way did property and capital ever fall into the hands of their present owners? This is a question which, when envisaged from the points of view of history, logic, and justice, cannot be answered in any other way but one which would serve as an indictment against the present owners. I shall therefore confine myself here to the statement that property owners and capitalists, *inasmuch as they live not by their own productive labor* but by getting land rent, house rent, interest upon their capital, or by speculation on land, buildings, and capital, or by the commercial and industrial exploitation of the manual labor of the proletariat, all live at the expense of the proletariat. (Speculation and exploitation no doubt also constitute a sort of labor, but altogether non-productive labor.)

The Crucial Test of the Institution of Property.   I know only too well that this mode of life is highly esteemed in all the civilized countries, that it is expressly and tenderly protected by all the States, and that the States, religions, and all the juridical laws, both criminal and civil, and all the political governments, monarchic and republican—with their immense judicial and police apparatuses and their standing armies—have no other mission but to consecrate and protect such practices. In the presence of these powerful and respectable authorities I cannot even permit myself to ask whether this mode of life is legitimate from the point of view of human justice, liberty, human equality, and fraternity. I simply ask myself: Under such conditions, are fraternity and equality possible between the exploiter and the exploited, are justice and freedom possible for the exploited?

The Gap in the Theoretic Vindication of Capitalism.   Let us even suppose, as it is being maintained by the bourgeois economists and with them all the lawyers, all the worshipers of and believers in the juridical right, all the priests of the civil and criminal code—let us suppose that this economic relationship between the exploiter and the exploited is altogether legitimate, that it is the inevitable consequence, the product of an eternal, indestructible social law, yet still it will always be true that exploitation precludes brotherhood and equality.

And it goes without saying that such relationship precludes economic equality.[3]

Class Monopoly of Means of Production Is a Basic Evil.   Can the emancipation of labor signify any other thing but its deliverance from the yoke of property and capital? And how can we prevent both from dominating and exploiting labor so long as, while separated from labor, they are monopolized by a class which, freed from the necessity of working for a living by virtue of its exclusive use of capital and property, continues to oppress labor by exacting from it land-rent and interest upon capital? That class, drawing its strength from its monopolistic position, takes possession of all the profits of industrial and commercial enterprises, leaving to the workers, who are crushed by the mutual competition for employment into which they are forced, only that which is barely necessary to keep them from starving to death.

No political or juridical law, severe as it may be, can prevent this domination and exploitation, no law can stand up against the power of this deeply rooted fact, no one can prevent this situation from producing its natural results. Hence it follows that so long as property and capital exist on the one hand, and labor on the other hand, the first constituting the bourgeois class and the other the proletariat, the worker will be the slave and the bourgeois the master.

Abolition of Inheritance of Right.   But what is it that separates property and capital from labor? What produces the economic and political class differences? What is it that destroys equality and perpetuates inequality, the privileges of a small number of people, and the slavery of the great majority? It is *the right of inheritance*.

So long as the right of inheritance remains in force, there never will be economic, social, and political equality in this world; and so long as inequality exists, oppression and exploitation also will exist.

Consequently, from the point of view of the integral emancipation of labor and of the workers, we should aim at *the abolition of the inheritance right*.

What we want to and what we should abolish is *the right to inherit*— a right based upon jurisprudence and constituting the very basis of *the juridical family* and *the State*.

Strictly speaking, inheritance is that which assures to the heirs, whether completely or only partly so, the possibility of living without working by levying a toll upon collective labor, whether it be land rent or interest on capital. From our point of view, capital as well as land, in a word, all the instruments and materials necessary for work, in ceasing to be transmissible by the law of inheritance, become forever the collective property of all the producers' associations.

Only at that price is it possible to attain equality and consequently the emancipation of labor and of the workers.[4]

CHAPTER 2   *The Present Economic Regime*

General Tendencies of Capitalism.   Capitalist production and banking speculation, which in the long run swallows up this production, must ceaselessly expand at the expense of the smaller speculative and productive enterprises devoured by them; they must become the sole monopolies, universal and world-embracing.[1]

Competition in the economic field destroys and swallows up the small and even medium-sized capitalist enterprises, factories, land estates, and commercial houses for the benefit of huge capital holdings, industrial enterprises, and mercantile firms.[2]

Growing Concentration of Wealth.   This wealth is exclusive and every day it tends to become increasingly so by concentrating in the hands of an ever smaller number of persons and by throwing the lower stratum of the middle class, the petty bourgeoisie, into the ranks of the proletariat, so that the development of this wealth is directly related to the growing poverty of the masses of workers. Hence it follows that the gulf separating the lucky and privileged minority from the millions of workers who maintain this minority through their own labor is ever widening and that the luckier the exploiters of labor become, the more wretched the great mass of workers are.[3]

Proletarianization of the Peasantry. The small peasant property, weighed down by debts, mortgages, taxes, and all kinds of levies, melts away and slips out of the owner's hands, helping to round out the ever-growing possessions of the big owners; an inevitable economic law pushes him in turn into the ranks of the proletariat.[4]

What is property, what is capital, in their present form? For the capitalist and the property owner they mean the power and the right, guaranteed by the State, to live without working. And since neither property nor capital produce anything when not fertilized by labor—that means the power and the right to live by exploiting the labor of someone else, the right to exploit the labor of those who possess neither property nor capital and who thus are forced to sell their productive power to the lucky owners of both. . . .

Exploitation Is the Essence of Capitalism. . . . Let us even suppose, as it is being maintained by the bourgeois economists,—and with them by all the lawyers, all the worshipers of and believers in the juridical right, by all the priests of the civil and criminal code—let us suppose that this economic relationship between the exploiter and the exploited is altogether legitimate, that it is the inevitable consequence, the product, of an eternal, indestructible social law—and still it will always remain true that exploitation precludes brotherhood and equality for the exploited.

Workers Forced to Sell Their Labor. It goes without saying that it precludes economic equality. Suppose that I am your worker and you are my employer. If I offer my labor at the lowest price, if I consent to have you live off my labor, it is certainly not because of devotion or brotherly love for you. And no bourgeois economist would dare to say that it was, however idyllic and naive their reasoning becomes when they begin to speak about the reciprocal affections and mutual relations which *should* exist between employers and employees. No, I do it because my family and I would starve to death if I did not work for an employer. Thus I am *forced* to sell you my labor at the lowest possible price, and I am forced to do it by the threat of hunger.

Selling of Labor Power Is Not a Free Transaction. But—the economists tell us—the property owners, the capitalists, the employers, are *likewise* forced to seek out and purchase the labor of the proletariat. Yes, it is true, they are forced to do it, *but not in the same measure.* Had there been equality between those who offer their labor and those who purchase it, between the necessity of selling one's labor and the necessity of buying it, the slavery and misery of the proletariat would not exist. But then there would be neither capitalists, nor property owners, nor the proletariat, nor rich, nor poor: there would be only workers. It is precisely because such equality does not exist that we have and are bound to have exploiters.

Growth of the Proletariat Outstrips the Productive Capacity of Capitalism. This equality does not exist because in modern society where wealth is produced by the intervention of capital paying wages to labor, the growth of the population outstrips the growth of population, which results in the supply of labor necessarily surpassing the demand and leading to a relative sinking of the level of wages. Production thus constituted, monopolized, exploited by bourgeois capital, is pushed on the one hand by the mutual competition of capitalists to concentrate evermore in the hands of an ever diminishing number of powerful capitalists, or in the hands of joint-stock companies which, owing to the merging of their capital, are more powerful than the biggest isolated capitalists. (And the small and medium-sized capitalists, not being able to produce at the same price as the big capitalists, naturally succumb in this deadly struggle.) On the other hand, all enterprises are forced by the same competition to sell their products at the lowest possible price.

It [capitalistic monopoly] can attain this two-fold result only by forcing out an ever-growing number of small or medium-sized capitalists, speculators, merchants, or industrialists, from the world of the exploiters into the world of the exploited proletariat, and at the same time squeezing out ever greater savings from the wages of the same proletariat.

Growing Competition for Jobs Forces Down Wage Levels. On the other hand, the mass of the proletariat, growing as a result of the general increase of the population—which, as we know, not even poverty can stop effectively—and through the increasing proletarianization of the petty-bourgeoisie, ex-owners, capitalists, merchants, and industrialists—growing, as I have already said, at a much more rapid rate than the productive capacities of an economy that is exploited by bourgeois capital—this growing mass of the proletariat is placed in a condition wherein the workers themselves are forced into disastrous competition against one another.

For since they possess no other means of existence but their own manual labor, they are driven, by the fear of seeing themselves replaced by others, to sell it at the lowest price. This tendency of the workers, or rather the necessity to which they are condemned by their own poverty, combined with the tendency of the employers to sell the products of *their* workers, and consequently to buy their labor, at *the lowest price*, constantly reproduces and consolidates the poverty of the proletariat. Since he finds himself in a state of poverty, the worker is compelled to sell his labor for almost nothing, and because he sells that product for almost nothing, he sinks into ever greater poverty.

Intensified Exploitation and Its Consequences.   Yes, greater misery, indeed! For in this galley-slave labor the productive force of the workers, bused, ruthlessly exploited, excessively wasted and underfed, is rapidly used up. And once it is used up, what can be its value on the market, of what worth is this *sole commodity* which he possesses and upon the daily sale of which he depends for a livelihood? Nothing! And then? Then nothing is left for the worker but to die.

What, in a given country, is the lowest possible wage? It is the price of that which is considered by the proletarians of that country as *absolutely necessary* to keep oneself alive. All the bourgeois economists are in agreement on this point. . . .

The Iron Law of Wages.   The current price of primary necessities constitutes the prevailing constant level above which workers' wages *can never* rise for a very long time, but beneath which they drop very often, which constantly results in inanition, sickness, and death, until a sufficient number of workers *disappear* to equalize again the supply of and demand for labor.

There Is No Equality of Bargaining Power Between Employer and Worker.   What the economists call equalized supply and demand does not constitute real equality between those who offer their labor for sale and those who purchase it. Suppose that I, a manufacturer, need a hundred workers and that exactly a hundred workers present themselves in the market—only one hundred, for if more came, the supply would exceed the demand, resulting in lowered wages. But since only one hundred appear, and since I, the manufacturer, need only that number—neither more nor less—it would seem at first that complete equality was established; that supply and demand being equal in number, they should likewise be equal in other respects.

Does it follow that the workers can demand from me a wage and conditions of work assuring them the means of a truly free, dignified, and human existence? Not at all! If I grant them those conditions and those wages, I, the capitalist, shall not gain thereby any more than they will. But then, why should I have to plague myself and become ruined by offering them the profits of my capital? If I want to work myself as the workers do, I will invest my capital somewhere else, wherever I can get the highest interest, and will offer my labor for sale to some capitalist just as my workers do.

If, profiting by the powerful initiative afforded me by my capital, I ask those hundred workers to fertilize that capital with their labor, it is not because of my sympathy for their sufferings, nor because of a spirit of justice, nor because of love for humanity. The capitalists are by no means philanthropists; they would be ruined if they practiced philanthropy. It is because I hope to draw from the labor of the workers sufficient profit to be able to live comfortably, even richly, while at the same time increasing my capital—and all that without having to work myself. Of course I shall work too, but my work will be of an altogether different kind, and I will be remunerated at a much higher rate than the workers. It will not be the work of production but that of administration and exploitation.

Monopolization of Administrative Work. But isn't administrative work also productive work? No doubt it is, for lacking a good and intelligent administration, manual labor will not produce anything or it will produce very little and very badly. But from the point of view of justice and the needs of production itself, it is not at all necessary that this work should be monopolized in my hands, nor, above all, that I should be compensated at a rate so much higher than manual labor. The co-operative associations already have proven that workers are quite capable of administering industrial enterprises, that it can be done by workers elected from their midst and who receive the same wage. Therefore if I concentrate in my hands the administrative power, it is not because the interests of production demand it, but in order to serve my own ends, the ends of exploitation. As the absolute boss of my establishment I get for my labor ten or twenty times more, and if I am a big industrialist I may get a hundred times more than my workers get for theirs, and this is true despite the fact that my labor is incomparably less painful than theirs.[5]

The Mechanics of the Fictitious Free Labor Contract. But since supply and demand are equal, why do the workers accept the conditions laid down by the employer? If the capitalist stands in just as great a need of employing the workers as the one hundred workers do of being employed by him, does it not follow that both sides are in an equal position? Do not both meet at the market as two equal merchants—from the juridical point of view at least—one bringing the commodity called *a daily wage*, to be exchanged for the *daily labor* of the worker on the basis of so many hours per day; and the other bringing *his own labor* as his commodity to be exchanged for the wage offered by the capitalist? Since, in our supposition, the demand is for a hundred workers and the supply is likewise that of a hundred persons, it may seem that both sides are in an equal position.

Of course nothing of the kind is true. What is it that brings the capitalist to the market? It is the urge to get rich, to increase his capital, to gratify his ambitions and social vanities, to be able to indulge in all conceivable pleasures. And what brings a worker to the market? Hunger, the necessity of eating today and tomorrow. Thus, while being equal from the point of view of juridical fiction, the capitalist and the worker are anything but equal from the point of view of the economic situation, which is the real situation.

The capitalist is not threatened with hunger when he comes to the market; he knows very well that if he does not find today the workers for whom he is looking, he will still have enough to eat for quite a long time, owing to the capital of which he is the happy possessor. If the workers whom he meets in the market present demands which seem excessive to im, because, far from enabling him to increase his wealth and improve even more his economic position, those proposals and conditions might, I do not say equalize, but bring the economic position of the workers somewhat close to his own—what does he do in that case? He turns down those proposals and waits.

After all, he was not impelled by an urgent necessity, but by a desire to improve a position, which, compared to that of the workers, is already quite comfortable, and so he can wait. And he will wait, for his business experience has taught him that the resistance of workers who, possessing neither capital, nor comfort, nor any savings to speak of, are pressed by a relentless necessity, by hunger, that this resistance cannot last very long, and that finally he will be able to find the hundred workers for whom he is looking—for *they will be forced to accept the conditions which he finds it profitable to impose upon them.* If they refuse, others will come who will be only too happy to accept such conditions. That is how things are done daily with the knowledge and in the full view of everyone. . . .

A Master-Slave Contract. . . . The capitalist then comes to the market in the capacity, if not of an absolutely free agent, at least that of an infinitely freer agent than the worker. What happens in the market is a meeting between a drive for lucre and starvation, between master and slave. Juridically they are both equal; but economically the worker is the serf of the capitalist, *even before the market transaction has been concluded* whereby the worker sells his person and his liberty for a given time. The worker is in the position of a serf because this terrible threat of starvation which daily hangs over his head and over his family, will force him to accept any conditions imposed by the gainful calculations of the capitalist, the industrialist, the employer.

Juridical Right Versus Economic Reality. And once the contract has been negotiated, the serfdom of the worker is doubly increased. . . . M. Karl Marx, the illustrious leader of German Communism, justly observed in his magnificent work *Das Kapital* that if the contract *freely* entered into by the vendors of money—in the form of wages—and the vendors of their own labor—that is, between the employer and the workers—were concluded not for a definite and limited term only, but for one's whole life, it would constitute real slavery. Concluded for a term only and reserving to the worker the right to quit his employer, this contract constitutes a sort of *voluntary* and *transitory* serfdom.

Yes, transitory and voluntary from the juridical point of view, but nowise from the point of view of economic possibility. The worker always has the *right* to leave his employer, but has he the means to do so? And if he does quit him, is it in order to lead a free existence, in which he will have no master but himself? No, he does it in order to sell himself to another employer. He is driven to it by the same hunger which forced him to sell himself to the first employer.

Thus the worker's liberty, so much exalted by the economists, jurists, and bourgeois republicans, is only a theoretical freedom, lacking any means for its possible realization, and consequently it is only a fictitious liberty, an utter falsehood. The truth is that the whole life of the worker is simply a continuous and dismaying succession of terms of serfdom—voluntary from the juridical point of view but compulsory in the economic sense—broken up by momentarily brief interludes of freedom accompanied by starvation; in other words, it is real slavery.

Labor Contracts Are Observed By the Employer Only in the Breach. This slavery manifests itself daily in all kinds of ways. Apart from the vexations and oppressive conditions of the contract which turn the worker into a subordinate, a passive and obedient servant, and the employer into a nearly absolute master—apart from all that it is well known that there is hardly an industrial enterprise wherein the owner, impelled on one hand by the two-fold instinct of an unappeasable lust for profits and absolute power, and on the other hand, profiting by the economic dependence of the worker, does not set aside the terms stipulated in the contract and wring some additional concessions in his own favor. Now he will demand more hours of work, that is, over and above those stipulated in the contract; now he will cut down the wages on some pretext; now he will impose arbitrary fines, or he will treat the workers harshly, rudely, and insolently.

But, one may say, in that case the worker can quit. Easier said than done. At times the worker receives part of his wages in advance, or his wife or children may be sick, or perhaps his work is poorly paid throughout this particular industry. Other employers may be paying even less than his own employer, and after quitting this job he may not even be able to find another one. And to remain without a job spells death for him and his family. In addition, there is an understanding among all the employers, and all of them resemble one another. All are almost equally irritating, unjust, and harsh.

Is this a calumny? No, it is in the nature of things, and in the logical necessity of the relationship existing between the employers and their workers.[6]

CHAPTER 3 *Class Struggle in Society Inevitable*

Citizens and slaves—such was the antagonism existing in the ancient world as well as in the slave States of the New World. Citizens and slaves —that is, forced laborers, slaves not by right but in fact—such is the antagonism of the modern world. And just as the ancient States perished from slavery, so will the modern States perish at the hands of the proletariat.

Class Differences Are Real Despite the Lack of Clear Demarcations. In vain would one try to console oneself that this antagonism is fictitious rather than real, or that it is impossible to lay down a clear line of demarcation between the possessing and dispossessed classes, since both merge into each other through many intermediary and imperceptible shadings. Nor for that matter do such lines of demarcation exist in the natural world; for instance, in the ascending series of beings it is impossible to show exactly the point where the plant kingdom ends and the animal kingdom begins, where bestiality ceases and humanity begins. Nevertheless, there is a very real difference between a plant and an animal, and between an animal and man.

It is the same in human society: notwithstanding the intermediary links which render imperceptible the transition from one political and social situation to another, the differences between classes is very marked, and everyone can distinguish the blue-blooded aristocracy from the financial aristocracy, the upper bourgeoisie from the petty-bourgeoisie, and the latter from the factory and city proletariat—just as we can distinguish the big land-owner, the *rentier*, from the peasant who works his own land, and the farmer from the ordinary land proletarian (the hired farm-hand.)

Basic Class Difference. All these different political and social groupings can now be reduced to two principal categories, diametrically opposed and naturally hostile to each other: the *privileged classes*, comprising all those who are privileged with respect to possession of land, capital, or even only of bourgeois education, and the *working classes*, disinherited with respect to land as well as capital, and deprived of all education and instruction.[1]

Class Struggle in Existing Society Is Irreconcilable. The antagonism existing between the bourgeois world and that of the workers takes on an ever more pronounced character. Every serious-minded man, whose feelings and imagination are not distorted by the influence, often unconscious, of biased sophisms, must realize that no reconciliation between these two worlds is possible. The workers want equality and the bourgeoisie wants to maintain inequality. Obviously one destroys the other. Therefore the great majority of bourgeois capitalists and property-owners who have the courage frankly to avow their wishes manifest with the same candor the horror which the present labor movement inspires in them. They are resolute and sincere enemies; we know them and it is well that we do.[2]

It is clear now that there can be no reconciliation between the fierce, starving proletariat, moved by social-revolutionary passions and persistently aiming to create another world upon the foundation of the principles of truth, justice, freedom, equality, and human brotherhood (principles tolerated in respectable society only as an innocent subject for rhetorical exercises) and the enlightened and educated world of privileged classes defending with desperate vigor the political, juridical, metaphysical, theological, and military regime as the last fortress guarding the precious privilege of economic exploitation. Between these two worlds, I say, between the plain working people and educated society (combining in itself, as we know, all the excellences, beauty, and virtues) no reconciliation is possible.[3]

Class Struggle in Terms of Progress and Reaction. Only two real forces have been left by now: the party of the past, of reaction, comprising all the possessing and privileged classes and now taking shelter, often outspokenly, under the banner of military dictatorship or the authority of the State; and the party of the future, the party of integral human emancipation, the party of revolutionary Socialism, of the proletariat.[4]

One must be a sophist or utterly blind to deny the existence of the abyss which today separates these two classes. As in the ancient world, our modern civilization, comprising a comparatively limited minority of privileged citizens, has for its basis the forced labor (forced by hunger) of the vast majority of the population, inevitably doomed to ignorance and brutality. . . .

Free Trade Is No Solution. It is in vain that one may say with the economists that the betterment of the economic situation of the working classes depends upon the general progress of industry and commerce in every country and their complete emancipation from the tutelage and protection of the State. Freedom of industry and commerce is of course a great thing, and is one of the basic foundations for the future international union of all the peoples of the world. Being friends of liberty at any price, and of all liberties, we should be equally the friends of those liberties as well. But, on the other hand, we must recognize that so long as the present States exist and so long as labor continues to be the serf of property and capital, this liberty, by enriching a very small section of the bourgeoisie at the expense of the vast majority of the population, will produce one good result: It will enervate and demoralize more completely the small number of privileged people, will increase the poverty, the resentment, and the just indignation of the working masses, and thereby will bring nearer the hour of destruction of the States.

Free-Trade Capitalism Is Fertile Soil for the Growth of Pauperism. England, Belgium, France, and Germany are certainly those countries in Europe where commerce and industry enjoy comparatively the greatest freedom, and where they have attained the highest degree of development. And likewise those are precisely the countries where pauperism is felt in the most cruel manner, and where the gulf between the capitalists and property-owners on one hand and the working classes on the other appears to have widened to an extent unknown in other countries.[5]

The Labor of the Privileged Classes. Thus we are compelled to recognize as a general rule that in the modern world, if not to the same degree as in the ancient world, the civilization of a small number is still based upon the forced labor and comparative barbarism of the great majority. Yet it would be unjust to say that this privileged class is altogether alien to work; on the contrary, in our day many of its members work hard. The number of absolutely unoccupied persons is perceptibly decreasing, and work is beginning to elicit respect in those circles; for the most fortunate members of society are beginning to understand that in order to remain at the high level of the present civilization, in order at least to be able to profit by their privileges and to safeguard them, one has to work a great deal.

But there is a difference between the work of the well-to-do classes and that of the workers: the first, being paid for at a rate proportionately much higher than the second, gives leisure to the privileged people, that supreme condition of all human development, intellectual as well as moral —a condition never yet enjoyed by the laboring classes. And then the work of the privileged people is almost exclusively of the nervous kind, that is, of imagination, memory, and thought—whereas the work of the millions of proletarians is of the *muscular* kind; and often, as in the case of factory work, it does not exercise man's whole system but develops only one part of him to the detriment of all the other parts, and it is generally done under conditions which are harmful to bodily health and which militate against his harmonious development.

In this respect, the worker on the land is much more fortunate: free from the vitiating effect of the stuffy and frequently poisoned air of factories and workshops, and free from the deforming effect of an abnormal development of some of his powers at the expense of others, his nature remains more vigorous and complete—but in return, his intelligence is nearly always more stationary, sluggish, and much less developed than that of the factory and city proletariat.

Respective Rewards of the Two Kinds of Labor. Altogether artisans, factory workers, and farm-laborers form one and the same category, that of *muscular work*, and are opposed to the privileged representatives of *nervous work*. What is the consequence of this quite real division which constitutes the very basis of the present situation, political as well as social?

To the privileged representatives of nervous work, who, incidentally, are called upon, in the present organization of society, to carry on this type of work, not because they are more intelligent but only because they were born into a privileged class—to them go all the benefits, but also all the corruptions of existing civilization. To them go wealth, luxury, comfort, well-being, family joys, exclusive enjoyment of political liberty with the power to exploit the work of millions of workers and to govern them at will and in their own interest—all the creations, all the refinements of imagination and thought . . . and with this power to become complete men —all the poisons of a humanity perverted by privilege.

And what is left for the representatives of *muscular work*, for the countless millions of proletarians or even small land-owners? Inescapable poverty, lack of even the joys of family life (for the family soon becomes a burden to the poor man), ignorance, barbarism, and we might almost say, forced bestiality, with the "consolation" that they serve as a pedestal for civilization, for liberty, and for the corruption of a small minority. But in return, they have preserved freshness of mind and heart. Morally invigorated by work, even though it has been forced upon them, they have retained a sense of justice of an altogether higher kind than the justice of learned jurists and of the law codes. Living a life of misery, they have a warm feeling of compassion for all the unfortunate; they have preserved sound sense uncorrupted by the sophisms of a doctrinaire science or by the falsehoods of politics—and since they have not abused life, nor even made use of life, they have retained their faith in it.

The Change in the Situation Wrought By the Great French Revolution. But, we are told, this contrast, this gulf between the privileged minority and the vast number of disinherited has always existed and continues to exist. Then what kind of change did take place? What changed was that in the past this gulf had been enveloped in thick religious mist so that the masses of people could not descry it; but that after the Great Revolution had begun to dispel this mist, the masses became aware of the gulf and began to ask the reason for its existence. The significance of that change is immense.

From the time when the Revolution brought down to the masses its Gospel—not the mystic but the rational, not the heavenly but the earthly, not the divine but the human Gospel, the Gospel of the Rights of Man— ever since it proclaimed that all men are equal, that all men are entitled to liberty and equality, the masses of all European countries, of all the civilized world, awakening gradually from the sleep which had kept them in bondage ever since Christianity drugged them with its opium, began to ask themselves whether they too had the right to equality, freedom, and humanity.

Socialism Is the Logical Consequence of the Dynamics of the French Revolution. As soon as this question was posed, the people, guided by their admirable sound sense as well as by their instincts, realized that the first condition of their real emancipation, or of their *humanization*, was a radical change in their economic condition. The question of daily bread was to them justly the first question, for, as Aristotle long ago had noted, man, in order to think, in order to feel himself free, in order to become a man, has to be liberated from the preoccupations of the material life. For that matter, the bourgeois, who are so vociferous in their attacks against the materialism of the people and who preach to the latter the abstinences of idealism, know it very well, for they themselves preach it only by word and not by example.

The second question for the people was leisure after work—an indispensable condition for humanity. But bread and leisure never can be obtained apart from a radical transformation of the present organization of society, and that explains why the Revolution, driven on by the implications of its own principle, gave birth to Socialism.[6]

CHAPTER 4 *Checkered History of the Bourgeoisie*

There was a time when the bourgeoisie, endowed with vital power and constituting the only historic class, offered the spectacle of union and fraternity, in its acts as well as in its thoughts. That was the finest period in the life of that class, no doubt always respectable but thereafter an impotent, stupid, and sterile class; that was the epoch of its most vigorous development. Such it was prior to the Great Revolution of 1793; such it also was though to a much lesser degree before the revolutions of 1830 and 1848. Then the bourgeoisie had a world to conquer, it had to take its place in society, and, organized for struggle, and intelligent, audacious, and feeling itself stronger than anyone else in point of right, it was endowed with an irresistible, almighty power. Alone it engendered three revolutions against the united power of the monarchy, the nobility, and the clergy.

Freemasonry: the International of the Bourgeoisie in Its Heroic Past. At that time the bourgeoisie also created a universal, formidable, international association: *Freemasonry.*

It would be a great mistake to judge the Freemasonry of the last century or even that of the beginning of the present century, by what it represents now. Pre-eminently a bourgeois institution, Freemasonry reflected in its history the development, the growing power, and the decadence of the intellectual and moral bourgeoisie. . . . Prior to 1793 and even before 1830 Freemasonry united in its midst, with few exceptions, all the chosen spirits, the most ardent hearts and most daring wills; it constituted an active, powerful, and truly beneficent organization. It was the vigorous embodiment and the practical realization of the humanitarian idea of the eighteenth century. All the great principles of liberty, equality, fraternity, reason, and human justice, worked out at first theoretically by the philosophy of the century, became within Freemasonry practical dogmas and the bases of a new morality and politics—they became the soul of a gigantic work of demolition and reconstruction. . . .

Decay of Freemasonry. The triumph of the Revolution killed Freemasonry; for, having seen its wishes partly fulfilled by the Revolution, and having taken, as a result of the latter, the place of the nobility, the bourgeoisie, after being for a long time an exploited and oppressed class, became in turn a privileged, exploiting, oppressing conservative, and reactionary class. . . . Following the *coup d'etat* of Napoleon I, Freemasonry became an imperial institution throughout the greater part of the European continent.

The Epigone of Bourgeois Revolutionism. To some extent the Restoration revived it. Seeing itself threatened by the return of the old regime, and forced to yield to the nobility and the Church coalition the place which it had won through the first Revolution, the bourgeoisie again became revolutionary by force of necessity. But what a difference between this warmed-up revolutionism and the ardent and powerful revolutionism which had inspired it toward the end of the last century. Then the bourgeoisie was sincere, it seriously and naively believed in the rights of man, it was inspired and driven on by a genius for destruction and reconstruction. And at that time the bourgeoisie found itself in full possession of its intelligence and in full development of its power.

It did not yet suspect that a gulf separated it from the people; it believed and felt itself to be—and for that matter it really was—the real representative of the people. The Thermidorian reaction and the Babeuf conspiracy cured it of this illusion. The gulf separating the working people from the exploiting, dominating, and prosperous bourgeoisie has widened ever more, and now nothing less than the dead body of the whole bourgeoisie, and its entire privileged existence, will ever be able to fill up this gulf.[1]

Class Antagonism Displaced the Bourgeoisie from Its Revolutionary Position as Leader of the People. The bourgeoisie of the last century sincerely believed that by emancipating themselves from the monarchistic, clerical, and feudal yoke, they would thereby emancipate the whole people. And this sincere but naive belief was the source of their heroic daring and of all their marvelous power. They felt themselves united with everyone, and they marched to the assault carrying within themselves the power and right for everybody. Owing to this right and this power which were, so to speak, embodied in their class, the bourgeois of the last century could scale and take the fortress of political power which their fathers had coveted for so many centuries.

But at the very moment when they had planted their banner there, a new light struck their minds. As soon as they had won that power, they

ealized that there actually was nothing in common between the interests
f the bourgeoisie and those of the great masses of people, but that, on
he contrary, they were radically opposed to each other, and that the
ower and the exclusive prosperity of the possessing class could rest only
pon the poverty and the political and social dependence of the proletariat.

After that the relations between the bourgeoisie and the people
hanged radically, but before the workers had realized that the bourgeois
vere their natural enemies, from necessity rather than from a wicked will,
he bourgeoisie had become aware of this inevitable antagonism. It is this
hat I call the bad conscience of the bourgeoisie.[2]

Flight From the Revolutionary Past. Now it is altogether different:
he bourgeoisie, in all the countries of Europe, is most of all afraid of the
ocial Revolution; it knows that against this storm it has no other refuge
ut the State. That is why it always desires and demands *a strong State,*
r, in plain language, a military dictatorship. And in order the easier to
amboozle the masses of the people, it aims to invest this dictatorship with
he forms of a popular representative government which would allow it
o exploit the great masses of the people *in the name of the people itself.*[3]

The Upper Bourgeoisie. . . In the upper layers of the bourgeoisie,
ollowing the consolidation of the unity of the State, there has come into
xistence and now is developing and expanding to an ever greater extent
he social unity of the privileged exploiters of the labor of the working
eople.

This class [the upper bourgeoisie] comprises the high officialdom, the
pheres of high bureaucracy, military officers, high police officials, and
udges; the world of large owners, industrialists, merchants, and bankers;
he official legal world and the press; and likewise the Parliament, the
ight wing of which already enjoys all the benefits of government, whereas
he left wing aims to take into its own hands the very same government.[4]

The Petty-Bourgeoisie. We realize quite well that even among the
ourgeoisie knowledge is not equally distributed. Here too there is a
hierarchy conditioned not by the capacity of the individuals therein, but
by the relative wealth of the social layer to which they belong by birth.
Thus, for instance, the education received by the children of the petty-
bourgeoisie, just slightly above that of the education of workers' children, is insignificant when compared to the education received by the
children of the upper and middle bourgeoisie. And what do we see? The
petty-bourgeoisie, which ranks itself with the middle classes because of a
ridiculous vanity on the one hand, and on the other because of its dependence upon the big capitalists, finds itself most of the time in an even more
miserable and more humiliating position than that of the proletariat.

Therefore when we speak of privileged classes we do not mean thereby
this miserable petty-bourgeoisie, which, if it had more courage and more
intelligence, would not fail to join us in order jointly to struggle against

the big bourgeoisie, which crushes it no less than it crushes the proletariat. And if the economic development of society is going to proceed in the same direction for another ten years, we shall see the greater part of the middle bourgeoisie sunk at first into the present position of the petty bourgeoisie, and then gradually lose themselves in the rank of the proletariat, all this taking place as the result of the same inevitable concentration of property in the hands of an ever smaller number of people, necessarily entailing the division of the social world into a small, very rich, learned and ruling minority, and the vast majority of miserable, ignorant proletarians and slaves.

Technical Progress Benefits Only the Bourgeoisie. There is a fact which should strike all conscientious people, all those who have at heart human dignity and justice; that is, the freedom of everyone in equality for all. This notable fact is that all the inventions of the mind, all the great applications of science to industry, to commerce, and generally to social life, have benefited up to now only the privileged classes and the power of the States, those eternal protectors of political and social iniquities, and they have never benefited the masses of the people. We need only point to machinery by way of an illustration, to have every worker and every sincere partisan of emancipation for labor agree with us on that score.

The State a Bourgeois-Controlled Institution. What power now sustains the privileged classes, with all their insolent well-being and iniquitous enjoyments of life, against the legitimate indignation of the masses of the people? That power is the power of the State, in which their children are holding, as they always have held, all the dominant positions and the middle and lower positions, except those of laborers and soldiers.

Administration of the Economy in Place of the State. The bourgeoisie is the dominant and exclusively intelligent class because it exploits the people and keeps it in a state of starvation. If the people become prosperous and as learned as the bourgeoisie, the domination of the latter must come to an end; and there will be no more room for political government, such government changing then into a simple apparatus for the administration of the economy.[6]

Moral and Intellectual Decay of the Bourgeoisie. The educated classes, the nobility, the bourgeoisie, who at one time flourished and stood at the head of a living and progressive civilization throughout Europe, now have sunk into torpor and have become vulgarized, obese, and cowardly, so much so that if they represent anything it is the most deleterious and vile attributes of man's nature. We see that these classes in a highly moral country like France are not even capable of defending the independence of their own country against Germans. And in Germany we see that all these classes are capable of is boot-licking loyalty to their Kaiser.[7]

No bourgeois, even of the reddest kind, wants to have economic equality, for that kind of equality would spell his death.[8]

The bourgeoisie do not see and do not understand anything lying outside of the State and the regulating powers of the State. The height of their ideal, of their imagination and heroism, is the revolutionary exaggeration of the power and action of the State in the name of public safety.[9]

Death Agony of a Historically Condemned Class. This class, as a political and social organism, after having rendered outstanding services to the civilization of the modern world, is now condemned to death by history itself. To die is the only service which it may still render to humanity, which it served during its life. But it does not want to die. And this reluctance to die is the only cause of its present stupidity and that shameful impotence now characterizing everyone of its political, national, and international enterprises.[10]

Is the Bourgeoisie Altogether Bankrupt? Has the bourgeoisie already become bankrupt? Not yet. Or has it lost the taste for liberty and peace? Not at all. It still continues to love liberty, with the condition, of course, that this liberty exist for the bourgeoisie only; that is, that the latter retain the liberty to exploit the slavery of the masses, who, while possessing, under existing constitutions, the right to liberty but not the means to enjoy it, remain forcibly enslaved under the yoke of the bourgeoisie. As for peace, never did the bourgeoisie feel so much the need thereof as it does today. Armed peace, which weighs down heavily upon the European world, disturbs, paralyzes, and ruins the bourgeoisie.[11]

Bourgeois Reaction Against Military Dictatorship. A large part of the bourgeoisie is tired of the reign of Caesarism and militarism, which it founded in 1848 because of its fear of the proletariat. . . .

There is no doubt that the bourgeoisie on the whole, including the radical bourgeoisie, was not, in the proper sense of the word, the creator of Caesarian and military despotism, the effects of which it already has come to deplore. Having availed itself of this dictatorship in its struggle against the proletariat, it now evinces the desire to get rid of it. Nothing is more natural: this regime humiliates and ruins it. But how can it get rid of this dictatorship? At one time it was courageous and powerful; it had the power to conquer worlds. Now it is cowardly and weak, and afflicted with the impotence of old age. It is keenly aware of this feebleness, and it feels that it alone cannot do anything. It needs assistance. This assistance can be rendered only by the proletariat, and that is why it feels that the latter must be won over to its side.

The Liberal Bourgeoisie and the Proletariat. But how can the proletariat be won over? By promises of liberty and political equality? No, those are words which do not touch the workers any more. They have learned, at their own cost, they have realized through their own harsh experience, that these words mean only the preservation of their economic slavery, often more harsh than what has gone before. . . . If you want to touch the hearts of those wretched millions of slaves of work, talk to them about their economic emancipation. There are hardly any workers now who do not realize that this is the only serious and real basis of all the other emancipations. Therefore they have to be approached from the point of view of economic reforms of society.

Bourgeois Socialism. "Well, then," the members of the League for Peace and Liberty will tell themselves, "let us also call ourselves Socialists. Let us promise them economic and social reforms, but on the condition that they respect the bases of civilization and bourgeois omnipotence, individual and hereditary property, interest on capital, and land rent. Let us persuade them that it is only upon these conditions, which incidentally assure our domination and the slavery of the proletariat, that the workers can be emancipated.

"Let us also convince them that in order to carry out those social reforms it is necessary first to have a good political revolution, exclusively political, and as red as they want to make it in the political sense, with a lot of head-chopping—if that becomes necessary—but with an even greater respect for sacrosanct property. In short, a purely Jacobin revolution which will render us the masters of the situation; and once we become masters we shall give the workers what we can and want to give them."

Distinguishing Marks of a Bourgeois Socialist. Here we have the infallible sign by which workers can detect a false Socialist, a bourgeois Socialist. If, in speaking to them of revolution, or, if you please, of social transformation, he tells them that political transformation *should precede* the economic transformation; if he denies that both have to be made at the same time, or holds that the political revolution has to be something apart from the immediate and direct carrying out of full and complete social liquidation—the workers should turn their backs upon him: for the one who speaks thus is either a fool or a hypocritical exploiter.[12]

The Buorgeoisie Has No Faith in the Future. What is very remarkable and what, besides, has been observed and established by a great number of writers of various tendencies, is that now only the proletariat possesses a constructive ideal toward which it aspires with the still virginal passion of its whole being. It sees ahead of it a star, a sun which illumines and already warms it (at least in its imagination) in its faith, and which shows it with a certain clarity the road to be followed, whereas all the privileged and so-called enlightened classes find themselves plunged at the same time into a frightful and desolating darkness.

The latter see nothing ahead of them, they do not believe in or aspire to anything but the everlasting preservation of the *status quo*, recognizing at the same time that this *status quo* has no value at all. Nothing proves better that these classes are condemned to die and that the future belongs to the proletariat. It is the "barbarians" (the proletarians) who now represent faith in human destiny and the future of civilization, whereas the "civilized people" find their salvation only in barbarism: the massacre of the Communards and return to the Pope. Such are the final two behests of the privileged civilization.[13]

CHAPTER 5 *Proletariat Long Enslaved*

At first men devoured one another like wild beasts. Then the cleverest and the strongest began to enslave the other people. Later the slaves became serfs. And at a still later stage, the serfs became free wage-slaves.[1]

The Proletariat Is a Class of Well-Defined Characteristics. The city proletariat and the peasantry constitute the real people, the former, of course, being more advanced than the peasants. The proletariat . . . constitutes a very unfortunate, very much oppressed class, but at the same time one that has clearly marked characteristics of its own. As a definite, well marked-off class, it is subject to the workings of a historic and inevitable law which determines the career and the durability of every class in accordance with what it has done and how it has lived in the past. Collective individualities, all classes, exhaust themselves in the long run just as individuals do.[2]

Economic Crises and the Proletariat. In countries with highly developed industries, particularly England, France, Belgium, and Germany, ever since the introduction of improved machinery and the application of steam power in industry, and ever since large-scale factory production came into existence, commercial crises became inevitable, recurring at ever more frequent periodic intervals. Where industry has flourished to the greatest extent, workers have been faced with the periodic threat of starving to death. Naturally this gave birth to labor crises, labor movements, and labor strikes, at first in England (in the Twenties of this nineteenth century), then in France (in the Thirties), and finally in Germany and Belgium (in the Forties). The wide-spread distress, and the general cause of that distress, created powerful associations in those countries, at first only local, for mutual aid, mutual defense, and mutual struggle.[3]

Proletarian Internationalism. The city and factory proletariat, although attached by their poverty, like slaves, to the locality where they have to work, have no local interests because they have no property. All their interests are of a general character: they are not even national, but rather international. For the question of work and wages, the only question which interests them directly, actually, and vividly, an everyday question which has become the center and the basis of all other questions—social as well as political and religious—tends now to take on, by the simple devel opment of the almighty power of capital in industry and commerce, an unconditionally international character. It is this that explains the marvelous growth of the International Workingmen's Association, an association which, though founded less than six years ago, already counts in Europe alone more than a million members.[4]

Aristocracy of Labor. In every country, among the millions of un skilled workers, there is a layer of more developed, literate individuals con stituting therefore a sort of aristocracy among the workers. This labor aristocracy is divided into two categories, of which one is highly useful and the other quite harmful.

Handicraft a Holdover from Medieval Age. Let us begin with the harmful category. It consists pre-eminently and almost exclusively not of factory workers but of artisans. We know that the situation of the artisans in Europe, though hardly to be envied, is still incomparably better than that of the factory workers. The artisans are exploited not by big but by small capital, which lacks by far the power to oppress and humiliate workers to the extent possessed by the vast aggregations of capital in the industrial world. The world of artisans, of handicraft and not machine work, is a vestige of the medieval economic structure. More and more it is being dislodged under the irresistible pressure of large-scale factory pro duction, which naturally aims to get hold of all the branches of industry.

But where handicraft does persist, the workers occupied in it live much better: and the relations between the not over-wealthy employers, who themselves sprang from the working class, and their workers are more intimate, more simple and patriarchal than in the world of factory pro duction. Among the artisans, then, one finds many semi-bourgeois, by their habits and convictions, hoping and aiming, consciously or uncon sciously, to become one hundred per cent bourgeois.

But craftsmen themselves are subdivided into three categories. The largest and least aristocratic category—that is, the least fortunate of all of them in the bourgeois sense—comprises all the least skilled and the crudest crafts (like blacksmithing, for instance), which demand considerable physi cal power. Workers belonging to this category, by their tendencies and convictions, stand nearer than others to factory workers. And in their midst valuable revolutionary instincts are preserved and are being devel oped. One frequently finds among them persons who are capable of com prehending, in all their scope and implications, the problems involved in the universal emancipation of the workers.

There is a middle category, comprising such trades as joiners, printers, tailors, shoemakers, and many other similar handicrafts, which require a certain degree of education and special knowledge, or at least less physical exertion, and therefore leave more time for thinking. Among these workers there is comparatively more well-being and accordingly more bourgeois smugness. Their revolutionary instincts are considerably weaker than in the first relatively unskilled category. But on the other hand one meets here a greater number of men who think and reason, though rather erratically at times, and whose convictions are consciously arrived at. At the same time this category contains a goodly portion of hair-splitters incapable of action because of their proneness for idle talk, and sometimes, under the influence of vanity and personal ambitions, even consciously blocking such action.

The Semi-Bourgeois Category. And, finally, there is a third category of hand trades producing luxury commodities and therefore tied up by their own interests with the existence and preservation of the well-to-do bourgeois world. Most of the workers belonging to this environment are almost completely permeated with bourgeois passions, bourgeois conceit, bourgeois prejudices. Fortunately, in the general mass of workers, these constitute only an insignificant minority. But where they do predominate, international propaganda moves very slowly and frequently takes on a clearly anti-social, purely bourgeois tendency. In these circles we see predominating the craving for an exclusively personal happiness, for individual —that is, bourgeois—self-promotion, and not for collective emancipation and happiness.

The wages of this category of workers are incomparably higher, their work being at the same time more of the white-collar type, lighter, cleaner, more respectable than in the first two categories. That is why there is more well-being, more rudimentary schooling, self-conceit, and vanity among them. They become Socialists only during commercial crises which, because of the concomitant slump in wages, remind them that they are not bourgeois but only day-laborers.

Bourgeois Socialism Finds Its Support Among Workers of the Third Category. It stands to reason that during the last ten years, when the peaceful co-operative system was still in the hey-day of its high-blown dreams and expectations, bourgeois Socialism found its principal support not in the world of factory workers but in that of artisans and mainly in the last two categories—the most privileged and the nearest to the bourgeois world. The universal failure of the co-operative system was a beneficent lesson to the detrimental workers' aristocracy.

The True Labor Aristocracy: the Revolutionary Vanguard. But along with the latter there also exists an aristocracy of a different kind, a beneficial and useful aristocracy; an aristocracy not by virtue of position but by that of conviction of revolutionary class-consciousness and of rational, energetic passion and will. Workers who belong to this category are the most thorough enemies of every aristocracy and every privilege—that of the nobility, the bourgeoisie, and even that of some workers' groups. They can be called aristocrats only in the most literal or original meaning of the word, in the sense of being *the best people*. And indeed they are the best people, not only among the working class but in society as a whole. They combine in themselves, in their comprehension of the social problem, all the advantages of free and independent thought, of scientific views combined with the sincerity of a sound folk-instinct.

They would find it quite easy to rise above their own class, to become members of the bourgeois caste, and to rise from the ranks of the ignorant, exploited, and enslaved people into those of the fortunate coterie of exploiters—but the desire for that kind of personal advancement is foreign to them. They are permeated with the passion for solidarity, and they do not understand any other liberty and happiness but that which can be enjoyed together with all the millions of their enslaved human brothers. And it stands to reason that those men enjoy a great and fascinating, although unsought, influence over the masses of workers. Add to this category of workers those who have broken away from the bourgeois class, and who have given themselves to the great cause of emancipation of labor, and you get what we call the useful and beneficent aristocracy in the international labor movement.[5]

Proletarian Humanism Tempered by Sound Sense. If true human feelings, so greatly debased and falsified in our days by official hypocrisy and bourgeois sentimentality, are still preserved anywhere, it is only among the workers. For the workers constitute the only class in existing society of whom one might say that it is really generous, too generous at times, and too forgetful of the atrocious crimes and odious betrayals of which it is frequently the victim. The proletariat is incapable of cruelty. But at the same time the proletariat is actuated by a realistic instinct which leads it straight toward the right goal, and by common sense which tells it that if it wants to put an end to evil-doing, it must first curb and paralyze the evil-doers.[6]

An Irrepressible Class. There is no power now in the world, there is no political nor religious means in existence, which can stop, among the proletariat of any country, and especially among the French proletariat, the drive toward economic emancipation and toward social equality.[7]

The great mass of unskilled workers in Italy, as well as in other countries, constitute in themselves the whole life, the power, and the future of existing society. Only a few persons from the bourgeois world have joined the workers, only those who have come to hate with all their souls the present political economic, and social order, who have turned their backs upon the class from which they sprang, and who have devoted all their energies to the cause of the people. Those persons are few and far between, but they are highly valuable, provided, of course, that they have stifled within themselves all personal ambition; in which case, I repeat, they are indeed highly valuable. The people give them life, elementary strength, and a soil from which they draw their sustenance, and in return they bring their positive knowledge, the power of abstraction and generalization, and organizational abilities, to be used in organizing labor unions, which in turn create the conscious fighting force without which no victory is possible.[8]

Possible Allies of the Proletariat. Deep as our scorn is for the modern bourgeoisie, with all the antipathy and distrust which it inspires within us, there are still two categories within this class with regard to whom we do not give up the hope, of seeing them, in part at least, become converted sooner or later by Socialist propaganda to the people's cause. One of them, driven on by the force of circumstances and the necessities of its own actual position, and the other by a generous temperament, they are without doubt bound to take part with us in wiping out existing iniquities and in the building of a new world.

We are referring to the petty-bourgeoisie and to the youth in the schools and universities.[9]

CHAPTER 6 *Peasants' Day is Yet to Come*

The peasants in almost all the countries of Western Europe—with the exception of England and Scotland, where peasants in the proper sense of the word do not exist, and with the exception of Ireland, Italy, and Spain, where they are poverty-stricken, and where they are revolutionary and Socialists without even being aware of it—outside of these countries the peasants of Western Europe, especially those of France and Germany, are semi-content with their position.

They enjoy, or believe they enjoy, certain advantages, and they imagine that it would be to their interest to preserve those advantages against the attacks of a social revolution. They have, if not the real profits of property, at least a vain-glorious dream about it. Besides, they are kept systematically in crass ignorance by governments and all the official and officious State churches. The peasants constitute the principal, almost sole, foundation upon which the safety and power of the State now rest. Therefore they have become the object of especial solicitude on the part of all governments. And the peasant mind is being worked upon by all the governmental and church agencies, who try to cultivate within that mind the tender flowers of Christian faith and loyalty to the reigning monarchs, and to sow salutary seeds of hatred for the city.

Peasants Are a Potentially Revolutionary Class. Yet in spite of all that the peasants can be stirred into action, and sooner or later they will be so stirred by the Social Revolution. This is true for three reasons:

1. Owing to their backward or relatively *barbarous* civilization, they have retained in all their integrity the simple, robust temperament and the energy germane to the folk nature. 2. They live from the labor of their hands, and are morally conditioned by this labor, which fosters within them an instinctive hatred for all privileged parasites of the State, and for all exploiters of labor. 3. Finally, being toilers themselves, they share common interests with city workers, from whom they are separated only by their prejudices.

A Workers-Peasants Revolution Under the Leadership of the Proletariat. A great, truly Socialist and revolutionary movement may at first startle them, but their instinct and their native common sense will soon make them realize that the Social Revolution does not aim to despoil them of what they have, but to lead to the triumph everywhere and for everyone, of the sacred right of work, a right to be established upon the ruins of privileged parasitism. And when the [industrial] workers, inspired by revolutionary passion, and abandoning the pretentious and scholastic language of a doctrinaire Socialism, come to tell them simply, without any evasions or phrase-mongering, what they want; when they come to the villages not as schoolmasters but as brothers and as equals, provoking the revolution but not imposing it upon the toilers on the land; when they have consigned to flames all the writs, lawsuits, property deeds and rents, private debts, mortgages, and criminal and civil laws; when they have made a bonfire of all these immense heaps of red tape—the sign and official consecration of the poverty and slavery of the proletariat—when the workers have done all these things, then, rest assured, the peasants will understand them and will rise together with them.

But in order that the peasants rise in rebellion, it is absolutely necessary that the city workers take upon themselves the initiative in this revolutionary movement, because it is only the city workers who today unite in themselves the instinct, the clear consciousness, the idea, and the conscious will of the Social Revolution. Consequently, the whole danger threatening the existence of the States is now mainly centered in the city proletariat.[1]

The Peasantry and the Communists. To the Communists, or Social Democrats, of Germany, the peasantry, any peasantry, stands for reaction; and the State, any State, even the Bismarckian State, stands for revolution. Far be it from us to traduce the German Social Democrats in this matter. We have cited to this effect speeches, pamphlets, magazine articles, and finally their letters, in proof of our assertion. Altogether, the Marxists cannot even think otherwise: protagonists of the State as they are, they have have to damn any revolution of a truly popular sweep and character, especially a peasant revolution, which is anarchistic by nature and which marches straightforward toward the destruction of the State. And in this hatred for the peasant rebellion, the Marxists join in touching unanimity all the layers and parties of the bourgeois society of Germany.[2]

Basic Solidarity of Peasants and Workers. One should not forget that the peasants of France, certainly a vast majority of them, although owning their lands, nevertheless live by their own labor. This is what separates them essentially from the bourgeois class, the great majority of which lives by the profitable exploitation of the work of the masses of the people. And this very circumstance unites the peasants with the city workers, notwithstanding the difference of their positions—a difference which is much to the disadvantage of the workers—and the difference of ideas, too often resulting in misunderstandings in matters of principles.

Proletarian Snobbishness Harmful to the Cause of Peasant-Worker Unity. What above all alienates the peasants from the workers of the cities is a certain *aristocracy of intelligence*, rather ill-founded on the part of the workers, which they flaunt before the peasants. The workers are no doubt the more literate, they are more developed so far as mind, knowledge, and ideas are concerned, and in the name of this petty scientific superiority, they sometimes treat the peasants condescendingly, openly showing their contempt for them. The workers are quite wrong in that respect, for by this very claim, and seemingly with much greater reason, the bourgeois, who are much more learned and developed than the workers, should have even a greater right to despise the latter. And as we know, the bourgeois certainly do not miss any occasion to emphasize their superiority.[3]

In the interests of the revolution, the workers should stop flaunting their disdain for the peasants. In the face of the bourgeois exploiter the worker should feel that he is the brother of the peasant.[4]

Revolutionary Unity of Workers and Peasants Will Lead to Abolition of Classes. The peasants in the greater part of Italy are miserably poor, much poorer than the workers in the cities. They are not proprietors like the peasants of France, which fact is of course highly fortunate from the point of view of the Revolution. And it is only in a few regions that the peasants manage to make some sort of living as share-croppers. That is why the masses of the Italian peasantry already constitute a vast and powerful army of the Social Revolution. Directed by the proletariat of the city and organized by the revolutionary Socialist youth, this army will be invincible.

Therefore, my dear friends, simultaneously with the organizing of the city workers, you should use all the means at your disposal to break the ice separating the proletariat of the cities from the people of the villages, and to unite and organize those two classes into one. And all the other classes should disappear from the face of the earth, not as individuals but as classes.[5]

CHAPTER 7 *The State: General Outlook*

Is the State the Embodiment of the General Interest? What is the
State? The metaphysicians and the learned jurists tell us that the State is a
public affair: it represents the collective well-being and the rights of all
as opposed to the disintegrating action of the egoistic interests and passions
of the individual. It is the realization of justice, morality, and virtue upon
the earth. Consequently, there is no greater or more sublime duty on the
part of the individual than to dedicate, to sacrifice himself, and if necessary,
to die for the triumph and the power of the State.

Here we have in a few words the theology of the State. Let us see then
whether this political theology does not conceal beneath an attractive and
poetic appearance rather vulgar and sordid realities.

The Idea of the State Analyzed. Let us analyze first the idea of the
State as presented to us by its panegyrists. It is the sacrifice of natural liberty and the interests of everyone—of individuals as well as of comparatively small collective units, associations, communes, and provinces—to the
interests and liberty of all, to the prosperity of the great whole.

But this totality, this great whole, what is it in reality? It is an agglomeration of all the individuals and of all the more circumscribed human
collectives which comprise it. And if this whole, in order to constitute itself
as such, demands the sacrifice of individual and local interests, how then
can it in reality represent them in their totality?

An Exclusive But Not an Inclusive Universality. It is then not a living
whole, giving everyone the chance to breathe freely and becoming the
richer, freer, and more powerful, the more extensive the development of
liberty and prosperity for everyone becomes in its midst. It is not a natural
human society which supports and reinforces the life of everyone by the
life of all—quite the contrary, it is the immolation of every individual as
well as of local associations, it is an abstraction which is destructive of a
living society, it is the limitation, or rather the complete negation, of the
life and of the rights of all the parts which go to make up the whole in
the purported interest of everybody. It is the State, it is the altar of political religion upon which natural society is always immolated: a devouring
universality, subsisting upon human sacrifices, just as the Church does. The
State, I repeat again, is the youngest brother of the Church.[1]

**The Premise of the Theory of the State Is the Negation of Man's
Liberty.** But if the metaphysicians affirm that men, especially those who
believe in the immortality of the soul, stand outside of the society of free
beings, we inevitably arrive at the conclusion that men can unite in a

ociety only at the cost of their own liberty, their natural independence, and by sacrificing first their personal and then their local interests. Such self-renunciation and self-sacrifice are thus all the more imperative the more numerous society is in point of membership and the greater the complexity of its organization.

In this sense the State is the expression of all individual sacrifices. Given his abstract and at the same time violent origin, the State must continue restricting liberty to an even greater extent, doing it in the name of the falsehood called "the good of the people", which in reality represents exclusively the interests of the dominant class. Thus the State appears as an inevitable negation and annihilation of all liberty, and of all individual and collective interests.[2]

The Abstraction of the State Hides the Concrete Factor of Class Exploitation. It is evident that all the so-called general interests of society supposedly represented by the State, which in reality are only the general and permanent negation of the positive interests of the regions, communes, associations, and a vast number of individuals subordinated to the State, constitute an abstraction, a fiction, a falsehood, and that the State is like a vast slaughterhouse and an enormous cemetery, where under the shadow and the pretext of this abstraction all the best aspirations, all the living forces of a country, are sanctimoniously immolated and interred. And since abstractions do not exist in themselves nor for themselves, since they have neither feet with which to walk, hands to create, nor stomachs to digest this mass of victims turned over to them to be devoured, it is clear that just as the religious or celestial abstraction God represents in reality the very positive and real interests of the clergy, so God's earthly complement, the political abstraction the State, represents no less positive and real interests of the bourgeoisie, which is now the principal if not the exclusive exploiting class. . . .[3]

The Church and the State. To prove the identity of the State and the Church, I shall ask the reader to take note of the fact that both are essentially based upon the idea of sacrifice of life and natural rights, and that both start equally from the same principle: the natural wickedness of men, which, according to the Church, can be overcome only by Divine Grace, and by the death of the natural man in God, and according to the State, only through law and the immolation of the individual on the altar of the State. Both aim to transform man—one, into a saint, the other, into a citizen. But the natural man has to die, for his condemnation is unanimously decreed by the religion of the Church and that of the State.

Such, in its ideal purity, is the identical theory of the Church and the State. It is a pure abstraction; but every historic abstraction presupposes historic facts. And these facts are of an altogether real and brutal character: they are violence, spoliation, conquest, enslavement. Man is so constituted that he is not content merely to commit certain acts; he also feels the need of justifying and legitimating those acts before the eyes of the whole world.

Thus religion came in the nick of time to bestow its blessing upon accomplished facts, and owing to this benediction, the iniquitous and brutal facts became transformed into "rights."

Abstraction of the State in Real Life. Let us see now what role this abstraction of the State, paralleling the historic abstraction called the Church, has played and continues to play in real life, in human society. The State, as I have said before, is in effect a vast cemetery wherein all the manifestations of individual and local life are sacrificed, where the interests of the parts constituting the whole die and are buried. It is the altar on which the real liberty and the well-being of peoples are immolated to political grandeur; and the more complete this immolation is, the more perfect is the State. Hence I conclude that the Russian Empire is a State *par excellence*, a State without rhetoric or phrase-mongering, the most perfect in Europe. On the contrary, all States in which the people are allowed to breathe somewhat are, from the ideal point of view, incomplete States, just as other churches, compared to the Roman Catholic, are deficient.

The Sacerdotal Body of the State. The State is an abstraction devouring the life of the people. But in order that an abstraction may be born, that it may develop and continue to exist in real life, it is necessary that there be a real collective body interested in maintaining its existence. This function cannot be fulfilled by the masses of the people, since it is they who are precisely the victims of the State. It has to be done by a privileged body, the sacerdotal body of the State, the governing and possessing class which holds the same place in the State that the sacerdotal class in religion —the priests—hold in the Church.

The State Could Not Exist Without a Privileged Body. And, indeed, what do we see throughout history? The State has always been the patrimony of some privileged class: the sacerdotal class, the nobility, the bourgeoisie—and finally, when all the other classes have exhausted themselves, the class of bureaucracy enters upon the stage and then the State falls, or rises, if you please, to the position of a machine. But for the salvation of the State it is absolutely necessary that there be some privileged class interested in maintaining its existence.[4]

The Liberal and Absolutist Theories of the State. The State is not a direct product of Nature; it does not precede, as society does, the awakening of thought in man. According to liberal political writers, the first State was created by man's free and conscious will; according to the absolutists, the State is a divine creation. In both cases it dominates society and tends altogether to absorb it.

In the second case [that of the absolutist theory] this absorption is self-evident: a divine institution must necessarily devour all natural organizations. What is more curious in this case is that the individualistic school, with its free-contract theory, leads to the same result. And, indeed, this school begins by denying the very existence of a natural society antedating the contract—inasmuch as such a society would presuppose the existence of natural relations among individuals, and consequently *a reciprocal limitation of their liberties,* which is contrary to the absolute liberty enjoyed, according to this theory, prior to the conclusion of the contract, and which would be neither less nor more than this contract itself, existing as a natural fact and preceding the free contract. According to this theory, human society began only with the conclusion of the contract. But what then is this society? It is the pure and logical realization of the contract, with all of its implied tendencies and legislative and practical consequences —it is the State.

The State Is the Sum of Negations of Individual Liberty. Let us examine it more closely. What does the State represent? The sum of negations of the individual liberties of all of its members; or the sum of sacrifices which all of its members make in renouncing a part of their liberty for the common good. We have seen that, according to the individualist theory, the freedom of everyone is the limit, or rather the natural negation of the freedom of all the others. And so it is this absolute limitation, this negation of the liberty of everyone in the name of liberty of all or of the common right, that constitutes the State. Thus where the State begins, individual liberty ceases, and *vice versa.*

Liberty Is Indivisible. It will be argued that the State, the representative of the public weal or of the interest common to all, curtails a part of everyone's liberty in order to assure the remainder of this liberty. But this remainder is security, if you please, yet it is by no means liberty. For liberty is indivisible: a part of it cannot be curtailed without destroying it as a whole. This small part of liberty which is being curtailed is the very essence of my liberty, it is everything. By a natural, necessary, and irresistible movement all my liberty is concentrated precisely in that part, small though it may be, which is being curtailed.

Universal Suffrage Is No Guarantee of Freedom. But, we are told, the democratic State, based upon free universal suffrage for all its citizens, surely cannot be the negation of their liberty. And why not? This depends absolutely upon the mission and the power which the citizens delegate to the State. And a republican State, based upon universal suffrage, could be exceedingly despotic, even more despotic than a monarchic State, when, under the pretext of representing the will of everyone, it bears down upon the will and the free movement of every one of its members with the whole weight of its collective power.

Who Is the Supreme Arbiter of Good and Evil? But the State, it will be argued again, restricts the liberty of its members only in so far as this liberty is bent upon injustice, upon evil-doing. The State prevents them from killing, robbing, and offending one another, and in general from doing evil, leaving them on the contrary full and complete liberty to do good. But what is good and what is evil?[5]

CHAPTER 8 *The Modern State Surveyed*

Capitalism and Representative Democracy. Modern capitalist production and banking speculations demand for their full development a vast centralized State apparatus which alone is capable of subjecting the millions of toilers to their exploitation.

A federal organization, from the bottom upward, of workers' associations, groups, city and village communes, and finally of regions and peoples, the sole condition of a real and not fictitious liberty, is just as contrary to capitalist production as any sort of economic autonomy. But capitalist production and banking speculation get along very well with the so-called *representative democracy;* for this most modern State form, based upon the pretended rule by the people's will, allegedly expressed by the would-be representatives of the people at the supposedly popular assemblies, unites in itself the two conditions necessary for the prosperity of the capitalistic economy: State centralization and the actual subjection of the Sovereign —The People—to the minority allegedly representing it but actually governing it intellectually and invariably exploiting it.

Modern State Must Have Centralized, Military Apparatus. The modern State, in its essence and aims, is necessarily a military State, and a military State is driven on by the very same logic to become a conquering State. If it does not conquer, it will be conquered by others, and that is true for the simple reason that where there is force, it must manifest itself in some form. Hence it follows that the modern State invariably must be a vast and powerful State: only under this indispensable condition can it preserve itself.

Dynamics of State and Capitalism Are Identical. And just as capitalist production and banking speculation, which in the long run swallows up that production, must, under the threat of bankruptcy, ceaselessly expand at the expense of the small financial and productive enterprises which they absorb, must become universal, monopolistic enterprises extending all over the world—so this modern and necessarily military State is driven on by an irrepressible urge to become a universal State. But a universal State, which of course never can be realized, can exist only in a singular number, the co-existence of two such States alongside of each other being utterly impossible.

Monarchy and Republic. Hegemony is only a modest manifestation, possible under the circumstances, of this unrealizable urge inherent in every State. And the first condition of this hegemony is the relative impotence and subjection of all the neighboring States.[1] At the present time, most

The Modern State Surveyed

serious in its implications, a strong State can have only one foundation; military and bureaucratic centralization. In this respect the essential difference between a monarchy and a democratic republic is reduced to the following: in a monarchy the bureaucratic world oppresses and plunders the people for the greater benefit of the privileged propertied classes as well as for its own benefit, and all that is done in the name of the monarch; in a republic the same bureaucracy will do exactly the same, but—in the name of the will of the people. In a republic the so-called people, the legal people, allegedly represented by the State, stifle and will keep on stifling the actual and living people. But the people will scarcely feel any better if the stick with which they are being belabored is called The People's Stick.

No State Can Satisfy the Aspirations of the People. No State, democratic though it may be in form—and not even the reddest *political* republic, which is a people's republic in the same sense in which this falsehood is known by the name of popular representation—can give the people what they need, that is, the free organization of their own interests, from the bottom upward, with no interference, tutelage, or violence from above, because every State, even the most Republican and the most democratic State—even the would-be popular State conceived by M. Marx—are in their essence only machines governing the masses from above, through an intelligent and therefore a privileged minority, allegedly knowing the genuine interests of the people better than the people themselves.

Inherent Antagonism Toward People Leads to Violence. Thus, not being able to satisfy the demands of the people or to allay popular passion, the propertied and ruling classes have only one means at their disposal: *State violence*, in a word, the State, because the *State* denotes *violence*, rule by disguised, or if necessary open and unceremonious, violence.[2]

The State, any State—even when it is dressed up in the most liberal and democratic form—is necessarily based upon domination, and upon violence, that is, upon despotism—a concealed but no less dangerous despotism.[3]

Militarism and Freedom. We have already said that society cannot remain a State without taking on the character of a conquering State. The same competition, which in the economic field annihilates and swallows up small and even medium-sized capital, industrial enterprises, and landed estates in favor of vast capital, factories, and commercial houses—is also operative in the lives of the States, leading to the destruction and absorption of small and medium-sized States for the benefit of empires. Henceforth every State, in so far as it wants to live not only on paper and not merely by sufferance of its neighbors, but to enjoy real independence—inevitably must become a conquering State.

But to be a conquering State means to be forced to hold in subjection many millions of alien people. And this requires the development of a huge military force. And where military force prevails, there freedom has to take its leave—especially the freedom and well-being of the working people.[4]

Expansion of State Leads to Growth of Abuse. Some believe that when the State has expanded and its population has doubled, trebled, or increased tenfold, it will become more liberal, and that its institutions, all the conditions of its existence, and its governmental action will become more popular in character and more in harmony with the instincts of the people. But upon what is this hope and this supposition based? Upon theory? Yet theoretically it is quite evident that the larger the State, the more complex its organism, and the more alien it becomes to the people—and because of that, the more do its interests militate against the interests of the masses of the people, the heavier the oppression of the people, and the farther apart the State government finds itself from genuine popular self-rule.

Or are their expectations based upon the practical experience of other countries? By way of answering this question, it is enough to point to the example of Russia, Austria, expanded Prussia, France, England, Italy, and even the United States of America, where everything is under the administrative control of a special, altogether bourgeois class, under the control of so-called politicians or business people in politics, whereas the great mass of toilers live under conditions which are just as wretched and frightful as those which prevail in the monarchic States.[5]

Social Control of State Power as a Necessary Safeguard for Liberty. Modern society is so convinced of this truth—that all political power, whatever its origin and form may be, necessarily tends toward despotism—that in any country where society succeeds in emancipating itself to some extent from the State, it hastens to subject the government, even when the latter has sprung from a revolution and from popular elections, to as severe a control as possible. It places the salvation of liberty in a real and serious organization of control to be exercised by the popular will and opinion upon men invested with public authority. In all the countries enjoying representative government, liberty can be valid only when this control is valid. On the contrary, where such control is fictitious, the freedom of the people likewise becomes a mere fiction.[6]

The best men easily become corrupted, especially when the environment itself promotes corruption on the part of individuals through lack of serious control and permanent opposition.[7]

Lack of permanent opposition and continuous control inevitably become a source of moral depravity for all the individuals who find themselves invested with some social power.[8]

Participation in Government as a Source of Corruption. Many times it has been established as a general truth that it suffices for anyone, even the most liberal and popular man, to become a part of a governmental machine in order to undergo a complete change in outlook and attitude.

Unless that person is frequently reinvigorated by contacts with the life of the people; unless he is compelled to act openly under conditions of full publicity; unless he is subjected to a salutary and uninterrupted regime of popular control and criticism, which is to remind him constantly that he is not the master nor even the guardian of the masses but only their proxy or their elected functionary who is always subject to recall—unless he is placed under those conditions, he runs the risk of becoming utterly spoiled by dealing only with aristocrats like himself, and he also runs the risk of becoming a pretentious and vain fool, all puffed up with the feeling of his ridiculous importance.[9]

Universal Suffrage as an Attempted Form of Popular Control; the Swiss Example. It would be easy to prove that in no part of Europe is there genuine control by the people. But we shall confine ourselves to Switzerland and see how this control is being applied. . . .

. . . Toward the period of 1830 the most advanced cantons in Switzerland sought to guarantee liberty by introducing universal suffrage. . . . Once this universal suffrage had been established, the belief became general that from then on liberty for the population would be firmly assured. This, however, turned out to be a great illusion, and one may say that the realization of this illusion led in some cantons to the downfall and everywhere to the demoralization, which today has become some flagrant, of the Radical Party. . . . [It] really acted on the strength of its convictions when it promised liberty to the people through universal suffrage. . . .

And, indeed, the whole thing seemed so natural and simple: Once the legislative and executive power emanate directly from popular elections, shall they not become the pure expression of the will of the people, and that will, can it produce anything else but freedom and prosperity of the people?[10]

Universal Suffrage Under Capitalism. I frankly confess, my dear friend, that I do not share the superstitious devotion of your bourgeois radicals or your republican bourgeois to universal suffrage. . . . *So long as universal suffrage is exercised in a society where the people, the mass of workers, are ECONOMICALLY dominated by a minority holding in exclusive possession the property and capital of the country, free or independent though the people may be otherwise, or as they may appear to be from a political aspect, these elections held under conditions of universal suffrage can only be illusory, anti-democratic in their results, which invariably will prove to be absolutely opposed to the needs, instincts, and real will of the population.*

Universal Suffrage in Past History. And all the elections held after the *coup d'etat* of December,* with the people of France directly partici-

---

* The *coup d'etat* effected by Louis Napoleon (Napoleon III) on December 2, 1851, which made him practically dictator of France.

pating in such elections, were they not in their results quite contrary to the interests of the people? And did not the last imperial plebiscite yield seven millions of "Yes" votes to the Emperor? No doubt it will be argued that universal suffrage was never freely exercised under the Empire, inasmuch as freedom of the press and freedom of association—the essential conditions of political liberty—had been proscribed and the defenseless people left to be corrupted by a subsidized press and an infamous administration. Be it so, but the elections of 1848 for the Constituent Assembly and the office of President, and also those held in May, 1849, for the Legislative Assembly, were, I believe, absolutely free. They took place with no undue pressure or intervention by the government, under conditions of the greatest freedom. And, still, what did they produce? Nothing but reaction.[11]

Why Workers Cannot Make Use of Political Democracy. One has to be greatly enamored of illusions to imagine that workers, under the economic and social conditions in which they now find themselves, can fully profit, or can make serious and real use of their political freedom. For this they lack two "small" things: leisure and material means. . . .

Certainly the French workers were neither indifferent nor unintelligent, and yet, notwithstanding the most extensive universal suffrage, they had to clear the stage of action for the bourgeoisie. Why? Because they lacked the material means which are necessary to make political liberty a reality, because they remained slaves forced to work by hunger while the radical, liberal, and even conservative bourgeois—some Republicans of quite recent date and others converted on the morrow of the Revolution—kept coming and going, agitated, harangued, and freely conspired. Some could do it because of their incomes from rent or from some other lucrative variety of bourgeois income, and others owed it to the State budget, which they naturally preserved and even increased to an unheard of extent.

The results are well known: first. the June days, and later, as a necessary sequel, the days of December.[12]

Proudhon on Universal Suffrage. "One of the first acts of the Provisional Government (of 1848)," says Proudhon,* "an act eliciting the greatest applause, was the application of universal suffrage. On the very day that the decree was promulgated, we wrote precisely these words, which at that time could have passed as a paradox: *Universal suffrage is counter-revolution.* One can judge by the events which followed whether we were right in this matter. The elections of 1848, in their great majority, were carried by priests, legitimists, partisans of monarchy, by the most reactionary and retrograde elements of France. And it could not be otherwise."

---

* *The General Idea of the Revolution in the Nineteenth Century.* Bakunin does not give the page number.

No, it could not be otherwise, and this will hold true to an even greater measure so long as inequality of economic and social conditions prevails in the organization of society, and so long as society continues to be divided into two classes, one of which—*the exploiting and privileged class*—enjoys all the advantages of fortune, education, and leisure, while the other class—comprising the whole mass of the proletariat—gets for its share only forced and wearisome labor, ignorance, and poverty, with their necessary accompaniment: slavery, not by right but in fact.

The Great Odds Which the Proletariat Must Face in Political Democracy.   Yes, slavery indeed; for wide as may be in scope the political rights accorded to these millions of wage-receiving proletarians—the true galley-slaves of hunger—you will never succeed in drawing them away from the pernicious influence, from the natural domination of diverse representatives of the privileged classes—beginning with the preacher and ending with the bourgeois Republican of the reddest, Jacobin variety—representatives who, divided though they may appear, or as they may actually be, on political questions, are nevertheless united by one common and supreme interest: the exploitation of the misery, ignorance, political inexperience, and good faith of the proletariat, for the benefit of the economic domination of the possessing class.

How could the city and rural proletariat resist the political intrigues of the clericals, the nobility, and the bourgeoisie? For self-defense it has only one weapon—its instinct, which tends almost always to be true and just because it is itself the principal, if not the sole victim of the iniquity and all the falsehoods which reign supreme in existing society. And because it is oppressed by privilege it naturally demands equality for all.

Workers Lack Education, Leisure, and Knowledge of Affairs.   But instinct as a weapon is not sufficient to safeguard the proletariat against the reactionary machinations of the privileged classes. Instinct left to itself, and inasmuch as it has not been transformed into consciously reflected, clearly determined thought, lends itself easily to falsification, distortion, and deceit. Yet it is impossible for it to rise to this state of self-awareness without the aid of education, of science; and science, knowledge of affairs and of people, and political experience—those are things which the proletariat completely lacks. The consequence can be easily foreseen: the proletariat wants one thing, but clever people, profiting by its ignorance, make it do quite another thing, without it even suspecting that it is doing the contrary of what it wants to do. And when it finally does take note of this, it is generally too late to repair the wrong of which it naturally, necessarily, and invariably becomes the first and principal victim.[13]

Workers' Deputies Lose Their Proletarian Outlook.   But, we are told, the workers, taught by the experience which they have gone through, will not send the bourgeoisie any more as their representatives to the

Constituent or Legislative Assemblies; instead they will send simple workers. Poor as they are, the workers can manage somehow to scrape up enough for the upkeep of their parliamentary deputies. And do you know what will be the result? The inevitable result will be that workers' deputies, transferred to a purely bourgeois environment and into an atmosphere of purely bourgeois political ideas, ceasing in fact to be workers and becoming statesmen instead, will become middle class in their outlook, perhaps even more so than the bourgeois themselves.

For men do not create situations; it is situations that create men. And we know from experience that *bourgeois workers* are frequently neither less egoistical than bourgeois exploiters, nor less baneful for the International than bourgeois Socialists; nor are they less ridiculous in their vanity than bourgeois commoners raised into nobility.

Political Liberty Without Socialism Is a Fraud. Whatever may be said and done, one thing is clear: so long as the workers remain in their present state, no liberty will be possible for them, and those who call upon them to win political liberties without touching upon the burning question of Socialism, without even uttering the phrase "social liquidation" which sets the bourgeois trembling, tell them in effect the following: "Win first this freedom for us in order that we may use it against you later."[14]

Under Capitalism the Bourgeoisie Is Better Equipped Than the Workers to Make Use of Parliamentarian Democracy. It is certain that the bourgeoisie knows better than the proletariat what it wants and what it should want. This is true for two reasons: first, because it is more learned than the latter, and because it has more leisure and many more means of all sorts to know the persons whom it elected; and second—and this is the principal reason—because the purpose which it is pursuing is, unlike that of the proletariat, neither new nor is it immensely large in scope. On the contrary, it is known and is completely determined by history as well as by all the conditions of the present situation of the bourgeoisie, this purpose being nothing else but the preservation of political and economic domination by the bourgeoisie. This is so clearly posed that it is quite easy to guess and to know which of the candidates who solicit the electoral votes of the bourgeoisie are capable of serving well its interests. Therefore it is certain, or nearly certain, that the bourgeoisie will always be represented in accordance with its most intimate desires.

Classes Do Not Abdicate Their Privileges. But it is no less certain that this representation, excellent from the point of view of the bourgeoisie, will prove to be detestable from the point of view of popular interests. The interests of the bourgeoisie being absolutely opposed to those of the working masses, it is certain that a bourgeois Parliament could never do anything else but legislate the slavery of the people, and vote all those measures which have for their aim the perpetuation of their

poverty and ignorance. Indeed, one must be extremely naive to believe
that a bourgeois Parliament could freely vote to bring about the intellectual, material, and political emancipation of the people. Has it ever been
witnessed in history that a political body, a privileged class, committed
suicide, or sacrificed the least of its interests and so-called rights for the
love of justice and liberty?

I believe I have already pointed out that even the famous night of
August 4, when the nobility of France generously sacrificed their interests
upon the altar of the fatherland, was nothing but a forced and belated
consequence of a formidable uprising of peasants who set fire to the
title deeds and the castles of their lords and masters. No, classes never
sacrifice themselves and will never do it—because it is contrary to their
nature, to the reason for their existence, and nothing is ever done or ever
can be done by them against Nature or against reason. Therefore one
would have to be mad, indeed, to expect from a privileged Assembly
measures and laws for the benefit of the people.[15]

It is clear to me that universal suffrage is the most extensive and at the
same time the most refined manifestation of the political charlatanism of
the State; a dangerous instrument without doubt, and demanding a great
deal of skill and competence by those who make use of it, but becoming
at the same time—that is, if those people learn to make use of it—the surest
means of making the masses co-operate in the building of their own
prison. Napoleon III built his power completely upon universal suffrage
and it never betrayed his trust. And Bismarck made it the basis of his
Knouto-Germanic Empire.[16]

CHAPTER 9 *Representative System
Based on Fiction*

The Basic Discrepancy.   The falsehood of the representative system
rests upon the fiction that the executive power and the legislative chamber
issuing from popular elections must, or even can for that matter, represent
the will of the people. The people want instinctively, want necessarily,
two things: the greatest material prosperity possible under the circumstances and the greatest liberty in their lives, liberty of movement and
liberty of action. That is, they want better organization of their economic
interests and complete absence of all power, of all political organization—

since every political organization inevitably ends in negation of the liberty of the people. Such is the essence of all popular instincts.

Gulf Between Those Who Govern and Those That Are Governed. But the instinctive aims of those who govern—of those who frame the laws of the country as well as of those who exercise the executive power, are, because of their exceptional position diametrically opposed to the instinctive popular aspirations. Whatever their democratic sentiments and intentions may be, viewing society from the high position in which they find themselves, they cannot consider this society in any other way but that in which a schoolmaster views his pupils. And there can be no equality between the schoolmaster and the pupils. On one side there is the feeling of superiority necessarily inspired by a superior position; on the other side there is the feeling of inferiority induced by the attitude of superiority on the part of the teacher exercising executive or legislative power. Whoever says political power says domination. And where domination exists, a more or less considerable section of the population is bound to be dominated by others. So it is quite natural that those who are dominated detest those who dominate them, while those who do the dominating necessarily must repress and consequently oppress those who are subject to their domination.

Change of Perspective Induced By Possession of Power. Such has been the eternal history of political power ever since that power was established in this world. It is that also which explains why and how men who were democrats and rebels of the reddest variety when they were a part of the mass of governed people, became exceedingly moderate when they rose to power. Usually these backslidings are attributed to treason. That, however, is an erroneous idea; they have for their main cause the change of position and perspective.

Labor Government Subject to the Same Change. Permeated with this truth, I can express without fear of being contradicted the conviction that if there should be established tomorrow a government or a legislative council, a Parliament made up exclusively of workers, those very workers who are now staunch democrats and Socialists, will become determined aristocrats, bold or timid worshipers of the principle of authority, and will also become oppressors and exploiters.

The Example of the Most Radical Political Democracy. In Switzerland, as in all other countries, much as the equalitarian principles have been embodied in its political constitutions, it is the bourgeoisie that governs, and it is the people, the workers, peasants included, who obey the laws made by the bourgeoisie. The people have neither the leisure nor the necessary education to occupy themselves with the matters of government. The bourgeoisie, possessing both, has in fact if not by right the exclusive privilege of governing. Therefore political equality in Switzerland, as in all other countries, is only a puerile fiction, an utter lie.

The Popular Will as Refracted Through the Bourgeois Prism. But being so far removed from the people by the conditions of its economic and social existence, how can the bourgeoisie give expression in the government and in the laws, to the feelings, the ideas, and the will of the people? This is an impossibility, and daily experience proves to us in effect that in legislation as well as in carrying on the government, the bourgeoisie is guided by its own interests and its own instincts without concerning itself much with the interests of the people.

True, all the Swiss legislators, as well as the members of the governments of the various Swiss cantons, are elected, directly or indirectly, by the people. True, on election days even the proudest bourgeois who have any political ambitions are forced to court His Majesty—The Sovereign People. They come to Him with their hats off and seemingly have no other will but that of the people. This, however, is for them only a brief interlude of unpleasantness. On the day after the elections every one goes back to his daily business: the people to their work, and the bourgeoisie to their lucrative affairs and political intrigues. They do not meet and they do not know each other any more.

How can the people—who are crushed by their toil and ignorant of most of the questions at issue—control the political acts of their elected representatives? And is it not evident that the control supposedly exercised by the electors over their representatives is in reality nothing but sheer fiction? Since popular control in the representative system is the sole guarantee of popular liberty, it is clear that this liberty itself is nothing but pure fiction.

The Referendum Comes Into Being. In order to obviate this inconvenience, the Radical-Democrats of the Zurich canton devised and put into practice a new political system—the *referendum*, or direct legislation by the people. But the *referendum* itself is only a palliative, a new illusion, a falsehood. In order to vote, with full knowledge of the issue in question and with the full freedom required for it, upon laws proposed to the people or which the people themselves are induced to propose, it is necessary that the people have the time and the education needed to study those proposals, to reflect upon them, to discuss them. The people must become a vast Parliament holding its sessions in the open fields.

But this is rarely possible, and only upon grand occasions when the proposed laws arouse the attention and affect the interests of everyone. Most of the time the proposed laws are of such a specialized nature that one has to accustom oneself to political and juridical abstractions to grasp their real implications. Naturally they escape the attention and comprehension of the people, who vote for them blindly, believing implicitly their favorite orators. Taken separately, every one of those laws appears too insignificant to be of much interest to the masses, but in their totality they form a net which enmeshes them. Thus, in spite of the *referendum,* the so-called sovereign people remain the instrument and the very humble servant of the bourgeoisie.

We can well see then that in the representative system, even when improved upon with the aid of the *referendum*, popular control does not exist, and since no serious liberty is possible for the people without this control, we are driven to the conclusion that popular liberty and self-government are falsehoods.[1]

Municipal Elections Are Nearer to the People. The people, owing to the economic situation in which they still find themselves, are inevitably ignorant and indifferent, and know only those things which closely affect them. They well understand their daily interests, the affairs of daily life. But over and above these there begins for them the unknown, the uncertain, and the danger of political mystification. Since the people possess a good deal of practical instinct, they rarely let themselves be deceived in municipal elections. They know more or less the affairs of their municipality, they take a great deal of interest in those matters, and they know how to choose from their midst men who are the most capable of conducting those affairs. In these matters control by the people is quite possible, for they take place under the very eyes of the electors and touch upon the most intimate interests of their daily existence. That is why municipal elections are always and everywhere the best, conforming in a more real manner to the feelings, interests, and will of the people.[2]

But Even in Municipalities the People's Will Is Thwarted. The greater part of the affairs and laws which have a direct bearing upon the well-being and the material interests of the communes, are consummated above the heads of the people, without their noticing it, caring about it, or intervening in it. The people are compromised, committed to certain courses of action, and sometimes ruined without even being aware of it. They have neither the experience nor the necessary time to study all that, and they leave it all to their elected representatives, who naturally serve the interests of their own class, their own world, and not the world of the people, and whose greatest art consists in presenting their measures and laws in the most soothing and popular character. The system of democratic representation is a system of hypocrisy and perpetual lies. It needs the stupidity of the people as a necessary condition for its existence, and it bases its triumphs upon this state of the people's minds.[3]

Bourgeois Republic Cannot Be Identified With Liberty. The bourgeois republicans are quite wrong in identifying *their* republic with liberty. Therein lies the great source of all their illusions when they find themselves in opposition,—and likewise the source of their deceptions and inconsistencies when they have the power in their hands. Their republic is based entirely upon this idea of power and a strong government, of a government which has to show itself the more energetic and powerful because it sprang from a popular election. And they do not want to understand this simple truth, one that is confirmed by the experience of all times and all peoples, that every organized, established power necessarily excludes the liberty of the people.

Since the political State has no other mission but to protect the exploitation of the labor of the people by the economically privileged classes, the power of that State can be compatible only with the exclusive liberty of those classes whom it represents, and for this very reason it is bound to run contrary to the liberty of the people. Who says the State says domination, and every domination presumes the existence of masses who are dominated. Consequently the State can have no confidence in the spontaneous action and free movement of the masses, whose most cherished interests militate against its existence. It is their natural enemy, their invariable oppressor, and although it takes good care not to avow it openly, it is bound to act always in this capacity.

It is this that most of the young partisans of the authoritarian or bourgeois republic do not understand so long as they remain in the opposition, inasmuch as they themselves have not yet had a taste of this power. Because they detest the monarchic despotism from the depth of their hearts, with all the passion of which their paltry, enervated, and degenerate natures are capable, they imagine that they detest despotism in general. Because they would like to have the power and the courage to subvert the throne, they believe themselves to be revolutionaries. And they do not even suspect that it is not despotism that they hate but only its monarchic form, and that this very despotism, when it takes on the guise of a republican form, will have found in them the most zealous adherents.

Radically There Is Little Difference Between Monarchy and Democracy. They do not know that despotism resides not so much in the *form* of the State or of power as in the very *principle* of the State and political power, and that consequently the republican State is bound by its very essence to be as despotic as a State governed by an Emperor or a King. There is only one real difference between the two States. Both have for their essential basis and aim the economic enslavement of the masses for the benefit of the possessing classes. What they do differ in is that in order to attain this aim the monarchic power, which in our days inevitably tends to be transformed into a military dictatorship, deprives every class of liberty, even the class which it protects to the detriment of the people. . . . It is compelled to serve the interests of the bourgeoisie, but it does so without permitting that class to interfere in any serious manner in the government of the affairs of the country. . . .

From Revolution to Counter-Revolution. Bourgeois republicans are the most rabid and passionate enemies of the Social Revolution. In moments of political crisis, when they need the powerful hand of the people to subvert the throne, they stoop to promise material improvements to this "so very interesting" class of workers; but since they are at the same time animated with the most firm resolve to preserve and maintain all the principles, all the *sacred foundations*, of existing society, and to preserve all those economic and juridical institutions which have for their necessary consequence actual slavery of the people—it stands to reason that their promises dissolve like smoke into thin air. Disillusioned, the people murmur, threaten, revolt, and then, in order to hold back the explosion of the people's discontent, they—the bourgeois revolutionists— see themselves forced to resort to all-powerful repression by the State. Hence it follows that the republican State is altogether just as oppressive as the monarchic State; only its oppression is directed not against the possessing classes but exclusively against the people.

Republic the Favorite Form of Bourgeois Rule. Accordingly no form of government was ever so favorable to the interests of the bourgeoisie nor was it ever so beloved by the bourgeoisie as the republic; and it would always remain so if only, in the present economic situation of Europe, the republic had the power to maintain itself against the ever more threatening Socialist aspirations of the masses of workers.[4]

The Moderate and Radical Wings of the Bourgeoisie. There is no substantial difference between the Radical Party of republicans and the moderate doctrinaire party of constitutional liberals. Both spring from the same source, differing only in temperament. Both put as the basis of the social organization: the State, and family law, with the resulting inheritance law and personal property, that is, the right of the propertied minority to exploit the labor of the propertyless majority. The difference between the two parties consists in that the doctrinaire liberals want to concentrate all the political rights exclusively in the hands of the exploiting minority, whereas radical liberals want to extend those rights to the exploited masses of the people. The doctrinaire liberals view the State as a fortress chiefly created for the purpose of securing to the privileged minority the exclusive possession of political and economic rights, while the radicals, on the contrary, uphold the States before the people as a defender against the despotism of the very same minority.

Democratic State a Contradiction in Terms. One must admit that logic and all historical experience are on the side of the doctrinaire liberals. So long as the people, by their toil, feed, maintain, and enrich the privileged groups of the population—until that time the people, incapable of self-government because of being compelled to work not for themselves but for others, invariably will be ruled and dominated by the exploiting classes. This cannot be remedied even by the broadest democratic constitution, because the economic fact is stronger than political rights, which can have meaning and actuality only inasmuch as they rest upon this economic fact.

And, finally, equality of *political rights*, or *a democratic State*, constitute in themselves the most glaring contradiction in terms. The State, or political right, denotes force, authority, predominance; it presupposes inequality in fact. Where all rule, there are no more ruled, and there is no State. Where all equally enjoy the same human rights, there all political right loses its reason for being. Political right connotes privilege, and where all are equally privileged, there privilege vanishes, and along with it goes political right. Therefore the terms *"democratic State"* and *"equality of political rights"* denote no less than the destruction of the State and abolition of all political right.[5]

The term "democracy" denotes government of the people, by the people, and for the people, with the latter denoting the whole mass of citizens—and nowadays one must add: citizenesses—who form a nation.

In this sense we certainly are all democrats.

Democracy As 'Rule of People' an Equivocal Concept. But at the same time we have to recognize that this term—*democracy*—is not sufficient for an exact definition, and that, viewed in isolation, like the term *liberty,* it can lend itself only to equivocal interpretations. Have we not seen the planters, the slave owners of the South and all their partisans in the North of the United States, calling themselves democrats? And modern Caesarism, hanging like a terrible threat over all humanity in Europe, does it not likewise name itself as democratic? And even the Muscovite and Saint Petersburg imperialism, this "State pure and simple," this ideal of all the centralized, military, and bureaucratic powers, was it not in the name of democracy that it recently crushed Poland?

Republic in Itself Holds No Solution For Social Problems. It is evident that democracy without liberty cannot serve as our banner. But what is this democracy based upon liberty if not a republic? The union of freedom with privilege creates a regime of constitutional monarchy, but its union with democracy can be realized only in a republic. . . . We are all republicans in the sense that, driven by the consequences of an inexorable logic, forewarned by the harsh but at the same time salutary lessons of history, by all the experiences of the past, and above all by the events that have cast their gloom over Europe since 1848, as well as by the dangers threatening us today, we have all equally arrived at this conviction—that *monarchic institutions are incompatible with the reign of peace, justice, and liberty.*

As for us, gentlemen, as Russian Socialists and as Slavs, we hold it our duty to declare openly that the word "republic" has only an altogether negative value, that of subverting and eliminating the monarchy, and that not only does the republic fail to elate us but, on the contrary, every time that it is represented to us as a positive and serious solution of all the questions of the day, and as the supreme end toward which all our efforts should tend—we feel that we have to protest.

We detest monarchy with all our hearts; we do not ask anything better than to see it overthrown all over Europe and the world, and like you we are convinced that its abolition is the indispensable condition of the emancipation of humanity. From this point of view we are frankly republicans. But we do not believe that it is sufficient to overthrow the monarchy in order to emancipate the people and give them justice and peace. We are firmly convinced of the contrary, namely: that a great, military, bureaucratic, and politically centralized republic can become and necessarily will become a conquering power in its relation to other powers and oppressive in regard to its own population, and that it will prove incapable of assuring to its subjects—even when they are called citizens—well-being and liberty. Have we not seen the great French nation twice constitute itself as a democratic republic, and twice lose its liberty and let itself be drawn into wars of conquest?[6]

Social Justice Incompatible With Existence of the State. The State denotes violence, oppression, exploitation, and injustice raised into a system and made into the cornerstone of the existence of any society. The State never had and never will have any morality. Its morality and only justice is the supreme interest of self-preservation and almighty power—an interest before which all humanity has to kneel in worship. The State is the complete negation of humanity, a double negation: the opposite of human freedom and justice, and the violent breach of the universal solidarity of the human race.

The World State, which has been attempted so many times, has always proved to be a failure. Consequently, so long as the State exists, there will be several of them; and since every one of them sets as its only aim and supreme law the maintenance of itself to the detriment of the others, it follows that the very existence of the State implies perpetual war—the violent negation of humanity. Every State must conquer or be conquered. Every State bases its power upon the weakness of other powers and—if it can do it without undermining its own position—upon their destruction.

From our point of view it would be a terrible contradiction and a ridiculous piece of naiveté to avow the wish to establish international justice, freedom, and perpetual peace, and at the same time to want to retain the State. It would be impossible to make the State change its nature, for it is such only because of this nature, and in foregoing the latter it would cease to be a State. Thus there is not and there could not be a good, just, and moral State.

All States are bad in the sense that by their nature, that is, by the conditions and objectives of their existence, they constitute the very opposite of human justice, freedom, and equality. And in this sense, whatever one may say, there is not much difference between the barbarous Russian Empire and the most civilized States of Europe. What difference there is consists in the fact that the Tsar's Empire does openly what the others do in an underhanded, hypocritical way. And the frank, despotic, and contemptuous attitude of the Tsar's Empire toward everything humane constitutes the deeply hidden ideal toward which all European statesmen aim and which they admire so greatly. All the European States do the same things that Russia does. A virtuous State can be only an impotent State, and even that kind of State is criminal in its thoughts and aspirations.

Universal Federation of Producers Upon the Ruins of the State Urged. Thus I come to the conclusion: He who wants to join with us in the establishment of freedom, justice, and peace, he who wants the triumph of humanity, and the full and complete emancipation of the masses of the people, should also aim toward the destruction of all States and the establishment upon their ruins of a Universal Federation of Free Associations of all the countries in the world.[7]

CHAPTER 10 *Patriotism's Part in Man's Struggle*

Patriotism Was Never a Popular Virtue.   Was patriotism, in the complex meaning usually given to this term, ever a popular passion, a popular virtue?

Basing myself upon the lessons of history, I shall not hesitate in answering this question with a resolute *Nay!* And in order to prove to the reader that I do not err in giving this answer, I will ask his permission to analyze the principal elements which, combined in diverse ways, constitute what is called patriotism.

The Components of Patriotism.   Those elements are four in number: 1. The natural or physiological element; 2. the economic element; 3. the political element; 4. the religious or fanatical element.

The physiological element is the chief foundation of all naive, instinctive, and brutal egoism. It is a natural passion, which, because it is too natural—that is, altogether animal—is in flagrant contradiction to any kind of politics, and, what is worse, it greatly handicaps the economic, scientific, and human development of society.

Natural patriotism is a purely bestial fact, to be found at every stage of animal life and, one might even say, to be found up to a certain point, even in the plant world. Taken in this sense, patriotism is a war of destruction, it is the first human expression of the great and inevitable struggle for life which constitutes all the development, all the life of the natural or real world—an incessant struggle, a universal devouring of one another which nourishes every individual, every species, with the flesh and blood of the individuals of other species, and which, inevitably renewing itself in every hour, at every instant, makes it possible for the stronger, more perfect, and intelligent species to live, prosper, and develop at the expense of all the others.

. . . Man, the animal endowed with speech, introduces the first word into this struggle, and that word is *patriotism*.

Hunger and Sex: the Basic Drives of the Animal World. The struggle for life in the animal and vegetable world is not only a struggle among individuals; it is a struggle among species, groups, and families, a struggle in which one is pitted against the other. In every living being there are two instincts, two great dominant interests: food and reproduction. From the point of view of nourishment every individual is the natural enemy of all the others, ignoring in this respect all kinds of bonds which link him with the family, group, and species.

. . . Hunger is a rude and invincible despot, and that is why the necessity of obtaining food, a necessity felt by the individual, is the first law, the supreme condition of life. It is the foundation of all human and social life as well as of the life of animals and plants. To revolt against it is to annihilate life, to condemn oneself to mere non-existence. But along with this fundamental law of living nature there is the equally essential law of reproduction. The first aims to preserve the individuals, the second aims to form families, groups, species. And the individuals, impelled by a natural necessity, seek, in order to reproduce themselves, to mate with other individuals who by their inner organization come the nearest to them and most closely resemble them.[1]

Boundaries of Animal Solidarity Are Determined by Sexual Affinity. Since the instinct of reproduction establishes the only tie of solidarity existing among the individuals of the animal world, it follows that where this capacity for mating ceases, there all animal solidarity ceases with it. Whatever remains outside of this possibility of reproduction for the individuals, constitutes a different species, an absolutely foreign world, hostile and condemned to destruction. And everything contained in this world of sexual affinity constitutes the vast fatherland of the species—like humanity for men, for instance.

But this destruction, or the devouring of one another by living individuals, takes place not only outside the limits of the circumscribed world which we call the fatherland of the species. We find it also within this world—in forms just as ferocious, or at times even more ferocious, than that taking place outside of this world. This is true because of the resistance and rivalries which individuals encounter, and also because of the struggle prompted by sex rivalries, a struggle no less cruel and ferocious than the one impelled by hunger. Besides, every animal species subdivides into different groups and families, undergoing constant modifications under the influence of the geographical and climatic conditions on their respective habitats.

The greater or lesser difference in conditions of life determines the corresponding difference in the structure of the individuals belonging to the same species. Besides, it is known that every individual animal naturally seeks to mate with an individual which is most similar to it, a tendency which naturally results in the development of the greatest number of variations within the same species. And since the differences separating those variations from one another are based mainly upon reproduction, and since reproduction is the sole basis of all animal solidarity, it is evident that the greater solidarity of the species necessarily will subdivide into a number of solidarity spheres of a more limited character, so that the greater fatherland is bound to break up into a multitude of small animal fatherlands, hostile to and destructive of one another.

Patriotism a Passion of Group Solidarity. I have shown how patriotism, taken as a natural passion, springs from a physiological law, to be exact, from the law which determines the separation of living beings into species, families, and groups.

The patriotic passion is manifestly a passion of social solidarity. In order to find its clearest expression in the animal world, one has to turn to those animal species which, like man, are endowed with a pre-eminently social nature: for example, the ants, the bees, the beavers, and many others which possess settled habitations in common, and also species that rove in herds. The animals which live in a collective and fixed dwelling represent, in its natural aspect, the patriotism of the agricultural people, while the animals roving in herds represent the patriotism of nomadic peoples.

Patriotism—the Attachment to Settled Patterns of Life. It is evident that the first is more complete than the latter, which implies only the solidarity of the individuals living in the herd, whereas the first adds to it the bonds tying the individual to the soil or to his natural habitat. Habits —constituting second nature for men as well as for animals—certain patterns of life, are much more determined and fixed among social animals which lead a settled life than among migratory herds; and it is these different habits, these particular modes of existence, which constitute an essential element of patriotism.

One can define natural patriotism as follows: It is an instinctive, mechanical, uncritical attachment to the socially accepted hereditary or traditional pattern of life—and the same kind of an instinctive, automatic hostility toward any other kind of life. It is love for one's own and aversion to anything having a foreign character. Patriotism then is collective egoism on one hand, and war on the other.

Its solidarity, however, is not sufficiently strong to keep the individual members of an animal group from devouring one another when the need arises; but it is sufficiently strong to make those individuals forget their civil discords and unite each time that they are threatened with invasion by another collective group.

Take, for instance, the dogs of some village. In the natural state dogs do not form a collective republic. Left to their instinct, they live like wolves, in roving packs, and it is only under the influence of man that they become settled in their mode of life. But when attached to one place they form in every village a sort of republic based upon individual liberty in accordance with the formula so well loved by bourgeois economists: everyone for himself and the Devil take the hindmost. There an unlimited *laissez-faire* and competition are in action, a civil war without mercy and without truce, in which the strongest always bites the weaker one—just as it is in the bourgeois republics. But let a dog from another village happen to pass their street, and immediately you will see all those brawling citizens of the canine republic hurl themselves *en masse* upon the unfortunate stranger.

Yet is this not an exact copy, or rather the original, of the copies repeating themselves from day to day in human society? Is it not the full manifestation of that natural patriotism which, as I already have said, and dare say again, is a purely bestial passion? It is without doubt bestial in character inasmuch as dogs are incontestably beasts, and since man himself, being an animal, like the dog and other animals upon the earth, and the only one endowed with the physiological faculty of thinking and speaking, begins his history with bestiality, and, after centuries of development, finally conquers and attains humanity in its most perfect form.

Once we know the origin of man, we should not wonder at his bestiality, which is a natural fact among so many other natural facts; nor should we grow indignant about it, for what follows from this fact is that we struggle against it still more vigorously, inasmuch as all human life is but an incessant struggle against man's bestiality for the sake of his humanity.

The Bestial Origin of Natural Patriotism. I simply wanted to establish here that patriotism, extolled by poets, politicians of all schools, by governments, and by all the privileged classes, as the highest and most ideal virtue, has its roots not in the humanity of man but in his bestiality.

And indeed, we see natural patriotism reigning supreme at the beginning of history and in the present day—in the least civilized sectors of human society. Of course, patriotism in human society is a much more complex emotion than in other animal societies; this is so for the reason that the life of man, an animal endowed with the faculties of thought and speech, encompasses an incomparably larger world than that of the animals of other species. With man the purely physical habits and customs are supplemented by the more or less abstract traditions of an intellectual and moral order—a multitude of true or false ideas and representations, which go together with various customs, religious, economic, political, and social. All that constitutes the elements of natural patriotism in man, in so far as those things, combining in one way or another, form, for a given society, a particular mode of existence, a traditional pattern of living, thinking, and acting, which differs from all other patterns.

But whatever differences, in respect to quantity and quality of the objects embraced, there may exist between the natural patriotism of human societies and that of animal societies, they have this in common— that both are instinctive, traditional, habitual, and collective passions, and that the intensity of one as well as of the other does not depend upon the character of their content. One might say on the contrary that the less complicated this content is, the more simple, more intense, and vigorously exclusive is the patriotic feeling which manifests and expresses it.

Intensity of Natural Patriotism Is in Inverse Ratio to the Development of Civilization. Obviously animals are much more attached to traditional customs of the society to which they belong than man. With animals this patriotic attachment is inevitable; not being capable of freeing themselves from such attachment through their own efforts, they often have to wait for man's influence in order to shake it off. The same holds true of human society: the less developed a civilization is, and the less complex the basis of its social life, the stronger the manifestations of natural patriotism—that is, the instinctive attachment of individuals to all the material, intellectual, and moral habits which constitute the traditional and customary life of a particular society as well as their hatred for anything alien, anything different from their own life. So it follows that natural patriotism is in inverse ratio to the development of civilization, that is, to the triumph of humanity in human societies.

Organic Character of the Patriotism of Savages. No one will deny that the instinctive or natural patriotism of the wretched tribes inhabiting the Arctic zone, hardly touched by human civilization and poverty-stricken even in respect to bare necessities of material life, is infinitely stronger and more exclusive than the patriotism of a Frenchman, an Englishman, or a German, for example. The Frenchman, the Englishman, and the German can live and acclimatize themselves anywhere, whereas the native of the polar regions would pine away longing for his country were he kept out of it. And still what could be more miserable and less human than his existence! This merely proves once more that the intensity of this kind of patriotism is an indication of bestiality and not of humanity.

Alongside this positive element of patriotism, which consists in the instinctive attachment of individuals to the particular mode of existence of the society to which they belong, there is a negative element just as essential as the first and inseparable from it. It is the equally instinctive revulsion from everything foreign, instinctive and consequently altogether bestial—yes, bestial indeed, for this horror is the more violent and overwhelming, the less the one experiencing it thinks of it and understands it, and the less of humanity there is in him.

Anti-Foreignism: Negative Aspect of Natural Patriotism. At present this patriotic revulsion from everything foreign is found only among savage peoples; in Europe it can be found among the semi-savage layers of population which bourgeois civilization has not deigned to educate, but which, however, it never forgets to exploit. In the big capitals of Europe, in Paris itself, and above all in London, there are slums abandoned to a wretched population which no ray of enlightenment has ever touched. It is enough that a foreigner show up in those streets, and a throng of those ragged wretches—men, women, and children, who show by their appearance signs of the most frightful poverty and the lowest state of degradation—will surround him, heap vile abuse upon him, and even maltreat him, solely because he is a foreigner. This brutal and savage patriotism, is it then not the most glaring negation of that which is called humanity?

I have said that patriotism, in so far as it is instinctive or natural, and inasmuch as it has all its roots in animal life, presents only a particular combination of collective habits—material, intellectual, moral, economic, political, and social—developed by tradition or by history, within a limited group of human society. Such habits, I added, can be good or bad, since the content or the object of this instinctive feeling has no influence upon the degree of its intensity.

Even if one had to admit in this respect the existence of certain differences, one would have to say that they rather inclined toward bad than toward good habits. For—by virtue of the animal origin of all human society and the effect of that force of inertia, which exercises as powerful an action in the intellectual and moral world as in the material world—in every society which has not degenerated but which progresses and marches ahead, bad habits have priority in point of time, have become more deeply rooted than good habits. This explains why out of the sum total of the present collective habits prevailing in the most advanced countries of the world, nine tenths of them are absolutely worthless.

Habits Are a Necessary Part of Social Life. But let it not be imagined that I intend to declare war upon the general tendency of men and society to be governed by *habits*. As in many other things, men necessarily obey a natural law, and it would be absurd to rebel against natural laws. The action of habit in the intellectual and moral life of the individual as well as of societies is the same as the action of vegetative forces in animal life. One and the other are conditions of existence and reality. The good as well as the bad, in order to become a real fact, must be embodied in habits, with man taken individually or in society. All the exercises, all the studies, which men undertake, have no other aim but this, and the best things can strike root and become second nature with a man only by force of habit.

It would be foolhardy to rebel against this force of habit, for it is a necessary force which neither intelligence nor will can upset. But, if enlightened by the reason of our century and by the idea which we have formed of true justice, we seriously want to rise to the full dignity of human beings, we shall have to do only one thing: constantly to train and direct our will power—that is, the habit of willing things developed within us by circumstances that are independent of us—toward the extirpation of bad habits and their replacement with good ones. In order to humanize society completely it is essential to destroy ruthlessly all the causes, all the political, economic, and social conditions which produce traditions of evil in individuals, and to replace them with conditions which will engender within the same individuals the practice and habit of good.

Natural Patriotism—an Outgrown Stage. From the point of view of modern conscience, of humanity and justice—which we have come to understand the better owing to past developments of history—patriotism is a bad, narrow, and baneful habit, for it is the negation of human solidarity and equality. The social question, nowadays posed in a practical manner by the proletarian world of Europe and America, and the solution of which is possible only through abolition of State boundaries, necessarily tends to destroy this traditional habit in the consciousness of the workers of all countries.

Already at the beginning of the present [nineteenth] century, this habit had been greatly undermined in the consciousness of the higher financial, commercial, and industrial bourgeoisie, owing to the prodigious and altogether international character of the development of its wealth and economic interest.

But first I shall have to show how, long before this bourgeois revolution, instinctive, natural patriotism, which by its very nature can be only a very narrow, restricted social habit of a purely local character, had been profoundly changed, distorted, and weakened at the very beginning of history by the successive formation of political States.

Natural Patriotism Necessarily Has Deep Local Roots. Indeed, patriotism, in so far as it is a purely natural feeling—that is, a product of the life of a social group united by bonds of genuine solidarity and not yet enfeebled by reflection or by the effect of economic and political interests as well as religious abstractions—this largely animal patriotism can embrace only a very restricted world: a tribe, a commune, a village. At the beginning of history, as is now the case with savage peoples, there was neither nation, nor national language, nor national cult—there was not even any country in the political sense of the word. Every small locality, every village, had its particular language, its god, its priest, or its sorcerer; it was but a multiplied, enlarged family, which, in waging war against all other tribes, denied by the fact of its own existence all the rest of humanity. Such is natural patriotism in its vigorous and simple crudity.

We still find vestiges of this patriotism even in some of the most civilized countries of Europe, in Italy for example, especially in the Southern provinces of that peninsula, where the physical contour of the earth, the mountains, and the sea have set up barriers between valleys, villages, and cities, separating and isolating them, rendering them virtually alien one to another. Proudhon, in his pamphlet on Italian unity, observed with much reason that this unity so far had been only an idea and a bourgeois idea at that, and by no means a popular passion; that the rural population at least remained to a very great extent aloof from—and I would add, even hostile to it. For on the one hand, that unity militates against their local patriotism, and on the other hand it has not brought them anything but ruthless exploitation, oppression, and ruin.

We have seen that even in Switzerland, especially in the most backward cantons, local patriotism often comes into conflict with the patriotism of the canton, and the latter with the political, national patriotism of the whole confederation of the republic.

March of Civilization Destroys Natural Patriotism. In conclusion I repeat, by way of summing up, that patriotism as a natural feeling, being in its essence and reality a purely local feeling, is a serious obstacle to the formation of States, and that consequently the latter, and along with them civilization as such, could not establish themselves except by destroying,— if not completely, at least to a considerable extent—this animal passion.[2]

CHAPTER 11 *Class Interests in Modern Patriotism*

The very existence of the State demands that there be some privileged class vitally interested in maintaining that existence. And it is precisely the group interests of this privileged class. that are called patriotism.[1]

This flagrant negation of humanity which is the very essence of the State is from the State's point of view the supreme duty and the greatest virtue; it is called patriotism and it constitutes the transcendent morality of the State.[2]

True patriotism is of course a very respectable feeling, but at the same time a narrow, exclusive, anti-human, and at times a simply bestial feeling. A consistent patriot is one who, though passionately loving his fatherland and everything that he calls his own, likewise hates everything foreign.[3]

Patriotism Without Freedom—a Tool of Reaction. Patriotism which aims toward unity that is not based upon freedom is bad patriotism; it is blameful from the point of view of *the real interests* of the people and of the country which it pretends to exalt and serve. Such patriotism becomes, very often against its will, a friend of reaction, an enemy of revolution,— that is, of the emancipation of nations and men.[4]

Bourgeois Patriotism. Bourgeois patriotism, as I view it, is only a very shabby, very narrow, especially mercenary, and deeply anti-human passion, having for its object the preservation and maintenance of the power of the national State—that is, the mainstay of all the privileges of the exploiters throughout the nation.[5]

The bourgeois gentlemen of all parties, even of the most advanced and radical kind, cosmopolitan as they may be in their official views, whenever it comes to making money by exploiting to an ever greater extent the work of the people, show themselves to be politically ardent and fanatical patriots of the State, this patriotism being in fact, as it was well said by M. Thiers—the illustrious assassin of the Parisian proletariat and the actual savior of the present-day France—nothing else but the cult and the passion of the national State.[6]

Bourgeois Patriotism Degenerates When Faced by Revolutionary Movement of Workers. The latest events have proven that patriotism, this supreme virtue of the State, this soul animating the power of the State, does not exist any more in France. In the upper classes it manifests itself only in the form of national vanity. But this vanity is already so feeble, and already has been so much undermined by the bourgeois necessity and habit of sacrificing *ideal interests* for the sake of *real interests* that during the last war [the Franco-Prussian conflict] it could not, even for a short time, make patriots out of storekeepers, businessmen, Stock Exchange speculators, Army officers, bureaucrats, capitalists, and Jesuit-trained noblemen.

They all lost their courage, they all betrayed their country, having only one thing on their minds—to save their property—and they all tried to turn to their own advantage the calamity befalling France. All of them, with no exception, outdid one another in throwing themselves at the mercy of the haughty victor who became the arbiter of French destinies. Unanimously they preached submission, and meekness, humbly begging for peace. . . . But now all those degenerate prattlers have become patriotic and nationalistic again, and have taken to bragging, yet this ridiculous and repulsive balderdash on the part of such cheap heroes cannot obscure the evidence of their recent villainy.

Patriotism of Peasants Undermined by Bourgeois Psychology. Of still greater importance is the fact that the rural population of France did not evince the slightest patriotism. Yes, contrary to the general expectation, the French peasant, ever since he became a proprietor, has ceased to be a patriot.

In the period of Joan of Arc, it was the peasants who bore the brunt of the fighting which saved France. And in 1792 and afterward it was mainly the peasants who held off the military coalition of the rest of Europe. But then it was quite a different matter. Owing to the cheap sales of the estates belonging to the Church and the nobility, the peasant came to own the land which prior to that he had been cultivating in the capacity of a slave—and that is why he justly feared that in the event of defeat the emigrés who followed in the wake of the German troops would take away from him his recently acquired property.

But now he had no such fear, and he showed the utmost indifference to the shameful defeat of his sweet fatherland. In the central provinces of France the peasants were chasing out the French and foreign volunteers who had taken up arms to save France, refusing any aid to those volunteers, frequently betraying them to the Prussians and, conversely, according the German troops a hospitable reception. Alsace and Lorraine, however, must be counted as exceptions. There, strangely enough, as if to spite the Germans, who persist in regarding those provinces as purely German, there were stirrings of patriotic resistance.[7]

When Patriotism Turns Into Treason.   No doubt the privileged layers of French society would like to place their country in a position where it would again become an imposing power, a splendid and impressive power among the rest of the nations. But along with that they are also moved by greed, money-grubbing, the get-rich-quick spirit, and anti-patriotic egoism, all of which make them quite willing to sacrifice the property, life, and freedom of the proletariat for the sake of some patriotic gain, but rather reluctant when it comes to giving up any of their own gainful privileges. They would rather submit to a foreign yoke than yield any of their property or agree to a general leveling of rights and fortunes.

This is fully confirmed by events taking place before our eyes. When the government of M. Thiers officially announced to the Versailles Assembly the conclusion of the final peace treaty with the Berlin Cabinet, by virtue of which the German troops were to clear out of the occupied provinces of France in September, the majority of that Assembly, representing a coalition of privileged classes of France, were visibly depressed. Stocks at the French Exchange, which represent those privileged interests even more truly than the Assembly, dropped with this announcement, as if heralding a genuine State catastrophe. . . . It turned out that to the privileged French patriots, those representatives of bourgeois valor and bourgeois civilization, the *hateful, forced,* and *shameful* presence of the victorious army of occupation was a source of consolation, was their mainstay and salvation, and to their minds the withdrawal of that army spelled ruin and annihilation.

It is clear then that the rather strange patriotism of the French bourgeoisie seeks its salvation in the shameful subjugation of their own country.

Those who doubt it should look in the conservative magazines. Open the pages of any of those magazines and you will find that they threaten the French proletariat with the legitimate wrath of Prince Bismarck and his Emperor. That is patriotism indeed! Yes, they simply invite Germany's aid against the threatened Social Revolution in France.[8]

Only the City Proletariat Is Genuinely Patriotic.   One can say with full conviction that patriotism has been preserved only among the city proletariat.

In Paris, as well as in all the other cities and provinces of France, it was only the proletariat that demanded the arming of the people and war to the end. And strangely enough it was precisely this which aroused the greatest hatred among the propertied classes, as if they took offense because their "lesser brothers" (Gambetta's expression) showed more virtue and patriotic loyalty than the older brothers.

Proletarian Patriotism Is International in Scope.   However, the well-to-do classes were partly right. The proletariat was altogether moved by patriotism in the ancient and narrow meaning of the word.

True patriotism is of course a very venerable but also a narrow, exclusive, anti-human, and at times a pure and simple bestial feeling. Only he is a consistent patriot who, loving his own fatherland and everything of his own, also hates passionately everything foreign—the very image, one might say, of our [Russian] Slavophiles. There is not a trace of this hatred left in the city proletarian of France. On the contrary, in the last decade— or one might say, beginning with 1848 and even much earlier—under the influence of Socialist propaganda, there was stirred up within him a brotherly feeling toward the whole proletariat, and that went hand in hand with just as decisive an indifference toward the so-called greatness and glory of France. The French workers were opposed to the war undertaken by Napoleon III, and on the eve of that war, in a manifesto signed by the members of the Parisian section of the International, they openly declared their sincere fraternal attitude toward the workers of Germany. The French workers were arming not against the German people but against the German military despotism.[9]

Boundaries of the Proletariat Fatherland.   The boundaries of the proletarian fatherland have broadened to the extent of embracing now the proletariat of the whole world. This of course is just the opposite of the bourgeois fatherland. The declarations of the Paris Commune are in this respect highly characteristic, and the sympathies shown now by the French proletariat, even favoring a Federation based upon emancipated labor and collective ownership of the means of production, ignoring in this case national differences and State boundaries—these sympathies and active tendencies, I say, prove that so far as the French proletariat is concerned, State patriotism is all in the past.[10]

Bourgeois Patriotism Exemplified by 1870.   Whatever the patriots of the French State may say, much as they can boast now, it is clear that France as a State is condemned to a second-rate position. Moreover, it will have to submit to the supreme leadership, the friendly, solicitous influence of the German Empire, just as it was with the Italian State which, prior to 1870, submitted to the politics of Imperial France.

This situation, perhaps, suits well the French speculators who get their consolations from the world Stock Exchange market, but it is hardly flattering from the point of view of national vanity held by the patriots of the French State. Until 1870 one might have thought that this vanity was so strong that it would swing even the stoutest champions of bourgeois privileges into the camp of the Social Revolution, if only to save France from the shame of being overrun and conquered by Germans. But no one can expect this from them after what took place in 1870. It is common knowledge now that they will agree to any shame, even to submit to German protectorship, rather than forego their profitable domination over their own proletariat.[11]

Worship of Property Incompatible With True Patriotism. [Destruction of property] is incompatible with bourgeois consciousness, with bourgeois civilization, because it is all built upon fanatical worship of property. The burgher or bourgeois will forego life, freedom, or honor, but he will not yield his property. The very thought of encroaching upon it, of destroying it for any purpose, appears sacrilegious to him. That is why he will never agree to have his cities or houses destroyed, as demanded by the defense aims. And that is why the French bourgeois in 1870 and the German burghers of 1813 yielded so easily to the invaders. We have seen that it was enough for the peasants to come into ownership of property to be corrupted and divested of the last spark of patriotism.[12]

In the eyes of all these ardent patriots, as well in the historically verified opinion of M. Jules Favre, *the Social Revolution* holds for France *a greater danger than even* invasion by foreign troops. I would very much like to believe that, if not all, at least the greater number of those worthy citizens would willingly sacrifice their lives to save the glory, greatness, and independence of France. But, on the other hand, I am sure that a still greater majority of them would prefer to see this noble France submit to the temporary yoke of the Prussians than to be indebted for their salvation to a genuine popular revolution, which inevitably would destroy with one blow the economic and political domination by their class. Hence their revolting but forced indulgence for the so numerous and unfortunately still powerful partisans of Bonapartist treason, and their passionate severity, the ruthless persecution they loosed against the social revolutionists—the representatives of the working class who alone take seriously the freeing of the country from the foreign yoke.[13]

CHAPTER 12 *Law, Natural and Invented*

Individual Freedom Is a Derivative of Society. Emerging from the condition of the gorilla, man arrives only with difficulty at awareness of his humanity and realization of his liberty. In the beginning he has neither liberty nor the awareness thereof; he comes into the world as a ferocious beast and as a slave, and becomes humanized and progressively emancipated only in the midst of a society which necessarily precedes the emergence of man's thought, speech, and will. Man can attain this only through the collective efforts of all the past and present members of that society, which therefore is the natural basis and starting point of his human existence.

Hence it follows that man realizes his individual freedom only by rounding out his personality with the aid of other individuals belonging to the same social environment. He can achieve that only by dint of work and the collective power of society, without which man would no doubt remain the most stupid and miserable of all the wild animals living upon the earth. According to the materialist system, which is the only natural and logical system, society, far from limiting and detracting from the freedom of individuals, creates, on the contrary, this freedom. *Society is the root and the tree, and freedom is its fruit.* Consequently, in every epoch man has to seek his liberty not at the beginning but at the end of history, and one may say the real and complete emancipation of every individual is the true and the great objective, and the supreme end of history.[1]

Origin of Ideas in General and of the Idea of Law in Particular. This is not the place to inquire into the origin of the first notions and ideas in primitive society. All we can say with full certainty is that those ideas, most of which were of course highly absurd, were not conceived spontaneously by the miraculously enlightened intelligence of isolated and inspired individuals. They were the product of the collective, in many cases hardly perceptible, mental labor of all the individuals belonging to those societies. The contributions of outstanding men of genius has never consisted in anything but their ability to give the most faithful and felicitous expression to this collective mental labor, for all men of genius, according to Voltaire, "gathered everything that was good wherever they found it." Those ideas were at first only the most simple, and, of course, quite inadequate representations of natural and social phenomena, and the even less valid conclusions inferred from those phenomena.

Such was the beginning of all human notions, fancies, and thoughts. The subject matter of those thoughts was not the spontaneous creation of man's mind, but was at first given to him by the actual world—whether external or internal. Man's mind, that is, the purely organic and consequently material functioning of his brain, stimulated by external as well as internal sensations transmitted by the nerves—introduced only the purely formal comparison of those impressions of facts and things into true or false systems. That was the origin of the first ideas. Through the medium of speech, those ideas, or rather those first products of the imagination, were given a more or less precise and invariable expression, in the process of being handed down from one generation to the next. And thus the products of individual imagination, mingling together, came to control, vary, and complete one another, merging more or less into a single system and ending by constituting the general consciousness, the collective thought, of society. This thought, handed down by tradition from one generation to another, and ever more developed by centuries of mental labor, constitutes the intellectual and moral heritage of society, class, and nation.

Every new generation receives in its cradle a whole world of ideas, mental impressions, and feelings bequeathed to it by all the past centuries. This world at first does not appear to the newly born man in its ideal form, as a system of notions and ideas, as a religion, nor as a doctrine. A child is not capable of apprehending and comprehending it in this form. Rather it is imposed upon the child as a world of facts embodied and realized in the people and things constituting the child's environment from the first day of his life, a world speaking to the child through everything he hears and sees. *For man's ideas were at first nothing but the product of actual facts, natural as well as social, in the sense that they were their reflection or echo in man's brain,* and, so to speak, their ideal and more or less true reproduction by means of this positively material organ of human thought.

Innate Ideas. Later, having become solidly established in a well-ordered system in the intellectual consciousness of a given society, they become the causal agents of new phenomena: phenomena of a social and not of a purely natural order. They end by modifying and transforming, very slowly to be sure, human customs and institutions—in a word, the whole field of human interrelationships in society, and, by their embodiment in common objects, they become tangible and perceptible, even to children. This process is so thorough that every new generation becomes permeated with it from a tender age; and when it reaches the age of maturity, when the work of its own thought begins to assert itself,—a work accompanied by new criticism—it finds within itself, as well as in the surrounding society, a whole world of established thoughts and ideas which serve as the starting point, the raw material, the texture, for its own intellectual and moral labor. Those ideas comprise the traditional and everyday notions created by imagination which the metaphysicians,—deceived by the wholly unsensory and unnoticeable way in which those notions, coming from the outside, penetrate and impress themselves upon the child's brain, even before they reach his consciousness,—erroneously call *innate ideas*.

Such are the general or abstract ideas or godhead and soul, ideas altogether absurd, but inevitable and necessary in the historical development of the human mind, which through the ages, only slowly arriving at a rational and critical awareness of itself and its own manifestations, has always started with absurdity in order to arrive at truth, and with slavery in order to win freedom. Such are the ideas consecrated in the course of centuries by general ignorance and stupidity, and likewise, of course, by the interests of the privileged classes—consecrated to such an extent that even now it is difficult to declare oneself against them in plain language without arousing against oneself considerable sections of the people and without running the hazard of being pilloried by bourgeois hypocrisy.

Along with these purely abstract ideas, and always closely connected with them, the youth finds in society—and because of the all-powerful influence exerted upon him by society in his childhood, he also discovers within himself—many other notions or ideas which are much more determined and nearer to man's real life and to his daily existence. Such are the notions of Nature, man, justice, the duties and rights of individuals and classes, social conventions, family, property, the State, and many other ideas regulating the relations of man to man.[2]

Authority and Natural Laws. What is authority? Is it the inevitable power of natural laws manifestating themselves in the concatenation and necessary sequences of phenomena in the physical and social worlds? Indeed, revolt against these laws is not only nonpermissible, but even impossible. We may ignore them or even not know them at all, but we cannot disobey them, for they constitute the basis and the very conditions of our existence; they envelop us, penetrate us, and govern all our movements, thoughts, and acts to such an extent that even when we believe we disobey them we in reality only manifest their omnipotence.

Yes, we are unconditionally the slaves of these laws. But in such slavery there is no humiliation, or rather it is not slavery at all. For slavery presupposes the existence of an external master, a legislator standing above those whom he commands, while those laws are not extrinsic in relation to us: they are inherent in us, they constitute our nature, our whole being, physically, intellectually, and morally. And it is only through those laws that we live, breathe, act, think, and will. Without them we would be nothing, *we simply would not exist.*[3]

It is a great misfortune that a large number of natural laws, already established as such by science, remain unknown to the masses, thanks to the vigilance of the tutelary governments which, as we know, exist only for the good of the people. And another difficulty consists in the fact that the major portion of natural laws inherent in the development of human society and just as necessary, invariable, and inevitable as the laws governing the physical world, have not been recognized and duly established by science itself.

Universal Knowledge of Natural Laws Spells Abolition of Juridical Right. Once they have been recognized by science, and then from science, by means of a broad system of popular education, have entered into the general consciousness, the question of freedom will be solved. The most obdurate protagonists of the State must admit that when that takes place there will be no need of political organization, administration, or legislation —those three institutions which, whether they emanate from the will of the sovereign or from the vote of a Parliament elected by universal suffrage, and even if they should conform to the system of natural laws (which never has been the case and never will be)—are ever equally hostile and fatal to the liberty of the masses, for they impose upon them a system of external and therefore despotic laws.[4]

Political Legislation Is Inimical to Freedom of the People and Contrary to Natural Laws. A scientific body entrusted with the government of society would soon end by devoting itself no longer to science at all, but to quite another affair. And that affair, as in the case of all established powers, would be its own perpetuation by rendering the society entrusted to its care ever more stupid and consequently ever more in need of its government and direction.[5]

Legislative Institutions Breed Oligarchies. And that which is true of scientific academies also is true of all constituent and legislative assemblies, even those issuing from universal suffrage. In the latter case, to be sure, they may renew their composition, but this does not prevent the formation in a few years' time of a body of politicians, privileged in fact though not in law, who, devoting themselves exclusively to the administration of a nation's public affairs, end by forming a sort of political aristocracy or oligarchy, as can be seen by the example of Switzerland and of the United States of America.

Thus it follows that no external legislation and no authority are necessary; for that matter, one is inseparable from the other, while both tend toward the enslavement of society and the degradation of the legislators themselves.[6]

Political Rights and Democratic State Are Contradictions in Terms. And finally, the terms themselves, *equality of political rights*, and *democratic State,* imply a flagrant contradiction. The State, *raison d'Etat*, and political law denote power, authority, domination; they presuppose inequality in fact. Where all govern, no one is governed, and the State as such does not exist. Where all equally enjoy human rights, all political rights automatically are dissolved. Political law denotes privilege, but where all are equally privileged, there privilege vanishes, and with that political law is reduced to naught. Therefore the terms *the democratic States* and *equality of political rights* connote nothing less nor more than destruction of the State and abolition of all political rights.[7]

The Negation of Juridical Law. In a word, we reject all legislation—privileged, licensed, official, and legal—and all authority, and influence, even though they may emanate from universal suffrage, for we are convinced that it can turn only to the advantage of a dominant minority of exploiters against the interests of the vast majority in subjection to them. It is in this sense that we are really Anarchists.[8]

We recognize all natural authority, and all influence of fact upon us, but none of right; for all authority and all influence of right, officially imposed upon us, immediately becomes a falsehood and an oppression, and because of this inevitably brings us to absurdity and slavery.[9]

The Various Kinds of Rights. It is necessary to distinguish clearly between historic, political, or juridical right and rational or simply human right. The first has ruled the world up to this very hour, making it a receptacle for bloody injustices and oppressions. The second right shall be the means of our emancipation.[10]

The Essence of Right. The predominance and the abiding triumph of force, that is the real core of the matter, and all that is called *right* in the language of politics is nothing but the consecration of fact created by force.[11]

Rationalization of Their Right by the Aristocracy and the Bourgeoisie. The aristocracy of nobility did not need science to prove its right. Its power rested upon two irrefutable arguments based upon violence, upon brutal physical force and its consecration by God's will. The aristocracy committed violence, and the Church bestowed its benediction upon this violence. Such was the nature of its right. It was this intimate bond between the triumphing fist and divine sanction that gave the aristocracy its great prestige, inspiring it with knightly valor which took all hearts by storm.

The bourgeoisie, lacking any valor or grace whatsoever, can base its right upon only one argument: the very prosaic but very substantial power of money. It is the cynical denial of any virtue whatever: with money every fool and brute, every scoundrel, can possess all sorts of rights; without money all individual virtues do not amount to anything—this is the basic principle of the bourgeoisie in its brutal reality. It stands to reason that this argument, valid as it might be in itself, is not sufficient to justify and consolidate the power of the bourgeoisie. Human society is so constituted that the more evil things can be established in it only under the cloak of apparent respectability. Hence the adage: Hypocrisy is the respect vice pays to virtue. Even the mightiest violence needs consecration.

The nobility disguised its violence with divine grace. The bourgeoisie could not obtain that high patronage, . . . and therefore it had to seek sanctions outside of God and the Church. And it did find such sanctions among the licensed intellectuals.[12]

The Basis of the Past and Present Social Organization. All the political and civil organizations existing in the past and the present rest upon the following foundations: upon the historic fact of violence, upon the right to inherit property, upon the family rights of the father and the husband, and the consecration of all these foundations by religion. And all that taken together constitutes the essence of the State.[13]

Convinced that the existence of the State, in any form whatever, is incompatible with the freedom of the proletariat, and that it will not permit the fraternal international union of peoples, we want the abolition of all States.

With the State there must go also all that is called juridical right, and all organization of social life from the top downward, via legislation and government—organization which never had any other aim but the establishment and systematization of the exploitation of the labor of the people for the benefit of the ruling classes.

Abolition of the State and juridical right will have for its sequel the abolition of personal inheritable property and of the juridical family, which is based upon this property, since both preclude human justice.[14]

Abolition of the Right of Inheritance. This question [of abolishing the right of inheriting property] falls into two parts—the first comprising the principle, and the second *the practical application of the principle.*

And the question of the principle itself should be considered from two points of view: that of *expediency* and that of *justice.*

From the point of view of the emancipation of labor, is it expedient, is it necessary, that the right of inheritance should be abolished?

To pose this question is, in our opinion, to solve it. Can the emancipation of labor signify any other thing but its deliverance from the yoke of private property and capital? But how can those two be prevented from dominating and exploiting labor if, divorced from labor as they are, they are the exclusive monopoly of a class which, freed from the necessity of working for a living, will continue to exist and crush labor by extracting from it land rent and interest on capital—a class which, made strong by this position, seizes, as it has done up to now, the profits of industry and commerce, leaving to the workers, who are crushed by the competition into which they are driven, only that which is strictly necessary in order to keep them from starving to death.

No political or juridical law, drastic though it may be, will be able to put a stop to this domination and exploitation, no law can prevail against the power of facts, no one can prevent a given situation from producing its natural results. From which it follows clearly that so long as property and capital remain on one side and labor on the other—one constituting the class of the bourgeoisie and the other that of the proletariat, the worker will be the slave and the bourgeoisie the master.

But what is it that separates property and capital from labor? What constitutes, economically and politically, the distinction between classes? What is it that destroys equality and perpetuates inequality, the privileged status of a small number of people and the slavery of the great majority? It is *the right of inheritance.*

Are any proofs necessary to show that the right of inheritance begets all the economic, political, and social privileges? It is evident that class differences maintain themselves only by virtue of this right. Natural differences among individuals, as well as the fleeting differences which are a matter of luck or fortune and which do not outlive the individuals, perpetuate themselves—or become petrified, so to speak—as a result of the right of inheritance, and becoming traditional differences, they create privileges of birth, give rise to classes, and become a permanent source of exploitation of millions of workers by mere thousands of "noble birth."

So long as the right of inheritance is in force, there can be no economic, social, or political equality in the world; and so long as inequality exists there will be oppression and exploitation.

In principle then, from the point of view of the integral emancipation of work and workers, we should want *abolition of the right of inheritance.*

Biological Heredity Not Denied. It stands to reason that we do not intend to abolish physiological heredity, or the natural transmission of bodily and intellectual faculties; or to be more precise, the transmission of the muscular and mental faculties of parents to their children. This transmission is very often a misfortune, for it frequently passes on the physical and moral maladies of the past to the present generations. But the baneful effects of that transmission can be combated only by the application of science to social hygiene, individual as well as collective, and by a rational and equalitarian organization of society.

What we want to and should abolish is *the right of inheritance*, founded by jurisprudence and constituting the very basis of *the juridical family* and of *the State*.

The Right of Inheritance With Respect to Objects Having Sentimental Value. But it should be understood that we do not intend to abolish the right of inheritance with respect to objects that have a sentimental value attached to them. By that we mean the passing on to children or friends of objects of small [money] value belonging to deceased parents or friends and which because of long usage have retained a personal imprint. The real heritage is that which assures to the heirs, whether in full or only in part, the possibility of living without working by assessing collective labor for land rent or interest on capital. We are of the opinion that capital as well as land, in a word, all the implements and the raw materials necessary for labor, should no longer be transmitted through the right of inheritance, and should forever become the collective property of all the productive associations.

Equality, and consequently the emancipation of labor and of the workers, can be obtained only at this price. Few indeed are the workers who do not realize that in the future abolition of the right of inheritance shall be the supreme condition of equality. But there are workers who fear that if this right should be abolished at present, before a new social organization has made secure the lot of all children, whatever the conditions under which they were born, their own children may find themselves in distress after the death of their parents.

"What!" they say. "We scraped up, by hard work and great privations, three or four hundred francs, and our children shall be deprived of those savings!" Yes, they shall be deprived of them, but in exchange they will receive from society, without prejudice to the natural rights of the father and mother, maintenance and education and an upbringing that you would not be able to provide for them even with thirty or forty thousand francs. For it is evident that as soon as the right of inheritance is abolished, society will have to take upon itself the costs of the physical, moral, and intellectual development of all the children of both sexes who are born in its midst. It will become the supreme guardian of all those children.

Right of Inheritance and Work Stimulus.   Many persons maintain that by the abolition of the right of inheritance there will be destroyed the greatest stimulus impelling man to work. Those who so believe still consider work a necessary evil, or, in theological parlance, as the effect of Jehovah's curse which he hurled in his wrath against the unfortunate human species, and in which, by a singular caprice, he has included the whole of creation.

Without entering into a serious theological discussion, but taking as our base the simple study of human nature, we shall answer the detractors of labor by stating that the latter, far from being an evil or a harsh necessity, is a vital need for every person who is in full possession of his faculties. One can convince himself of this by submitting himself to the following experiment: Let him condemn himself for a few days to absolute inaction, or to sterile, unproductive, stupid work, and toward the end of it he will come to feel that he is a most unfortunate and degraded human being. Man, by his very nature, is compelled to work, just as he is compelled to eat, to drink, to think, to talk.

If work is an accursed thing nowadays, it is because it is excessive, brutalizing, and forced in character, because it leaves no room for leisure and deprives men of the possibility of enjoying life in a humane way, and because everyone, or nearly everyone, is compelled to apply his productive power to a kind of work which is the least suitable for his natural aptitudes. And finally, it is because, in a society based upon theology and jurisprudence, the possibility of living without working is deemed an honor and a privilege, while the necessity of working for a living is regarded as a sign of degradation, as a punishment, and as a shame.

The day when work of mind and body, intellectual and physical, is regarded as the greatest honor among men, as the sign of their manhood and humanity, society will be saved. But that day will never arrive so long as inequality reigns, and so long as the right of inheritance has not been abolished.

Will such an abolition be *just?*

But how could it be unjust if it is effected in the interests of everyone, in the interests of humanity as a whole?

Origin of the Right of Inheritance. Let us examine the right of inheritance from the point of view of human justice.

A man, we are told, acquires by his labor ten thousand or a hundred thousand, or perhaps a million francs—should he not have the right to bequeath this sum to his children? Would not [forbidding such a legacy] be a violation of the natural right of parents, an unjust spoliation?

To begin with, it already has been proven many times that an isolated worker cannot produce very much over and above what he consumes. We challenge anyone to produce a real worker, that is, one who does not enjoy any privileges, who earns tens of thousands, hundreds of thousands, or millions of francs. That would be a sheer impossibility. Therefore, if in existing society there are individuals who earn such big sums, this comes not as a result of their labor but is due to their privileged position; that is, to a juridically legalized injustice. And since anything that is not derived from one's own labor is necessarily taken from the labor of someone else, we have a right to say that all such gains are nothing but a form of theft committed by persons in privileged positions with regard to collective labor, and committed with the sanction of, and under the protection of, the State.

Let us proceed with this analysis.

The Dead Hand of the Past. The law-protected thief dies. He passes on, with or without a testamentary will, his lands or his capital to his children or other relatives. This, we are told, is the necessary corollary of his personal freedom and his individual right; his will is to be respected.

But a dead man is dead for good. Outside of the altogether moral and sentimental existence built up by the pious memories of his children, relatives, and friends (if he deserved such memories), or by public recognition (if he rendered some real service to the public)—outside of that he does not exist at all. Therefore he can have neither liberty, nor right, nor personal will. Phantoms should not rule and oppress the world which belongs only to living persons.

In order that he continue willing and acting after his death, it is necessary to have a juridical fiction or a political lie, and as this dead person is incapable of acting for himself, it is necessary that some power, the State, undertake to act in his name and for his sake; the State must execute the will of a man who, being no longer alive, cannot have any will whatever.

And what is the power of the State, if not the power of the people as a whole, organized to the detriment of the people and in favor of the privileged classes? And above all, it is the production and the collective force of the workers. Is it therefore necessary that the working classes guarantee to the privileged classes the right of inheritance, that is, the principal source of [the workers'] misery and slavery? Must they forge with their own hands the irons which keep them fettered?

Sequence of Abolition of Rights of Inheritance.   We conclude. It is sufficient that the proletariat declare the withdrawal of its support from the State, which sanctions its slavery, to have the right of inheritance, which is exclusively political and juridical—and consequently contrary to human right—collapse all by itself. It is enough to abolish the right of inheritance in order to abolish the juridical family and the State.

All social progress, for that matter, has proceeded by way of successive abolitions of rights of inheritance.

The first to be abolished was the divine right of inheritance, the traditional privileges and chastisements which for a long time were considered the consequence of the divine blessings or the divine curse.

Then the political right of inheritance was abolished, which had for its consequence recognition of the sovereignty of the people and equality of citizens before the law.

And now we must abolish the economic right of inheritance in order to emancipate the worker, the man, and in order to establish the reign of justice upon the ruins of all political and theological iniquities. . . .

Means of Abolishing the Right of Inheritance.   The last question to be solved is the question of practical measures for the abolition of the right of inheritance. This abolition could be effected in two ways: through successive reforms or by means of a social revolution.

It could be effected through reforms in those fortunate countries (the very rare, or if not altogether unknown countries) where the class of property owners and capitalists, the bourgeoisie, imbued with a spirit of wisdom which it now totally lacks, and realizing that the Social Revolution finally is imminent, would try to come to a settlement with the world of labor. In this case, but only in this case, the way of peaceful reforms presents itself as a possibility. By a series of successive modifications, cleverly combined and amiably agreed upon by the worker and the bourgeoisie, it would become possible to abolish the right of inheritance completely in twenty or thirty years, and to replace the present form of property ownership, and of existing work and education, by collective property and collective labor, and by integral education or instruction.

It is impossible for us to determine the precise character of those reforms, for they will have to conform to the particular situation in each country. But in all the countries the goal remains the same: the establishment of collective property and labor, and the freedom of everyone with equality for all.

The method of revolution will naturally be the shortest and simplest one. Revolutions are never made by individuals or associations. They are brought about by the force of circumstances. It should be definitely understood among us that on the first day of the Revolution the right of inheritance shall simply be abolished, and along with that, the State and juridical right, so that upon the ruins of all these iniquities, cutting athwart all political and national frontiers, there may arise a new international world, the world of labor, of science, of freedom, and of equality, a world organized from below upward, by the free association of all producers' associations.[15]

Rational or Human Right. Aiming at the actual and final emancipation of the people, we hold out the following program:

Abolition of the right of property inheritance.

Equalization of the rights of women—political as well as socio-economic rights—with those of men. Consequently, we want abolition of the family right and of marriage—ecclesiastical as well as civil marriage—[which are] inseparably bound up with the right of inheritance.

Basic economic truth rests upon two fundamental premises:

The land belongs only to those who cultivate it with their own hands: to the agricultural communes. The capital and all the tools of production belong to the workers: to the workers' associations.

The future political organization should be a free federation of workers, a federation of producers' associations of agricultural and factory workers.

And therefore, in the name of political emancipation, we want in the first place abolition of the State, and the uprooting of the State principle, with all the ecclesiastical, political, military, bureaucratic, juridical, academic, financial, and economic institutions.

National Right. We want full freedom for all nations, with the right of full self-determination for every people in conformity with their own instincts, needs, and will.[16] Every people, like every person, can be only what it is, and unquestionably it has the right to be itself.

This sums up the so-called national right. But if a people or a person exists in a certain form and cannot exist in any other, it does not follow that they have the right (nor that it would be of any benefit to them) to raise nationality in the one case or individuality in the other into specific principles, or that they should make much ado about such alleged principles.[17]

CHAPTER 13 *Power and Authority*

The Instinct for Power. All men possess a natural instinct for power which has its origin in the basic law of life enjoining every individual to wage a ceaseless struggle in order to insure his existence or to assert his rights. This struggle among men began with cannibalism; then continuing throughout the centuries under various religious banners, it passed successively through all forms of slavery and serfdom, becoming humanized very slowly, little by little, and seeming to relapse at times into primitive savagery. At the present time that struggle is taking place under the double aspect of exploitation of wage labor by capital, and of the political, juridical, civil, military, and police oppression by the State and Church, and by State officials; and it continues to arouse within all the individuals born in society the desire, the need, and sometimes the inevitability of commanding and exploiting other people.

The Power Instinct Is the Most Negative Force in History. Thus we see that the instinct to command others, in its primitive essence, is a carnivorous, altogether bestial and savage instinct. Under the influence of the mental development of men, it takes on a somewhat more ideal form, and becomes somewhat ennobled, presenting itself as the instrument of reason and the devoted servant of that abstraction, or political fiction, which is called the public good. But in its essence it remains just as baneful, and it becomes even more so when, with the application of science, it extends its scope and intensifies the power of its action. If there is a devil in history, it is this power principle. It is this principle, together with the stupidity and ignorance of the masses, upon which it is ever based and without which it never could exist,—it is this principle alone that has produced all the misfortunes, all the crimes, and the most shameful facts of history.

Growth of Power Instinct Determined by Social Conditions. And inevitably this cursed element is to be found, as a natural instinct, in every man, the best of them not excepted. Everyone carries within himself the germs of this lust for power, and every germ, as we know, because of a basic law of life, necessarily must develop and grow, if only it finds in its environment favorable conditions. These conditions in human society are the stupidity, ignorance, apathetic indifference, and servile habits of the masses—so one may say justly that it is the masses themselves that produce those exploiters, oppressors, despots, and executioners of humanity, of whom they are the victims. When the masses are deeply sunk in their sleep, patiently resigned to their degradation and slavery, the best men in their midst, the most energetic and intelligent of them, those who in a different environment might render great services to humanity, necessarily become despots. Often they become such by entertaining the illusion that they are working for the good of those whom they oppress. On the contrary, in an intelligent, wide-awake society, jealously guarding its liberty and disposed to defend its rights, even the most egoistic and malevolent individuals become good members of society. Such is the power of society, a thousand times greater than that of the strongest individuals.[1]

Exercise of Power a Negative Social Determinant. Man's nature is so constituted that, given the possibility of doing evil, that is, of feeding his vanity, his ambition, and his cupidity at the expense of someone else, he surely will make full use of such an opportunity. We of course are all sincere Socialists and revolutionists; and still, were we endowed with power, even for the short duration of a few months, we would not be what we are now. As Socialists we are convinced, you and I, that social environment, social position, and conditions of existence, are more powerful than the intelligence and will of the strongest and most powerful individual, and it is precisely for this reason that we demand not natural but social equality of individuals as the condition for justice and the foundation of morality. And that is why we detest power, all power, just as the people detest it.[2]

No one should be entrusted with power, inasmuch as anyone invested with authority must, through the force of an immutable social law, become an oppressor and exploiter of society.[3]

We are in fact enemies of all authority, for we realize that power and authority corrupt those who exercise them as much as those who are compelled to submit to them. Under its baneful influence some become ambitious despots, lusting for power and greedy for gain, exploiters of society for their own benefit or that of their class, while others become slaves.[4]

Exercise of Authority Cannot Be Claimed on the Ground of Science. The great misfortune is that a large number of natural laws, already established as such by science, remain unknown to the masses, thanks to the solicitous care of these tutelary governments that exist, as we know, only for the good of the people. And there also is another difficulty: namely, that the greater number of the natural laws inherent in the development of human society, which are quite as necessary, invariable, and inevitable as the laws which govern the physical world, have not been duly recognized and established by science itself.

Once they have been recognized, at first by science and then by means of an extensive system of popular education and instruction—once they have become part and parcel of the general consciousness—the question of liberty will be solved. The most recalcitrant authorities will then have to admit that henceforth there will be no need of political organization, administration, or legislation. Those three things—whether emanating from the will of the sovereign or issuing from the will of a Parliament elected by universal suffrage, or even conforming to the system of natural laws (which has never yet happened and never will happen)—are always equally baneful and hostile to the liberty of the people because they impose upon the latter a system of external and therefore despotic laws.

Natural Laws Must Be Freely Accepted.   The liberty of man consists solely in that he obeys natural laws because he has recognized them as such *himself*, and not because they have been imposed upon him by any external will whatever—divine or human, collective or individual.

Dictatorship by Scientists.   Suppose a learned academy, composed of the most illustrious representatives of science; suppose this academy were charged with legislation for, and the organization of, society, and that, inspired only by the purest love for truth, it would frame none but laws in absolute conformity with the latest discoveries of science. Well, I maintain that that legislation and that organization would be monstrosities, and this for two reasons.

First, human science is always and necessarily imperfect, and, comparing what it has discovered with what remains to be discovered, we may say that it is still in its cradle. This is true to such an extent that were we to force the practical life of men, collective as well as individual, into strict and exclusive conformity with the latest data of science, we should condemn society as well as individuals to suffer martyrdom on a Procrustean bed, which would soon end by dislocating and stifling them, life always remaining an infinitely greater thing than science.

The second reason is this: a society obeying legislation emanating from a scientific academy, not because it understood the reasonableness of this legislation (in which case the existence of that academy would become useless) but because the legislation emanated from the academy and was imposed in the name of science, which was venerated without being understood—that society would be a society of brutes and not of men. It would be a second edition of the wretched Paraguayan republic which submitted so long to the rule of the Society of Jesus. Such a society would rapidly sink to the lowest stage of idiocy.

But there is also a third reason rendering such a government impossible. This reason is that a scientific academy invested, so to speak, with absolute, sovereign power, even if it were composed of the most illustrious men, would unavoidably and quickly end by becoming morally and intellectually corrupted. Such has been the history of academies when the privileges allowed them were few and scanty. The greatest scientific genius, from the moment that he becomes an academician, an officially licensed savant, inevitably deteriorates and becomes sluggish. He loses his spontaneity, his revolutionary boldness, that wild and troublesome characteristic of the greatest geniuses who are always called upon to destroy old decrepit worlds and lay the foundations of new worlds. Doubtless our academician gains in good manners, in worldly and utilitarian wisdom, what he loses in power of thought.

Scientists Are Not Excepted From the Workings of the Law of Equality. It is the characteristic of privilege and of every privileged position to destroy the minds and hearts of men. A privileged man, whether politically or economically so, is a man depraved intellectually and morally. This is a social law which admits of no exception, and which is equally valid with respect to entire nations as well as social classes, social groups, and individuals. It is the law of equality, the supreme condition of freedom and humanity.

A scientific body entrusted with the government of society would soon end by devoting itself no longer to science but to some other effort. And this effort, as is the case with all established powers, would be to try to perpetuate itself by rendering the society entrusted to its care ever more stupid and consequently more in need of its direction and government.

And that which is true of scientific academies is equally true of all constituent assemblies and legislative bodies, even those elected on the basis of universal suffrage. It is true that the make-up of these latter bodies can be changed, but that does not prevent the formation in a few years' time of a body of politicians, privileged in fact if not in law, and who, devoting themselves exclusively to the direction of the public affairs of a country, end by forming a sort of political aristocracy or oligarchy. Witness the United States of America and Switzerland.

Thus no external legislation and no authority are necessary; for that matter, one is separable from the other, and both tend to enslave society and to degrade mentally the legislators themselves.[5]

In the good old times when the Christian faith, still unshaken and mainly represented by the Roman Catholic Church, flourished in all its might, God had no difficulty in designating his elect. It was understood that all the sovereigns, great and small, reigned by the grace of God, if only they were not excommunicated; the nobility itself based its privileges upon the benediction of the Holy Church. Even Protestantism, which contributed powerfully toward the destruction of faith, against its will of course, left, in this respect at least, the Christian doctrine wholly intact. "For there is no power (it repeated the words of St. Paul) but of God." Protestantism even reinforced the authority of the sovereign by proclaiming that it proceeded directly from God, without needing the intervention of the Church, and by subjecting the latter to the power of the sovereign.

But ever since the philosophy of the last century [the eighteenth], acting in union with the bourgeois revolution, delivered a mortal blow to faith and overthrew all the institutions based upon that faith, the doctrine of authority has had a hard time re-establishing itself in the consciousness of men. The present sovereigns continue, of course, to designate themselves as rulers "by the grace of God," but these words which once possessed a meaning that was real, powerful, and palpitating with life, are now considered by the educated classes and even by a section of the people itself, as an obsolete, banal, and essentially meaningless phrase. Napoleon III tried to rejuvenate it by adding to it another phrase: "and by the will of the people," which, added to the first one, either annuls its meaning and thereby becomes annullled in turn, or signifies that God wills whatever the people will.

What remains to be done is to ascertain the will of the people and to find out which political organ faithfully expresses that will. The Radical Democrats imagine that it is an Assembly elected on the basis of universal suffrage that will prove to be the most adequate organ for that purpose. Others, even more radical democrats, add to it the *referendum,* the direct voting of the whole people upon every more or less important law. All of them—conservatives, liberals, moderates, and extreme radicals—agree on one point, that the people should be governed; whether the people themselves elect their rulers and masters, or such are imposed upon them—but rulers and masters they should have. Devoid of intelligence, the people should let themselves be guided by those who do possess such intelligence.

The Reason of the Privileged Classes in the Light of Their Acceptance of Barbarous Dictatorship.   Whereas in past centuries authority was demanded in the name of God, now the doctrinaires demand it in the name of reason. It is not any more the priests of a decayed religion who demand power, but the licensed priests of the doctrinaire reason, and this is done at a time when the bankruptcy of that reason has become evident. For never did educated and learned people—and in general the so-called enlightened classes—show such moral degradation, such cowardice, egoism, and such a complete lack of convictions as in our own days. Because of this cowardice they have remained stupid in spite of their learning, understanding only one thing—and that is to conserve whatever exists, madly hoping to arrest the course of history with the brutal force of a military dictatorship before which they now have shamefully prostrated themselves.

Moral Bankruptcy of the Old Intelligentsia.   Just as in the days of old the representatives of divine reason and authority—the Church and the priests—too obviously allied themselves with the economic exploitation of the masses—which was the principal cause of their downfall—so now have the representatives of man's reason and authority, the State, the learned societies, and the enlightened classes—too obviously identified themselves with the business of cruel and iniquitous exploitation to retain the slightest moral force or any prestige whatever. Condemned by their own conscience, they feel themselves exposed, and have no other recourse against the contempt which, as they know, has been well merited by them, but the ferocious arguments of an organized and armed violence. An organization based upon three detestable things—bureaucracy, police, and a standing army—this is what now constitutes the State, the visible body of the exploiting and doctrinaire reasoning of the privileged classes.

Emergence of a New Reasoning and the Rise of a Libertarian Outlook.

In contrast to this rotting and dying reasoning a new, young, and vigorous spirit is awakening and crystalizing in the midst of the people. It is full of life and hope for the future; it is of course not yet fully developed with respect to science, but it eagerly aspires toward a new science cleared from all the stupidities of metaphysics and theology. This new logic will have neither licensed professors nor prophets nor priests, nor, drawing its power from each and all, will it found a new Church or a new State. It will destroy the last vestiges of this cursed and fatal principle of authority, human as well as divine, and, rendering everyone his full liberty, it will realize the equality, solidarity, and fraternity of mankind.[6]

The Proper Role and Function of the Expert. Does it follow that I reject all authority? No, far be it from me to entertain such a thought. In the matter of boots, I defer to the authority of the bootmaker. When it is a question of houses, canals, or railroads, I consult the authority of the architect or engineer. For each special type of knowledge I apply to the scientist of that respective branch. I listen to them freely, and with all the respect merited by their intelligence, their character, and their knowledge, though always reserving my indisputable right of criticism and control. I do not content myself with consulting a single specialist who is an authority in a given field; I consult several of them. I compare their opinions and I choose the one which seems to me the soundest.

But I recognize no infallible authority, not even on questions of an altogether special character. Consequently, whatever respect I may have for the honesty and sincerity of such and such individuals, I have no absolute faith in any person. Such faith would be fatal to my reason, to my liberty, and to the success of my undertakings: it would immediately transform me into a stupid slave, an instrument of the will and interests of others.

If I bow before the authority of the specialists and declare myself ready to follow, to a certain extent and so long as it may seem to me to be necessary, their general indications and even their directions, it is because their authority is imposed upon me by no one, neither by men nor by God. Otherwise I would reject them with horror and send to the Devil their counsels, their directions, and their knowledge, certain that they would make me pay, by the loss of my liberty and self-respect, for such odd bits of truth enveloped in a multitude of lies, as they might give me.

I bow before the authority of specialists because it is imposed upon me by my own reason. I am aware of the fact that I can embrace in all its details and positive developments only a very small part of human knowledge. The greatest intelligence would not be equal to the task of embracing the whole. Hence there results, for science as well as for industry, the necessity of division and association of labor. I take and I give —such is human life. Each is an authoritative leader and in turn is led by others. Accordingly there is no fixed and constant authority, but a continual exchange of mutual, temporary, and, above all, voluntary authority and subordination.

Government By Supermen.   This same reason forbids me, then, to recognize a fixed, constant, and universal authority, for there is no universal man capable of embracing all the sciences, all the branches of social life, in all their wealth of details, without which the application of science to life is impossible. And if such universality ever could be realized in a single man, and if he wanted to make use of that universality to impose his authority upon us, it would be necessary to drive that man out of society—because the exercise of such authority by him would reduce all the others to slavery and imbecility.

I do not believe that society ought to maltreat men of genius as it has done up to now; but neither do I believe that it should pamper them, still less accord them any exclusive privileges or rights whatever. And that is so for three reasons: first, because it has often happened that society mistook a charlatan for a man of genius; second, because, through such a system of privileges, it might transform even a real man of genius into a charlatan, demoralize and degrade him; and finally, because it might thus set up a despot over itself.

I recapitulate. We recognize, then, the absolute authority of science, for science has for its object only the mentally elaborated reproduction, as systematic as possible, of the natural laws inherent in the material, intellectual, and moral life of both the physical and social worlds, those two worlds constituting in fact one and the same natural world. Outside of this only legitimate authority, legitimate because it is rational and is in harmony with human liberty, we declare all other authorities false, arbitrary, and fatal.

Authority of Science Is Not Identical With Authority of Savants. We recognize the absolute authority of science, but we reject the infallibility and universality of the representatives of science. In our Church—if I may be permitted to use for a moment an expression which otherwise I detest; Church and State are my two bugbears—in our Church, as in the Protestant Church, we have a chief, an invisible Christ, science; and, like the Protestants, being even more consistent than the Protestants, we will suffer neither Pope, nor Council, nor conclaves of infallible Cardinals, nor Bishops, nor even priests. Our Christ differs from the Protestant and Christian Christ in this—that the latter is a personal being, while ours is impersonal. The Christ of Christianity, already completed in an eternal past, appears as a perfect being, whereas the completing and perfecting of our Christ, science, are ever in the future; which is equivalent to saying that these ends never will be realized. So, in recognizing *absolute science* as the only absolute authority, we in no way compromise our liberty.

Absolute Science Is a Dynamic Concept of an Infinite Process of Becoming. By the words "absolute science" I mean the truly universal science which would reproduce ideally, to its full extent and in all its infinite detail, the universe, the system, or the co-ordination of all the natural laws manifested by the incessant development of worlds. It is evident that such a science, the sublime object of all the efforts of the human mind, will never be fully and absolutely realized. Our Christ, then, will remain uncompleted throughout eternity, a circumstance which must take down the pride of his licensed representatives among us. Against God the Son, in whose name they assume to impose upon us their insolent and pedantic authority, we appeal to God the Father, who is the real world, the real life, of which he (the Son) is only a too imperfect expression—whereas we, real beings, living, working, struggling, loving, aspiring, enjoying, and suffering, are its direct representatives.

But, while rejecting the absolute, universal, and infallible authority of men of science, we willingly bow before the respectable, although relative, temporary, and closely restricted authority of the representatives of special sciences, asking for nothing better than to consult them by turns, and feeling very grateful for such valuable information as they may want to extend to us—on condition, however, that they be willing to receive similar counsel from us on occasions when, and concerning matters about which, we are more learned than they.

In general, we ask nothing better than to see men endowed with great knowledge, great experience, great minds, and above all great hearts, exercise over us a natural and legitimate influence, freely accepted, and never imposed in the name of any official authority whatever—celestial or terrestrial. We accept all natural authorities and all influences of fact, but none of right; for every authority and every influence of right, officially imposed as such, becoming directly an oppression and a falsehood, would inevitably impose upon us . . . slavery and absurdity.[7]

The Authority Flowing From the Collective Experience of Free and Equal Men. The only great and omnipotent authority, at once natural and rational, the only one which we may respect, will be that of the collective and public spirit of a society founded on equality and solidarity and the mutual human respect of all its members.

Yes, this is an authority which is not at all divine, which is wholly human, but before which we shall bow willingly, certain that, far from enslaving them, it will emancipate men. It will be a thousand times more powerful than all your divine, theological, metaphysical, political, and judicial authorities, established by the Church and State, more powerful than your criminal codes, your jailers, and your executioners.[8]

The Ideal of Anarchism. In a word, we reject all privileged, licensed, official, and legal legislation and authority, even though it arise from universal suffrage, convinced that it could turn only to the benefit of a dominant and exploiting minority, and against the interests of the vast enslaved majority. It is in this sense that we are really Anarchists.[9]

CHAPTER 14 *State Centralization and Its Effects*

Political Centralization Is Destructive of Liberty. The political centralization created by the Radical Party [of Switzerland] is destructive of liberty. . . . The old regime of cantonal autonomy guaranteed the freedom and national independence of Switzerland much better than the present system of centralization.

If liberty has of late made notable progress in several of the erstwhile reactionary cantons, it is not at all due to the new powers with which the Constitution of 1848 invested the federal authorities; this [the progress in backward cantons] is due solely to intellectual development meanwhile, and to the march of time. All the progress achieved since 1848 in the federal domain is of the economic order, like the introduction of a single currency, a single standard of weights and measures, large scale public works, commercial treaties, etcetera.

Economic and Political Centralization. It will be contended that economic centralization can be attained only by political centralization, that one implies the other, and that both are necessary and beneficial to the same extent. Not at all, we say. Economic centralization, the essential condition of civilization, creates liberty; but political centralization kills it, destroying for the benefit of the government and the governing classes the life and spontaneous action of the population. Concentration of political power can produce only slavery, for freedom and power are mutually exclusive. Every government, even the most democratic one, is the natural enemy of freedom, and the stronger it is, the more concentrated its power, the more oppressive it becomes. These truths, for that matter, are so simple and clear that one feels ashamed in having to repeat them.[1]

The Lesson of Switzerland. The experience of the last twenty-two years [1848-1870] shows that political centralization has likewise proven fatal to Switzerland. It destroys the liberty of the country, endangers its independence, turns it into a complacent and servile *gendarme* in the service of all the powerful despots of Europe. In reducing its moral force, political centralization jeopardizes the material existence of the country.[2]

The Last Word in Political Centralization. Cavaignac, who rendered such valuable service to both the French and international reaction, was, however, a man of sincere republican convictions. Is it not remarkable that it was a republican who was destined to lay the first basis for the military dictatorship in Europe, to be the forerunner, in the direct line of Napoleon III and the German Emperor; just as it was the lot of another republican, his famous predecessor, Robespierre, to pave the road for the State despot-ism personified by Napoleon? Does it not prove that the all-absorbing and overwhelming military discipline—the ideal of the pan-German Empire—is the inevitable last word in bourgeois State centralization, in bourgeois civilization?

Centralization in Germany. Whatever the case may be, the noble-men, the bureaucracy, the ruling caste, and the princes conceived a great liking for Cavaignac, and, greatly aroused by his success, they visibly took courage and began preparing for new struggles.[3]

The conquered rich provinces, and the immense quantities of cap-tured war materials, have enabled Germany to maintain a huge standing army. The creation of the Empire and its organic subjection to the Prussian autocracy, the building and arming of new fortresses, and, finally, the building of the fleet—all that, of course, has contributed greatly toward the strengthening of German might. But its cheif support consists above all in the deep and undeniable popular sympathy.

As one of our Swiss friends has said: "Now every German tailor living in Japan, China, and Moscow feels behind him the German Navy and the whole German power. And this proud realization makes him madly exul-tant. At last the German has come to see the day when, leaning upon the armed might of the State, he can say, just as proudly as the Englishman or the American [speaks of his own nationality], 'I am a German.' " True, but the Englishman or the American, in saying 'I am an Englishman' or 'I am an American,' says thereby 'I am a free man,' while the German says 'I am a slave, but my Emperor is stronger than all the other sovereigns, and the German soldier, who is strangling me, will finally have strangled all of you.' "

The German People Turn Toward Discipline. Will the German people content themselves for long with this realization? Who can say?

The Germans have been yearning so long for a single [totalitarian] State with a single stick—that they probably will be enjoying their present bliss for a long time. Every people to its taste, and the taste of the German people runs toward a stout stick to be wielded by the State.

Moral Effects of State Centralization. No one can seriously doubt that with State centralization rampant, there will begin—for that matter, there already has begun—to develop in Germany all the evil principles, all the corruption, all the causes of inner disintegration which always go hand in hand with political centralization.

One can doubt it the less inasmuch as this process of moral and intel-lectual disintegration already has set in; one has only to read the German magazines, of conservative or moderate orientation, to find there descrip-tions of the corruption sweeping through the German public, which until now, as we know, has been the most honest in the world.

This inevitable result of capitalist monopoly is always and everywhere accompanied by the intensification and extension of State centralization.[4]

Political Centralization Instrumental in Distorting Political Progress of French Nation.   We are convinced that if France twice lost its freedom, and saw its democratic republic turn into a military dicatorship, the fault does not lie with the character of the people, but with *political centralization*. This centralization, long since prepared by the French kings and statesmen, later personified in a man whom the fawning rhetoric of the court named the Great King, then hurled into the abyss by the shameful disorders of a decrepit monarchy—this political centralization would have perished in the mire, had it not been raised by the mighty hand of the Revolution. Yes, strange indeed, that great Revolution, which for the first time in history had proclaimed the liberty not only of the citizen but of man, by making itself the heir of the monarchy which it had destroyed, revived at the same time this negation of all liberty: *centralization and omnipotence of the State.*

Recreated by the Constituent Assembly and combated, although with little success, by the Girondists, this political centralization was completed by the National Convention. Robespierre and Saint-Just were the true restorers of centralization. Nothing was overlooked by this new governmental machine, not even the Supreme Being with the cult of the State. This machine awaited only a clever mechanic to show to the astonished world the possibilities for powerful oppression with which it had been endowed by its imprudent builders . . . and then came Napoleon.

Thus this Revolution, which at first was inspired by love for liberty and humanity, only because it came to believe in the possibility of reconciling those two concepts with State centralization, committed suicide, and killed both, begetting in their place only a military dictatorship, Caesarism.

Federalism the Political Ideal of a New Society.   Is it not clear then, gentlemen, that in order to save liberty and peace in Europe, we ought to oppose to this monstrous and oppressive centralization of the military, bureaucratic, despotic, monarchic, constitutional, or even republican States, the great salutary principles of federalism?

Henceforth it ought to be clear to all those who really want the emancipation of Europe that, while retaining our sympathies for the great Socialist and humanitarian ideas proclaimed by the French Revolution, we must reject its State policy and resolutely adopt the policy of liberty pursued by the Americans of the North.[5]

CHAPTER 15   *The Element of Discipline*

The Mystic Cult of Authority in the France of Napoleon III. With discipline and confidence it is the same as with union. All those are excellent things when put in the right place, but they are disastrous when applied to people who do not deserve them. Passionate lover of freedom that I am, I confess that I greatly distrust those who always have the word *discipline* on their lips. It is exceedingly dangerous, especially in France, where most of the time discipline signifies despotism on one hand and automatism on the other. In France the mystic cult of authority, the love of commanding and the habit of submitting to orders, has destroyed in society, as well as among the vast majority of individuals, every feeling for liberty and all faith in the spontaneous and living order which liberty alone can create.

Speak to them of liberty, and they raise an outcry about disorder. For it seems to them that no sooner would this ever oppressive and violent discipline of the State stop functioning than everyone would be at the next one's throat and society would have collapsed. Therein lies the astounding secret of the slavery which French society has put up with ever since its Great Revolution. Robespierre and the Jacobins bequeathed to it the cult of State discipline. This cult—which you will find in its entirety among your bourgeois republicans, whether official or officious—is now ruining France.

It is ruining it by paralyzing the only source and the only means of deliverance that is left open to it—the unleashing of the popular forces of the country. It is ruining France by making it seek salvation in authority and the illusory action of the State, which at the present moment represents only vain despotic pretensions going hand in hand with absolute impotence.

Freedom Is Compatible with Discipline. Hostile as I am to that which in France is called discipline, nevertheless I recognize that a certain kind of discipline, not automatic but voluntary and thoughtful discipline, which harmonizes perfectly with the freedom of individuals, is, and ever will be, necessary when a great number of individuals, freely united, undertake any kind of collective work or action. Under those conditions, discipline is simply the voluntary and thoughtful co-ordination of all individual efforts toward a common goal.

At the moment of action, in the midst of a struggle, the roles are naturally distributed in accordance with everyone's attitudes, evaluated and judged by the whole collective; some direct and command, while others execute commands. But no function remains fixed and petrified, nothing is irrevocably attached to one person. Hierarchic order and advancement do not exist, so that the executive of yesterday may become the subordinate of today. No one is raised above the others, or, if he does rise for some time, it is only to drop back at a later time into his former position, like the sea wave ever dropping back to the salutary level of equality.

The Diffusion of Power.   In such a system power, properly speaking, no longer exists. Power is diffused in the collective and becomes the sincere expression of the liberty of everyone, the faithful and serious realization of the will of all; everyone obeys because the executive-for-the-day dictates only what he himself, that is, every individual, wants.

This is the only true human discipline, the discipline necessary for the organization of freedom. It is not this kind of discipline that is preached by the republican statesmen. They want the old French discipline, automatic, routine-like, blind discipline. They want a chief, not freely elected and for only one day, but one that is imposed by the State for a long time, if not forever; this executive commands and the rest obey. The salvation of France, they tell you—and even the freedom of France—is possible only at this price. Thus passive obedience—the foundation of every despotism—will be the cornerstone upon which you are going to found your republic.

But if this chief of mine orders me to turn my weapons against this very republic, or to betray France to the Prussians, must I or must I not obey such an order? If I obey, I betray France; if I disobey, I violate, I break the discipline which you want to impose upon me as the only means of salvation for France.

Authoritarian Discipline in the Face of the Profound Political Crisis of 1871.   And do not tell me that this dilemma which I ask you to solve is an idle problem. No, it is a problem of palpitating urgency, for it is with the painful choices of this dilemma that the soldiers are now faced. Who does not know that their chiefs, their generals, and the great majority of their superior officers, are devoted body and soul to the Imperial regime? Who does not know that they are everywhere openly conspiring and plotting against the Republic? What are the soldiers to do? If they obey, they will betray France. And if they disobey, they will destroy what is left of your regular Army.

Revolution Destroys Blind Discipline.   For the republicans, for the partisans of the State, of public order and discipline, this dilemma is insoluble. But for us revolutionary Socialists it does not present any difficulty. Yes, they should disobey, they should revolt, they should break this discipline and destroy the present organization of the regular Army, they should destroy, in the name of the salvation of France, this phantom State, powerless to do good, but powerful for evil.[1]

PART III

The System of Anarchism

Freedom and Equality

Natural and Man-Made Laws. Man can never be altogether free in relation to natural and social laws.[1]

What is freedom? What is slavery? Does man's freedom consist in revolting against all laws? We say *No*, in so far as laws are natural, economic, and social laws, not authoritatively imposed but inherent in things, in relations, in situations, the natural development of which is expressed by those laws. We say *Yes* if they are political and juridical laws, imposed by men upon men: whether violently by the right of force; whether by deceit and hypocrisy—in the name of religion or any doctrine whatever; or finally, by dint of the fiction, the democratic falsehood called *universal suffrage*.[2]

Man Cannot Revolt Against Nor Escape from Nature. Against the laws of Nature no revolt is possible on the part of man, the simple reason being that he himself is a product of Nature and that he exists only by virtue of those laws. A rebellion on his part would be . . . a ridiculous attempt, it would be a revolt against himself, a veritable suicide. And when man has a determination to destroy himself, or even when he carries out such a design, he again acts in accordance with those same natural laws, from which nothing can exempt him: neither thought, nor will, nor despair, nor any other passion, nor life, nor death.

Man himself is nothing but Nature. His most sublime or most monstrous sentiments, the most perverted, the most egoistic, or the most heroic resolves or manifestations of his will, his most abstract, most theological, or most insane thoughts—all that is nothing else but Nature. Nature envelops, permeates, constitutes his whole existence. How can he ever escape this Nature?[3]

The Sources of Escapism. It is really to be wondered at how man could ever conceive this idea of escaping from Nature. Separation from Nature being utterly impossible, how could man ever dream of such a thing? Whence this monstrous dream? Whence does it come if not from *theology*, the science of Non-Being, and later from *metaphysics*, which is the impossible reconciliation of Non-Existence with reality?[4]

We must distinguish well between natural laws and authoritarian, arbitrary, political, religious, criminal, and civil laws which the privileged classes have established in the course of history, always in the interest of exploitation of the labor of the toiling masses—laws which, under the pretense of a fictitious morality were ever the source of the deepest immorality: consequently, involuntary and inescapable obedience to all laws which, independently of human will, constitute the very life of Nature and society; and at the same time independence as complete as possible for everyone in relation to all pretensions to command, coming from any human will whatever, individual as well as collective, and tending to assert themselves not by way of natural influence, but by imposing their law, their despotism.[5]

Freedom Does Not Imply Foregoing Any Exertion of Influence. The freedom of every man is the result produced ever anew by a multitude of physical, mental, and moral influences to which he is subjected by the environment in which he was born, and in which he lives and dies. To wish to escape from this influence in the name of some transcendental, divine freedom, self-sufficient and absolutely egoistical, is to aim at nonexistence; to forego influencing others means to forego social action, or even giving expression to one's thoughts and feelings—which again is to tend toward non-existence. This notorious independence, so greatly extolled by the idealists and metaphysicians, and individual freedom conceived in this sense, are just mere nothingness.[6]

The worse it is for those who are ignorant of the natural and social law of human solidarity to the extent of imagining that the absolute mutual independence of individuals or the masses is possible or desirable. To will that is to will the very annihilation of society, for all social life is simply this incessant mutual dependence of individuals and masses. All individuals, even the strongest and the most intelligent of them, are, at every instant of their lives, at once producers and the product of the will and action of the masses.[7]

In Nature as in human society, which in itself is nothing but Nature, everything that lives does so only under the supreme condition of intervening in the most positive manner in the life of others—intervening in as powerful a manner as the particular nature of a given individual permits it to do so. To do away with this reciprocal influence would spell death in the full sense of the word. And when we demand liberty for the masses, we do not pretend to have abolished any of the natural influences exerted upon the masses by any individual or group of individuals. What we want is the abolition of fictitious, privileged, legal, and official influences.[8]

Liberty in Conformity with Natural Laws. Man's freedom consists solely in this: that he obeys natural laws because he has *himself* recognized them as such, and not because they have been imposed upon him by any extrinsic will whatever, divine or human, collective or individual.[9]

As against natural laws there is only one kind of liberty possible for man—and that is to recognize and apply them on an ever-extending scale in conformity with the goal of emancipation, or humanization—individual or collective—which he pursues. These laws, once recognized, exercise an authority which has never been disputed by the great mass of mankind. One must, for instance, be a madman or a theologian, or at least a metaphysician, a jurist, or a bourgeois economist to revolt against the law according to which twice two makes four. One must have faith to imagine that one will not burn in fire or that he will not drown in water unless he has recourse to some subterfuge, which, in its turn, is founded on some other natural law. But these revolts, or rather these attempts at or wild fancies of impossible revolts, constitute only very rare exceptions; for in general it may be said that the mass of mankind, in their daily lives, let themselves be governed, in an almost absolute fashion, by common sense, that is, by the sum of generally recognized natural laws.[10]

Rational Liberty.   True, man, with the aid of knowledge and the thoughtful application of the laws of Nature, gradually emancipates himself, but he achieves this emancipation not in regard to the universal yoke, which is borne by all living beings, himself included, and by all existing things that are produced and that vanish in this world. Man frees himself only from the brutal pressure of *his* external material and social world, including that of all the things and people surrounding him. He dominates things through science and by work; and as to the arbitrary yoke of men, he throws it off through revolutions.

Such then is the only rational meaning of the word *liberty*: it is the domination over external things, *based upon the respectful observance of the laws of Nature;* it is independence from the pretentious claims and despotic acts of men; it is science, work, political rebellion, and, finally, it is the organization, at once planned and free, of a social environment, in conformity with the natural laws inherent in every human society. The first and last condition of this liberty remains then the most absolute submission to the omnipotence of Nature, our mother, and the observance, the most rigorous application of her laws.[11]

Wide Diffusion of Knowledge Will Lead to Full Freedom.   The great misfortune is that a large number of natural laws, already established as such by science, remain unknown to the masses, thanks to the solicitous care of the tutelary governments that exist, as we know, only for the good of the people. There also is another difficulty: namely, that the greater number of the natural laws inherent in the development of human society, which are quite as necessary, invariable, and inevitable, as the laws which govern the physical world, have not been duly recognized and established by science itself.[12]

Once they have been recognized, first by science and then by means of an extensive system of popular education and instruction, once they have become part and parcel of the general consciousness—the question of liberty will be completely solved. The most recalcitrant authorities must admit that there will then be no need of political organization, administration, or legislation, three things which, whether emanating from the will of the sovereign or from that of a parliament elected on the basis of universal suffrage, and even if they should conform to the system of natural laws—which has never happened yet and never will happen—are always equally baneful and hostile to the liberty of the people because they impose upon the latter a system of external and therefore despotic laws.[13]

Freedom Is Valid Only When Shared by Everyone. The materialist, realist, and collectivist definition of liberty is altogether opposed to that of the idealists. The materialist definition runs like this: Man becomes man and arrives at awareness as well as realization of his humanity only in society and only through the collective action of the whole society. He frees himself from the yoke of external Nature only by collective and social labor, which alone is capable of transforming the surface of the earth into an abode favorable to the development of humanity. And without this material emancipation there can be no intellectual or moral emancipation for anyone.

Man cannot free himself from the yoke of his own nature, that is, he can subordinate his instincts and his bodily movements to the direction of his ever-developing mind only with the aid of education and upbringing. Both, however, are pre-eminently and exclusively social phenomena. For outside of society man would always remain a wild beast or a saint, which is about the same. Finally, an isolated man cannot have awareness of his liberty. To be free signifies that man shall be recognized and treated as such by another man, by all men who surround him. Liberty then is not a fact springing from isolation but from reciprocal action, a fact not of exclusion, but, on the contrary, of social interaction—for the freedom of every individual is simply the reflection of his humanity or his human right in the consciousness of all free men, his brothers, his equals.[14]

I can call myself and feel myself a free man only in the presence of and in relation to other men. In the presence of an animal of inferior species, I am neither free nor am I a man, for that animal is incapable of conceiving, and consequently incapable of recognizing my humanity. I myself am human and free only inasmuch as I recognize the freedom and humanity of all people surrounding me. It is only when I respect their human character that I respect my own humanity.

A cannibal who eats his captives, treating them as savage animals, is not a man but a beast. The master of slaves is not a man but a master. In ignoring the humanity of his slaves, he ignores his own humanity. Every ancient society furnishes good proofs thereof: the Greeks, the Romans, did not feel free as men, they did not consider themselves as such from the point of view of human right. They believed themselves privileged as Greeks, as Romans, only in their own fatherland, and only so long as the latter remained unconquered and on the contrary conquering other countries because of the special protection of their national gods. And they did not wonder and did not hold it their right or duty to revolt when, having been vanquished, they themselves fell into slavery.[15]

Christian Freedom. It was the great merit of Christianity that it proclaimed the humanity of all human beings, including that of women, and the equality of all men before God. Yet how was it proclaimed? In the sky, in the future life, but not for the existing real life upon earth. Besides, this equality to come constitutes a falsehood because, as we know, the number of the elect is greatly restricted. On this point all the theologians of the various Christian sects are in full agreement. Accordingly, the so-called Christian equality entails the most flagrant privilege on the part of the several thousands elected by Divine Grace over the millions of the damned. For that matter, the equality of all before God, even if it were all-inclusive to embrace everyone, would only be equality of nothingness, and equal slavery of all before a supreme master.[16]

And is not the basis of the Christian cult and the first condition of salvation the renunciation of human dignity and the cultivation of contempt for this dignity in the presence of Divine Grandeur? A Christian then is not a man, in the sense that he lacks the consciousness of his humanity, and because, not respecting human dignity in himself, he cannot respect it in others; and not respecting it in others, he cannot respect it in himself. A Christian can be a prophet, a saint, a priest, a king, a general, a minister, a State functionary, a representative of some authority, a gendarme, an executioner, a nobleman, an exploiting bourgeois, an enthralled proletarian, an oppressor or one of the oppressed, a torturer or one of the tortured, an employer or a hired man, but he has no right to call himself man, for one becomes a man only when he respects and loves the humanity and liberty of everyone else and when his own freedom and his humanity are respected, loved, stimulated, and created by all others.[17]

Freedom of Individual Increased and Not Limited by Freedom of All. I am free only when all human beings surrounding me—men and women alike—are equally free. The freedom of others, far from limiting or negating my liberty, is on the contrary its necessary condition and confirmation. I become free in the true sense only by virtue of the liberty of others, so much so that the greater the number of free people surrounding me and the deeper and greater and more extensive their liberty, the deeper and larger becomes my liberty.

On the contrary, it is the slavery of men that sets up a barrier to my liberty, or (which practically amounts to the same) it is their bestiality which constitutes a negation of my humanity because, I repeat again, I can call myself a truly free person only when my freedom or, (which is the same) my human dignity, my human right, the essence of which is to obey no one and to follow only the guidance of my own ideas—when this freedom, reflected by the equally free consciousness of all men, comes back to me confirmed by everybody's assent. My personal freedom, thus confirmed by the freedom of everyone else, extends to infinity.

The Constituent Elements of Freedom. We can see then that freedom, as understood by materialists, is something very positive, very complex, and above all eminently social, since it can be realized only by society and only under conditions of strict equality and solidarity of each person with all his fellows. One can distinguish in it three phases of development, three elements, the first of which is highly positive and social. It is the full development and the full enjoyment by everyone of all the faculties and human powers through the means of education, scientific upbringing, and material prosperity, and all that can be given to everyone only by collective labor, and by the material and mental, muscular, and nervous labor of society as a whole.[18]

Rebellion the Second Element of Liberty. The second element or phase of liberty is negative in character. It is the element of *revolt* on the part of the human individual against all divine and human authority, collective and individual. It is first of all a revolt against the tyranny of the supreme phantom of theology, against God. . . .

. . . Following that and coming as a consequence of the revolt against God, there is the revolt against the tyranny of man, against authority, individual as well as collective, represented and legalized by the State.[19]

The Implication of the Theory of the Pre-Social Existence of Individual Freedom. But if the metaphysicians affirm that men, especially those who believe in the immortality of the soul, stand outside of the society of free beings, we inevitably arrive at the conclusion that men can unite in a society only at the cost of their own liberty, their natural independence, and by sacrificing first their personal and their local interests. Such self-renunciation and self-sacrifice are thus all the more imperative the more numerous society is in point of membership and the greater the complexity of its organization. In this sense the State is the expression of all the individual sacrifices. Given this abstract and at the same time violent origin, the State has to restrict liberty to an ever greater extent, doing it in the name of a falsehood called "the good of the people," which in reality represents exclusively the interests of the dominant class. Thus the State appears as an inevitable negation and annihilation of all liberty, of all individual and collective interests.[20]

Freedom the Ultimate Aim of Human Development. But we who believe neither in God nor in the immortality of the soul, nor in the freedom of will, we maintain that liberty should be understood in its larger connotation as the goal of the historic progress of humanity. By a strange, although logical contrast, our adversaries, the idealists of theology and metaphysics, take the principle of liberty as the foundation and the starting point of their theories, to deduce from it the indispensability of slavery for all men. We, materialists in theory, aim in practice to create and consolidate a rational and noble idealism. Our enemies, the divine and transcendental idealists, sink into a practical bloody, and vile materialism, impelled by the same logic according to which every development is the negation of the basic principle.

We are convinced that all the wealth and all the intellectual, moral, and material development of man, as well as the degree of independence he already has attained—that all this is the product of life in society. Outside of society, man would not only fail to be free; he would not even grow to the stature of a true man, that is, a being aware of himself and who feels and has the power of speech. It was only the intercourse of minds and collective labor that forced man out of the stage of being a savage and a brute, which constituted his original nature, or the starting point of his ultimate development.[21]

Freedom and Socialism Are Mutually Complementary. *The serious realization of liberty, justice, and peace will be impossible so long as the vast majority of the population remains dispossessed in point of elementary needs, so long as it is deprived of education and is condemned to political and social insignificance and slavery—in fact if not by law—by the poverty as well as the necessity of working without rest or leisure, producing all the wealth, upon which the world now prides itself, and receiving in return only such a small part thereof that it hardly suffices to assure [the worker's] bread for the next day; . . . we are convinced that freedom without Socialism is privilege and injustice, and that Socialism without freedom is slavery and brutality.*[22]

It is characteristic of privilege and of every privileged position to kill the minds and hearts of men. The privileged man, whether politically or economically, is a mentally and morally depraved man. That is a social law which admits of no exception and which holds good in relation to whole nations as well as to classes, groups, and individuals. It is the law of equality, the supreme condition of freedom and humanity.[23]

Socialism and Equality. Much as one may resort to all kinds of subterfuges, much as one may try to obscure the issue, and to falsify social science for the benefit of bourgeois exploitation, all sensible people who have no interest in deceiving themselves, now understand that so long as a certain number of people possessing economic privileges have the means to lead a life which is beyond the reach of the workers; that so long as a more or less considerable number inherit, in various proportions, capital and land which is not the product of their own labor, while on the other hand the vast majority of workers do not inherit anything at all; so long as land rent and interest on capital enable those privileged people to live without working—so long as such a state of things exists, equality is inconceivable.

Even assuming that everyone in society works—whether by compulsion or by free choice—but that one class in society, thanks to its economic situation and enjoying as a result thereof special political and social priv-ileges, can devote itself exclusively to mental work, while the vast majority of people struggle hard for a bare living; in a word, so long as individuals on coming into life do not find in society the same means of livelihood, the same education, upbringing, work, and enjoyment—political, economic, and social equality will be impossible.

It was in the name of equality that the bourgeoisie overthrew and massacred the nobility. And it is in the name of equality that we now demand either the violent death or the voluntary suicide of the bourgeoisie, only with this difference—that being less bloodthirsty than the bour-geoisie of the revolutionary period, we do not want the death of men but the abolition of positions and things. If the bourgeoisie resigns itself to the inevitable changes, not a hair on its head will be touched. But so much the worse for it, if, forgetting prudence and sacrificing its individual interests to the collective interests of its class, a class doomed to extinction, it places itself athwart the course of the historic justice of the people, in order to save a position which will soon become utterly untenable.[24]

The Nature of True Freedom. I am a fanatical lover of freedom, viewing it as the only milieu in the midst of which the intelligence, dignity, and happiness of men can grow; but not of that formal liberty, vouchsafed, measured, and regulated by the State, which is an eternal falsehood and which in reality represents only the privilege of the select few based upon the slavery of the rest; and not of that individualist, egoistic, jejune, and fictitious liberty proclaimed by Jean Jacques Rousseau as well as by all the other schools of bourgeois liberalism, which regard the so-called public right represented by the State as being the limit of the right of everyone, which necessarily and always results in the whittling down of the right of everyone to the zero point.

No, I have in mind the only liberty worthy of that name, liberty consisting in the full development of all the material, intellectual, and moral powers latent in every man; a liberty which does not recognize any other restrictions but those which are traced by the laws of our own nature, which, properly speaking, is tantamount to saying that there are no restrictions at all, since these laws are not imposed upon us by some out-side legislator standing above us or alongside us. Those laws are imminent, inherent in us; they constitute the very basis of our being, material as well as intellectual and moral; and instead of finding in them a limit to our liberty we should regard them as its real conditions and as its effective reason.[25]

I have in mind this liberty of everyone which, far from finding itself checked by the freedom of others, is, on the contrary, confirmed by it and extended to infinity. And I have in mind the freedom of every individual unlimited by the freedom of all, freedom in solidarity, freedom in equality, freedom triumphing over brute force and the principle of authority (which was ever the ideal expression of this force); a freedom which, having over-thrown all the heavenly and earthly idols, will have founded and organized a new world, the world of human solidarity, upon the ruins of all the churches and states.[26]

I am a convinced partisan *of economic and social equality* because I know that outside of this equality, freedom, justice, human dignity, morality, and the well-being of individuals as well as the flourishing of nations, are a lie.[27]

We already have said that by freedom we understand on one hand the development, as complete as possible, of all the natural faculties of every individual, and on the other hand his independence not in relation to natural and social laws, but in relation to all laws imposed by other human wills, whether collective or isolated.[28]

We understand by freedom, from the positive point of view, the development, as complete as possible, of all faculties which man has within himself, and, from the negative point of view, the independence of the will of everyone from the will of others.[29]

We are convinced—and modern history fully confirms our conviction—that so long as humanity is divided into an exploiting minority and an exploited majority, freedom is impossible, becoming instead a falsehood. If you want freedom for all, you must strive together with us to attain universal equality.[30]

How Can Freedom and Equality Be Assured? Do you want to make it impossible for anyone to oppress his fellow-man? Then make sure that no one shall possess power. Do you want men to respect the liberty, rights, and personality of their fellows? Make sure that they shall be compelled to respect them, *forced not by the will nor by the oppressive action of other men, and not by the repression of the State and its laws, necessarily represented and applied by men,* which in turn makes slaves of them, but by the very organization of social environment—an organization so constituted that by affording everyone the fullest enjoyment of his liberty, it does not permit anyone to rise above others nor dominate them in any way but through the natural influence of the intellectual and moral qualities which he possesses, *without this influence ever being imposed as a right and without leaning upon any political institution whatever.*[31]

CHAPTER 2 *Federalism: Real and Sham*

Is Municipal Self-Government a Sufficient Counter-Balance for a Centralized State? The illustrious Italian patriot Joseph Mazzini . . . maintains that autonomy of the communes is quite sufficient to counterbalance the omnipotence of a solidily built republic. But he is mistaken about that: no isolated commune would be capable of resisting such a formidable centralization; it would be crushed by it. In order not to succumb in this struggle, each commune will have to combine with neighboring communes in a federation with a view to common defense; that is, it will have to form together with them an autonomous province. Besides, if the provinces are not autonomous, they will have to be governed by State-appointed functionaries. There is no midway between a rigorously consistent federalism and a bureaucratic regime. . . . In 1793, under the regime of terror, the autonomy of communes was recognized, but that did not prevent their being crushed by the revolutionary despotism of the Convention or rather of the Commune of Paris, of which Napoleon was the heir.[1]

Organic Social Unity Versus State Unity. Mazzini and all the advocates of unity place themselves in a contradictory position when on one hand they tell you of the deep, intimate, brotherly feeling existing among this group of twenty-five millions of Italians, united by language, traditions, morals, faith, and common aspirations, while on the other hand they want to maintain—nay, to augment—the power of the State, which, they say, is necessary for the preservation of that unity. But if the Italians are so effectively and indissolubly linked by ties of solidarity, it would be a luxury and even sheer nonsense to force them into a union. If, on the contrary, you believe it necessary to force them to unite, it simply shows that you are convinced that the natural bonds are not so strong, and that you lie to them, that you wish to mislead them when you talk of union.

A social union, the real outcome of a combination of traditions, habits, customs, ideas, present interests, and common aspirations, is a living, fertile, real unity. The political unity of the State is a fiction, an abstraction of unity; and not only does it conceal discord, but it artificially produces such discord where, without this intervention by the State, a living unity would not fail to spring up.[2]

Socialism Must Be Federalistic in Character. That is why Socialism is federalistic in character and why the International as a whole enthusiastically hailed the program of the Paris Commune.* On the other hand, the Commune proclaimed explicitly in its manifestoes that what it wanted was not the dissolution of the national unity of France but its resurrection, its consolidation, its revival, and real and full liberty for the people. It wanted the unity of the nation, of the people, of French society, but not the unity of the State.

Medieval and Modern Communes. Mazzini, in his hatred of the Paris Commune, has gone to the extreme of sheer foolishness. He maintains that the system proclaimed by the last revolution in Paris would lead us back

---

* This refers to the Commune of 1871, and is not to be confused with the Commune of 1793, cited earlier in this chapter.

to the medieval ages, that is, to the breaking up of the civilized world into a number of small centers, foreign to and ignoring one another. He does not understand, poor fellow, that between the commune of the Middle Ages and the modern commune there is the vast difference which the history of the last five centuries wrought not just in books but in the morals, aspirations, ideas, interests, and needs of the population. The Italian communes were, at the beginning of their history, really isolated centers of social and political life, independent of one another, lacking any solidarity, and forced into a certain kind of self-sufficiency.

How different that was from what is in existence today! The material, intellectual, and moral interests created among all the members of the same nation—nay, even of different nations—a social unity of so powerful and real a nature that whatever is being done now by the States to paralyze and destroy such unity is of no avail. That unity resists everything and it will survive the States.[3]

The Living Unity of the Future. When the States have disappeared, a living, fertile, beneficent unity of regions as well as of nations—first the international unity of the civilized world and then the unity of all of the peoples of the earth, by way of a free federation and organization from below upward—will unfold itself in all its majesty, not divine but human.[4]

The patriotic movement of the Italian youth under the direction of Garibaldi and Mazzini was legitimate, useful, and glorious; not because it created political unity, the unified Italian State—on the contrary, that was its mistake, for it could not create that unity without sacrificing the liberty and prosperity of the people—but because it destroyed the various political centers of domination, the different States which violently and artificially obstructed the social unification of the Italian people.

That glorious work having been accomplished, the youth of Italy is called upon to perform an even more glorious task. That is to aid the Italian people in destroying the unitary State which it founded with its own hands. It [the youth of Italy] should oppose to the unitary banner of Mazzini the federal banner of the Italian nation, of the Italian people.

Real and Sham Federalism. One has to distinguish between federalism and federalism.

There exists in Italy the tradition of a regional federalism, which by now has become a political and historical falsehood. Let us say once for all, the past will never come back; it would be a great misfortune if it were revived. Regional federalism could be only an institution of the merging aristocratic and plutocratic classes (*consorteria*), for, in relation to the communes and workers' associations—industrial and agricultural—it would still be a political organization built from the top downward. A truly popular organization begins, on the contrary, from below, from the association, from the commune. Thus, starting out with the organization of the lowest nucleus and proceeding upward, federalism becomes a political institution of Socialism, the free and spontaneous organization of popular life.[5]

In conformity with sentiment unanimously expressed at the first Congress of the League for Peace and Freedom [held in Geneva, Switzerland, in September, 1867], we now declare:

The Principle of Federalism. 1. There is only one way of insuring the triumph of freedom, justice, and peace in the international relations of Europe, of rendering impossible any civil war among peoples comprising the European family, and that is: *by building up a United States of Europe.*

2. The United States of Europe can never be formed out of the present European States, in view of the monstrous inequality existing among their respective forces.

3. The example of the defunct German Confederation proved in a peremptory manner that a confederation of monarchies is a mockery, that it is powerless to guarantee peace and liberty to the populations.[6]

4. No centralized, bureaucratic, military State, even if it calls itself republican, can seriously and sincerely enter into an international confederation. By its constitution, which will always be a negation of freedom within the State, either open or masked, it will necessarily be a permanent war declaration, a standing menace to the existence of the neighboring countries. Based essentially upon a preceding act of violence, upon conquest, or what in private life is called burglary—an act blessed by the Church, consecrated by time, and therefore transformed into a historic right, and resting upon this divine consecration of a triumphant violence as an exclusive and supreme right—every centralized State thereby poses itself as an absolute negation of the rights of all other States, recognizing them in the treaties it concludes only in view of some political interest or owing to its impotence.

5. All the adherents of the League should direct their efforts to rebuild their respective countries, in order to replace the old organization, founded from above downward upon violence and the principle of authority, by a new organization having no other foundation but the interests, needs, and natural affinities of the population, and admitting no other principle but the free federation of individuals into communes, of communes into provinces, of provinces into nations, and finally, of nations into the United States of Europe and then into the United States of the World.

6. Consequently, the absolute abandonment of all that is called the historic rights of the States; all questions relating to natural, political, strategic, and commercial boundaries should henceforth be considered as belonging to ancient history and be vigorously rejected by League adherents.[7]

7. Recognition of the absolute right of every nation, small or large, of every people, weak or strong, and of every province, of every commune, to a complete autonomy, provided the internal constitution of any

such unit is not in the nature of a menace to the autonomy and freedom of its neighbors.

8. Because a certain country constitutes a part of some State, even if it joined that State of its own free will, it does not follow that it is under obligation to remain forever attached to that State. No perpetual obligation can be admitted by human justice, the only justice which we recognize as having authority with us, and we will never recognize any duties that are not founded upon freedom. The right of free reunion, as well as the right of secession, is the first and most important of all political rights; lacking that right, a confederation would simply be disguised centralization. . . .[8]

12. The League recognizes *nationality* as a natural fact, having the incontestable right to exist and to develop freely, but it does not recognize it as a *principle*—for every principle should possess the character of universality, whereas nationality, on the contrary, is an exclusive and isolated fact. The so-called *principle of nationalities*, such as has been posed in our day by the governments of France, Russia, and Prussia, and even by many German, Polish, Italian, and Hungarian patriots, is only a derivative of reaction and is opposed to the spirit of revolution. A highly aristocratic principle at heart, going so far as to despise the local dialects of the illiterate population, implicitly denying the liberty of the provinces and the real autonomy of the communes, and lacking the support of the masses whose real interests it sacrifices for the sake of the so-called public good, this principle expresses only the pretended historic rights and ambitions of the States. Thus the right of nationality can be considered only as the natural result of the supreme principle of liberty, ceasing to be a right from the moment it is posed against or even outside of liberty.[9]

13. Unity is the goal toward which humanity irresistibly tends. But it becomes fatal and destructive of the intelligence, dignity, and prosperity of individuals and peoples whenever it is formed by excluding liberty, whether by violence or by the authority of any theological, metaphysical, political, or even economic ideas. . . . The League can recognize only one kind of unity: that which is freely constituted by the federation of the autonomous parties into a single whole, so that the latter, no longer being the negation of rights and particular interests, and ceasing to be the cemetery wherein all the local prosperities are interred, will become, on the contrary, the source and the confirmation of all these autonomies and all these prosperities. The League shall then vigorously attack every religious, political, economic, and social organization which is not permeated by this great principle of liberty. Without that principle there can be neither enlightenment, nor prosperity, nor justice, nor humanity.[10]

Such then are the developments and the necessary consequences of the great principle of federalism. Such are the necessary conditions of peace and freedom. The necessary conditions, yes—but the only ones? We do not think so.[11]

. . . The abolition of every political State, the transformation of the political federation into an economic, national, and international federation. It is toward this aim that Europe as a whole is now marching.[12]

The Federalism of the Southern States Was Based Upon a Hideous Social Reality. The Southern States, in the great republican confederation of North America, were, from the time of the proclamation of independence by the American republic, pre-eminently democratic and federalist States, going to the length of clamoring for secession. And still they have, of late, drawn upon themselves the condemnation of all partisans of liberty and humanity, and by their iniquitous and sacrilegious war against the republican States of the North, they nearly succeeded in overthrowing and destroying the finest political organization that mankind has ever known.

What is the main cause behind this strange fact? Is it a political cause? No, the cause is wholly social in character. The internal political organization of the Southern States was in many respects more perfect, more completely in harmony with the ideal of liberty than the political organization of the Northern States. But this magnificent political structure *had its dark side*, like the republics of antiquity: *the freedom of citizens was founded upon the forced labor of slaves.*[13]

The Stirrings of Equality Produced by the French Revolution. From the time when the Revolution brought down to the masses its Gospel— not the mystic but the rational, not the heavenly but the earthly, not the divine but the human Gospel, the Gospel of the Rights of Man—and after it proclaimed that all men are equal, and that all men are entitled to liberty and equality—the masses of . . . all the civilized world, awakening gradually from the sleep which had kept them in bondage ever since Christianity drugged them with its opium, began to ask themselves whether they too had the right to equality, freedom, and humanity.

Socialism—the Explicit Expression of the Hopes Raised by the French Revolution. As soon as this question was posed, the people, guided by their admirable sound sense as well as by their instincts, realized that the first condition of their real emancipation, or of their *humanization*, must be a radical change in their economic situation. The question of daily bread was, justly, the first question to them, for, as Aristotle noted, man, in order to think, to feel himself free, and to become a man, must be freed from the preoccupations of the material life. For that matter, the bourgeois, who are so vociferous in their outcries against the materialism of the people and who preach to the latter the abstinences of idealism, know it very well, for they themselves preach it by word and not by example.

The second question arising for the people is that of leisure after work, an indispensable condition for humanity; but bread and leisure can never be obtained apart from a radical transformation of society, and that explains why the Revolution, driven on by the implications of its own principle, *gave birth to Socialism.*[14]

CHAPTER 3 *State Socialism Theories Weighed*

Babeuf: the Link Between the French Revolution and Socialism.
The French Revolution, having proclaimed the right and the duty of
every human individual to become *a man,* arrived in its ultimate conclusions at Babeuvism. Babeuf, one of the last energetic and pure-hearted
citizens whom the Revolution created and then killed off in such a great
number, and who had the good fortune to count among his friends such
men as Buonarotti, combined in a singular conception the political tradition of antiquity with the altogether modern ideas of a social revolution.

Seeing that the Revolution was failing for lack of a radical change,
which, in all probability, was then impossible in view of the economic
structure of that period (and faithful, on the other hand, to the spirit of
the Revolution, which ended by substituting the omnipotent action of
the State for all individual initiative), he had conceived a political and
social system, according to which the Republic—the expression of the
collective will of the citizens—after having confiscated all individual
property, was to administer it in the interest of all, allotting to everyone
in equal shares: education, instruction, the means of existence, and pleasures,
and compelling all, without exception, in the measure of each one's
capacity, to do physical or mental labor.

Babeuf's conspiracy failed, and he was guillotined with some of his
friends. But his ideal of a Socialist republic did not die with him. Taken
up by his friend, Buonarotti, the greatest conspirator of this century, that
idea was transmitted by the latter as a sacred trust to new generations, and,
owing to the secret societies which he founded in Belgium and France,
Communist ideas blossomed forth in the popular imagination. From 1830
to 1848 they found capable interpreters in the persons of Cabet and Louis
Blanc, who definitively established revolutionary Socialism.[1]

Doctrinaire Socialism.   Another Socialist current, issuing from the
same revolutionary source, and tending toward the same goal, but by
altogether different means, a current which we should gladly call doctrinaire *Socialism,* was founded by two eminent men: Saint-Simon and
Fourier. Saint-Simonism was expounded, developed, transformed, and
established as a quasi-practical system, as a Church, by "Father" Enfantin,
together with many of his friends, most of whom [later] became financiers
and statesmen, singularly devoted to the empire. Fourierism found its
exponent in *Démocratie Pacifique* [Peaceful Democracy], edited until
December 2, 1852, by Victor Considerant.[2]

The Historic Role of Saint-Simonism and Fourierism. The merits of those two systems, differing from each other in many respects, consist mainly in the profound, scientific, and severe criticism of the present system, the monstrous contradictions of which they boldly uncovered, and in the important fact that they attacked and shook Christianity in the name of rehabilitation of matter and human passions, calumniated and at the same time so widely practiced by Christian priests.

The Saint-Simonians wanted to replace Christianity with a new religion, based upon the mystic cult of the flesh, with a new hierarchy of priests, new exploiters of the multitude by the privilege of genius, ability, and talent. The Fourierists, democrats to a much greater extent—and one might say, more sincerely democratic—conceived their phalansteries as being governed and administered by chiefs elected through universal suffrage, and in which, they believed, each would find the kind of work and kind of place most suitable to his natural passions. The fallacies of the Saint-Simonians are too evident to be discussed here.

The two-fold error of the Fourierists consisted, first, in believing sincerely that through the power of persuasion and peaceful propaganda they would be able to touch the hearts of the rich to such an extent that the latter would come themselves and lay down the surpluses of their riches at the doors of their phalansteries; and their second error was that they imagined it would be possible to construct theoretically, *a priori*, a social paradise in which humanity would settle down forever. They did not understand that all we can do now is to indicate the great principles of the development of humanity, and that we should leave it to . . . future generations to carry those principles into practice.

In general, regimentation was the common passion of all the Socialists, except one, prior to 1848. Cabet, Louis Blanc, the Fourierists, the Saint-Simonians—all these were possessed by the passion to indoctrinate and to organize the future; all of them were authoritarians to a greater or lesser extent.

Proudhon. But then came Proudhon: the son of a peasant, and, by his works and instinct, a hundred times more revolutionary than all the doctrinaire and bourgeois Socialists, he equipped himself with a critical point of view, as ruthless as it was profound and penetrating, in order to destroy all their systems. Opposing liberty to authority, he boldly proclaimed himself an Anarchist by way of setting forth his ideas in contradistinction to those of the State Socialists, and, in the face of their deism or pantheism, he had the courage simply to declare himself an atheist, or rather a *positivist*, like Auguste Comte.[3]

Proudhon's Socialism,—based upon individual and collective freedom and upon the spontaneous actions of free associations, and obeying no other laws but the general laws of the social economy, those that already had been discovered or would be discovered in the future; a Socialism functioning outside of any governmental regulation and all State protection, and subordinating politics to the economic, intellectual, and moral interests of society—that kind of Socialism was bound in the course of time to arrive at Federalism.[4]

Such was the state of social science prior to 1848. The polemics voiced through newspapers, leaflets, and Socialist pamphlets carried a multitude of new ideas into the midst of the working class; the latter became permeated with those ideas toward 1848, and when the revolution broke out in that year, Socialism emerged as a powerful force.[5]

The June Defeat of the Workers of Paris Was the Defeat of State Socialism, But Not of Socialism in General. It was not Socialism in general that succumbed in June, 1848, but only *State Socialism*, the authoritarian, regimenting Socialism which hoped and believed that the State would be able to satisfy the needs and the legitimate aspirations of the working class, and that, armed with full and unlimited power, it would be desirous and capable of inaugurating a new social order. Thus it was not Socialism that died in the month of June; on the contrary, it was the State that went bankrupt. Proclaiming itself incapable of paying the debt which it had contracted toward Socialism, the State attempted to kill the latter to rid itself in this easy manner of the debt it had incurred.

The State did not succeed in destroying Socialism, but it did kill the faith in the State entertained by Socialism. By this very act the State annihilated the theories of authoritarian or doctrinaire Socialism, some of which, like Cabet's *Icaria* and Louis Blanc's *The Organization of Labor*, counseled the people to repose full confidence in the State, while others demonstrated their absurdity by a number of ridiculous experiments. Even Proudhoun's bank, which might have prospered under more favorable circumstances, succumbed under the crushing weight of the universal hostility of the bourgeois.

Why Socialism Lost Out in the Revolution of 1848. Socialism lost this first battle for a very simple reason: It was full of instinctive drives and negative ideas, it was a thousand times right when it fought against privilege. But it still lacked positive and practical ideas necessary to build a new system, a system of popular justice, upon the ruins of the bourgeois system. The workers who fought in June for the emancipation of the people, were united by instinct and not by ideas—the ideas which they did have formed a veritable tower of Babel, a chaos from which nothing could come out. Such was the principal cause of their defeat. Should one on that account doubt the present and future power of Socialism? Christianity, which set for itself the task of founding the Kingdom of Justice in Heaven, needed several centuries to conquer Europe. Is it to be wondered then that Socialism, which set for itself a more difficult task—the founding of the Kingdom of Justice upon the earth—has not triumphed in a few years?[6]

The Ruined Petty Bourgeois Will Be Swept into the Social Struggle Under the Leadership of the Proletariat. . . . At the present time the petty bourgeoisie, small industry, and petty trade begin to suffer almost as much as the working masses, and, if things continue moving in the same direction and at the same rate, this respectable bourgeois majority will, in all probability, soon merge with the proletariat. Large-scale commerce, big industry, and above all, big and dishonest speculation, crush the petty bourgeoisie, devour, and push it toward the abyss. Thus the position of the petty bourgeoisie becomes more and more revolutionary, and its ideas, which have been reactionary until now, must take an opposite direction. The most intelligent of its members begin to understand that no other salvation remains for the honest bourgeoisie but to ally themselves with the people—and that the petty bourgeoisie is interested in the social problem no less than and *in the same manner* as the people.[7]

This progressive change in the climate of opinion among the petty bourgeoisie in Europe is a fact as consoling as it is indisputable. We should not, however, entertain any illusions on that score: *the initiative in this new development will belong to the people and not to the petty bourgeoisie; in the West, to the factory and city workers; and in Russia, Poland, and most of the Slavic countries, to the peasants.* The petty bourgeoisie has become too cowardly, too timid, too skeptical, to take any initiative whatever; it lets itself be carried away, but it does not show initiative in this respect, for it is poverty-stricken in regard to ideas to the same extent that it lacks faith and social passion. The passion which sweeps away all obstacles and creates new worlds can be found now only among the people. Therefore it is with the people that the initiative of this new movement will belong in the future.[8]

The Party of Reaction and the Party of Social Revolution. In our time, everywhere—in America, and throughout Europe, as well as in Russia—there exist only two serious, truly strong parties: the *Party of Reaction*, embracing the whole world of State and class privilege and resting upon personal, inheritable property and the resulting exploitation of the people's toil, resting upon divine right, family authority, and State law, and the *Party of Social Revolution*, which steadfastly aims at the final annihilation of this decrepit, criminal world, in order to build upon its ruins a world in which no special privilege will exist, a world based upon common labor obligatory for all, upon free human right, and upon human truth illuminated by science.[9]

Thus, without hesitation, we include in the hostile party of reaction not only outspoken reactionaries and Jesuits, but likewise Liberal Constitutionalists and also the Radical Party—the party of political republicans.

Bourgeois Socialism. Let us turn now to the Socialists, who also divide into three essentially different parties. First of all, we shall divide them into two categories: the party of peaceful or bourgeois Socialists, and the party of Social Revolutionists. The latter is in turn subdivided into revolutionary State Socialists and revolutionary Anarchist-Socialists, the enemies of every State and every State principle.[10]

The party of peaceful bourgeois Socialists or, political social Jesuits, belongs by its essence to the party of reaction. It comprises men of various political categories, who are flirting with Socialism only with the view of strengthening their own party. There are conservatives who are Socialists, there are Socialist priests, and liberal and radical Socialists. All of them recognize in Socialism a formidable rising force, and every one of them pulls it in his direction, hoping with its aid to restore the sinking and decrepit vitality of his respective party.

Among the great number of these malicious exploiters of Socialism are to be found, here and there, sincere and well-meaning people who really want to see an improvement in the lot of the proletariat, but who lack sufficient energy of mind and will to place before themselves the social problem in all its formidable reality, in order to recognize the absolute irreconcilability of the past with the future or even the present day with the morrow, and who waste their days in vain, idle efforts to reconcile those contradictions. They are sincere, it is true, but their sincerity causes great harm, covering up the insincerity of the malicious exploiters of Socialism.[11]

The peaceful Socialists of all denominations agree upon one essential point which determines quite concretely their reactionary trend and dooms even the most sincere among them to merge sooner or later with the party of deliberate and conscious reaction—that is, if they do not prefer to throw in their lot beforehand with the party of revolutionary Socialism.[12]

Class Ties Stronger Than Convictions With Bourgeois Socialists. *Life dominates thought and determines the will.* Here is a truth which should never be lost sight of whenever we want to get our bearings in the realm of political and social phenomena. If we want to establish a sincere and complete community of thought among men, we must found it upon the same conditions of life, upon a community of interests. And since, by the very conditions of their respective existence, there exists a gulf between the bourgeois and the proletarian worlds, one being the exploiting and the other the exploited world, I conclude that if a man, born and raised in a bourgeois environment, wishes sincerely and without any phrase-mongering to become a friend and brother of the workers, he must renounce all the conditions of his past existence, all his bourgeois habits, break off all ties of feelings, vanity, and mind which bind him to the bourgeois world, and, turning his back upon the latter, becoming its enemy and declaring relentless war upon it, plunge completely and unreservedly into the workers' world.[13]

If he does not find within himself a passion for justice sufficiently strong to inspire this resolution and courage, let him in that case not deceive himself and let him not deceive the workers: he will never become their friend. His abstract thoughts, his dreams of justice, may carry him away to the point of joining the cause with the exploited in moments of reflection, in moments of theoretic contemplation and calm when nothing is stirring, when quiet reigns in the world of exploiters. But let there come a moment of great social crisis when those two worlds opposed to each other meet in a supreme struggle—and all the bonds tying him to his present life inevitably will pull him back into the world of exploiters. This already has happened to many of our former friends and always will happen to the bourgeois republicans and Socialists.[14]

The Intermediary Group of Socialists.   In between the reactionary majority and the small minority of people wholly and sincerely devoted to the cause of freedom for the people, there is in the world of State and class privilege a category of persons, quite considerable in number and in the deleterious influence which it has exercised upon the toiling people. This category embraces all those who have devoted themselves, with their minds and hearts, to the cause of the people, but who, by their social position, by the material political advantages accruing from that position, and by their habits, and social and family ties, belong to a world which is dead set against that cause.

Those are unfortunate individuals, but they are harmful nevertheless. Fooling themselves and the masses of people by the candor of their aspirations, and apparently motivated by a genuine love for the people, the best of them, obeying the iron law, according to which the social position of a given person outweighs as a determining factor his subjective wishes, they serve the cause of reaction, without even being aware of it, as it happens quite often, ever mouthing phrases conveying their alleged interest in the people's weal and the people's emancipation. It is such persons that crowd the ranks of the parties of political republicans and bourgeois Socialists, and also the ranks of the party of *social-revolutionary dictatorship or the social-revolutionary State.*[15]

Danger of the State Cult Among Socialists.   Men belonging to this category, by joining the International, may become really dangerous to it. Like true demagogues, they aim to abolish the existing States only in order to create a new form of State—that is, domination, if not for the benefit of their material interests, at least for the gratification of their ambition and vanity, and incidentally resulting in perceptible material benefits. Those persons are dangerous because they carry with them the masses of the people, conniving at the same time at a dangerous passion and a dangerous prejudice on the part of the latter: the passion for revenge which makes the people seek, to its own detriment, self-satisfaction, emancipation, and salvation in the wholesale annihilation of persons but not of things, not of the regimes which constitute the power of the individuals belonging to the State and class hierarchy, whose moral degeneration can be laid directly at the door of this social order.

The dangerous prejudice on the part of the people consists in the bias, unfortunately deep-seated, in favor of *a strong State power*—of the people, of course, and not of a class hierarchy—as if the official power of the State can ever become the power of the people and as if such power is not in itself the unquestionable source and origin of classes and class hierarchy.[16]

The Distinguishing Characteristic of a Bourgeois Socialist. Here is an infallible sign by which workers can discern a sham Socialist, a bourgeois Socialist: If, in speaking to them of revolution, or, if you please, of social transformation, he tells them that a political change *must precede* the economic change; if he denies that both those revolutions have to take place at once, or even that a political revolution should be something else than the immediate and direct carrying out of a full social liquidation —let the workers turn their back upon him, for he is nothing but a fool, or a hypocritical exploiter.[17]

One cannot really be a "free thinker" without being at the same time a Socialist in the larger sense of the word; it is ridiculous to talk about "free thought" and at the same time to aspire toward a unitary, authoritarian, and bourgeois republic.[18]

CHAPTER 4 *Criticism of Marxism*

Not only are we averse to the idea of persuading our Slav brothers to join the ranks of the Social-Democratic party of German workers, headed by the duumvirate invested with dictatorial power—Marx and Engels— followed by Bebel, Liebknecht, and a few Jewish litterateurs. On the contrary, we shall use all efforts to turn the Slavic proletariat away from a suicidal union with that party, which, by its tendency, aims, and means, is not a folk party, but a purely bourgeois party, and is in addition a German party, that is, anti-Slavic.[1]

The Fallacious Premise of the Doctrinaire Revolutionists. Idealists of all sorts, metaphysicians, positivists, those who uphold the priority of science over life, the doctrinaire revolutionists—all of them champion, with equal zeal although differing in their argumentation, the idea of the State and State power, seeing in them, quite logically from their point of view, the only salvation of society. *Quite logically*, I say, having taken as their basis the tenet—a fallacious tenet in our opinion—that thought is prior to life, and abstract theory is prior to social practice, and that therefore sociological science must become the starting point for social upheavals and social reconstruction—they necessarily arrived at the conclusion that since thought, theory, and science are, for the present at least, the property of only a very few people, those few should direct social life, and not only foment and stimulate but rule all movements of the people; and that on the morrow of the Revolution the new social organization should be set up not by the free integration of workers' associations, villages, communes, and regions from below upward, conforming to the needs and instincts of the people, but solely by the dictatorial power of this learned minority, allegedly expressing the general will of the people.[2]

The Common Ground of the Theory of Revolutionary Dictatorship and the Theory of the State. It is upon this fiction of people's representation and upon the actual fact of the masses of people being ruled by a small handful of privileged individuals elected, or for that matter not even elected, by throngs herded together on election day and ever ignorant of why and whom they elect; it is upon this fictitious and abstract expression of the fancied general will and thought of the people, of which the living and real people have not the slightest conception—that the theory of the State and that of revolutionary dictatorship are based in equal measure.

Between revolutionary dictatorship and the State principle the difference is only in the external situation. In substance both are one and the same: the ruling of the majority by the minority in the name of the alleged stupidity of the first and the alleged superior intelligence of the second. Therefore both are equally reactionary, both having as their result the invariable consolidation of the political and economic privileges of the ruling minority and the political and economic enslavement of the masses of people.[3]

Doctrinaire Socialists Are the Friends of the State. Now it is clear why the doctrinaire Socialists who have for their aim the overthrow of the existing authorities and regimes in order to build upon the ruins of the latter a dictatorship of their own, never were and never will be enemies of the State, but on the contrary that they were and ever will be its zealous champions. They are enemies of the powers-that-be only because they cannot take their places. They are enemies of the existing political institutions because such institutions preclude the possibility of carrying out their own dictatorship, but they are at the same time the most ardent friends of State power, without which the Revolution, by freeing the toiling masses, would deprive this would-be revolutionary minority of all hope of putting the people into a new harness and heap upon them the blessings of their governmental measures.[4]

This is true to such an extent that at the present time, when reaction is triumphing all over Europe, when all the States, moved by the wicked spirit of self-preservation and oppression, clad in the triple armor of military, police, and financial power, and getting ready, under the supreme leadership of Prince Bismarck to wage a desperate struggle against social revolution; when all sincere revolutionists should, as it seems proper to us, unite in order to repulse the desperate assaults of international reaction, we see, on the contrary, that the doctrinaire revolutionists, under the leadership of Marx, are ever taking the side of the State protagonists against the people's revolution.[5]

Lassalle's Program.   No one, outside of Lassalle, could explain and prove so convincingly to the German workers that under the given economic conditions of today the situation of the proletariat not only cannot be radically changed, but, on the contrary, by virtue of inevitable economic law, it must and will become worse every year, notwithstanding the efforts of the co-operatives, which can benefit only a small number of workers and only for a very brief period.

Thus far we agree with Lassalle. But from this point on, we begin to differ with him. As against Schulze-Delitzsch, who advised the workers to seek salvation only through their own energy and not to expect nor demand anything from the State, Lassalle, having proved, first, that under the economic conditions of today the workers cannot expect even the mitigation of their lot, and second, that so long as the bourgeois State exists, bourgeois privileges will remain impregnable—having proved that, he arrived at the following conclusion: in order to attain freedom, real freedom, based upon economic equality, *the proletariat must capture the State* and turn the power of the State against the bourgeoisie for the benefit of the workers, in the same manner in which this power is now turned against the workers by the bourgeoisie for the benefit of the exploiting class.[6]

Socialism Via Peaceful Reform.   How is the proletariat to capture the State? There are but two means available for that purpose: a political revolution or a lawful agitation on behalf of a peaceful reform. Lassalle chose the second course.

In this sense, and for that purpose, he formed a political party of German workers possessing considerable strength, having organized it along hierarchical lines and submitted it to rigorous discipline and to a sort of personal dictatorship; in other words, he did what M. Marx had tried to do to the International during the last three years. Marx's attempt proved to be a failure, while Lassalle was wholly successful. As his direct aim Lassalle set himself the task of impelling a popular movement and agitation for the winning of universal suffrage, for the right of the people to elect State representatives and authorities.

Having won this right, the people would send their own representatives to the Parliament, which in turn, by various decrees and enactments, would transform the given State into a People's State (*Volks-Staat*). And the first task of this People's State would be to open unlimited credit to the producers' and consumers' associations, which only then will be able to combat bourgeois capital, finally succeeding in conquering and assimilating it. When this process of absorption has been completed, then the period of the radical change of society will dawn upon mankind.[7]

The Fiction of the People's State.   Such is the program of Lassalle, such is the program of the Social-Democratic Party. Properly speaking, it belongs not to Lassalle but to Marx, who fully expressed it in the well-known *Manifesto of the Communist Party* published by Marx and Engels in 1848. This program is likewise alluded to in the first *Manifesto of the International Association* written by Marx in 1864, in the words: "The first duty of the working class should be to conquer for itself political power," or as the *Manifesto of the Communist Party* says in that respect: "The first step in the revolution by the working class, is to raise the proletariat to the position of a ruling class. . . . The proletariat will centralize the instruments of production in the hands of the State, that is, the proletariat raised to the position of a ruling class."[8]

We already have expressed our abhorrence for the theories of Lassalle and Marx, theories which counseled the workers—if not as their ultimate ideal, at least as their next chief aim—*to form a People's State*, which, according to their interpretation, will only be "the proletariat raised to the position of a ruling class."[9]

. . . But the State connotes domination, and domination connotes exploitation, which proves that the term *the People's State* (*Volks-Staat*), which unfortunately still remains the watchword of the German Social-Democratic Party, is a ridiculous contradiction, a fiction, a falsehood—doubtless an unconscious falsehood—and for the proletariat a very dangerous pitfall. The State, however popular it be made in form, will always be an institution of domination and exploitation, and it will therefore ever remain a permanent source of slavery and misery. Consequently there is no other means of emancipating the people economically and politically, of providing them with well-being and freedom, but to abolish the State, all States, and once and for all do away with that which until now has been called *politics*.[10]

The Implication of the Dictatorship of the Proletariat.   One may ask then: if the proletariat is to be the ruling class, over whom will it rule? The answer is that there will remain another proletariat which will be subjected to this new domination, this new State. It may be, for example, the peasant "rabble," which, as we know, does not stand in great favor with the Marxists, and who, finding themselves on a lower level of culture, probably will be ruled by the city and factory proletariat; or considered from the national point of view, the Slavs, for instance, will assume, for precisely the same reason, the same position of slavish subjection to the victorious German proletariat which the latter now holds with respect to its own bourgeoisie.[11]

If there is a State, there must necessarily be domination, and therefore slavery; a State without slavery, overt or concealed, is unthinkable—and that is why we are enemies of the State.

What does it mean: "the proletariat raised into a ruling class?" Will the proletariat as a whole be at the head of the government? There are about forty million Germans. Will all the forty million be members of the government? The whole people will govern and there will be no one to be governed. It means that there will be no government, no State, but if there is a State in existence there will be people who are governed, and there will be slaves.

This dilemma is solved very simply in the Marxist theory. By a people's government they mean the governing of people by means of a small number of representatives elected by the people. Universal suffrage—the right of the whole people to elect its so-called representatives and rulers of the State—this is the last word of the Marxists as well as of the demo-cratic school. And this is a falsehood behind which lurks the despotism of a governing minority, a falsehood which is all the more dangerous in that it appears as the ostensible expression of a people's will.[12]

Thus, from whatever angle we approach the problem, we arrive at the same sorry result: the rule of great masses of people by a small privileged minority. But, the Marxists say, this minority will consist of workers. Yes, indeed, of *ex-workers*, who, once they become rulers or representatives of the people, cease to be workers and begin to look down upon the toiling people. From that time on they represent not the people but themselves and their own claims to govern the people. Those who doubt this know precious little about human nature.[13]

Dictatorship Cannot Beget Freedom. But these elected representa-tives will be convinced Socialists, and learned Socialists at that. The words "learned Socialist" and scientific Socialism" which are met with con-stantly in the works and speeches of the Lassalleans and Marxists, prove only that this would-be people's State will be nothing else but despotic rule over the toiling masses by a new, numerically small aristocracy of genuine or sham scientists. The people lack learning and so they will be freed from the cares of government, will be wholly regimented into one common herd of governed people. Emancipation indeed!

The Marxists are aware of this contradiction, and, realizing that gov-ernment by scientists (the most distressing, offensive, and despicable type of government in the world) will be, notwithstanding its democratic form, a veritable dictatorship,—console themselves with the thought that this dictatorship will be only temporary and of brief duration. They say that the only care and aim of this government will be to educate and uplift the people—economically and politically—to such an extent that no government will be necessary, and that the State, having lost its political character, that is, its character of rule and domination, will turn all by itself into an altogether free organization of economic interests and communes.[14]

Here we have an obvious contradiction. If their State is going to be a genuine people's State, why should it then dissolve itself—and if its rule is necessary for the real emancipation of the people, how dare they call it a people's State? Our polemic had the effect of making them realize that freedom or Anarchism, that is, the free organization of workers from below upward, is the ultimate aim of social development, and that every State, their own people's State included, is a yoke, which means that it begets despotism on one hand and slavery on the other.[15]

They say that this State yoke—the dictatorship—is a necessary transitional means in order to attain the emancipation of the people: Anarchism or freedom is the goal, the State or dictatorship is the means. Thus to free the working masses, it is first necessary to enslave them.

That is as far as our polemic went. They maintain that only a dictatorship—their dictatorship, of course—can create the will of the people, while our answer to this is: No dictatorship can have any other aim but that of self-perpetuation, and it can beget only slavery in the people tolerating it; freedom can be created only by freedom, that is, by a universal rebellion on the part of the people and free organization of the toiling masses from the bottom up.

Powerfully Centralized State the Goal of the Marxists. While the political and social theory of the anti-State Socialists or Anarchists leads them steadily toward a full break with all governments, and with all varieties of bourgeois policy, leaving no other way out but a social revolution, the opposite theory of the State Communists and scientific authority also inevitably draws and enmeshes its partisans, under the pretext of political tactics, into ceaseless compromises with governments and political parties; that is, it pushes them toward downright reaction.[16]

The basic point of Lassalle's politico-social program and the Communist theory of Marx is *the (imaginary) emancipation of the proletariat by means of the State*. But for that it is necessary that the State consent to take upon itself the task of emancipating the proletariat from the yoke of bourgeois capital. How can the State be imbued with such a will? There are only two means whereby that can be done.

The proletariat ought to wage a revolution in order to capture the State—a rather heroic undertaking. And in our opinion, once the proletariat captures the State, it should immediately proceed with its destruction as the everlasting prison for the toiling masses. Yet according to the theory of M. Marx, the people not only should not destroy the State but should strengthen and reinforce it, and transfer it in this form into the hands of its benefactors, guardians, and teachers, the chiefs of the Communist Party

—in a word, to M. Marx and his friends, who will begin to emancipate it in their own fashion.

They will concentrate all the powers of government in strong hands, because the very fact that the people are ignorant necessitates strong, solicitous care by the government. They will create a single State bank, concentrating in its hands all the commercial, industrial, agricultural, and even scientific production; and they will divide the mass of people into two armies—industrial and agricultural armies under the direct command of the State engineers who will constitute the new privileged scientific-political class.

One can see then what a shining goal the German Communist school has set up before the people.[17]

CHAPTER 5 *Social-Democratic Program Examined*

The Workers' Social-Democratic Party and the General Association of German Workers founded by Lassalle are both Socialist organizations in the sense that they want a socialist reform in the relations between capital and labor. The Lassalleans, as well as the party of Eisenach, are unanimous on that point—that in order to obtain this reform, *it is necessary first to reform the State*, and that if this cannot be achieved in a peaceful manner, by means of extensive propaganda and a peaceful, legal labor movement, then force should be resorted to in order to bring about State reform—in other words, the change is to be effected through a political revolution.

According to the almost unanimous view of the German Socialists, *a political revolution should precede a social revolution*, which in my opinion is a great and fatal error, because every political revolution taking place prior to and consequently without a social revolution must necessarily be a bourgeois revolution, and a bourgeois revolution can only be instrumental in bringing about bourgeois Socialism—that is, it is bound to end in a new, more hypocritical and more skilful, but no less oppressive, exploitation of the proletariat by the bourgeoisie.[1]

This unfortunate idea of a political revolution which, so the German Socialists say, is to precede the Social Revolution, opens wide the door of the Workers' Social-Democratic Party to all the exclusively political radical democrats of Germany who have very little Socialism in them. Thus it has happened that on several occasions the Workers' Social-Democratic Party was prevailed upon by its leaders—not by its own collective instinct, which is socialistic to a much greater degree than the ideas of its leaders—to fraternize with the bourgeois democrats of the People's Party (*Volkspartei*), an exclusively political party which is not only foreign but downright hostile to any serious Socialism.[2]

The Program of the Eisenach Congress. During the whole year, from August, 1868, to August, 1869, diplomatic relations were carried on between the chief representatives of both the workers' and bourgeois parties, the final result of those negotiations being the famous program of the Eisenach Congress (August 7-9, 1869), at which the Workers' Social-Democratic Party constituted itself as such. This program was a true compromise between the socialist and revolutionary program of the International Workingmen's Association, so clearly set forth at the Brussels and Basel Congresses, and the well known program of bourgeois democratism.[3]

Article I of this program strikes us first of all because of its utter disagreement with both the text and the spirit of the International Association's basic program. The Social-Democratic Party wants to institute a free people's State. Those words—*free* and *people's*—sound well, but the third word, *State*, does not ring true to the ears of a real revolutionary Socialist, a resolute and sincere enemy of all bourgeois institutions with no exception; it is in flagrant contradiction to the very aim of the International Association, and it takes all meaning out of the words *free* and *people's*.[4]

The International Workingmen's Association implies the negation of the State, every State necessarily being a *national* State. Or do the authors of the program understand by it an international State, a universal State, or, in a more restricted sense, a State embracing all the countries of Western Europe, where there exists (using the favorite expression of the German Social-Democrats) "modern society or civilization," that is, a society wherein capital, which has become the sole owner of labor, is concentrated in the hands of a privileged class, the bourgeoisie, reducing the workers to poverty and slavery? Or do the Social-Democratic Party leaders aim to set up a State which would embrace all western Europe: England, France, Germany, all the Scandinavian countries, all the Slavic countries subject to Austria, Belgium, Holland, Switzerland, Italy, Spain, and Portugal?[5]

No, their imagination and political appetite do not embrace so many countries at once. All they want now, with a passion which they do not even take the trouble to conceal, is the organization of their *German fatherland*, of a great pan-German unity. It is the setting up of *an exclusively German* State that the first article of their program poses as the principal and supreme goal of the *workers'* democratic *socialistic* party. They are political patriots above everything else.

Where then does their internationalism come in? What do these *German patriots* have to offer to the international brotherhood of workers of all countries? Nothing but socialist phrases having no possibility of realization, phrases belied by the principal, exclusively political basis of their program—*the German State*.[6]

Indeed, since the German workers are to aim above all at the setting up of a German State, the solidarity which should, from the point of view of their economic and social interests, unite them with their brothers, the exploited workers of the whole world, and which should, in my opinion, be the principal and only basis for workers' associations in all countries— this international solidarity is necessarily sacrificed to patriotism, to the national passion. It may therefore happen that the workers of a certain country, divided between two loyalties, between two contradictory tend- encies—*the socialist solidarity of labor and the political patriotism of the national State*—and sacrificing (as, for that matter, they must if they obey the first article of the German Social-Democratic Party), sacrificing, as I said, international solidarity to patriotism, the workers may find themselves in the rather unfortunate position of having to unite themselves with their own bourgeoisie against the workers of a foreign State. And this is pre- cisely what has happened to the German workers at the present moment.[7]

Loyalty to National State Incompatible With Socialism. It is clear that so long as the goal of the German workers consists in setting up a national State, no matter how free or how much of a people's State they imagine it to be—and there is quite a distance between imagining those things and carrying them out, especially when that imagination presup- poses an impossible reconciliation of two elements, of two principles mutu- ally canceling each other (the State and the freedom of the people)—it is clear that they will ever continue to sacrifice the liberty of the people to the greatness of the State, Socialism to politics, and justice and international brotherhood to patriotism. It is clear that their own economic emancipa- tion will remain a beautiful dream relegated to the far-off future.[8]

It is impossible to attain simultaneously two contradictory ends. Since Socialism and social revolution imply destruction of the State, it is clear that those who aim to set up a State must renounce Socialism and must sacrifice the economic emancipation of the masses to the political might of some privileged party.

The German Social-Democratic Party has to sacrifice the economic emancipation, and consequently the political emancipation of the prole- tariat—*or rather its emancipation from politics*—to the ambition and the triumph of bourgeois democracy. This follows plainly from the second and third articles of the program of the Social-Democratic Party.

The first paragraphs of Article 2 are in full agreement with the social- istic principle of the International Workingmen's Association, whose pro- gram they almost literally reproduce. But the fourth paragraph of the same article, declaring that political liberty is the *preliminary* condition of economic emancipation, completely destroys the practical value of this recognition in principle. It can only signify the following:

"Workers, you are the slaves, the victims, of property and capital. You wish to free yourselves from this economic yoke. Very well, your wishes are completely legitimate. But in order to realize them, *you must first help us to effect a political revolution. Later on, we will help you to wage the Social Revolution.* Let us first establish, with your strength, a democratic State, a good bourgeois democracy, as in Switzerland, and then—then we will give you the same kind of prosperity that the workers enjoy in Switzerland." (Observe, for instance, the strikes in Geneva and Basel.[9])

In order to convince oneself that this incredible delusion fully expresses the tendencies and the spirit of the German social democracy (of the program and not the natural aspirations of the German workers comprising that party) one has only to study Article 3, which enumerates *all the immediate* and "next" demands (*die nächsten Forderungen*) to be put forth by the party in its peaceful and legal campaign agitation.

All these demands, except the tenth, which was not even suggested by the authors of the program, but was added during the discussion provoked by a motion introduced by a member of the Eisenach Congress—all those demands have an exclusively political character. All the clauses recommended as the principal objects of the immediate practical action of the party amount to nothing but the well-known program of bourgeois democracy—universal suffrage, with direct legislation by the people; abolition of all political privileges; arming of the nation; separation of the Church from the State, and the School from the Church; free and compulsory education; freedom of press, association, assembly, and coalition; and converting all indirect taxes into a single, direct and progressive income tax.[10]

This then constitutes for the present the veritable object, the real aim of this party: an exclusively political reform of the State, of the institutions and laws of the State. Was I not right in saying that this program is socialistic only so far as its dreams of a far away future are concerned, and that in reality it is nothing but a purely political and bourgeois program? And would I not be right in saying also that, were the Social-Democratic Party of the German workers to be judged by this program —which I would never do, knowing that the genuine aspirations of the German workers go much beyond it—we should have the right to think that the aim pursued in creating this party was that of making use of the working masses as a blind tool for attaining the political objectives of the German bourgeois democracy?[11]

Protection of Labor and State Credit to Co-operatives. This program has only two planks which will not be to the liking of the bourgeoisie. The first is contained in the second half of the eighth paragraph, Article 3, which demands the establishing of *a normal working day, the abolition of child labor,* and *the limitation of women's work,* three things at the mention of which the bourgeois make wry faces, because, being passionate lovers of all liberties which they can turn to their own advantage, they loudly demand for the proletariat freedom to let itself be exploited, and freedom to oppress and overwhelm it with work without the State having the right to interfere. However, times have become so difficult for our poor capitalists that they have finally agreed to such State intervention even in England, the social organization of which is, so far as I know, far from being socialistic.[12]

Another plank, even more important and of a more definitely socialistic character, is contained in the tenth paragraph of Article 3, . . . which demands State assistance and State credit for workers' co-operation, and especially for producers' associations, with all the desirable guarantees of freedom.

No bourgeois will accept this plank of his own free will, it being in absolute contradiction to what bourgeois democracy and bourgeois Socialism call freedom—in reality, the freedom to exploit the proletariat, which is compelled to sell its labor to capital at the lowest price, compelled not by any political or civil law whatever, but by the economic situation in which it finds itself through fear and terror of starvation.

This freedom, I say, does not fear the competition of workers' associations—neither consumers', producers', nor mutual credit associations—for the simple reason that workers' organizations, left to their own resources, will never be able to accumulate sufficiently strong aggregations of capital capable of waging an effective struggle against bourgeois capital. Yet when workers' associations are supported by the power of the State, when they are backed by the credit of the State, not only will they be able to fight, but, in the long run, they will be able to vanquish the industrial and commercial enterprises of the bourgeoisie, founded only with private capital—whether individual or collective capital, represented by joint-stock companies—the State, of course, being the strongest of all such companies.[13]

Labor financed by the State—such is the fundamental principle of *authoritarian Communism*, of State Socialism. The State, *having become the sole proprietor,*—at the end of a certain period of transition necessary to have society pass, without any severe economic or political shocks, from the present organization of bourgeois privilege to the future organization of official equality for all—the State also will have become the sole capitalist, banker, money-lender, organizer, director of all national work, and the distributor of its profits. Such is the ideal, the fundamental principle of modern Communism.[14]

Political and Social Revolution Must Go Together. We should ruthlessly eliminate the politics of bourgeois democrats or bourgeois Socialists who, in declaring that "political liberty is the *preliminary* condition of economic emancipation," understand by those words only the following: "Political reforms, or a political revolution, must precede economic reforms or an economic revolution; therefore the workers must ally themselves with the more or less radical bourgeois in order to carry out a political revolution together with the bourgeoisie, and then wage an economic revolution against the latter."

We loudly protest against this baneful theory, which can end only with the workers being used once more as an instrument against themselves and being turned over again to bourgeois exploitation.[15]

To win political freedom first can signify no other thing but to win this freedom only, leaving for the first days at least economic and social relations in the same old state,—that is, leaving the proprietors and capitalists with their insolent wealth, and the workers with their poverty.[16]

But, it is argued, this freedom, once won, shall serve the workers later as an instrument with which to win *equality* or *economic justice*.

Freedom is indeed a magnificent and powerful instrument. The question, however, is whether workers really can make use of it, whether it will actually be in their possession, or whether, as has been the case until now, their *political liberty* will prove to be only a deceitful appearance, a mere fiction.[17]

CHAPTER 6 *Stateless Socialism: Anarchism*

Effect of the Great Principles Proclaimed by the French Revolution. From the time when the Revolution brought down to the masses its Gospel —not the mystic but the rational, not the heavenly but the earthly, not the divine but the human Gospel, the Gospel of the Rights of Man—ever since it proclaimed that all men are equal, that all men are entitled to liberty and equality, the masses of all European countries, of all the civilized world, awakening gradually from the sleep which had kept them in bondage ever since Christianity drugged them with its opium, began to ask themselves whether they too, had the right to equality, freedom, and humanity.

As soon as this question was posed, the people, guided by their admirable sound sense as well as by their instincts, realized that the first condition of their real emancipation, or of their *humanization*, was above all a radical change in their economic situation. The question of daily bread is to them justly the first question, for as it was noted by Aristotle, man, in order to think, in order to feel himself free, in order to become man, must be freed from the material cares of daily life. For that matter, the bourgeois, who are so vociferous in their outcries against the materialism of the people and who preach to the latter the abstinences of idealism, know it very well, for they themselves preach it only by word and not by example.

The second question arising before the people—that of leisure after work—is the indispensable condition of humanity. But bread and leisure can never be obtained apart from a radical transformation of existing society, and that explains why the Revolution, impelled by the implications of its own principles, gave birth to Socialism.[1]

Socialism Is Justice.   . . . Socialism is *justice*. When we speak of justice, we understand thereby not the justice contained in the Codes and in Roman jurisprudence—which were based to a great extent upon facts of violence achieved by force, violence consecrated by time and by the benedictions of some church or other (Christian or pagan), and as such accepted as absolute principles, from which all law is to be deduced by a process of logical reasoning—no, we speak of that justice which is based solely upon human conscience, the justice to be found in the consciousness of every man—even in that of children—and which can be expressed in a single word: *equity*.

This universal justice which, owing to conquests by force and religious influences, has never yet prevailed in the political or juridical or economic worlds, should become the basis of the new world. Without it there can be neither liberty, nor republic, nor prosperity, nor peace. It then must govern our resolutions in order that we work effectively toward the establishment of peace. And this justice urges us to take upon ourselves the defense of the interests of the terribly maltreated people and demand their economic and social emancipation along with political freedom.

The Basic Principle of Socialism.   We do not propose here, gentlemen, this or any other socialist system. What we demand now is the proclaiming anew of the great principle of the French Revolution: that *every human being should have the material and moral means to develop all his humanity*, a principle which, in our opinion, is to be translated into the following problem:

To organize society in such a manner that every individual, man or woman, should find, upon entering life, approximately equal means for the development of his or her diverse faculties and their utilization in his or her work. And to organize such a society that, rendering impossible the exploitation of anyone's labor, will enable every individual to enjoy the social wealth, which in reality is produced only by collective labor, but to enjoy it only in so far as he contributes directly toward the creation of that wealth.

State Socialism Rejected.   The carrying out of this task will of course take centuries of development. But history has already brought it forth and henceforth we cannot ignore it without condemning ourselves to utter impotence. We hasten to add here that we vigorously reject any attempt at social organization which would not admit the fullest liberty of individuals and organizations, or which would require the setting up of any regimenting power whatever. In the name of freedom, which we recognize as the only foundation and the only creative principle of any organization, economic or political, we shall protest against anything even remotely resembling State Communism, or State Socialism.[2]

Abolition of the Inheritance Law.   The only thing which, in our opinion, the State can and should do, is first to modify little by little the inheritance law so as to arrive as soon as possible at its complete abolition. That law being purely a creation of the State, and one of the essential conditions of the very existence of the authoritarian and divine State, it can and should be abolished by freedom in the State. In other words, the State should dissolve itself into a society freely organized in accordance with the principles of justice. Inheritance right, in our opinion, should be abolished, for so long as it exists there will be hereditary economic inequality, not the natural inequality of individuals, but the artificial man-made inequality of classes—and the latter will always beget hereditary inequality in the development and shaping of minds, continuing to be the source and consecration of all political and social inequalities.

The task of justice is to establish equality for everyone, inasmuch as that equality will depend upon the economic and political organization of society—an equality with which everyone is going to begin his life, so that everyone, guided by his own nature, will be the product of his own efforts. In our opinion, the property of the deceased should accrue to a social fund for the instruction and education of children of both sexes, including their maintenance from birth until they come of age. As Slavs and as Russians, we shall add that with us the fundamental social idea, based upon the general and traditional instinct of our populations, is that land, the property of all the people, should be owned only by those who cultivate it with their own hands.[3]

We are convinced, gentlemen, that this principle is just, that it is the essential and inevitable condition of all serious social reform, and that consequently Western Europe in turn will not fail to recognize and accept this principle, notwithstanding the difficulties of its realization in some countries, as in France, for instance, where the majority of peasants own the land which they cultivate, but where most of those very peasants will soon end up by owning next to nothing, owing to the parceling out of land coming as the inevitable result of the political and economic system now prevailing in France. We shall, however, refrain from offering any proposals on the land question. . . . We shall confine ourselves now to proposing the following declaration:

The Declaration of Socialism.   "Convinced that the serious realization of liberty, justice, and peace will be impossible so long as the vast majority of the population remains dispossessed of elementary needs, so long as it is deprived of education and is condemned to political and social insignificance and slavery—in fact if not by law—by poverty as well as by the necessity of working without rest or leisure, producing all the wealth upon which the world now prides itself, and receiving in return only such a small part thereof that it hardly suffices to assure its livelihood for the next day;

"Convinced that for all that mass of population, terribly maltreated for centuries, the problem of bread is the problem of mental emancipation, of freedom and humanity;

"Convinced that freedom without Socialism is privilege and injustice, and that Socialism without freedom is slavery and brutality;

"The League [for Peace and Freedom] loudly proclaims the necessity of a radical social and economic reconstruction, having for its aim the emancipation of people's labor from the yoke of capital and property owners, a reconstruction based upon strict justice—neither juridical nor theological nor metaphysical justice, but simply human justice—upon positive science and upon the widest freedom."[4]

Organization of Productive Forces in Place of Political Power. It is necessary to abolish completely, both in principle and in fact, all that which is called political power; for, so long as political power exists, there will be ruler and ruled, masters and slaves, exploiters and exploited. Once abolished, political power should be replaced by an organization of productive forces and economic service.[5]

Notwithstanding the enormous development of modern states—a development which in its ultimate phase is quite logically reducing the State to an absurdity—it is becoming evident that the days of the State and the State principle are numbered. Already we can see approaching the full emancipation of the toiling masses and their free social organization, free from governmental intervention, formed by economic associations of the people and brushing aside all the old State frontiers and national distinctions, and having as its basis only productive labor, humanized labor, having one common interest in spite of its diversity.[6]

The Ideal of the People. This ideal of course appears to the people as signifying first of all the end of want, the end of poverty, and the full satisfaction of all material needs by means of collective labor, equal and obligatory for all, and then, as the end of domination and the free organization of the people's lives in accordance with their needs—not from the top down, as we have it in the State, but from the bottom up, an organization formed by the people themselves, apart from all governments and parliaments, a free union of associations of agricultural and factory workers, of communes, regions, and nations, and finally, in the more remote future, the universal human brotherhood, triumphing above the ruins of all States.[7]

The Program of a Free Society. Outside of the Mazzinian system, which is the system of the republic in the form of a State, there is no other system but that of the republic as a commune, the republic as a federation, a Socialist and a genuine people's republic—the system of Anarchism. It is the politics of the Social Revolution, which aims at the abolition of the State, and the economic, altogether free organization of the people, an organization from below upward, by means of a federation.[8]

. . . There will be no possibility of the existence of a political government, for this government will be transformed into a simple administration of common affairs.[9]

Our program can be summed up in a few words:

Peace, emancipation, and the happiness of the oppressed.

War upon all oppressors and all despoilers.

Full restitution to workers: all the capital, the factories, and all the instruments of work and raw materials to go to the associations, and the land to those who cultivate it with their own hands.

Liberty, justice, and fraternity in regard to all human beings born upon the earth.

Equality for all.

To all, with no distinction whatever, all the means of development, education, and upbringing, and the equal possibility of living while working.[10]

Organizing of a society by means of a free federation from below upward, of workers' associations, industrial as well as agricultural, scientific as well as literary associations—first into a commune, then a federation of communes into regions, of regions into nations, and of nations into an international fraternal association.[11]

Correct Tactics During a Revolution. In a social revolution, which in everything is diametrically opposed to a political revolution, the actions of individuals hardly count at all, whereas the spontaneous action of the masses is everything. All that individuals can do is to clarify, propagate, and work out ideas corresponding to the popular instinct, and, what is more, to contribute their incessant efforts to revolutionary organization of the natural power of the masses—but nothing else beyond that; the rest can and should be done by the people themselves. Any other method would lead to political dictatorship, to the re-emergence of the State, of privileges, of inequalities, of all the oppressions of the State—that is, it would lead in a roundabout but logical way toward re-establishment of political, social, and economic slavery of the masses of people.

Varlin and all his friends, like all sincere Socialists, and in general like all workers born and brought up among the people, shared to a high degree this perfectly legitimate bias against the initiative coming from isolated individuals, against the domination exercised by superior individuals, and being above all consistent, they extended the same prejudice and distrust to their own persons.

Revolution by Decrees Is Doomed to Failure. Contrary to the ideas of the authoritarian Communists, altogether fallacious ideas in my opinion, that the Social Revolution can be decreed and organized by means of a dictatorship or a Constituent Assembly—our friends, the Parisian Socialists, held the opinion that that revolution can be waged and brought to its full development only through the spontaneous and continued mass action of groups and associations of the people.[12]

Our Parisian friends were a thousand times right. For, indeed, there is no mind, much as it may be endowed with the quality of a genius,—or if we speak of a collective dictatorship consisting of several hundred supremely endowed individuals—there is no combination of intellects so vast as to be able to embrace all the infinite multiplicity and diversity of the real interests, aspirations, wills, and needs constituting in their totality the collective will of the people; there is no intellect that can devise a social organization capable of satisfying each and all.

Such an organization would ever be a Procrustean bed into which violence, more or less sanctioned by the State, would force the unfortunate society. But it is this old system of organization based upon force that the Social Revolution should put an end to by giving full liberty to the masses, groups, communes, associations, and even individuals, and by destroying once and for all the historic cause of all violence—the very existence of the State, the fall of which will entail the destruction of all the iniquities of juridical right and all the falsehood of various cults, that right and those cults having ever been simply the complaisant consecration, ideal as well as real, of all violence represented, guaranteed, and authorized by the State.[13]

It is evident that only when the State has ceased to exist humanity will obtain its freedom, and the true interests of society, of all groups, of all local organizations, and likewise all the individuals forming such organization, will find their real satisfaction.[14]

Free Organization to Follow Abolition of the State. Abolition of the State and the Church should be the first and indispensable condition of the real enfranchisement of society. It will be only after this that society can and should begin its own reorganization; that, however, should take place not from the top down, not according to an ideal plan mapped by a few sages or savants, and not by means of decrees issued by some dictatorial power or even by a National Assembly elected by universal suffrage. Such a system, as I have already said, inevitably would lead to the formation of a governmental aristocracy, that is, a class of persons which has nothing in common with the masses of people; and, to be sure, this class would again turn to exploiting and enthralling the masses under the pretext of common welfare or of the salvation of the State.[15]

Freedom Must Go Hand-in-Hand With Equality. I am a convinced partisan of *economic and social equality*, for I know that outside of this equality, freedom, justice, human dignity, morality, and the well-being of individuals as well as the prosperity of nations are all nothing but so many falsehoods. But being at the same time a partisan of freedom—the first condition of humanity—I believe that equality should be established in the world by a spontaneous organization of labor and collective property, by the free organization of producers' associations into communes, and the free federation of communes—but nowise by means of the supreme and tutelary action of the State.

The Difference Between Authoritarian and Libertarian Revolutionists. It is this point which mainly divides the Socialists or revolutionary collectivists from the authoritarian Communists, the partisans of the absolute initiative of the State. The goal of both is the same: both parties want the creation of a new social order based exclusively upon collective labor, under economic conditions that are equal for all—that is, under conditions of collective ownership of the tools of production.

Only the Communists imagine that they can attain through development and organization of the political power of the working classes, and chiefly of the city proletariat, aided by bourgeois radicalism—whereas the revolutionary Socialists, the enemies of all ambiguous alliances, believe, on the contrary, that this common goal can be attained not through the political but through the social (and therefore anti-political) organization and power of the working masses of the cities and villages, including all those who, though belonging by birth to the higher classes, have broken with their past of their own free will, and have openly joined the proletariat and accepted its program.[16]

The Methods of the Communists and the Anarchists. Hence the two different methods. The Communists believe that it is necessary to organize the forces of the workers in order to take possession of the political might of the State. The revolutionary Socialists organize with the view of destroying, or if you prefer a more refined expression, of liquidating the State. The Communists are the partisans of the principle and practice of authority, while revolutionary Socialists place their faith only in freedom. Both are equally the partisans of science, which is to destroy superstition and take the place of faith; but the first want to impose science upon the people, while the revolutionary collectivists try to diffuse science and knowledge among the people, so that the various groups of human society, when convinced by propaganda, may organize and spontaneously combine into federations, in accordance with their natural tendencies and their real interests, but never according to a plan traced in advance and *imposed upon the ignorant masses* by a few "superior" minds.[17]

Revolutionary Socialists believe that there is much more of practical reason and intelligence in the instinctive aspirations and real needs of the masses of people than in the profound minds of all these learned doctors and self-appointed tutors of humanity, who, having before them the sorry examples of so many abortive attempts to make humanity happy, still intend to keep on working in the same direction. But revolutionary Socialists believe, on the contrary, that humanity has permitted itself to be ruled for a long time, much too long, and that the source of its misfortune lies not in this nor in any other form of government but in the principle and the very existence of the government, whatever its nature may be.

It is this difference of opinion, which already has become historic, that now exists between the scientific Communism, developed by the German school and partly accepted by American and English Socialists, and Proudhonism, extensively developed and pushed to its ultimate conclusions, and by now accepted by the proletariat of the Latin countries. Revolutionary Socialism has made its first brilliant and practical appearance in the Paris Commune.[18]

On the Pan-German banner is written: *Retention and strengthening of the State at any cost.* On our banner, the social-revolutionary banner, on the contrary, are inscribed, in fiery and bloody letters: the destruction of all States, the annihilation of bourgeois civilization, free and spontaneous organization from below upward, by means of free associations, the organization of the unbridled rabble of toilers, of all emancipated humanity, and the creation of a new universally human world.[19]

Before creating, or rather aiding the people to create, this new organization, it is necessary to achieve a victory. It is necessary to overthrow that which is, in order to be able to establish that which should be. . . .[20]

CHAPTER 7 *Founding of the Workers' International*

Awakening of Labor on the Eve of the International. In 1863 and 1864, the years of the founding of the International, in nearly all of the countries of Europe, and especially those where modern industry had reached its highest development—in England, France, Belgium, Germany, and Switzerland—two facts made themselves manifest, facts which facilitated and practically made mandatory the creation of the International. The first was the simultaneous awakening in all the countries of the consciousness, courage, and spirit of the workers, following twelve or even fifteen years of a state of depression which came as a result of the terrible debacle of 1848 and 1851. The second fact was that of the marvelous development of the wealth of the bourgeoisie and, as its necessary accompaniment, the poverty of the workers in all the countries. This was the fact which spurred these workers to action, while their awakening consciousness and spirit endowed them with the essential faith.[1]

The Central Sections. But, as it often happens, this renascent faith did not manifest itself at once among the great masses of the European workers. Out of all the countries of Europe there were only two—soon followed by others—in which it made its first appearance. Even in those privileged countries it was not the whole mass but a small number of little, widely scattered workers' associations which felt within themselves the stirrings of a reborn confidence, felt it strongly enough to resume the struggle; and in those associations it was at first a few rare individuals, the more intelligent, the more energetic, the more devoted among them, and in most cases those who already had been tried and developed by previous struggles, and who, full of hope and faith, mustered the courage to take the initiative of starting the new movement.

Those individuals, meeting casually in London in 1864, in connection with the Polish question—a problem of the highest political importance, but one that was completely alien to the question of international solidarity of labor—formed, under the direct influence of the founders of the International, the first nucleus of this great association. Then, having returned to their respective countries—France, Belgium, Germany, and Switzerland—the delegates formed nuclei in those lands. That is how the initial Central Sections (of the International) were set up.[2]

The Central Sections do not represent any special industry, since they comprise the most advanced workers in all kinds of industries. Then what do those sections represent? They represent the idea of the International itself. What is their mission? The development and propagandizing of this idea. And what is this idea? It is the emancipation not only of workers in such and such an industry or in such and such a country, but of all workers in all industries—the emancipation of the workers of all the countries in the world. It is the general emancipation of all those who, earning with difficulty their miserable livelihood by any productive labor whatever, are economically exploited and politically oppressed by capital, or rather by the owners and the privileged brokers of capital.

Such is the negative, militant, or revolutionary power of this idea. And the positive force? It is the founding of a new social world, resting only upon emancipated labor and spontaneously created upon the ruins of the old world, by the organization and the free federation of workers' associations liberated from the economic and political yoke of the privileged classes.[3]

Those two aspects of the same question, one negative and the other positive, are inseparable from each other.[4]

Central Sections Are Mere Ideological Groupings. The Central Sections are the active and living centers where the new faith is preserved, where it develops, and where it is being clarified. No one joins them in the capacity of a special worker of such and such a trade with the view of forming any particular trade union organizations. Those who join those sections are workers in general, having in view the general emancipation and organization of labor, and of the new social world based on labor. The workers comprising the membership of those sections leave behind them their character of special or "real" workers, presenting themselves to the organization as workers "in general." Workers for what? Workers for the idea, the propaganda and organization of the economic and militant might of the International, workers for the Social Revolution.

The Central Sections represent an altogether different character from that of the trade sections, even being diametrically opposed to them. Whereas the latter, following a natural course of development, begin with the fact in order to arrive at the idea, the Central Sections, following, on the contrary, the course of ideal or abstract development, begin with the idea in order to arrive at the fact. It is evident that in contradistinction to the fully realistic or positivist method of the trade sections, the method of the Central Sections appears to be artificial and abstract. This manner of proceeding from the idea to the fact is precisely the one used by the idealists of all schools, theologians, and metaphysicians, whose final impotence has by now become a matter of historical record. The secret of this impotence lies in the absolute impossibility of arriving at the real and concrete fact by taking the absolute idea as the starting point.[5]

The Central Sections in Themselves Would be Powerless to Draw in Great Masses of Workers. If the International Workingmen's Association were made up only of Central Sections, undoubtedly it would never attain even one hundredth part of the impressive power upon which it is priding itself now. Those sections would be merely so many workers' academies where all questions would perpetually be discussed, including of course the question of organization of labor, but without the slightest attempt being made to carry it into practice, nor even having the possibility of doing it. . . .[6]

. . . If the International were made up only of Central Sections, the latter probably would have succeeded by now in forming conspiracies for the overthrow of the present order of things; but such conspiracies would be confined only to mere intentions, being too impotent to attain their goal since they would never be able to draw in more than a very small number of workers—the most intelligent, most energetic, most convinced and devoted among them. The vast majority, the millions of proletarians, would remain outside of those conspiracies, but in order to overthrow and destroy the political and social order which now crushes us, it would be necessary to have the co-operation of those millions.

The Empirical Approach of Workers to Their Problems. Only individuals, and a small number of them at that, can be carried away by an abstract and "pure" idea. The millions, the masses, not only of the proletariat but also of the enlightened and privileged classes, are carried away only by the power and logic of "facts," apprehending and envisaging most of the time only their immediate interests or moved only by their monetary, more or less blind, passions. Therefore, in order to interest and draw the whole proletariat into the work of the International, it is necessary to approach it not with general and abstract ideas, but with a living and tangible comprehension of its own pressing problems, of which evils those workers are aware in a concrete manner.

Their daily tribulations, although presenting to a social thinker a problem of a general character and being actually only the particular effects of general and permanent causes, are in reality infinitely diverse, taking on a multitude of different aspects, produced by a multitude of transitory and contributory causes. Such is the daily reality of those evils. But the mass of workers who are forced to live from hand to mouth and who find hardly a moment of leisure in which to think of the next day, apprehend the evils from which they suffer precisely and exclusively in the context of this particular reality but never or scarcely ever in their general aspect.[7]

Concrete Statement Offers the Only Effective Approach to the Great Mass of Workers. It follows then that in order to touch the heart and gain the confidence, the assent, the adhesion, and the co-operation of the illiterate legions of the proletariat—and the vast majority of proletarians unfortunately still belong in this category—it is necessary to begin to speak to those workers not of the general sufferings of the international proletariat as a whole, but of their particular, daily, altogether private misfortunes. It is necessary to speak to them of their own trade and the conditions of their work in the specific locality where they live; of the harsh conditions and long hours of their daily work, of the small pay, the meanness of their employer, the high cost of living, and how impossible it is for them properly to support and bring up a family.

And in laying before them the means to combat those evils and to better their position, it is not necessary at all to speak to them at first of the general and revolutionary means which now constitute the program of action of the International Workingmen's Association, such as the abolition of individual hereditary property and the collectivization of property, the abolition of the juridical right and that of the State, and their replacement by the organization and free federation of producers' associations. The workers, in all probability, would hardly understand all that. It also is possible that, finding themselves under the influence of the religious, political, and social ideas which governments and priests have tried to implant in their minds, they will turn away in anger and distrust from any imprudent propagandist who tries to convert them by using such arguments.

No, they should be approached only by way of holding up before them such means of struggle the usefulness of which they cannot fail to comprehend, and which they are prone to accept upon the promptings of their good sense and daily experience. Those first elementary means are, as we already have said, the establishing of complete solidarity with their fellow-workers in the shop, in their own defense and in the struggle against their common master; and then the extension of this solidarity to all workers in the same trade and in the same locality in their joint struggle against the employers—that is, their formal entrance as active members into the section of their trade, a section affiliated with the International Working-men's Association.[8]

The economic fact, the conditions in a special industry and the particular conditions of exploitation of that industry by capital, the intimate and particular solidarity of interests, of needs, sufferings, and aspirations which exist among all workers who are members of the same trade section—all that forms the real basis of their association. The idea comes afterward as the explanation or the adequate expression of the development and the mental reflection of this fact in the collective consciousness.

Solidarity of Trade Union Members Rooted in Actuality. A worker does not need any great intellectual preparation to become a member of the trade union section [of the International] representing his trade. He is a member of it, in quite a natural way, before even being aware of it. All he has to know is that he is being worked to death and that this killing work, so poorly paid that he has hardly enough to provide for his family, enriches his employer, which means that the latter is his ruthless exploiter, his tireless oppressor, his enemy, his master, toward whom he owes no other feeling but that of hate and the rebelliousness of a slave, to give place much later, after he has vanquished the employer in the final struggle, to a sense of justice and a feeling of brotherhood toward the former employer, as one who is now a free man.

The worker also must realize—and this is not difficult for him to understand—that by himself he is powerless against his master and that to prevent his being utterly crushed by the latter, he must first unite with his fellow-workers in the shop, and be loyal to them in all the struggles arising there against the master.[9]

Internationalism Growing Out of Actual Experiences of Proletarian Struggles. He also must know that merely a union of workers in the same shop is not sufficient, that it is necessary that all the workers in the same trade employed in the same locality should unite. Once he realizes this—and if he is not exceedingly stupid, his daily experience will teach him as much as that—he consciously becomes a devoted member of his corporative section. The latter already exists as a matter of fact, but it is still devoid of international consciousness, it is still only a local fact. The same experience, at this time collective, will soon overcome in the consciousness of the least intelligent worker the narrow limits of exclusively local solidarity.

There comes a crisis, a strike. The workers in a certain locality belonging to the same trade make common cause, demanding from their employers a wage increase or a reduction of hours of work. The employers do not want to grant those demands; and since they cannot do without workers, they bring them from other localities or other provinces of the same country or even from foreign countries. But in those countries the workers work longer hours for less pay; and the employers there can sell their products cheaper, successfully competing against countries where workers working less earn more, and thus force the employers in the latter countries to cut wages and increase the hours of their workers.

Hence it follows that in the long run the relatively tolerable position of the workers in one country can be maintained only on condition that it be more or less the same in other countries. All this repeats itself too often to escape the attention of even the most simple-minded workers. Then they come to realize that in order to protect themselves against the ever-growing exploitation by the employers, it is not enough to organize solidarity on a local scale, but that it is necessary to unite the workers of the same trade not in one province only—and not even in just one country —but in all countries, and above all in those countries which are interlinked by commercial and industrial ties. When the workers come to realize all this, then an organization will be formed, not only on a local nor even on a national scale, but a truly international organization embracing all the workers in a given trade.[10]

But this is not yet an organization of workers in general, it is only an international organization of a single trade. And in order that non-educated workers realize and recognize the actual solidarity existing among all the trade unions of all the countries of the world, it is necessary that the other workers, intellectually more developed than the rest and having some knowledge of economic science, should come to their aid. Not that the ordinary worker lacks daily experience in that respect, but the economic phenomena through which this solidarity manifests itself are exceedingly complex, so that their true meaning may be above the comprehension of the unenlightened worker.[11]

If we assume that international solidarity has been established in a single trade while lacking in the others, it follows that in this organized industry wages will be higher and hours of work shorter than in all other industries. And it having been proven that because of the competition of employers and capitalists, the source of real profits of both is the comparatively low wages and the long hours imposed upon workers, it is clear that in the industry in which the workers are organized along international lines, the capitalists and the employers will earn less than in all the others, as a result of which the capitalists will gradually transfer their capital and credit, and the employers their exploiting activity, into the less organized or altogether unorganized branches of industry.

This will necessarily lead to a falling off in the demand for labor in the internationally organized industry, which will naturally result in a worsening of the situation of the workers in that industry, who will have to accept lower wages in order not to starve. Hence it follows that conditions of labor cannot get worse or better in any particular industry without immediately affecting the workers in other industries, and that workers of all trades are interlinked with real and indissoluble ties of solidarity.[12]

Internationalism Issues from the Living Experiences of the Proletariat. This solidarity has been proven by science as well as by experience—science for that matter being simply universal experience, clearly expressed, systematically and properly explained. But solidarity manifests itself in the workers' world by a mutual, profound, and passionate sympathy, which, —in a measure that economic factors and their political and social consequences keep on developing, factors telling more and more distressingly upon the workers of all trades—grows and becomes ever more of an intense passion with the proletariat.

The workers in every trade and in every country,—owing on one hand to the material and moral support which in the course of their struggle they find among workers in other trades and other countries, and on the other hand, because of the condemnation and the systematic, hate-breathing opposition with which they meet not only from their own employers but also from employers in other, even very remote industries, and from the bourgeoisie as a whole—become fully aware of their situation and the principal conditions necessary to their emancipation. They see that the social world is in reality divided into three main categories: 1. The countless millions of exploited workers; 2. A few hundred thousand second- or third-rank exploiters; 3. A few thousand, or, at the most, a few tens of thousands of the larger beasts of prey, big capitalists who have grown fat on directly exploiting the second category and indirectly the first category, pocketing at least half the profits obtained from the collective labor of humanity.[13]

As soon as the worker takes note of this special and abiding fact, he must soon realize, backward though he may be in his development, that if there is any means of salvation for him, it must lie along the lines of establishing and organizing the closest practical solidarity among the proletarians of the whole world, regardless of industries, or countries, in their struggle against the exploiting bourgeoisie.

The Necessary Historic Premises of the International. Here then is the ready framework of the International Workingmen's Association. It was given to us not by a theory born in the head of one or several profound thinkers, but by the actual development of economic facts, by the hard trials to which those facts subject the working masses, and the reflections, the thoughts, which they naturally engender in the minds of the workers.

That the International Association could come into existence it was necessary that the elements involved in its making—the economic factors, the experience, strivings, and thoughts of the proletariat—should already have been developed strongly enough to form a solid base for it. It was

necessary that there already should have been, in the midst of the proletariat, groups or associations of sufficiently advanced workers who, scattered throughout the world, could take upon themselves the initiative of
the great emancipatory movement of the workers. Following that comes,
of course, the personal initiative of a few intelligent individuals fully
devoted to the cause of the people.[14]

It is not enough that the working masses come to realize that international solidarity is the only means of their emancipation; it also is necessary that they have faith in the real efficacy and certainty of this means
of salvation, that they have faith in the possibility of their impending
deliverance. This faith is a matter of temperament, collective disposition,
and mental state. Temperament is given to various peoples by nature,
but it is subject to historic development. The collective disposition of
the proletarian is always a two-fold product: first, of all preceding events,
and then, especially, of his present economic and social situation.[15]

CHAPTER 8 *Economic Solidarity
at its Widest*

The Crystalization of a Class-Conscious International Union. Having
joined the trade union section of the International, the newly converted
worker learns many things there. He learns that the same solidarity existing among all members of that section has likewise been established among
various sections or among all the trades in the same locality, and that the
wider organization of this solidarity, embracing the workers of all trades,
became necessary because the employers in all industries act in concert in
order to drive down the standard of living of people who are forced to
live by selling their labor. The new member of the section is being educated to the idea that this two-fold solidarity—first of workers of one and
the same trade or of all crafts organized into various sections, is not confined to a single given locality, but, spreading far beyond the frontiers of
one country, encompasses the whole labor world, the proletariat of all
countries, powerfully organized for its own defense, for waging war upon
bourgeois exploitation.[1]

Having become a member of the International, he will learn—much
more than he would be able to learn from verbal explanations that he
might get from his comrades—from his personal experience, which now becomes one and the same with the experiences of the other members of the

section. The workers in his trade, losing patience with the greed of their employers, declare a strike. But any strike is a harsh trial for workers who live on wages. They don't make anything, yet their families, their children, their own stomachs clamor for daily food. The strike fund which they built up with so much difficulty is not sufficient to keep them up for many weeks or even many days. They are faced by starvation or by the prospect of having to submit to the harshest conditions imposed upon them by the greed or insolence of their employers. They will have to accept those conditions if help does not come.

But who will offer them this aid? Of course not the bourgeoisie, which is leagued against the workers; help can come only from workers in other trades and in other countries. And lo and behold, this help does arrive, brought or sent by other sections of the International, and by both local and foreign sections. This ever-recurring experience shows more than words can do the beneficent power of the international solidarity of the labor world.[2]

No Ideological Conditions for Joining the Trade Union Section of the International. The worker joining the trade union section of the International is not asked any questions about his political or religious principles. He is asked only one thing: Does he wish to accept, along with the benefits of the association, his share of the duties, which are quite arduous at times? Does he intend to remain loyal to the section through thick and thin, through all the vicissitudes of the struggle, at first exclusively economic, and is he henceforth willing to conform all his acts to the decisions of the majority, in so far as those decisions have a direct or indirect bearing upon this struggle against the employers? In a word, the only solidarity which is offered to him as a benefit, and which at the same time is inculcated into him as a duty, is *economic solidarity* in the widest sense of the word.

But once this solidarity is seriously accepted and established, it produces everything else: the most sublime and the most subversive principles of the International, the principles most destructive of religion, of the juridical right of the State, of divine and human authority—the most revolutionary ideas, in a word, being from the Socialist point of view the necessary, natural development of this economic solidarity. And the immense practical advantage of the trade union sections over the central sections consists exactly in that this development, and those principles, are being proved to workers not by theoretic reasoning but by the living and tragic experience of a struggle which is becoming wider, deeper, and more terrible with every day, so that even the most ignorant, the least prepared, the most submissive worker, ever driven on by the very consequences of the struggle, ends up by avowing himself a revolutionist, Anarchist, and atheist, very often being unaware as to the process whereby he became such.[3]

It is clear that only the trade union sections can give their members this practical education and consequently only they can draw into the organization of the International the masses of the proletariat, those masses without whose practical co-operation, as I have said, the Social Revolution will never be able to triumph.[4]

International Founded Not by Doctrinaires but by Socialist Workers. If there were only central sections in the International, they would be like souls without bodies, magnificent dreams impossible of realization. Fortunately, however, the central sections, the branches of the main center formed in London, were founded not by bourgeois people, not by professional scientists, not by men of prominence in political activity, but by Socialist workers. Workers—and therein lies their great advantage over the bourgeoisie—because of their economic position, because they were spared the doctrinaire, classical, idealistic, and metaphysical education which poisons the minds of the bourgeois youth, have highly practical and positive minds.

They do not content themselves merely with ideas; they need facts, and they believe ideas only in so far as they rest upon facts. This fortunate circumstance has enabled them to escape the two reefs upon which thus far all bourgeois revolutionary attempts have run aground: academic wranglings and platonic conspiracies. For that matter, the program of the International Workingmen's Association drawn up in London and definitely accepted by the Geneva Congress (1866), in proclaiming that *the economic emancipation of the working classes is the great aim to which all political movement should be subordinated as a simple means and that all the efforts hitherto made failed because of lack of solidarity among the workers of various professions in each country and of a fraternal union among the workers of various countries,* showed clearly the only road which they could and should follow.[5]

Proper Functioning of the Central Sections.   Before all, the central sections had to address themselves to the masses in the name of economic emancipation and not in the name of political revolution; and at first in the name of their material interests in order to arrive at moral interests, the latter being, in their capacity of collective interests, only the expression and the logical consequence of the first. They could not wait until the masses came to them; they had to go out to the masses and approach them at the point of their daily actualities—those actualities being their daily labor specialized and divided into crafts. They had to address themselves to various trades already organized by the exigencies of collective labor into separate branches of industry, in order to have them adhere to the economic goal; in other words, in order to have them affiliate with the International, retaining their autonomy and particular organizations. The first thing they had to do, and which they succeeded in doing, was to organize around every central section as many trade union sections as there were different industries.

Thus the central sections, which in every country represent the soul or mind of the International, took on a body, and became real and powerful organizations. Many are of the opinion that once this mission had been fulfilled, the central sections should have been dissolved, leaving behind only trade union organizations. That, in our opinion, is a big mistake.[6]

The Dynamic Forces of the International: the Economic Struggle and the New Social Philosophy. The great task which the International Workingmen's Association set itself, the task of the ultimate and complete emancipation of workers from the yoke of all the exploiters of their labor —of the employers, the owners of raw materials and tools of production, in a word, of all the representatives of capital—is not only an economic or a purely material task. It is at the same time a social, philosophical, and moral task; and it is likewise . . . a highly political task, but only in the sense of the destruction of all politics through abolition of the States.

We believe there is no need to prove that the economic emancipation of the workers is impossible under the political, juridical, religious, and social organization now prevailing in most of the civilized countries, and that consequently, in order to attain and realize this task in full, it will be necessary to destroy all existing institutions: the State, the Church, the courts, the banks, the universities, the Administration, Army, and police, which are in effect nothing but fortresses erected by the privileged classes against the proletariat. And it is not enough to destroy them in one country; they must be destroyed in all countries. For ever since the formation of modern States in the seventeenth and eighteenth centuries there has been a growing solidarity among those institutions—cutting across the frontiers of all countries—and a very strong international alliance.

Thus the task which the International Workingmen's Association set for itself is no less than the complete liquidation of the existing political, religious, juridical, and social world and its replacement by a new economic, philosophical, and social world. But such a gigantic enterprise could never be realized if there were not at the service of the International two equally powerful, equally gigantic and complementary levers. The first of these is the ever growing intensity of needs, sufferings, and economic demands of the masses; the other is the new social philosophy, a highly realistic popular philosophy, resting theoretically only upon real science—that is, upon a science that is experimental and rational, and at the same time admits no other basis but that of human principles, (the expression of the eternal instincts of the masses), the principles of equality, freedom, and universal solidarity.[7]

Why Political and Anti-Religious Principles Were Eliminated from the International. We believe that the founders of the International acted very wisely in eliminating from its program all political and religious questions. Beyond doubt they did not lack political opinions or clear-cut anti-religious views, but they refrained from embodying them in this program, their aim above all being to unite the working masses of the civilized world into one common action. Necessarily they had to seek out a common basis, a set of elementary principles upon which all real workers —that is, all those who were ruthlessly exploited and who were suffering, might come together, irrespective of the political and religious aberrations which still hold sway over the minds of many of those workers.

Had the founders of the International hoisted the banner of some political or anti-religious school, far from uniting all the workers of Europe, they would have divided them even more than at present. This would be so because, aided by the ignorance of the masses, the self-interested and highly corrupting propaganda of the priests, governments, and bourgeois political parties, including the reddest variety of them, have succeeded in disseminating a great number of fallacies among the masses of the people, and because unfortunately those blinded masses have often let themselves be taken in by all kinds of falsehoods which had no other aim but to make the masses voluntarily and stupidly serve the interests of the privileged classes, to their own detriment.

For that matter, the difference in the degree of the industrial, political, mental, and moral development of the working masses of various countries is still too great to have them united on the platform of one and the same political and anti-religious program. To make this a part of the program of the International, and to make it an absolute condition for those joining it, would be to aim at the organizing of a sect, not a universal association; and it would spell the break-up of the International.[8]

A True People's Politics.   There is also another reason which led at the outset to the elimination from the International's program—in appearance at least, and only in appearance—of all political tendencies.

Until now, from the beginning of history, there has never been a true politics of the people, and by "the people" we mean the people of low station in life, "the rabble" which sustains the whole world by its labor. Until now it has been only the privileged classes that engaged in politics. Those classes have made use of the physical prowess of the people to overthrow one another and take the place of the overthrown groups. The people in turn have always taken sides in such struggles, vaguely hoping that at least one of these political revolutions, none of which could get along without the people, but none of which was waged for its sake, would alleviate to some extent its poverty and its age-long slavery. And it has always ended in deception. Even the great French Revolution cheated the people. It destroyed the aristocratic nobility and put in its place the bourgeoisie. The people are no longer called slaves or serfs, they are proclaimed free men, possessing all their rights from birth, but their slavery and poverty remain the same.

And they will ever remain the same so long as the working masses will serve as tools of bourgeois politics, whether this be called conservative, liberal, progressive, or radical—even if it takes on the most revolutionary coloring. For all bourgeois politics, of any color or name whatever, can have only one aim: *to maintain the domination of the bourgeoisie and the slavery of the proletariat.*

The Elimination of Bourgeois Politics. What was the International to do? First of all, it had to detach the working masses from any kind of bourgeois politics, it had to eliminate from its program all the political programs of the bourgeoisie. But at the time it was founded there was no other politics in the whole world but the politics of the Church, monarchy, aristocracy, or bourgeoisie. The latter, especially the politics of the radical bourgeoisie, was no doubt more liberal and humane than the others, but they all were equally based upon the exploitation of the working masses and had no other aim than to contest the monopolizing of this exploitation. The International then had to begin by clearing the ground, and since every form of politics, from the point of view of the emancipation of labor, was tainted by the touch of reactionary elements, the International had to throw out of its midst all the known political systems in order to found, upon the ruins of the bourgeois world, the true politics of the workers, the politics of the International Workingmen's Association.[9]

The Politics of the International. The International does not reject politics of a general kind; it will be compelled to intervene in politics so long as it is forced to struggle against the bourgeoisie. It rejects only bourgeois politics and bourgeois religion, for one establishes the predatory domination of the bourgeoisie and the other sanctifies and consecrates it.[10]

There is no other means of freeing the people economically and politically, of giving them at the same time well-being and liberty, except to abolish the State, all the States, and therewith once and for all destroy that which until now has been called *politics*—politics being precisely nothing but the functioning, the manifestation, external and internal, of the action of the State; that is, the art and science of dominating and exploiting the masses in favor of the privileged classes.

Wherein the Politics of the International Differs from that of Political Parties. It is not true then to say that we completely ignore politics. We do not ignore it, for we definitely want to destroy it. And here we have the essential point separating us from political parties and bourgeois radical Socialists. Their politics consists in making use of, reforming, and transforming the politics of the State, whereas our politics, the only kind we admit, is the total *abolition* of the State, and of the politics which is its necessary manifestation.

And only because we frankly want the abolition of this politics do we believe that we have the right to call ourselves internationalists and revolutionary Socialists; for he who wants to pursue politics of a different kind, who does not aim with us at the total abolition of politics—he must accept the politics of the State, patriotic and bourgeois politics; and that is to deny in the name of his great or small national State the human solidarity of the nations beyond the pale of his particular State, as well as the economic and social emancipation of the masses within the State.[11]

What type of politics can there be? Apart from Mazzini's system—that of the Republic-State—there is only one other: the system of the Republic-Commune, the Republic-Federation, i.e., the system of *Anarchism*. This is the politics of the Social Revolution, which aims at abolition of the *State* and establishment of the economic, entirely free organization of the people —organization from bottom to top by means of federation.[12]

The founders of the International Workingmen's Association acted wisely in refraining from placing political and philosophical principles as the basis of this association, and in imparting to it at the beginning the character of an organization exclusively waging "an economic struggle against capital." They did so because they were certain that once the workers, drawing confidence from their right as well as from the numerical power of their class, became involved in a battle of solidarity against bourgeois exploitation, they would necessarily be led, in the natural course of things and by the development of this struggle, soon to recognize the political, social, and philosophical principles of the International, principles which in effect are the true expression of their point of departure and their goal.[13]

If you start off by announcing first those two aims to ignorant workers, burdened by their daily toil and demoralized and poisoned—consciously, one might say—by the perverse doctrines with which the governments, acting in concert with all the privileged castes (priests, the nobility, and the bourgeoisie) have been overwhelming the people, you will frighten the workers. They may repulse you without even suspecting that those ideas are actually the most faithful expression of their own interests, that those aims carry within themselves the possibility of realizing their most cherished wishes, and that, on the contrary, the political and religious prejudices in the name of which they have spurned those ideas are perhaps the direct cause of the prolongation of their slavery and misery.

The Prejudices of the People and Those of the Educated Classes. One has to distinguish between the prejudices of the people and those of the privileged classes. The prejudices of the masses are based only upon their ignorance, and run contrary to their own interests, whereas the prejudices of the bourgeoisie are based precisely upon the interests of that class, and they hold out against the disintegrating effect of bourgeois science itself only through the strength of the collective egoism of the bourgeoisie. The people want, but they do not know; the bourgeoisie knows, but it does not want. Which of the two is incurable? The bourgeoisie, without any doubt.[14]

Workers Are Socialistic by Instinct. We are referring to the great mass of toilers, which, worn out by daily drudgery, is ignorant and miserable. This mass, whatever its political and religious prejudices may be,— prejudices which, as a result of the specific efforts of the bourgeoisie in that direction, have become dominant in its consciousness—is unconsciously socialistic. Instinctively, by virtue of its social position, it is socialistic in a more serious and real fashion than all the bourgeois and scientific Socialists put together. It is socialistic by virtue of all the conditions of its material existence, by virtue of all the needs of its being, and not through the dictates of the intellect as is the case with the bourgeois Socialists. In actual life the needs of the first category exercise a much greater power than the needs of the intellect, which are, as is the case always and everywhere, the expression of the being, the reflection of its successive developments, but never its principle.[15]

CHAPTER 9   *What the Workers Lack*

What the workers lack is not a sense of reality, nor the necessity of Socialist aspirations, but only Socialist thought. What every worker aspires to deep down in his heart is a fully human existence with respect to his material well-being and intellectual development, an existence based upon justice—that is, upon equality and the liberty of everyone and all in work. But this ideal obviously cannot be realized in the present political and social world, which is based upon injustice and cynical exploitation of the labor of the toiling masses. Hence every serious-minded worker is necessarily a revolutionary Socialist, inasmuch as his emancipation can be realized only through the overthrow of the system which now exists. Either this organization of injustice, with all of its display of iniquitous laws and privileged institutions, must perish or the working masses will remain condemned to perpetual slavery.[1]

This is the Socialist thought, the germs of which are found in the instinct of every serious-minded worker. The Socialist aim then consists in making every worker fully conscious of what he wants by awakening in him an intelligence which corresponds to his instinct, for when the intelligence of workers rises to the level of their instinct, their will crystalizes and their might becomes irresistible.

What is it that obstructs the more rapid development of this salutary intelligence among the working masses? Their ignorance, and to a great extent the political and religious prejudices with which the classes interested in keeping them ignorant try to becloud their consciousness and their natural intelligence. How can this ignorance be dissipated, how can these disastrous prejudices be destroyed? Will it be achieved through education and propaganda?[2]

Both of course are excellent means. But in the situation of the working masses in the present day they are insufficient. The isolated worker is weighed down by his toil and his daily cares to such an extent that he hardly has any time for education. And, for that matter, who will carry on this propaganda? Will it be some sincere Socialists who came from bourgeois ranks? These no doubt are imbued with a generous will, but, to begin with, they are too few in numbers to impart to their propaganda the necessary sweep; and, in addition, because in view of their social position they belong to a different world, they cannot exercise adequate influence over the workers, but arouse in them more or less legitimate distrust.[3]

"The emancipation of the workers should be the task of the workers themselves," says the preamble of our general statute. And it is a thousand times right in saying so. This is the principal basis of our great association. But the world of workers is generally ignorant, it is almost innocent of any theory. Consequently, there remains only one way, *the way of a practical emancipation*. What is and what should be the method?

There is only one way: That is complete solidarity in the struggle of workers against the employers. It is the organization and federation of workers' resistance funds.[4]

The people are ready. They suffer greatly and, what is more important, they are beginning to understand that there is no need for that suffering. They are weary of keeping their eyes turned Heavenward and will not remain patient for long on earth. In a word, the masses—even independently of any propaganda—have consciously turned to Socialism. The general and profound sympathy aroused by the Paris Commune among the proletariat of all countries, serves as a proof of this. And the masses—they constitute power, or, at least, a significant element of power. . . .[5]

Organization and Science. What do the masses lack to be able to overthrow the prevailing social order, so detestable to them? They lack two things: organization and science—precisely the two things which constitute now, and always have constituted, the power of governments. Above all, there must be organization, which is impossible without the help of science. Thanks to military organization, one battalion, a thousand armed men, can hold in fear, and in reality they do that, a million people who may be just as well armed but who are not organized. And thanks to its bureaucratic organization, the State, with the aid of a few hundred thousand officials, holds in subjection vast countries. Consequently, in order to create a popular force capable of crushing the military and civil power of the State, the proletariat must organize.[6]

Organization of the International.   It is exactly this which the International Workingmen's Association is doing now, and when it has embraced or organized in its midst a half, a third, a fourth, or even a tenth of the European proletariat, the States will cease to exist. The organization of the International, having for its aim not the creation of States or new forms of despotism, but the radical destruction of all kinds of domination, must differ essentially from the State organization. Just as much as the State is authoritarian, artificial, and violent, alien, and hostile to the natural development of the people's interests and instincts, so must the organization of the International be free and natural, conforming in every respect to those interests and instincts.

But what is this natural organization of the masses? It is an organization based upon the various manifestations of their actual daily life, and upon the various forms of labor—organization by trades or professions. Once all the industries are represented in the International, including the various forms of agricultural labor, its organization, the organization of the masses of the people, will have been achieved.[7]

For it is indeed enough that one worker out of ten, *seriously and with full knowledge of the cause,* join the International, while the nine remaining outside of this organization become subject to its invisible influence, and, when a critical moment arrives, they will follow, without even suspecting it, its directions, in so far as this is necessary for the salvation of the proletariat.

An Organized Minority But Not a State Government. It may be objected that this manner of organizing the influence of the International upon the masses of the people seems to tend to establish upon the ruins of old authorities and existing governments, a new system of authority and government. But to think so would be a great error.[8]

A government by the International, if it is a government, or rather the organized action of the International upon the masses, will ever differ from the action of all the States in this essential characteristic, that it will always be only the organization of action—not official and not vested with any authority or any political power, but altogether natural in character—on the part of a more or less numerous group of individuals inspired by a general idea and tending toward the same goal, at first upon the opinion of the masses and only then, by means of this opinion more or less modified under the influence of the International, upon their will and their acts. Whereas the governments, armed with authority and material power—which some claim to have received from God, while others claim it on the strength of their alleged intellectual superiority or derive it from the popular will expressed by means of the legerdemain called universal suffrage—impose themselves forcibly upon the masses, force the latter to obey their decrees without even making apparent efforts to ascertain the sentiments of the masses, their needs, or their will.

Between the power of the State and that of the International there is the same difference which exists between the official action of the State and the natural action of a club. The International does not have and never shall have any other power but the great power of opinion and it will never be anything else but the organization of the natural action of the individuals upon the masses. In contrast the State and all its institutions —the Church, the University, the courts, financial science, the police, and the Army—demand the passive obedience of their subjects, no doubt within the very elastic limits recognized and determined by the laws, and of course without neglecting to corrupt as much as possible the opinion and the will of those subjects, ignoring and often defying their explicit wishes.[9]

The International Versus the State.   The State is authority, it is the domination and the organized power of the possessing and so-called enlightened classes upon the masses; the International spells the deliverance of the masses. The State, never seeking and never being able to seek anything but the enslavement of the masses, calls for their submission. The International, seeking nothing else but complete liberty for the working people, calls upon them to revolt. But in order to make this revolt powerful and capable of overthrowing the domination of the State and the privileged classes, solely represented by the State, the International has to organize. In order to realize this aim, it employs only two means which, far from being legal, (and legality in all countries is most of the time only the juridical consecration of privilege, that is, of injustice), are legitimate from the point of view of human right. Those two means, as we already have said, are the propaganda of the ideas of the International and the organizing of the natural influence of its members upon the masses.[10]

Natural Influence Is No Infringement Upon Liberty.   Whoever contends that activity organized in this fashion constitutes infringement upon the freedom of the masses, or an attempt to create a new authoritarian power, is, in our opinion, a sophist or a fool. The worse it is for those who are ignorant of the natural and social law of human solidarity to the extent of imagining that absolute mutual independence of individuals and the masses is possible or desirable. To will that would be to will the very annihilation of society, for all social life is simply this incessant mutual dependence of individuals and masses. All individuals, even the strongest and most intelligent of them, are, at every instant of their lives, at once producers and the products of the will and action of the masses.

The liberty of every individual is the result, ever reproduced anew, of the multitude of material, intellectual, and moral influences exercised by the individuals surrounding him, by the society in which he was born, and in which he develops and dies. To wish to escape this influence in the name of a transcendental, divine, absolutely egoistic, self-sufficient freedom is to condemn oneself to non-existence; to want to forego exercising this freedom upon others, is to forego all social action, the very expression of one's thoughts and feelings. It means ending up in non-existence. This independence, so highly extolled by the idealists and metaphysicians, and individual freedom conceived in this sense, are non-being.[11]

In Nature as in human society, which is somewhat different from Nature, every being lives only by the higher principle of the most positive intervention in the existence of every other being. The extent of this intervention varies only according to the nature of the individual. Destruction of this mutual influence would mean death. And when we demand freedom for the masses, we do not pretend to do away with any of the natural influences exercised upon them by individuals or groups of individuals. We want abolition of artificial, privileged, legal, official influences.

If the State and the Church were private institutions, we, to be sure, would be their adversaries, yet we would not protest against their right to exist. But we do protest against them because, doubtless being private institutions in the sense that they exist in fact only for the particular interest of the privileged classes, they nevertheless make use of the collective power of the masses organized for that purpose in order, officially and violently, to force their authority upon the masses. If the International became organized into a State, we, its convinced and impassioned partisans, would become its most implacable enemies.[12]

The International Cannot Become a State. But the point is precisely that the International cannot organize itself into a State. It cannot do it because, in the first place, as its name indicates, it abolishes all frontiers; and there can be no State without frontiers, inasmuch as a universal State, the dream of conquering peoples and of the greatest despots in the world, has been proven by historic experience impossible of realization. Who says the State necessarily says several States—oppressors and exploiters within their boundaries, conquering or at least hostile to one another beyond their frontiers—and says the negation of humanity. The universal State, or the People's State, of which the German Communists speak, thus can denote only one thing: *the destruction of the State.*[13]

The International Workingmen's Association would have no meaning if it did not aim at abolition of the State. It organizes the working masses of the people only for the purpose of this destruction. How does it organize them? Not from the top down, imposing upon the social diversity produced by the diversity of labor, or imposing upon the natural life of the masses fictitious unity and order as is done by the States—but, on the contrary, from the bottom up, taking for its starting point the social existence of the masses, their real aspirations, and inducing them to group, harmonize, and balance their forces in accordance with the natural diversity of occupations and situations, and aiding them in it. Such is the proper aim of the organization of trade union sections.

The Role of an Organized Minority During a Revolutionary Crisis.
We already have said that in order to organize the masses, in order to
establish with them the salutary and solid influence of the International
Workingmen's Association, all that is necessary, strictly speaking, is that
one worker out of ten belonging to a given trade join the respective trade
union section. This can easily be understood. In moments of great political
and economic crises, when the instinct of the masses, sharpened by events
to the utmost point of keenness, lays itself open to all worth-while suggestions, at a time when these herds of human slaves, crushed and flattened
down but still unresigned to their position, rise up at last to throw off
their yoke, feeling, however, bewildered and powerless because of being
completely disorganized—ten, twenty, or thirty well organized persons,
acting in concert and knowing where they are going and what they want,
can easily carry along a hundred, two hundred, or three hundred people,
or even more. We saw an example of this in the Paris Commune. A serious
organization, just beginning its life during the siege, and far from a strong
or anything like a strong organization, was sufficient to create a formidable
power, a vast resistance potential.[14]

**An Adequate Class-Conscious Membership Will Make the Interna-
tional Invincible.** What will happen then when the International Association is organized much better, when it embraces in its ranks a much
greater number of sections, and especially a great number of agricultural
sections, every section having twice or three times its present membership?
What will happen then when every one of its members learns much better
than he knows now, the final aim and the true principles of the International as well as the means of realizing its triumph? The International then
will have become an invincible power.[15]

The Germs of a Despotic State. We are convinced that if the International is split into two groups—one comprising the vast majority and
consisting of members whose only science reduces itself to a blind faith in
the theoretical and practical wisdom of its leaders, and the other consisting
only of a few scores of leaders—this organization, the mission of which is
to emancipate humanity, will itself be transformed into a sort of *an oligarchic State*, the worst of all States. And what is more, this sagacious,
learned, and clever minority which, together with all the responsibility,
has assumed all the rights of an autocratic government, which is the more
despotic in that its despotism is carefully hidden under the appearance of
obsequious respect for the will and decisions of a sovereign people, decisions ever suggested to this popular will by the government itself—this
minority, we say, obeying the necessities and conditions of its privileged
position and suffering the fate of all governments, will become more and
more despotic, pernicious, and reactionary.[16]

The International Workingmen's Association can become an instrument
of the emancipation of humanity only when it has emancipated itself first,

and that will happen only when it has ceased dividing into two groups—the majority as blind tools and the minority of learned savants who do all the directing—and when every member of the Association has become permeated with the science, philosophy, and politics of Socialism.[17]

Free Criticism Essential to the Life of the International. The International is not a bourgeois and decrepit institution maintained only by artificial means. It is young and has the future ahead of it, and therefore it should be able to stand criticism. Only truth, candor, boldness in judgements and acts, and permanent self-exercised control can make it prosper. Since the International is not an association which has to be organized from the top down in the authoritarian way, by the despotic rule of its committees, and since it can be organized only from the bottom up, and only in the popular way, by a spontaneous and free movement of the masses, it is necessary that the masses know everything, that there be no governmental secrets so far as they are concerned, that they never accept fictions or appearances for realities, that they have a clear idea of the aims and methods of their course, and above all that they always be clearly aware of their real situation. Therefore all questions touching the International should be discussed boldly and in the open, and its institutions and the real state of its organizations should not be treated as administrative secrets but as abiding topics of a frank and public discussion.[18]

Wide Latitude of Programs Permitted Within the Framework of General Principles. As to the mode of organization of social life, of work and collective property, the program of the International does not impose anything absolute. The International has neither dogmas nor uniform theories. In this respect, as is the case with every living and free society, there are many different theories stirring in its midst. But it accepts as its fundamental basis the development and spontaneous organization of all the associations and all the communes in complete autonomy, on condition that the associations and the communes take as the basis of their organization the aforementioned general principles which are obligatory upon all who want to join the International. As to the rest, the International counts upon the salutary effect of the free circulation and advocacy of ideas and upon identity and natural equilibrium of interests.[19]

The International and the Revolution. Is the International Workingmen's Association revolutionary in the sense of barricades and violent overthrow of the political order now existing in Europe? No, it occupies itself very little with that kind of politics, or rather, it does not occupy itself with it at all. Bourgeois revolutionists are greatly vexed with the International because of its indifference to their aims and plans. . . .

The International then ignores completely all the daily political intrigues, and up to the present time it has known only one kind of politics—its propaganda, the expansion of its work, its organization. On the day when the great majority of workers in America and Europe join the

International and become well organized within it, there will be no longer any need for a revolution; justice will have been achieved without violence. And should there be broken heads, it will be only because the bourgeois want it.

A few more years of peaceful development, and the International will have become a power against which it would be ludicrous to take up a struggle. The bourgeoisie understand this only too well, and that is why they try to provoke a struggle now. Today they still hope that they have sufficient power to crush us, but they realize that tomorrow it will be too late. Therefore they want to force the International to battle today.[20]

Are we going to let ourselves fall into this crude trap? No, if we did, we would greatly oblige the bourgeoisie but ruin our own cause for a long time. We have justice and right on our side, but our forces are still inadequate for a real struggle. Let us then refrain from giving vent to our indignation, let us remain firm, unshakable, and calm, however provoked we may be by the insolent bourgeois whippersnappers. Let us keep on suffering, but let us not forget anything.

And while biding our time, let us continue, redouble, and expand ever more widely our propaganda work. It is necessary that the workers of all countries, the peasants of the villages as well as the factory workers of the cities, know what the International Association wants. It is necessary that they understand that apart from the triumph of the International there is no other means of emancipation; that the International is the fatherland of all the oppressed workers, their only refuge against exploitation by the bourgeoisie, the only force capable of overthrowing the insolent power of the latter.[21]

Let us organize and enlarge our Association, but at the same time let us not forget to strengthen it in order that our solidarity, which is our whole power, may become more real from day to day. Let us have more and more of this solidarity in study, in work, in public action, in life. Let us rally our forces in common enterprises in order to render existence somewhat more tolerable and less difficult; and let us form everywhere, and as far as it is possible, consumers' and producers' co-operatives and mutual credit societies, which, though unable to free us in any adequate and serious manner, under present economic conditions, are important inasmuch as they train the workers in the practice of managing the economy and prepare the precious germs for the organization of the future.[22]

Propaganda and Economic Struggle.   The International Workingmen's Association, true to its principle, will never extend its backing to a political agitation which does not have for its immediate and direct aim *the complete economic emancipation of the worker*, that is, the abolition of the bourgeoisie as a class, separated in the economic sense from the great mass of the population—nor will it support any revolution which does not inscribe on its banner from the very first day: *social liquidation*.

But revolutions are not improvised. They are not made arbitrarily by individuals nor even by the most powerful associations. They come independently of all will and all conspiracies, and are always brought on by the natural force of circumstances. One can foresee them, one can anticipate their approach, but one cannot accelerate their explosion. Convinced of this truth, we ask ourselves the question: What policy should the International pursue during this more or less protracted period, separating us from the terrible social revolution which all of us feel is in the process of coming?[23]

While ignoring, as demanded by its statutes, all national and local politics, the International imparts to the labor agitation of all countries *an exclusively economic character*, setting as its aim: reduction of the hours of labor and increase of wages; and as the means: *the rallying of the mass of workers into one association and the building up of "resistance funds."*

The International will keep on propagating its principles inasmuch as these tenets, being the purest expression of the collective interests of the workers of the whole world, constitute the soul and the vital force of the Association. It will carry on this propaganda extensively, having no regard for bourgeois susceptibilities, so that every worker, emerging from the state of mental and moral torpor in which he is being kept by the deliberate efforts of the ruling class, comes to understand the situation, so that he knows well what he should want and under what conditions he can win for himself the rights of man.

The International will have to carry on this propaganda all the more energetically and sincerely because in the International itself we often meet with influences which, affecting disdain for those principles, try to pass them off as useless theory, and strive to lead the workers back to the political, economic, and religious catechism of the bourgeoisie.

It will finally expand and become strongly organized, cutting athwart the frontiers of all countries so that when the Revolution, brought about by the natural force of circumstances, breaks out, there will be a real force at hand which knows what to do and by virtue thereof is capable of taking the Revolution into its own hands and imparting to it a direction salutary for the people: a serious international organization of workers' associations of all countries, capable of replacing the departing political world of the States and the bourgeoisie.

We conclude this faithful presentation of the policy of the International by quoting the last paragraph of the preamble of our general statutes:

"The movement produced among the workers of the most industrious countries of Europe, in giving rise to new hopes, gives us a solemn warning not to relapse into the old errors."[24]

CHAPTER 10 *Fatherland and Nationality*

The State is not the Fatherland, it is the abstraction, the metaphysical, mystical, political, juridical fiction of the Fatherland. The common people of all countries deeply love their fatherland; but that is a natural, real love. The patriotism of the people is not just an idea, it is a fact; but political patriotism, love of the State, is not the faithful expression of that fact: it is an expression distorted by means of a false abstraction, always for the benefit of an exploiting minority.

Fatherland and nationality are, like individuality, each a natural and social fact, physiological and historical at the same time; neither of them is a principle. Only that can be called a human principle which is universal and common to all men; and nationality separates men, therefore it is not a principle. What is a principle is the respect which everyone should have for natural facts, real or social. Nationality, like individuality, is one of those facts. Therefore we should respect it. To violate it is to commit a crime, and, to speak the language of Mazzini, it becomes a sacred principle each time it is menaced and violated. And that is why I feel myself always sincerely the patriot of all oppressed fatherlands.[1]

The Essence of Nationality. A fatherland represents the incontestable and sacred right of every man, of every human group, association, commune, region, and nation to live, to feel, to think, to want, and to act in its own way—and this manner of living and feeling is always the incontestable result of a long historic development.[2]

Therefore we bow before tradition, before history; or rather, we recognize them, not because they appear to us as abstract barriers raised metaphysically, juridically, and politically by the learned interpreters and professors of the past, but only because they have actually passed into the flesh and blood, into the real thoughts and the will of actual populations. We are told that such and such a region—the canton of Tessin [in Switzerland], for instance—evidently belongs to the Italian family: it has language, morals, and everything in common with the populace of Lombardy, and therefore it should become a part of the united Italian State.

Our answer is that this is an utterly false conclusion. If there really exists a substantial identity between the Tessin canton and Lombardy, there is no doubt that Tessin will spontaneously join Lombardy. If it does not do it, if it does not feel the slightest desire for it, that will simply go to prove that real history—which continues from generation to generation in the real life of the people of the Tessin canton, the history which produced its reluctance to join Lombardy—is something altogether different from the history written in books.[3]

On the other hand, it should be noted that the real history of individuals, as well as that of peoples, does not proceed only by positive development but very often by the negation of the past and revolt against it; and this is the right of life, the inalienable right of the present generation, the guarantee of their liberty.[4]

Nationality and Universal Solidarity.   There is nothing more absurd and at the same time more harmful, more deadly, for the people than to uphold the fictitious principle of nationality as the ideal of all the people's aspirations. Nationality is not a universal human principle; it is a historic, local fact which, like all real and harmless facts, has the right to claim general acceptance. Every people and the smallest folk-unit has its own character, its own specific mode of existence, its own way of speaking, feeling, thinking, and acting; and it is this idiosyncrasy that constitutes the essence of nationality, which is the result of the whole historic life and the sum total of the living conditions of that people.[5]

Every people, like every person, is involuntarily that which it is and therefore has a right to be itself. Therein consists the so-called national rights. But if a certain people or person exists in fact in a determinate form, it does not follow that it or he has a right to uphold nationality in one case and individuality in the other as specific principles, and that they have to keep on forever fussing over them. On the contrary, the less they think of themselves and the more they become imbued with universal human values, the more vitalized they become, the more charged with meaning nationality becomes in the one instance, and individuality in the other.[6]

The Historic Responsibility of Every Nation.   The dignity of every nation, like that of every individual, should consist mainly in each accepting full responsibility for its acts, without seeking to shift it to others. Are they not very foolish—all these lamentations of a big boy complaining with tears in his eyes that someone has corrupted him, and put him on the evil path? And what is unbecoming in the case of a boy is certainly out of place in the case of a nation, whose very feeling of self-respect should preclude any attempts to shift the blame for its own mistakes upon others.[7]

Patriotism and Universal Justice.   Every one of us should rise above the narrow, petty patriotism to which one's own country is the center of the world, and which deems itself great in so far as it makes itself feared by its neighbors. We should place human, universal justice above all national interests. And we should once and for all time abandon the false principle of nationality, invented of late by the despots of France, Russia, and Prussia for the purpose of crushing the sovereign principle of liberty. Nationality is not a principle; it is a legitimate fact, just as individuality is. Every nationality, great or small, has the incontestable right to be itself, to live according to its own nature. This right is simply the corollary of the general principle of freedom.

Everyone who sincerely wishes peace and international justice, should once and for all renounce what is called the glory, the might, and the greatness of the Fatherland, should renounce all egoistic and vain interests of patriotism.[8]

CHAPTER 11   *Women, Marriage, and Family*

Equal Rights for Women.   As much as any one else I am a partisan of the complete emancipation of women and their social equality with men.[1]

The expression "social equality with men" implies that we demand, along with freedom, equal rights and duties for men and women[2]—that is, equalization of the rights of women, political as well as social and economic rights, with those of men; consequently, we want the abolition of family and marriage law, and of the ecclesiastic as well as the civil law, indissolubly bound up with the right of inheritance.[3]

Abolition of the Juridical Family.   In accepting the Anarchist revolutionary program, which alone, in our opinion, offers conditions for a real and complete emancipation of the common people, and convinced that the existence of the State in any form whatever is incompatible with the freedom of the proletariat, and that it does not permit the international fraternal union of nations, we therefore put forth the demand for the abolition of all States.

Abolition of States and of the juridical right will necessarily entail the abolition of personal inheritable property and the juridical family based upon this property, since both do not admit of human justice.[4]

Free Marriage Union.   [Against marriage by compulsion we have raised the banner of the free nation.] We are convinced that in abolishing religious, civil, and juridical marriage, we restore life, reality, and morality to natural marriage based solely upon human respect and the freedom of two persons; a man and woman who love each other. We are convinced that in recognizing the freedom of either party to the marriage to part from the other whenever he or she wishes to, without having to ask anyone's permission for it—and that likewise in denying the necessity of needing any permission to unite in marriage and rejecting in general the interference of any authority with that union, we make them more closely united to each other. And we are equally convinced that when the accursed State power is no longer with us to force individuals, associations, communes, provinces, and regions to live together against their will, all these will constitute a much closer union, a much more living unity, more real and more powerful than that which was forced upon them by the crushing power of the State.[5]

The Upbringing of Children. With the abolition of marriage there comes to the fore the question of the upbringing of children. Their upkeep from the time of their mother's pregnancy until their maturity, their training and education, equal for all—industrial and intellectual training combining preparation for both manual and mental labor—must be mainly the concern of the free society.[6]

Society and Children. Children do not constitute anyone's property: they are neither the property of the parents nor even of society. They belong only to their own future freedom. But in children this freedom is not yet real; it is only potential. For real freedom,—that is, the full awareness and the realization thereof in every individual, pre-eminently based upon a feeling of one's dignity and upon the genuine respect for someone else's freedom and dignity, i.e., upon justice—such freedom can develop in children only through the rational development of their minds, character, and will.

Hence it follows that society, the whole future of which depends upon adequate education and upbringing of children, and which therefore has not only the right but also the duty to watch over them, is the sole guardian of the children of both sexes. And since, as a result of the forthcoming abolition of the right of inheritance, society is to become the only heir, it will then deem as one of its first duties the furnishing of all the necessary means for the maintenance, upbringing, and education of children of both sexes, irrespective of their origin or of their parents.

The rights of the parents shall be confined to loving their children and exercising over them the only authority compatible with that love, in so far as this authority does not run counter to their morality, their mental development, or their future freedom. Marriage, in the sense of being a civil and a political act, like any intervention of society in questions of love, is bound to disappear. The children will be entrusted—naturally and not by right—to the mother, her prerogative under rational supervision of society.[7]

CHAPTER 12 *Upbringing and Education*

Integral, Equal Education an Indispensable Condition of Workers' Emancipation. The first demand of the International is an integral, equal education for all; the first thing the Paris Commune thought of in the midst of the terrible struggle of which you know, was to establish excellent elementary schools for boys and girls, conducted upon humanitarian principles and without priests.[1]

Can the emancipation of the workers be complete so long as the education received by the masses is inferior to that given to the bourgeoisie, or so long as there is in general any class whatever, large or small in numbers, enjoying by virtue of birth the privileges of superior and more thoroughgoing instruction? . . .

Is it not evident that out of two persons endowed with a nearly equal natural intelligence, the one who knows more, whose mind has been broadened to a greater extent by science and who, having a better understanding of the interlinking system of natural and social facts, or what one calls natural and social laws, will grasp more readily and in a broader light the character of the environment in which he finds himself? And is it not evident also that that person will feel more free, and that in practice he will prove the cleverer and stronger of the two?

It stands to reason that the one who knows more will dominate the one who knows less. And if there were, to begin with, only this difference in upbringing and education between two classes, it would in itself produce in a comparatively short time all the other differences, and human society would relapse into its present state; that is, it would be split up again into a mass of slaves and a small number of masters, the first working for the latter as they do now in existing society.[2]

One understands then why bourgeois Socialists demand only a little more education for the people, only a little more than what the people are getting now, and why we, the democratic Socialists, demand for the people *a full integral education,* as complete as the present state of the intellectual development of society will permit, so that there will be no class standing above the working masses by virtue of its superior education and being in a position, on account of it, to dominate and exploit the workers.[3]

So long as there exist two or several degrees of education for various layers of society, there inevitably will be classes in existence; that is, economic and political privileges for a small number of fortunate people, and poverty and slavery for a vast number of others.[4]

Education and Labor.   As members of the International Association we want equality, and because we want that we must likewise want integral education, equal for all. But we are asked: If everyone is going to be educated, who will want to work? Our answer is simple: *Everyone shall work, and everyone shall be educated.* One objection to that, frequently raised, is that this mixing of mental and mechanical labor will only be detrimental to both; that manual workers will make very poor scientists and scientists will always remain very poor manual workers.

Yes, that is true in existing society, wherein both manual and mental labor are equally distorted by the altogether artificial isolation to which both are condemned. But we are convinced that in a living and integral man each of these activities—muscular and nervous—should be equally developed, and that, far from harming each other, those two activities are bound to support, enlarge, and reinforce each other. Thus the knowledge of the savant will become more fruitful, useful, and broader in scope when he is no more a stranger to physical work, and the labor of the educated worker will be more intelligently done and consequently more productive than that of an ignorant one. Hence it follows that it is to the interest of both labor and science that there be no more workers nor scientists but only men.[5]

Science and Technique at the Disposal of Labor. Men who by virtue of their intellectual superiority are now exclusively preoccupied with the world of science and who, once established in that world, and yielding to the exigencies of a completely bourgeois position, turn all their inventions to the exclusive use of the privileged class, of which they themselves are a part,—all these men, once they make common cause with the rest of mankind, once they become fellow-workers with the common people, not only in imagination and in words, but in fact, and by actual work, will necessarily place their discoveries and applications of science at the disposal of society, for the benefit of everyone, and, in the first place, for the alleviation and ennoblement of labor, the only legitimate and real basis of human society.[6]

Science in the Transitional Period. It is possible and even probable that in the more or less prolonged transitional period, which will naturally follow in the wake of a great social crisis, sciences of the highest standing will sink to a level much below that held by each at present. . . . But does this temporary eclipse of the higher sciences really mean a great misfortune? What science loses in sublime loftiness, will it not regain by broadening its base? No doubt at first there will be fewer illustrious scientists, but there will be a greatly reduced number of ignorant people.

There will be no more of the gifted few who reach for the skies, but in their place there will be millions who are now debased and crushed by the conditions of their lives, and who then will bestride the world like free and proud men. There will be no demi-gods, but neither will there be slaves. The demi-gods and the slaves will become humanized; the first will step down a little, and the others will rise a great deal. There will be no place then for deification nor for contempt. All men will unite and march with fresh vigor toward new conquests in science as well as in life.

Equal Education and the Differential of Individual Abilities. But here another question arises: *Are all individuals equally capable of rising to the same levels of education?* Let us imagine a society organized upon the principles of utmost equality, and wherein all the children from their birth will have the same start in life, in economic, social, and political respects—that is, they will have the same maintenance, the same education, the same upbringing. Will there not be among those thousands of little individuals infinite differences in point of energy, natural tendencies, and aptitudes?

There we have one of the strong arguments of our adversaries, the bourgeois pure and simple and the bourgeois Socialists, who deem it irrefutable.[7]

Only under conditions of full equality can individual freedom—not privileged but human freedom—and the real capacities of individuals obtain their complete development. When equality has become the starting point in the lives of all people upon the earth, only then—safeguarding, however, the supreme rights of human solidarity, which is and will ever remain the greatest producer of all social values: material goods and the riches of the human mind—only then can one say that every individual is the product of his own efforts. From which we conclude that in order that individual capacities prosper in full, in order that they be not hindered in bearing full fruit, it is necessary to do away with all individual privileges—of political as well as economic nature—that is, it is necessary to abolish all classes. It is necessary to do away with individual property and the right of inheritance, it is necessary to attain the economic, political, and social triumph of equality.[8]

But once equality has triumphed and become established, will there be no difference in the capacities and degrees of energy possessed by various individuals? Such differences will continue to exist, not to the same extent, perhaps, as they now exist, but no doubt they will not altogether disappear. It is a truth, which has passed into a proverb, that there are no two leaves alike on one and the same tree. And this holds true even to a greater extent in regard to human beings, the latter being so much more complex than the leaves. But this diversity, far from being an evil, on the contrary, as it was well observed by the German philosopher Feuerbach, constitutes the wealth of humanity. Thanks to this diversity, humanity is a collective unit in which every individual member completes all the others and himself needs all the rest—so that this infinite diversity of human individuals is the very cause, the principal basis of their solidarity, constituting an all-powerful argument in favor of equality.[9]

Natural Differences Among Individuals not Denied. But then, we may be asked, how can one explain the fact that education, being almost identical, in appearance at least, often yields widely diverse results in point of development of character, heart, and mind? And to begin with, do not individual natures themselves differ at birth? This natural and innate difference, small though it may be, is nevertheless positive and real: difference in temperament, in vital energy, in the predominance of one sense or of a group of organic functions over others, difference in intensity of sense impressions and natural capacities.

We have tried to prove that vices as well as moral qualities—facts of individual and social consciousness—cannot be physically inherited, and that man cannot be physiologically pre-determined toward evil or irrevocably rendered incapable of good. But we never meant to deny that individual natures differ widely among themselves, or that some of them are endowed to a greater extent than others for a large human development. However, we believe that these natural differences are much exaggerated, and that most of them should be attributed not to Nature but to educational differences prevailing in existing society.[10]

The Great Majority of Differences in Ability Are Due to Differences in Education. The power to think, as well as the power of will, is conditioned in every individual by his *organism* and *upbringing.* How matters will stand in this respect a few centuries hence, after full social equality has been established upon the earth, we do not know. But it cannot be denied now that intelligence and stupidity in men are to some extent a matter of differences in their organisms. Equal brain power does not exist in present-day humanity. By way of consolation one may observe that the number of inordinately intelligent men, or those endowed with real genius, as well as the number of men egregiously stupid by nature, idiots, is quite small compared with the average run of humanity. The vast majority consists of persons endowed with average moderate and almost equal capacities, which do, however, differ widely in kind. And it is the majority that matters now and not the minority.

The major part of the differences now existing with respect to mental capacities are not innate but owe their origin to upbringing. Power of thought develops by *exercise in thinking* and by proper, expeditious guidance of the infant and adolescent brain in the great task of assimilating rational knowledge.[11]

In order to solve this question it is necessary that the two sciences which are called upon to solve it—physiological psychology, or the science of the brain, and pedagogy, or the science of upbringing or of the social development of the brain—should emerge from the infantile state in which both still find themselves. But once the physiological differences of individuals, of whatever degree they may be, are admitted, it clearly follows that a system of education, though excellent in itself as an abstract system, may be good for one and bad for the other.

Equal and Humanitarian Education Will Tend to Do Away with Many of the Present Differences. In order to be perfect, education must become more individualized than it is today, individualized in the sense of freedom, and based upon respect for freedom, even among children. Such an education should have for its object not merely *the mechanical training* of character, mind, and affections, but awakening them to an independent and free activity. It should have no other aim than the development of freedom, no other cult (or rather no other morality, no other object of respect) than the liberty of each and all; simple justice, not juridical but human; simple reason, neither theological nor metaphysical, but scientific; and labor, mental and physical, as the first and the obligatory basis of all dignity, freedom, and right. Such an education, widely diffused and embracing all men and women, an education promoted under economic and social conditions based upon strict justice, would be instrumental in doing away with many so-called natural differences.[12]

Society Owes an Integral Education to All. It follows that society, without taking into consideration the real or fictitious differences in individual propensities and capacities and not having the means to determine, nor the right to decree, the future career of the young, owes to all children, without any exception, *an absolutely equal education and upbringing*.[13]

Education of all degrees should be equal for all and therefore it should be an integral education, that is, it should prepare every child of either sex for a life of thought as well as of work, so that all will become equally complete and integral individuals.

The positivist philosophy, having dethroned in the minds of men the religious fables and the day-dreams of metaphysics, enables us to catch a glimpse of the character of scientific education in the future. It will have as its basis the study of Nature, and sociology as its completion. The ideal, ceasing to be the tyrant and distorter of life, as is ever the case in all the metaphysical and religious systems, will henceforth be only the ultimate and most beautiful expression of the real world. Ceasing to be a dream, it will itself become a reality.[14]

Since no mind, powerful as it may be, is capable of embracing in their particular concreteness all the sciences, and on the other hand, since a general knowledge of all sciences is absolutely necessary for the complete development of the mind, instruction divides naturally into two parts: the general one, giving the principal elements of all sciences, with no exception, as well as the knowledge (not superficial but real) of their totality; and the special part, necessarily divided into several groups or faculties, every one of which embraces a certain number of mutually complementary sciences.[15]

The first, the general part, will be obligatory for all children; it will constitute, if we may thus express ourselves, the humane education of their minds, completely replacing metaphysics and theology and at the same time developing the children to a point where they may knowingly choose, when they reach the age of adolescence, the special faculty of sciences best suited to their individual tastes and aptitudes.[16]

In the system of integral education, along with *scientific* or *theoretical* education, it is essential that there be *industrial* or *practical* education. Only in this way will it be possible to develop the integral man of the future: the worker who understands what he is doing.

Industrial teaching, paralleling scientific education, will be divided into two parts: general teaching, giving the children a general idea of, and the first practical knowledge of, all industries, as well as the idea of their totality constituting the material aspect of civilization, the totality of human labor; and the special part divided into groups of industries forming special closely interlinked units.

General teaching should prepare adolescents to choose freely the special group of industries, and among them that branch for which they have a particular taste. Having entered the second phase of industrial education, the young people will serve their first apprenticeship in real work under the guidance of their teachers.

Alongside of scientific and industrial education there will necessarily be a practical education, or rather a series of experiments, in morality, not divine but human morality. Divine morality is based upon two immoral principles, respect for authority and contempt for humanity; but human morality, on the contrary, is based upon contempt for authority and respect for freedom and humanity. Divine morality considers work degradation and punishment; but human morality sees in it the supreme condition of human happiness and human dignity. Divine morality, by its own logic, leads to a politics which recognizes only the right of those who, thanks to their privileged economic position, can live without working. Human morality grants those rights only to those who live by working; it recognizes that by work alone does man become a man.

The education of children, taking authority as its starting point, must gradually attain the fullest liberty.[17]

Rational Education.   Let us agree that, in the real meaning of the word, schools, in a normal society based upon equality and on respect for human freedom, will exist only for children and not for adults; and in order that they may become schools of emancipation and not of enslavement, it will be necessary to eliminate, in the first place, this fiction of God, the eternal and absolute enslaver. Education of children and their upbringing must be founded wholly upon the scientific development of reason and not that of faith; upon the development of personal dignity and independence, not upon piety and obedience; on the cult of truth and justice at any cost; and above all, upon respect for humanity, which must replace in everything the divine cult.

From Authority to Complete Liberty.   The principle of authority in the education of children constitutes the natural starting point: it is legitimate and necessary when applied to those of a tender age, at a time when their intelligence is still not in any way developed. But inasmuch as the development of everything, and consequently of education, implies the gradual negation of the point of departure, this principle must gradually diminish in the same measure in which instruction and education advance, giving place to increasing liberty.

All rational education is at bottom nothing but the progressive immola-tion of authority for the benefit of freedom, the final aim of education necessarily being the development of free men imbued with a feeling of respect and love for the liberty of others. Thus the first day of school life, if the school takes pupils at an age when they have just begun to prattle, must be that of the greatest authority and almost total absence of liberty; but its last day must be that of the greatest liberty and the absolute aboli-tion of every vestige of the animal or divine principle of authority.[18]

The Training of Will.   It is to be observed that lax system in up-bringing, now advocated by some on the pretext of freedom and consisting in continuous yielding to all the whims and caprices of the child, contrib-utes little toward the development of a strong will. On the contrary, the will develops by having it exercised; at first, of course, through compul-sory exercises, in the process of checking instinctive drives and cravings, and with this accumulation and concentration of inner power in the child there gradually comes concentration of attention, memory, and independent thought. A man who is incapable of self-control, of repressing cravings, of holding in check involuntary and harmful reflexes and actions, of resisting inward and outward pressure—in a word, one who lacks will power—is just an ordinary weakling.[19]

Extra-Mural Education. The principle of authority, applied to men who have come to age or grown beyond maturity, becomes a monstrosity, a flagrant denial of humanity, a source of slavery and intellectual and moral depravity. Unfortunately, paternal governments have left the masses to stagnate in an ignorance so profound that it will be necessary to estab-lish schools not only for the people's children, but also for the people themselves.

But these schools should be free from even the slightest application or manifestation of the principle of authority. They will not be schools in the accepted meaning, but popular academies, in which neither pupils nor masters will be known, but where the people will come freely to get, if they find it necessary, free instruction, and in which, rich in experience, they will teach many things to their professors who shall bring them the knowledge that they lack. This, then, will be a sort of intellectual fraternity between educated youth and the people.[20]

The real school for the people and for all grown men is life. The only great and all-powerful authority, at once natural and rational, the only one which we may respect, will be that of the collective and public spirit of a society founded on equality and solidarity as well as on liberty and the mutual respect of all of its members.[21]

Socialist Education Is Impossible in Existing Society.   Three things are necessary in order that men may become moral (that is, complete men in the true sense of the word): birth under hygienic conditions; a rational and integral education accompanied by an upbringing based upon respect for work, reason, equality, and liberty; and a social environment wherein the human individual, enjoying his full liberty, will be equal, both in fact and by right, to all others.

Does such an environment exist? It does not. So it follows that it must be created. If it were even possible to found in the existing environment schools which would give their pupils instruction and education as perfect as we can imagine, would those schools succeed in developing just, free, and moral men? No, they would not, for upon leaving school the graduates would find themselves in a social environment governed by altogether contrary principles, and since society is always stronger than individuals, it would soon come to dominate them, and it would demoralize them. For social life embraces everything, pervading schools as well as the life of the families and of all individuals comprised in it.[22]

Public education, not fictitious but real education, can exist only in a truly equalitarian society. . . . And since life itself and the influence of social environment are far more powerful educational factors than the teaching of all the licensed professors of the "duty" of sacrifice, and of all the virtues—then how can education ever be the common possession of all in a society wherein the social situation of individuals as well as of families differs so widely and is so unequal?[23]

Social Environment Shapes the Mentality of Teachers. Educators live and work in a certain society, and they are permeated throughout their whole being, and in the smallest particulars of their life—mostly without even being aware of it—by the convictions, prejudices, passions, and habits of that society. They transmit all those influences to the children in their charge, and since because of the natural tendency of man to exert pressure against those weaker than himself, most educators are oppressors and despots with respect to children—and likewise since the salutary spirit of contrariness, guarantee of freedom and of all progress, awakens within humans almost at infancy,—children and adolescents usually hate their educators, distrust them, and, protesting against their routine and their social teachings, the younger generation becomes capable of accepting or creating new things.

Here is one of the principal reasons why adolescents, while still attending school, and not yet taking a direct and constructive part in social life, are capable, to a greater extent than adults, of espousing a new truth. But no sooner do they leave school, no sooner do they come to take a definite place in society and become permeated with the habits, interests, and, so to speak, the logic of a certain more or less privileged position, no sooner does that happen than they—or the majority of them—take their places alongside the older generation against which they had rebelled, as the slaves of society, becoming in turn the oppressors of the next younger generation because of social prejudices.

Social environment, and social opinion, which always expresses the material and political interests of that environment, weigh down heavily upon free thought, and it takes a great deal of power of thought and even more so of anti-social interest and passion to withstand that heavy oppression.[24]

A Socialist Attitude Can be Developed in Children only in a Socialist Society. The teachers, professors, and parents are all members of this society, are all stultified or demoralized by it. So how can they give to their pupils that which they themselves lack? Morality can be effectively preached only by example, and since Socialist morality is altogether contrary to existing morality, the teachers who are necessarily dominated to a greater or smaller extent by the latter, will act in the presence of the pupils in a manner wholly contrary to what they preach. Consequently, Socialist education is impossible in the existing schools as well as in present-day families.

But integral education is equally impossible under existing conditions. The bourgeois have not the slightest desire that their children should become workers, and workers are deprived of the means necessary to give their offspring a scientific education.

I am very much amused by those good bourgeois Socialists who are always telling us: "Let us first educate the people and emancipate them." We say, on the contrary: Let them first emancipate themselves and then they will look after their own education.

Who will teach the people? You? But you do not teach them, you poison them by trying to inculcate all the religious, historical, political, juridical, and economic prejudices which guarantee your existence, but which at the same time destroy their intelligence, take the mettle out of their legitimate indignation, and debilitate their will. You let the people be crushed by their daily work and by their poverty and then you tell them: "Study, get educated." We should like to see you, with your children, take to study after thirteen, fourteen, or sixteen hours of brutalizing labor, with poverty and insecurity next day as your whole recompense.[25]

No, gentlemen, notwithstanding our respect for the great question of integral education, we declare that right now this is not the most important question confronting the people. The first question for the people is that of economic emancipation, which necessarily and immediately begets political emancipation, and only following that comes intellectual and moral emancipation of the people.[26]

Education for the People Must Go Hand-in-Hand with Improvement of Economic Conditions. Schools for the people are an excellent thing indeed; and yet one has to ask oneself whether the average man of the people, who leads a precarious hand-to-mouth existence, who lacks education and leisure and is forced to work himself to exhaustion in order to keep up his family—whether such a worker can have the wish, the idea, or the opportunity to send his children to school and maintain them during the study period? Will he not need them, need the help of their weak, childish hands, their labor in order to support the family? It is a distinct sacrifice on his part when he lets them have a year or two of schooling, enough to learn the three R's and have their hearts and minds poisoned with the Christian catechism, of which there is an inordinate abundance in the schools of all countries. Will this meager education ever be able to raise the working masses to the level of bourgeois education? Will the gulf ever be bridged?[27]

It is evident that this important question of the education and upbringing of the people depends upon the solution of the much more difficult problem of radical reorganization of the existing economic conditions of the working masses. Elevate those conditions, give back to labor what belongs to it by justice, and you thereby enable the workers to acquire knowledge, prosperity, leisure, and then, you may be sure, they will have created a broader, healthier, and loftier civilization than yours.[28]

Does it follow that we must eliminate all education and abolish all schools? Far from it! Education must be spread among the masses unsparingly, transforming all the churches, all those temples dedicated to the glory of God and to the slavery of men, into so many schools of human emancipation.[29]

That is why we fully subscribe to the resolution adopted by the Congress of Brussels in 1867:

"Recognizing that for the moment it is impossible to organize a rational system of education, the Congress urges its various sections to organize study courses which would follow a program of scientific, professional, and industrial education, that is, a program of integral instruction, in order to remedy as much as possible the present-day lack of education among workers. It is well understood that a reduction of working hours is to be considered an indispensable preliminary condition."

Yes, without doubt, the workers will do all within their means to give themselves the education which it is possible to obtain under the material conditions of their present life. But, without letting themselves be led astray by the siren voices of the bourgeoisie and of the bourgeois Socialists, they should above all concentrate their efforts upon the solving of this great problem of *economic emancipation*, which should be the source of all other emancipations.[30]

CHAPTER 13 *Summation*

I. *The negation of God and the principle of authority, divine and human, and also of any tutelage by a man over men*—Even when such tutelage is attempted upon adult persons wholly deprived of education, or the ignorant masses, and whether that tutelage is exercised in the name of higher considerations, or even of *scientific reasons* presented by a group of individuals of generally recognized intellectual standing, or by some other class—in either case it would lead to the formation of a sort of *intellectual aristocracy*, exceedingly odious and harmful to the cause of freedom.

Note 1. Positive and rational knowledge is the only torch lighting up man's road toward the recognition of truth and the regulation of his behavior and his relation to the society surrounding him. But this knowledge is subject to errors, and even were this not the case, it would still be presumptuous to claim to govern men in the name of such knowledge against their will. A genuinely free society can grant to knowledge only a two-fold right, enjoyment of which constitutes at the same time a duty: *first,* the upbringing and education of persons of both sexes, equally accessible to and compulsory upon children and adolescents until they become of age, after which all tutelage is to cease; and, *second,* the spreading of ideas and systems of ideas based upon exact science, and the endeavor, with the aid of absolutely free propaganda, to have those ideas deeply permeate the universal convictions of mankind.

Note 2. While definitely rejecting any tutelage (in whatever form it asserts itself) which the intellect developed by knowledge and experience —by business, worldly, and human experience—may attempt to set up over the ignorant masses, we are far from denying *the natural and beneficial influence of knowledge and experience* upon the masses, provided that that influence asserts itself very simply, by way of the natural incidence of higher intellects upon the lower intellects, and provided also that that influence is not invested with any official authority or endowed with any privileges, either political or social. For both these things necessarily produce upon one hand the enslavement of the masses, and on the other hand corruption, disintegration, and stupefaction of those who are invested and endowed with such powers.

II. *The negation of free will and the right of society to punish,*— since every human individual, with no exception whatever, is but an involuntary product of natural and social environment. There are four basic causes of man's immorality: 1. *Lack of rational hygiene and upbringing;* 2. *Inequality of economic and social conditions;* 3. *The ignorance of the masses flowing naturally from this situation;* 4. *And the unavoidable consequence of those conditions—slavery.*

Rational upbringing, education, and the organization of society upon a basis of freedom and justice, are to take the place of *punishment.* During the more or less prolonged transitional period which is bound to follow the Social Revolution, society, having to defend itself against incorrigible individuals—not criminal, but dangerous—shall never apply to them any other form of punishment except that of placing them beyond the pale of its guarantees and solidarity, that is, of having them *expelled.*

III.   The negation of free will does not connote the negation of freedom. *On the contrary, freedom represents the corollary, the direct result of natural and social necessity.*

Note 1. Man is not free in relation to the laws of Nature, which constitute the first basis and the necessary condition of his existence. They pervade and dominate him, just as they pervade and dominate everything that exists. Nothing is capable of saving him from their fateful omnipotence; any attempt to revolt on his part would simply lead to suicide. But thanks to the faculty inherent in his nature, by virtue of which he becomes conscious of his environment and learns to master it, *man can gradually free himself from the natural and crushing hostility of the external world—physical as well as social—with the aid of thought,* knowledge, and the application of thought to the conative instinct, that is, *with the aid of his rational will.*

Note 2. Man represents the last link, the highest level in the continuous scale of beings who, beginning with the simplest elements and ending with man, constitute the world known to us. Man is an animal who, thanks to the higher development of his organism, especially the brain, possesses the faculty of thought and speech. Therein lie all the differences separating him from all other animal species—his brothers, older in point of time and younger in point of mental faculties. That difference, however, is vast. It is the sole cause of what we call our history, the meaning of which can be briefly expressed in the following words: *Man starts with animality in order to arrive at humanity, that is, the organization of society with the aid of science, conscious thought, rational work, and freedom.*

Note 3. Man is a social animal, like many other animals which appeared upon the earth before he did. *He does not create society by means of a free agreement: he is born in the midst of Nature, and apart from it he could not live as a human being—he could not even become one, nor speak, think, will, or act in a rational manner.* In view of the fact that society shapes and determines his human essence, man is dependent upon it as completely as upon physical Nature, and there is no great genius who is exempt from its domination.

IV. *Social solidarity is the first human law; freedom is the second law.* Both laws interpenetrate and are inseparable from each other, thus constituting the very essence of humanity. Thus freedom is not the negation of solidarity; on the contrary, it represents the development of, and so to speak, the humanization of the latter.

V. *Freedom* does not connote man's independence in relation to the immutable laws of Nature and society. *It is first of all* man's ability gradually to emancipate himself from the oppression *of the external physical world with the aid of knowledge and rational labor; and, further, it signifies man's right to dispose* of himself and to act in conformity with his own views and *convictions*: a right opposed to the despotic and authoritarian claims of another man, a group, or class of people, or society as a whole.

Note 1. One should not confuse sociological laws, otherwise called the laws of social physiology, and which are just as immutable and necessary for every man as the laws of physical Nature, for in substance they also are physical laws—one should not confuse those laws with political, criminal, and civil laws, which to a greater or lesser extent express the morals, customs, interests, and views dominant in a given epoch, society, or section of that society, a separate class of society. It stands to reason that, being recognized by the majority of people, or even by one ruling class, they exert a powerful influence upon every individual. That influence is beneficial or harmful, depending upon its character, but so far as society is concerned, it is neither right nor useful to have these laws imposed upon anyone by force, by the exercise of authority, and contrary to the convictions of the individual. Such a method of imposing laws would imply an attempted infringement of freedom, of personal dignity, of the very human essence of the members of society.

VI. *A natural society, in the midst of which every man is born and outside of which he could never become a rational and free being*, becomes humanized only in the measure that all men comprising it become, individually and collectively, free to an ever greater extent.

Note 1. *To be personally free* means for every man living in a social milieu not to surrender his thought or will to any authority but his own reason and his own understanding of justice; in a word, not to recognize any other truth but the one which he himself has arrived at, and not to submit to any other law but the one accepted by his own conscience. Such is the indispensable condition for the observance of human dignity, the incontestable right of man, the sign of his humanity.

To be free collectively means to live among free people and to be free by virtue of their freedom. As we have already pointed out, man cannot become a rational being, possessing a rational will, (and consequently he could not achieve individual freedom) apart from society and without its aid. Thus the freedom of everyone is the result of universal solidarity. But if we recognize this solidarity as the basis and condition of every individual freedom, it becomes evident that a man living among slaves, even in the capacity of their master, will necessarily become the slave of that state of slavery, and that only by emancipating himself from such slavery will he become free himself.

Thus, too, the freedom of all is essential to my freedom. And it follows that it would be fallacious to maintain that the freedom of all constitutes a limit for and a limitation upon my freedom, for that would be tantamount to the denial of such freedom. On the contrary, universal freedom represents the necessary affirmation and boundless expansion of individual freedom.

VII. *Individual freedom of every man becomes actual and possible only through the collective freedom of society of which man constitutes a part by virtue of a natural and immutable law.*

Note 1. Like humanity, of which it is the purest expression, freedom presents not the beginning but the final moment of history. Human society, as we have indicated, begins with animality. Primitive people and savages hold their humanity and their human rights in so little esteem that they begin by devouring one another, which unfortunately still continues at full speed. The second stage in the course of human development is slavery. The third—in the midst of which we now live—is the period of economic exploitation, of wage labor. The fourth period, toward which we are aiming and which, it is to be hoped, we are approaching, is the epoch of *justice*, of freedom and equality, the epoch of mutual solidarity.

VIII. *The primitive, natural man becomes a free man, becomes humanized, a free and moral agent; in other words, he becomes aware of his humanity and realizes within himself and for himself his own human aspect and the rights of his fellow-beings.* Consequently man should wish the freedom, morality, and humanity of all men in the interest of his own humanity, his own morality, and his personal freedom.

IX. *Thus respect for the freedom of others is the highest duty of man. To love this freedom and to serve it—such is the only virtue. That is the basis of all morality; and there can be no other.*

X. Since freedom is the result and the clearest expression of solidarity, that is, of mutuality of interest, it can be realized only under conditions of equality. Political equality can be based only upon economic and social equality. And realization of freedom through equality constitutes justice.

XI. Since labor is the only source of all values, utilities, and wealth in general, man, who is primarily a social being, must work in order to live.

XII. Only associated labor, that is, labor organized upon the principles of reciprocity and co-operation, is adequate to the task of maintaining the existence of a large and somewhat civilized society. Whatever stands for civilization could be created only by labor organized and associated in this manner. The whole secret of the boundless productivity of human labor consists first of all in applying to a greater or lesser extent scientifically developed reason—which in turn is the product of the already organized labor—and then in the division of that labor, but under the necessary condition of simultaneously combining or associating this divided labor.

XIII. The basis and the main content of all historic iniquities, of all political and social privileges, is the enslavement and exploitation of organized labor for the benefit of the strongest—for conquering nations, classes, or individuals. Such is the true historic cause of slavery, serfdom, and wage labor; and that is, by way of a summary, the basis of the so-called right of private and inherited property.

XIV. From the moment that property rights became generally accepted, society had to split into two parts: on the one hand the property-owning, privileged minority, exploiting organized and forced labor, and on the other hand millions of proletarians, enthralled as slaves, serfs, or wageworkers. Some—thanks to leisure based upon the satisfaction of needs and material comfort—have at their disposal the highest blessings of civilization, education, and upbringing; and others, the millions of people, are condemned to forced labor, ignorance, and perpetual want.

XV. Thus the civilization of the minority is based upon the forced barbarism of the vast majority. Consequently the individuals who by virtue of their social position enjoy all sorts of political and social privileges, and all men of property, are in reality the natural enemies, the exploiters, and oppressors of the great masses of the people.

XVI. Because leisure—the precious advantage of the ruling classes—is necessary for the development of the mind, and because the development of character and personality likewise demands a certain degree of well-being and freedom in one's movements and activity, it was therefore quite natural that the ruling classes have proved to be more civilized, more intelligent, more human, and to a certain extent more moral than the great masses of the people. But in view of the fact that on the other hand inactivity and the enjoyment of all sorts of privileges weaken the body, dry up one's affections, and misdirect the mind, it is evident that sooner or later the privileged classes are bound to sink into corruption, mental torpor, and servility. We see this happening right now.

XVII. On the other hand, forced labor and utter lack of leisure doom the great masses of the people to barbarism. By themselves they cannot foster and maintain their own mental development since, because of their inherited burden of ignorance, the rational elements of their toil—the application of science, the combining and managing of productive forces—are left exclusively to the representatives of the bourgeois class. Only the muscular, irrational, mechanical elements of work, which become even more stupefying as a result of the division of labor, have been apportioned to the masses, who are stunned, in the full sense of the word, by their daily, galley-slave drudgery.

But despite all that, thanks to the prodigious moral power inherent in labor, because in demanding justice, freedom, and equality for themselves,

the workers therewith demand the same for all, there being no other social
group (except women and children) who are getting a rougher deal in life
than the workers; because they have enjoyed life very little and therefore
have not abused it, which means that they have not become satiated with it;
and also because, lacking education, they, however, possess the enormous
advantage of not having been corrupted and distorted by egoistic interests
and falsehoods prompted by acquisitiveness, and thus have retained their
natural energy of character while the privileged classes sink ever deeper,
become debilitated, and rot away—it is due to all this that only the workers
believe in life, that only the workers love and desire truth, freedom, equality,
and justice, and that it is only the workers to whom the future belongs.

XVIII.Our Socialist program demands and should unremittingly demand:

1. Political, economic, and social equalization of all classes and
all people living on the earth.

2. Abolition of inheritance of property.

3. Appropriation of land by agricultural associations, and of
capital and all the means of production by the industrial associations.

4. Abolition of the patriarchal family law, based exclusively
upon the right to inherit property and also upon the equalization
of man and woman in point of political, economic, and social
rights.

5. The upkeep, upbringing, and educating of the children of
both sexes until they become of age, it being understood that
scientific and technical training, including the branches of higher
teaching, is to be both equal for and compulsory for all.

The school is to replace the church and to render unnecessary criminal
codes, gendarmes, punishments, prisons, and executioners.

Children do not constitute anyone's property; they are not the property of their parents nor even of society. They belong only to their own
future freedom.

But in children this freedom is not yet real. It is only potential; for real
freedom, that is, the full awareness and the realization thereof in every individual, pre-eminently based upon the feeling of one's dignity and upon
genuine respect for the freedom and dignity of others, that is, upon justice
—such freedom can develop in children only by virtue of the rational
development of their minds, character, and rational will.

Hence it follows that society, the whole future of which depends upon
the adequate education and upbringing of children, and which therefore
has not only the right but also the duty to watch over them, is the only
natural guardian of children of both sexes. And since, as a result of the
forthcoming abolition of the right of inheritance, society is to become the

only heir, it will then deem it as one of its primary duties to furnish all the necessary means for the upkeep, upbringing, and education of children of both sexes, irrespective of their origin and of their parents.

The rights of the parents shall reduce themselves to loving their children and exercising over them the only authority compatible with that, inasmuch as such authority does not run counter to their morality, their mental development, and their future freedom.

Marriage, in the sense of being a civil and political act, like any intervention of society in questions of love, is bound to disappear. The children will be *entrusted*—naturally and not by right—*to the mother*, as her prerogative under rational supervision of society.

In view of the fact that minors, especially children, are largely incapable of reasoning and consciously governing their acts, *the principle of tutelage and authority*, which is to be eliminated from the life of society, will still find a natural sphere of application in the upbringing and education of children. However, such authority and tutelage should be *truly humane and rational*, and altogether alien to all the refrains of theology, metaphysics, and jurisprudence. They should start from the premise that from his birth not a single human being is either bad or good, and that *good*, that is, the love of freedom, the consciousness of justice and solidarity, the cult of or rather the respect for truth, reason, and labor, can be developed in men only through rational upbringing and education. Thus, we emphasize here, the sole aim of this *authority* should be to prepare all children for the utmost freedom. This aim can be achieved only by gradual self-effacement on the part of authority, and its giving place to self-activity on the part of the children, in the measure that they approach maturity.

Education should embrace all the branches of science, technique, and knowledge of crafts. It should be at once scientific and professional, general, compulsory for all children, and special—conforming to the tastes and proclivities of every one of them, so that every young boy and girl, upon leaving school, and becoming of age would be fit for either mental or manual work.

Freed from the tutelage of society, they are at liberty to enter or not to enter any of the labor associations. However, they will necessarily want to enter such associations, for with the abolition of the right of inheritance and the passing of all the land, capital, and means of production into the hands of the international federation of free workers' associations, there will be no more room nor opportunity for competition, that is, for the existence of isolated labor.

No one will be able to exploit the labor of others: everyone will have to work in order to live. And anyone who does not want to work will have the alternative of starving if he cannot find an association or a commune which will feed him out of considerations of pity. But then it also will be found just not to grant him any political rights, since, though being an able-bodied man, he prefers the shameful state of living at the expense of someone else; for social and political rights will have only one basis—the labor contributed by everyone.

During the transitional period, however, society will be confronted with the problem of individuals (and unfortunately there will be many of them) who grew up under the prevailing system of organized injustice and special privileges and who were not brought up with a realization of the need for justice and true human dignity and likewise with respect for and the habit of work. In regard to those individuals revolutionary or revolutionized society will find itself facing a distressing dilemma: it will either have to force them to work, which would be despotism, or let itself be exploited by idlers; and that would be a new slavery and the source of a new corruption of society.

In a society organized upon the principles of equality and justice, which serve as the basis of true freedom, given a rational organization of education and upbringing and likewise the pressure of public opinion, which, being based upon respect for labor, must despise idlers—in such a society idleness and parasites will be impossible. Having become exceedingly rare exceptions, those cases of idleness shall be regarded as special maladies to be subjected to clinical treatment. Only children—until they reach a certain degree of strength, and afterward only inasmuch as it is necessary to give them time to acquire knowledge and not to overload them with work —invalids, old people, and sick persons can be exempted from labor without resulting in the loss of anyone's dignity or the impairment of the rights of free men.

XIX. *In the interests of their radical and full economic emancipation, workers should demand the complete and resolute abolition of the State with all of its institutions.*

Note 1. What is the State? It is the historic organization of authority and tutelage, divine and human, extended to the masses of people in the name of some religion, or in the name of the alleged exceptional and privileged ability of one or sundry property-owning classes, to the detriment of the great mass of workers whose forced labor is cruelly exploited by those classes.

Conquest, which became the foundation of property right and of the right of inheritance, is also the basis of every State. The legitimized exploitation of the labor of the masses for the benefit of a certain number of property-owners (most of whom are fictitious, there being only a very small number of those who exist in reality) consecrated by *the Church* in the name of a fictitious Divinity which has always been made to side with the strongest and cleverest—that is what is called *right*. The development of prosperity, comfort, luxury, and the subtle and distorted intellect of the privileged classes—a development necessarily rooted in the misery and ignorance of the vast majority of the population—is called *civilization;* and the organization guaranteeing the existence of this complex of historic iniquities is called *the State*.

So the workers must wish for the destruction of the State.

Note 2. The State, necessarily reposing upon the exploitation and enslavement of the masses, and as such oppressing and trampling upon all the liberties of the people, and upon any form of justice, is bound to be brutal, conquering, predatory, and rapacious in its foreign relations. The State—any State, whether monarchy or republic—is the negation of humanity. It is the negation of humanity because, while setting as its highest or absolute aim *the patriotism of its citizens*, and placing, in accordance with its principles, above all other interests in the world the interests of its own self-preservation, of its own might within its own borders and its outward expansion, the State negates all particular interests and the human rights of its subjects as well as the rights of aliens. And thereby the State violates international solidarity among peoples and individuals, placing them outside of justice, and outside of humanity.

Note 3. The State is the younger brother of the Church. It can find no other reason for its existence apart from the theological or metaphysical idea. Being by its nature contrary to human justice, it has to seek its rationale in the theological or metaphysical fiction of divine justice. The ancient world lacked entirely the concept of nation or society, that is, the latter was completely enslaved and absorbed by the State, and every State deduced its origin and its special right of existence and domination from some god or system of gods deemed to be the exclusive patron of that State. In the ancient world man as an individual was unknown; the very idea of humanity was lacking. There were only citizens. That is why in that civilization slavery was a natural phenomenon and the necessary basis for the fruits of citizens.

When Christianity destroyed polytheism and proclaimed the only God, the States had to revert to the saints from the Christian paradise; and every Catholic State had one or several patron saints, its defenders and intercessors before the Lord God, who on that occasion may well have found himself in an embarrassing position. Besides, every State still finds it necessary to declare that the Lord God patronizes it in some special manner.

Metaphysics and the science of law, based in its idea upon metaphysics but in reality upon the class interests of the propertied classes, also sought to discover a rational basis for the fact of the existence of the State. They reverted to the fiction of the general and tacit agreement or contract, or to the fiction of objective justice and the general good of the people allegedly represented by the State.

According to the Jacobin democrats, the State has the task of making possible the triumph of the general and collective interests of all citizens over the egoistic interests of separate individuals, communes, and regions. The State is universal justice and collective reason triumphing over the egoism and stupidity of individuals. It is the declaration of the worthlessness and the unreasonableness of every individual in the name of the wisdom and the virtue of all. It is the negation of fact, or, which is the same thing, infinite limitation of all particular liberties, individual and collective, in the name of freedom for all—the collective and general freedom which in reality is only a depressing abstraction, deduced from the negation or the limitation of the rights of separate individuals and based upon the factual slavery of everyone.

In view of the fact that every abstraction can exist only inasmuch as it is backed up by the positive interests of a real being, the abstraction *State* in reality represents the positive interests of the ruling and property-owning, exploiting, and so-called intelligent classes, and also the systematic immolation for their benefit of the interests and freedom of the enslaved masses.*

* According to Max Nettlau, this summation by Bakunin was written March 25-30, 1871.

PART IV

Tactics and Methods of Realization

The Rationale of Revolutionary Tactics

The Historic-Economic Rationale. I admit that the present order, that is, the political, civil, and social order now existing in any country, is the final summary, or rather the result of the clash, struggle, worsting, and mutual annihilation of one another, and also of the combination and inter-action of all the heterogeneous forces, both inward and outward, operating within and acting upon a country. What follows from this? In the first place, it follows that a change in the prevailing order is possible and that it can take place only as a result of a change in the equilibrium of forces operating in a given society.

In order to solve the important problem as to how the existing equilibrium of social forces was changed in the past and how it can be changed in the present, we must look closer into the essential nature of those forces.

Just as it is the case in the organic and the non-organic world, wherein everything that lives, or that merely exists in a mechanical, physical, or chemical sense, invariably influences the surrounding world in some degree, so is it in society, where even the most lowly human being embodies a modicum of the social force. Of course, taken in isolation, this force, compared to the vast totality of all social forces, is insignificant and almost nil in its effect. Therefore if I alone, with no aid from anyone, intended to change the existing order only because it did not suit me—and me alone—I should prove to be a damned fool, and nothing else but that.

If, however, we had ten, twenty, or thirty persons aiming at the same goal, that would be a much more serious affair, although still woefully inadequate whenever the goal in question is not of a petty, trivial kind. The co-ordinated efforts of a few dozen persons are to be taken much more seriously than the efforts of a single person, and this is true not just because the sum of a few dozen people is numerically greater than one person—in a society of many millions the sum of a few dozen insignificant units is almost nil compared with the total social force—but because whenever a few dozen persons combine their efforts to achieve a common objective, this gives birth to a new force which far exceeds the simple arithmetical sum of their isolated individual efforts.

In political economy this fact was noted by Adam Smith and ascribed to the natural effect of *division of labor*. But in the particular case analyzed by us it is not only division of labor which works, that is, creates the new force—but to an even greater extent it is the *agreement*, and then the evolving of a plan of action, invariably followed by the best *distribution and the mechanical or calculated combination of the few forces* in accordance with the evolved plan.

The point is that from the beginning of history, in all countries—even in the most enlightened and intelligent ones—the whole sum of social forces is divided into two main categories, essentially differing from and nearly always opposed to each other. One category comprises the sum of unconscious, instinctive, traditional, and as if elemental forces, which are almost totally unorganized although astir with life—while the other category represents an incomparably smaller sum of conscious, concerted, purposefully combined forces which act according to a given plan and which are mechanically organized in keeping with the latter. The first category embraces the mass of many millions of people and in many respects a considerable majority of the educated and privileged classes and even of the lower ranks of the bureaucracy and soldiery—although the ruling orders, the bureaucracy, and the military, because of their essential nature, the advantages of their position, and their expeditious, more or less mechanical organization, belong to the second category, with the government as its center. In a word, society is divided into a minority consisting of exploiters and a majority comprising the vast mass of people, more or less consciously exploited by the others.

It stands to reason that it is almost impossible to draw a hard and fast line separating one world from the other. In society, as in Nature, the most contrary forces coalesce at their extremes. But one can say that with us, for instance, it is the peasantry and the burgesses or commoners that represent the great masses of exploited people. Above them rise in hierarchical order all the strata, which, the nearer they are to the plain people, the more they belong to the exploited category and the less they themselves exploit others; while, on the other hand, the further they are from the people, the more they are part of the exploiting category and the less do they themselves suffer from exploitation.

Thus the social layers rising one level above the peasantry and the commonalty are the *kulaks* in the villages and the Merchant Guilds, which without doubt exploit the people but which in turn are exploited by the priests, noblemen, and above all by both the lower and higher officials of the government. The same can be said of the lower ranks of the priesthood which are severely exploited by the higher ranks, and the gentry, who are over-shadowed by the rich land-owners and ex-merchants on one hand and on the other hand by officialdom and the court aristocracy. The bureaucracy and the military represent a strange mixture of passive and active elements in the matter of State exploitation, there being more of passivity in the lower ranks and more of conscious activity in the higher ranks.

At the top of this ladder stands a small group representing the category of exploiters in its purest and most active sense: all the higher officials of the military, civil, and ecclesiastical departments, and alongside of them, the high men of the financial, industrial and commercial world, devouring, with the connivance and under the protection of the government, the wealth or rather the poverty of the people.

Here we have a true picture of the distribution of the social forces in the Russian dominions. So let us trace the numerical ratio of those three categories. Out of the seventy millions constituting the population of the whole empire, the first or the lower category of exploited people comprises no less than sixty-seven or even sixty-eight millions. The number of conscious, pure and simple exploiters does not exceed three, four, or at its utmost, ten thousand individuals. There remains then about two or three million for the middle category, consisting of people who are at the same time exploited and exploiters of others. This category can be divided into two sections: the vast majority, who are being exploited to an extent greater than their own share of the exploitation of others, and a minority who are exploited only to a small degree and who are more or less conscious of their own role as exploiters. If we add this latter section to that of the top-ranking exploiters we get about 200,000 deliberate and avaricious exploiters out of 70,000,000 population, so that the ratio is about one to three hundred and fifty.

Now the question is: How could such a monstrous ratio ever come into existence? How is it that 200,000 are capable of exploiting 70,000,000 with impunity? Have those 200,000 people more physical vigor or more natural intelligence than the other 70,000,000? It is enough to pose this question to have it answered in the negative. Physical vigor is of course out of the question, and as to native intelligence, if we take at random 200,000 people from the lower strata and compare them with the 200,000 exploiters in point of mental capacity, we shall convince ourselves that the former possess greater native intelligence than the latter. But the latter do have an enormous advantage over the mass of people, the advantage of *education*.

Yes, education is a force, and however bad, superficial, and distorted the education of the higher classes may be, there is no doubt that, together with other causes, it contributes mightily toward the retaining of power in the hands of a privileged minority. But here the question comes up: Why is the minority educated while the vast majority remains uneducated? Is it because the minority has more ability in that direction than the majority? Again it is enough to ask this question to have it answered in the negative. There is much more of such ability among the mass of people than among the minority. It means that the minority enjoys the privilege of education for altogether different reasons.

What are those reasons? They are, of course, known to everyone: The minority has long been in a position where education has been accessible to it, and still is in such a position, while the masses of people cannot obtain any education; that is, the minority is in the advantageous position of exploiters while the people are the victims of their exploitation. It means then that the attitude of the exploiting minority toward the exploited people had been determined prior to the moment when the minority began to strive to regain power by means of education. What could have been the basis of its power prior to that time? It could have been only the power of agreement.

All States, past and present, had *agreement* as their invariable and chief starting point. In vain is this principal basis for the formation of States sought in religion. There is no doubt that religion, that is, people's ignorance, wild fanaticism, and the stupidity conditioned by those factors, contributed greatly toward the systematic organization for the exploitation of the mass of people called the State. But in order that this stupidity might be exploited it was necessary that there should be exploiters who *would enter into a mutual understanding* and form a State.

Take a hundred fools and invariably you will find a few among them who are somewhat more clever than the rest, although still being foolish as the average run goes. Therefore it is natural that they should become leaders, and as such they probably would fight one another until they came to realize that in doing so they would destroy each other to no one's advantage or profit. Having realized this, they begin to strive toward unity. They may not unite altogether, but they will band into two or three or several groups, with as many agreements. Then a struggle will ensue among those groups, each of them using every possible means to win the great mass of people to its side—specious services, bribery, cheating, and of course religion. There you have the beginning of State exploitation.

Finally one party, based upon the most extensive and intelligent compact, having vanquished all the others, attains exclusive power and creates *the law of the State*. That victory naturally attracts to the victor many persons from the camps of the vanquished, and if the victorious party is clever enough, it willingly accepts them into its midst, shows respect and grants all sorts of privileges to the strongest and most influential members of the vanquished party, distributing them in accordance with their special qualifications—that is, the means and methods, acquired by habit or inheritance, whereby they exploit, more or less consciously, all the other fools— some into the priesthood, some into the nobility, and others into the mercantile field. That is how estates of the realm are created, and the State emerges into the open. Afterward, one or another religion explains it; that is, it deifies the accomplished fact of violence, and thereby lays the foundation for the so-called *raison d'Etat*.

Once consolidated, the privileged orders continue to develop and strengthen their hold upon the masses by means of natural growth and inheritance. The children and grandchildren of the founders of the ruling classes become ever greater exploiters, more so by virtue of their social position than because of any conscious or calculated plan. As a result of a premeditated plot, power is concentrated more and more in the hands of a sovereign government and the minority standing nearest to it, making, so far as the great majority of the exploiting classes go, the exploitation of the masses more and more of a habitual, traditional, ritualistic, and more or less naively accepted function.

Little by little, and the further the more so, the majority of exploiters by birth and inherited social position, begin to believe seriously in *their innate and historic rights*. And not only they, but also the exploited masses, subjected to the influence of the same traditional habit and the baneful effect of *ill-intentioned* religious doctrines, begin likewise to believe in the rights of their exploiters and tormentors; and continue to believe in them until the measure of their sufferings is filled to the brim, awakening in them a different consciousness.

This new consciousness awakens and develops in the masses of people very slowly. Centuries may pass before it begins stirring; but once it commences to stir, no force is capable of stemming its course. That is why the great task of statecraft is to prevent this awakening of rational consciousness in the people, or at least to slow it down to the utmost.

The slowness of the development of rational consciousness in the people is due to two causes: first, the people are overwhelmed by hard work and even more by the distressing cares of daily life; and second, their political and economic position condemns them to ignorance. Poverty, hunger, exhausting toil, and continuous oppression are sufficient to break down the strongest and the most intelligent man. Add to these ignorance, and you soon come to wonder how these poor people do manage, albeit slowly, to advance, and not, on the contrary, to become ever more stupid from year to year.

Knowledge is power, ignorance is the cause of social impotence. The situation would not be so bad if all sank to the same level of ignorance. If that were the case the ones whom Nature endowed with greater intelligence would be the stronger. But in view of the advancing education of the dominant classes, the natural vigor of the people's minds loses its significance. What is education, if not mental capital, the sum of the mental labor of all past generations? How can an ignorant mind, vigorous though it may be by nature, hold out in a struggle against collective mental power produced by centuries of development? That is why we often see intelligent men of the people stand in awe before educated fools. These fools overwhelm one not by their own intelligence but by acquired knowledge.

This, however, happens only when an astute peasant meets an educated fool on some plane of affairs which lie beyond the scope of the peasant's understanding. In his own realm of familiar matters the peasant is more than a match for the average educated person. The trouble is that because of the ignorance of the plain people the scope of the latter's thinking is very narrow. Those peasants are rare whose mental outlook reaches beyond their villages, whereas the most mediocre educated man learns to embrace with his superficial mind the interests and the life of whole countries. It is mainly ignorance which prevents the people from becoming aware of their common interests, and of their immense numerical power. It is ignorance that prevents them from evolving a common understanding among themselves and building up an organization of rebellion against organized robbery and oppression—against the State. Therefore every discreet State will use all sorts of means to preserve this condition of people's ignorance upon which the power and the very existence of the State rest.

Just as in the State the people are doomed to ignorance, so the ruling classes are bound, by their position in the State, to advance the cause of State civilization. Until now there was no other civilization in history apart from ruling-class civilization. The real people, the drudge-people, were only tools and victims of that civilization. Their hard unskilled labor created the material for social enlightenment which in turn increased the dominant power of the ruling classes over them, while rewarding the people with poverty and slavery.

If class education kept on progressing while the people's minds remained in the same state, the slavery of the people would become more intensified with each new generation. But fortunately we have neither an uninterrupted forward march by the ruling classes, nor absolute inertia on the part of the people. And the kernel of ruling-class education contains a worm, hardly noticeable at first but growing in the measure that this enlightenment keeps on advancing, a worm gnawing at its vitals and finally destroying it altogether. This worm is nothing else but privilege, falsehood, the exploitation and oppression of the people, which constitute the essence of all class rule and therefore of the consciousness of the ruling classes.

In the first heroic period of rule by the estates of the realm all this is scarcely felt or realized. Estate egoism is screened at the beginning of history by the heroism of individuals who sacrifice themselves, by no means for the benefit of the people, but for the benefit and the glory of the class which to them constitutes the whole people and outside of whom they see only enemies or slaves. Such were the celebrated republicans of Greece and Rome. But this heroic period soon passes, and is followed by a period of prosaic use and enjoyment, when privilege, appearing in its true form, begets egoism, cowardice, meanness, and stupidity. And gradually the estate vigor turns into decrepitude, corruptions, and impotence.

During the period of decay of the estates, there rises up in their midst a minority of persons who are not corrupted, or rather less corrupted—spirited, intelligent, and magnanimous individuals who prefer truth to their own interests and who have arrived at the idea of people's rights, which are being trampled upon by estate privileges. Those individuals usually begin by making attempts to awaken the conscience of the estate to which they belong by birth. Then, convinced of the futility of these efforts, they turn their back upon the estate, disown it, and become apostles of people's emancipation and people's rebellion. Such were our Decembrists.

If the Decembrists failed, that was due to two principal causes. In the first place, they were noblemen, which means that they did not have much intercourse with the people, and that they knew but little about what needed to be done. Second, for the same reason, they could not approach the people, could not awaken within them the requisite faith and passion, since they spoke to the masses in the language of their own class and did not express the thoughts of the people. Only men of the people can be real leaders of the struggle for their emancipation. But can such liberators ever arise out of the depths of the people's ignorance?

In the measure that the intelligence and vigor of the estates deteriorate, the intelligence and then the power of people keep on rising. With the people, slow as their forward movement has been, and however much book learning may be out of their reach, the process of real advancement has never altogether stopped. The people have two books to learn from: the first is bitter experience, of want, oppression, plunder, and torments dealt to them by the government and the ruling classes; the other book is living, oral tradition, passing from one generation to another and becoming ever broader in scope and ever more rational in content. With the exception of the rather rare moments when the people have entered upon the stage of history as the leading actors, they have confined themselves to the role of spectators of the historic drama, and if they happened to take part in it, it was more often in the part of supernumeraries used whenever the people or troops were shown upon the stage.

In the internecine struggles of the estate parties, the people have always been called upon for aid by every faction, and were promised all kinds of benefits in return for this help. But no sooner did a struggle end with victory for one or another faction, or with mutual compromise, than the promises made to the people were forgotten. Moreover, it is the people who always have to pay for all the losses suffered in such conflicts. Reconciliation or victory could take place only at the people's expense. For that matter, it could not happen any other way, and it will always be this way, until economic and political conditions undergo a radical change.

Around what do all the wranglings of the estate parties revolve? Around wealth and power. And what is wealth and power if not two inseparable forms of exploitation of the people's labor and the people's unorganized power? All the estate parties are strong and wealthy only by virtue of the power and wealth stolen from the people. It means that the defeat of any of those parties is indeed the defeat of a certain portion of the people's power; the losses and material ruin suffered by it represent the ruin of the people's wealth.

Yet the triumph and enrichment of the victorious faction not only fail to benefit the people, but in reality make their position worse; first, because it is solely the people who foot the bill for this struggle; and second, because the victorious faction, having removed all rivals in the field of exploitation, sets about the business of exploiting the people with a heightened zest and more outspoken unscrupulousness.

Such is the experience which the people have gone through from the beginning of history, an experience which finally leads them to rational consciousness, to a clear understanding of things acquired at the expense of no end of suffering, ruin, and shedding of blood.[1]

CHAPTER 2 *Economic Problem*
Underlies All Others

Underlying all historic problems, national, religious, and political, there has always been the economic problem, the most important and essential problem not only for the drudge-people but likewise for all the estates, for the State, and for the Church. Wealth has always been and still is the indispensable condition for the realization of everything human: authority, power, intelligence, knowledge, freedom. This is true to such a degree that the most ideal church in the world—the Christian—which preaches contempt for worldly blessings, no sooner had it succeeded in vanquishing paganism and set up its own power upon the ruins of the latter than it directed all its energy toward acquiring wealth.

Political power and wealth are inseparable. Those who have power have the means to gain wealth and must center all their efforts upon acquiring it, for without it they will not be able to retain their power. Those who are wealthy must become strong, for, lacking power, they run the risk of being deprived of their wealth. The drudge-people have always been powerless because they were poverty-stricken, and they were poverty-stricken because they lacked organized power. In view of this, it is no wonder that among all the problems confronting them, they saw and see first and chiefly *the economic problem*—the problem of obtaining bread.

The drudge-people, the perpetual victims of civilization, the martyrs of history, did not always see and understand this problem as they do now, but they have always felt it strongly, and one may say that among all the historic problems which evoked their passive sympathy, in all their instinctive strivings and efforts in the religious and political fields, they always felt more intensely the economic problem, always aiming at solving it. Every people, taken in its totality, [is socialistic], and every toiler who is of the people, is a Socialist by virtue of his position. And this manner of being a Socialist is incomparably more serious than the manner of those Socialists who, belonging to the ruling classes by virtue of the advantageous conditions of their lives, arrived at Socialist convictions only via science and thinking.

I am by no means inclined to underestimate science or thought. I realize that it is those two factors which mainly distinguish man from other animals; I acknowledge them as the guiding stars of any human prosperity. But at the same time I realize that theirs is only a cold light, that is, whenever they do not go hand-in-hand with life, and that their truth becomes powerless and sterile when it does not rest upon the truth of life. Whenever they contradict life, science and thought degenerate into sophistry, into the service of untruth—or at least into shameful cowardice and inactivity.

For neither science nor thought exist in isolation, in abstraction; they manifest themselves only in the real man, and every real man is an integral being who cannot at the same time seek rigorous truth and theory and enjoy the fruits of untruth in practice. In every man, even the most sincere Socialist, belonging, not by birth but through accidental circumstances in his life, to the ruling classes, that is, one who is exploiting others, you can detect this contradiction between thought and life; and this contradiction invariably paralyzes him, renders him impotent. That is why he can become a wholly sincere Socialist only when he has broken *all ties* binding him to the privileged world and has renounced all its advantages.

The drudge-people have nothing to renounce and nothing to break away from; they are Socialists by virtue of their position. Poverty-stricken, injured, downtrodden, the toiler becomes by instinct the representative of all indigent people, all the injured and down-trodden—and what is this social problem if not the problem of the ultimate and integral emancipation of all down-trodden people? The essential difference between the educated Socialist belonging even though it be only by virtue of his education, to the ruling classes, and the unconscious Socialist of the toiling people, lies in the fact that the former, while desiring to be a Socialist, can never become one to the full extent, whereas the latter, while being a Socialist, is not aware of it, does not know there is a social science in this world, and has never even heard the name of Socialism.

One knows all about Socialism, but he is not a Socialist; the other is a Socialist, yet does not know about it. Which is preferable? In my opinion, it is preferable to *be* a Socialist. It is almost impossible to pass, so to speak, from abstract thought into life, from thought unaccompanied by life and lacking the driving power of life-necessity. But the reverse, the possibility of passing from being to thought, has been proven by the whole history of mankind. And it is now finding its additional substantiation in the history of the drudge-people.

The entire social problem is now reduced to a very simple question. The great multitudes of people have been and still are doomed to poverty and slavery. They have always constituted a vast majority in comparison to the oppressing and exploiting minority. It means that the power of numbers was always on their side. Then why have they not used it until now in order to throw off the ruinous and hateful yoke? Can one really conceive that there ever was a time when the masses of people loved oppression, when they did not feel that distressing yoke? That would be contrary to sound sense, to Nature itself. Every living being strives for prosperity and freedom, and in order to hate an oppressor, it is not necessary even to be a man, it is enough to be an animal. So the long-suffering patience of the masses is to be accounted for by other reasons.

One of the principal causes no doubt lies in the people's ignorance. Because of that ignorance they do not conceive of themselves as an all-powerful mass bound by the ties of solidarity. They are disunited in their conception of themselves as much as they are disunited in life, as a result of the oppressing circumstances. This two-fold disunion is the chief source of the daily impotence of the people. Because of that, among ignorant people, or people standing on the lowest level of education or possessing a meager historic and collective experience, every person, every community, views the troubles and oppressions which they suffer as a personal or particular phenomenon, and not as a general phenomenon affecting all in the same measure and one which therefore should bind all in one common venture, in resistance or in work.

What happens is just the contrary: every region, commune, family, and individual regard the others as enemies ready to impose their yoke upon and despoil the other party; and while this mutual alienation continues, every concerted party, even one that is hardly organized, every caste or State power which may represent a comparatively small number of people, can easily bamboozle, terrorize, and oppress millions of toilers.

The second reason—also a direct sequel of the very same ignorance—consists in the fact that the people do not see and do not know the principal sources of their misery, often hating only the manifestation of the cause and not the cause itself, just as a dog may bite the stick with which a man is hitting it but not the man who does the hitting. Therefore the governments, castes, and parties which until now have based their existence upon the mental aberrations of the people, could easily cheat the latter. Ignorant of the real causes of their woes, the people, of course, could not have any idea of the ways and means of their emancipation, letting themselves be shunted from one false road to another, seeking salvation where there could be none, and lending themselves as tools to be used against their own numbers by the exploiters and oppressors.

Thus the masses of the people, impelled by the same social need of improving their lives and freeing themselves of intolerable oppression, let themselves be carried from one form of religious nonsense to another, from one political form designed for the oppression of the people into another form, just as oppressive, if not even worse—like a man tormented by illness, and tossing from one side to the other, but actually feeling worse with every turn.

Such has been the history of the drudge-people in all countries, throughout the world. A hopeless, odious, horrible story capable of driving to despair anyone seeking human justice. And still one should not let himself be carried away by this feeling. Disgusting as that history has been until now, one cannot say that it was in vain or that it did not result in some benefits. What can one do if by his very nature man is condemned to work his way, through all kinds of abominations and torments, from pitch darkness to reason, from a brutish state to humanity? The historic errors, and the woes going hand-in-hand with them, have produced multitudes of illiterate people. And those people have paid with their sweat and blood, with poverty, hunger, slave drudgery, with torment and death—for every new movement into which they were drawn by the minorities exploiting them. Instead of books which they could not read, history registered those lessons upon their hides. Such lessons cannot be easily forgotten. By paying dearly for every new faith, hope, and error, the masses of people attain reason via historic stupidities.

Through bitter experience they have come to realize the vanity of all religious beliefs, of all national and political movements, as a result of which the social problem came to be posed for the first time with sufficient clarity. This problem corresponds to the original and century-long instinct, but through centuries of development, from the beginning of the history of the State, it was obscured by religious, political, and patriotic mists. Those mists have now rolled away and Europe is astir with the social problem.

Everywhere the masses are beginning to perceive the real cause of their misery, are becoming aware of the power of solidarity, and are beginning to compare their immense numbers with the insignificant number of their age-long despoilers. But if they have attained such consciousness, what prevents them from liberating themselves now?

The answer is: *Lack of organization, and the difficulty of bringing them into mutual agreement.*

We have seen that in every historically developed society, like present-day European society, for instance, the mass of people is divided into three main categories:

> The vast majority, utterly unorganized, exploited but not exploiting others.
>
> A considerable majority embracing all the estates of the realm, a minority exploiting and exploited in the same measure, oppressed and oppressing others.
>
> And finally, the smallest minority of exploiters and oppressors pure and simple, conscious of their function and fully agreed as to a common plan of action among themselves: the supreme governing estate.

We have seen also that in the measure in which it grows and develops, the majority of those who make up the estates of the realm becomes in itself a semi-instinctive mass, if you like, State-organized but lacking mutual understanding or conscious direction in its mass movements and actions. In relation to the drudge-masses who are not organized at all, they, the members of the State estates, of course, play the role of exploiters, continuing to exploit them not by means of a deliberate, mutually agreed-upon plan, but through force of habit, and traditional and juridical right, mostly believing in the lawfulness and sacredness of that right.

But at the same time, in regard to the minority in control of the government, the group which has explicit mutual understanding as to its course of action, this middle group, plays the more or less passive role of an exploited victim. And since this middle class, although insufficiently organized, still has more wealth, education, greater freedom of movement and action, and more of other means necessary to organize conspiracies and to set up an organization—more so than the drudge-people have—it frequently happens that rebellions break forth from among this middle class, rebellions often ending in victory over the government and the replacing of the latter with another government. Such has been the nature of all the internal political upheavals of which history tells us.

Out of these upheavals and rebellions nothing good could come for the people. For the estate rebellions are waged because of injuries to the estates of the realm, and not because of injuries to the people; they have as an object the interests of the estates, and not the interests of the people. No matter how much the estates fight among themselves, no matter how much they may rebel against the existing government, none of their revolutions has had, or ever could have, for their purpose the overthrow of the economic and political foundations of the State which make possible the exploitation of the toiling masses, that is, the very existence of classes and the class principle. No matter how revolutionary in spirit those privileged classes might be, and much as they might hate a particular form of the State, the State itself is sacred to them; its integrity, power, and interests are unanimously held up as supreme interests. Patriotism, that is, the sacrifice of oneself, of one's person and property, for the purposes of the State, always has been and still is deemed the highest virtue by them.

Therefore no revolution, bold and violent though it may be in its manifestations, has ever dared to put its sacrilegious hand upon the holy ark of the State. And since no State is possible without organization, administration, an army, and a considerable number of men invested with authority—that is, it is impossible without a government—the overthrow of one government is necessarily followed by the setting up of another, more sympathetic government, one that is of greater use to the classes which triumphed in the struggle.

But useful though it may be, the new government, after its honeymoon, begins to incur the indignation of the same classes which brought it into power. Such is the nature of any authority: it is doomed to work evil. I am not referring to evil from the point of view of the people's interests: the State as the fortress of the estates and the government as the guardian of the State's interests always constitute an absolute evil so far as the people are concerned. No, I am referring to the evil felt as such by the estates for the exclusive benefit of which the existence of the State and the government is necessary. I say that notwithstanding this necessity, the State always falls as a heavy burden upon these classes, and, while serving their essential interests, it nevertheless fleeces and oppresses them, though to a lesser extent than it does the masses.

A government which does not abuse its power, and which is not oppressive, an impartial and honest government acting only for the interests of all classes and not ignoring such interests in exclusive concern for the persons standing at its head—such a government is, like squaring the circle, an unattainable ideal because it runs counter to human nature. And human nature, the nature of every man, is such that, given power over others, he will invariably oppress them; placed in an exceptional position, and withdrawn from human equality, he becomes a scoundrel. Equality and the absence of authority are the only conditions essential to the morality of every man. Take the most radical revolutionist and place him upon the all-Russian throne or give him dictatorial power, of which so many of our green revolutionists day-dream, and within a year he will have become worse than the Emperor himself.

The estates of the realm long ago convinced themselves of it, and gave currency to an adage proclaiming that *"government is a necessary evil,"*— necessary of course for them but by no means for the people, to whom the State, and the government necessitated by it, is not a necessary but a fatal evil. If the ruling classes could get along without a government, retaining only the State—that is, the possibility and the right of exploiting the labor of the people—they would not set up one government instead of another. But historic experience—for instance, the sorry fate which befell the Polish gentry-ridden republic—showed them that it would be impossible to maintain a State without a government. The lack of a government begets anarchy, and anarchy leads to the destruction of the State, that is, to the enslavement of the country by another State, as was the case with the unfortunate Poland, or the full emancipation of the toiling people and the abolition of classes, which, we hope, will soon take place all over Europe.

In order to minimize the evil worked by every government, the ruling classes of the State devised various constitutional orders and forms which now have doomed the existing European States to oscillate between class anarchy and government despotism, and which have shaken the governmental edifice to such an extent that even we, though old men, may hope to become witnesses and contributing agents of its final destruction. There is no doubt that when the time of the smash-up arrives, the vast majority of the persons belonging to the ruling classes in the State, will close their ranks around the latter, irrespective of their hatred toward existing governments, and will defend it against the enraged toiling people in order to save the State, save the corner-stone of their existence as a class.

But why is a government necessary for the maintenance of the State? Because no State can exist without *a permanent conspiracy*, a conspiracy directed, of course, against the masses of drudge-people, for the enslavement and fleecing of which all States exist. And in every State the government is nothing but a permanent conspiracy on the part of the minority against the majority which it enslaves and fleeces. It follows clearly from the very essence of the State that there never has been and could not be such a State organization which did not run counter to the interests of the people and which was not deeply hated by the latter.

Because of the backwardness of the people, it often happens that, far from rising against the State, they show a sort of respect and affection toward it, expecting justice from it and the avenging of the people's wrongs, and therefore they seem to be imbued with patriotic feelings. But when we look more closely into the real attitude of any of them, of even the most patriotic people, toward the State, we find that they love and revere in it only the ideal conception thereof and not the actual manifestation. The people hate the essence of the State in so far as they come in touch with it, and are always ready to destroy it in so far as they are not restrained by the organized force of the government.

We have already seen that the larger the exploiting minority in the State grows, the less it becomes capable of directly governing the State's affairs. The many-sidedness and heterogeneity of the interests of the governing classes give rise in turn to disorder, anarchy, and the weakening of the State regime necessary to keep the exploited people in requisite obedience. Therefore the interests of all the ruling classes necessarily demand that an even more compact governmental minority crystalize from their midst, one that is capable, on account of being few in number, of *agreeing between themselves* to organize their own group and all the forces of the State for the benefit of the estates and against the people.

Every government has a two-fold aim. One, the chief and avowed aim, consists in preserving and strengthening the State, civilization, and civil order, that is, the systematic and legalized dominance of the ruling class over the exploited people. The other aim is just as important in the eyes of the government, though less willingly avowed in the open, and that is the preservation of its exclusive governmental advantages and its *personnel*. The first aim is pertinent to the general interests of the ruling classes; the second to the vanity and the exceptional advantages of the individuals in the government.

By its first aim the government places itself in a hostile attitude toward the people; by its second aim toward both the people and the privileged classes, there being moments in history when the government seemingly becomes even more hostile toward the possessing classes than toward the people. This happens whenever the former, growing dissatisfied with it, try to overthrow it or curtail its power. Then the feeling of self-preservation impels the government to forget its chief aim constituting the whole meaning of its existence: the preservation of the State or class rule and class welfare as against the people. But those moments cannot last long because the government, of whatever nature it may be, cannot exist without the estates, just as the latter cannot exist without a government. For the lack of any other class, the government creates a bureaucratic class of its own, like our nobility in Russia.

The whole problem of the government consists in the following: how, by the use of the smallest possible but best organized forces taken from the people to keep them obedient or in civil order, and at the same time preserve the independence, not of the people, which of course is out of the question, but of its State, against the ambitious designs of the neighboring powers, and, on the other hand, to increase its possessions at the expense of those same powers. In a word, war within and war without—such is the life of the government. It must be armed and ceaselessly on guard against both domestic and foreign enemies. Though itself breathing oppression and deceit, it is bound to regard all, within and outside of its borders, as enemies, and must be in a state of conspiracy against all of them.

However, the mutual enmity of the States and the governments ruling them cannot compare with the enmity of every one of them toward their own toiling people: and just as two ruling classes engaged in fierce warfare are ready to forget their most intransigent hatreds whenever a rebellion of the drudge-people looms up, so are two States and governments ready to forsake their enmities and their open warfare as soon as the threat of a social revolution appears on the horizon. The principal and most essential problem for all governments, States, and ruling classes, whatever form, name, or pretext they may use to disguise their nature, is to subdue the people and keep them in thralldom, because this is a problem of life and death for everything now called civilization or civil State.

All means are permitted to a government to attain those aims. What in private life is called infamy, vileness, crime, assumes with governments the character of valor, virtue, and duty. Machiavelli was a thousand times right in maintaining that the existence, prosperity, and power of *every* State—monarchic as well as republican—must be based upon crime. The life of every government is necessarily a series of mean, foul, and criminal acts against all alien peoples and also to a much larger extent against its own toiling people. It is a never-ending conspiracy against their prosperity and freedom.

Governmental science has been worked out and improved for centuries. I do not believe that anyone will accuse me of overstating the case if I call this science the highest form of State knavery evolved amid the constant struggle of, and by the experience of all past and present States. This is the science of fleecing the people in the way which they will feel least but which should not leave any surpluses with them—for any such surplus would give the people additional power—and which at the same time should not deprive them of the bare minimum necessary to sustain their wretched lives and for the further production of wealth.

It is the science of taking soldiers from the people and organizing them by means of skilful discipline, and of building up a regular army, the principal force of the State, a repressive force, maintained for the purpose of keeping the people in subjection. It is the science of distributing, cleverly and expeditiously, a few tens of thousands of soldiers and placing them in the most important spots of a specific region so as to keep the population in fear and obedience. It is the science of covering whole countries with the finest net of bureaucratic organization, and, by means of regulations, decrees, and other measures, shackling, disuniting, and enfeebling the working people so that they shall not be able to get together, unite, or advance, so that they shall always remain in the salutary condition of relative ignorance—that is, salutary for the government, for the State, and for the ruling classes—a condition rendering it difficult for the people to become influenced by new ideas and dynamic personalities.

This is the sole aim of any governmental organization, of the permanent conspiracy of the government against the people. And this conspiracy, openly avowed as such, embraces the entire diplomacy, the internal administration—military, civil, police, courts, finances, and education—and the Church.

And it is against his huge organization, armed with all means, mental and material, lawful and lawless, and which in an extremity can always count on the co-operation of all or nearly all the ruling classes, that the poor people have to struggle. The people, though having an overwhelming preponderance in numbers, are unarmed, ignorant, and deprived of any organization! Is victory possible? Has the struggle any chance of success?

It is not enough that the people wake up, that they finally become aware of their misery and the causes thereof. True, there is a great deal of elemental power, more power indeed than in the government, taken together with all the ruling classes; but an elemental force lacking organization is not a real power. It is upon this incontestable advantage of organized force over the elemental force of the people that the might of the State is based.[1]

Consequently, the question is not whether they [the people] have the capacity to rebel, but whether they are capable of building up an organization enabling them to bring the rebellion to a victorious end—not just to a casual victory but to a prolonged and ultimate triumph.

It is herein, and exclusively so, one may say, that this whole urgent problem is centered.[2]

Therefore the first condition of victory by the people is *agreement among the people* or *organization* of the people's forces.[3]

CHAPTER 3 *Socio-Economic and Psychological Factors*

Folk Instincts and Social Science.   Social science as a moral doctrine merely serves to develop and formulate folk instincts. Yet there exists a considerable gulf between the latter and that science. If those instincts had been all-sufficient to emancipate the people, such liberation would have taken place a long time ago. Folk instincts, however, have not been strong enough to prevent the masses from being victimized, throughout the long course of their sad and tragic history, by various religious, political, economic, and social absurdities.[1]

Folk Instinct as a Revolutionary Element.   True, the ordeals through which the masses of people passed were not altogether lost on them. Those ordeals left in their wake something approaching a historical consciousness, quite as if they had built up a practical science, based upon traditions, which often takes the place of theoretical science. Thus, for instance, one can say now with a certain degree of confidence that no nation in Western Europe will let itself be swept away by some religious impostor, new

Messiah, or political trickster. One can likewise assert that the need for an economic and social revolution is strongly felt by the European masses; if the instinct of the people did not assert itself so forcefully, deeply, and resolutely in this direction, no Socialists in the world, even though they might be geniuses of the highest order, would be capable of stirring up the people.[2]

How would the rural and city proletariat ever be able to resist the political intrigues of the clericals, the nobility, and the bourgeoisie? It has for its defense only one weapon, and that is its instinct, which nearly always tends toward the true and the just because it is the principal, if not the sole, victim of the iniquity and falsehoods reigning supreme in existing society, and, because, oppressed by privilege, it naturally demands equality for all.[3]

Instinct Is Not an Adequate Weapon.   But instinct is not an adequate weapon to safeguard the proletariat against the reactionary machinations of the privileged classes. Instinct, left to itself, and in so far as it has not yet been transformed into conscious, clearly defined thought, easily lets itself be misled, perverted, and deceived. And it is impossible for it to rise to this self-awareness without the aid of education and of science; and science—the knowledge of affairs and of men, and political experience—all this is lacking so far as the proletariat is concerned. The sequel to it can easily be foreseen: the proletariat wants one thing, but clever people, taking advantage of its ignorance, make it do something else, without the proletariat even suspecting that what it is doing is quite contrary to what it wishes to do. And when it finally does take note of what is happening, it is usually too late to undo the evil already committed, of which the proletariat is naturally and necessarily the first and principal victim.[4]

. . . Governments, those officially authorized guardians of public order and the security of property and persons, never fail to resort to such measures when necessary to their preservation. When they must, they become revolutionaries and exploit, divert to their profit, "the evil passions," the socialist passions. And we Socialist revolutionaries, we would not know how to direct these same passions toward their true goal, toward a goal in keeping with the profound instincts animating them! These instincts, I repeat again, are profoundly socialist, for they are the instincts of every man of labor against all the exploiters of labor—and just this is the whole of elementary, natural, and real Socialism. Everything else—all the various systems of social and economic organization—all that is only an experimental elaboration, more or less scientific, unfortunately too often doctrinaire, of this primitive and fundamental instinct of the people.[5]

Class Solidarity Is Stronger Than Solidarity of Ideas.   *Social hatreds, like religious hatreds, are much more intense, much deeper, than political hatreds.*[6]

As a general rule, a bourgeois, even if he is a republican of the reddest variety, will be more affected, impressed, and moved by the misfortunes of another bourgeois—even if the latter is a die-hard imperialist—than by the misfortunes of a worker, a man of the people. This difference of attitude of course represents a great injustice, but that injustice is not premeditated—it is instinctive. It comes from the fact that the conditions and habits of life which always exercise upon men a more powerful influence than their ideas and political convictions, those conditions and habits, that special manner of existence, of developing, thinking, and acting, all those social relations, so numerous and at the same time so regularly converging upon one point, which is the bourgeois life, the bourgeois world—all these establish among men belonging to this world (whatever differences of opinion may exist in their midst in regard to political matters) a solidarity which is infinitely more real, profound, powerful, and above all more sincere than that which may be established between the bourgeoisie and the workers by virtue of a more or less wide community of convictions and ideas.[7]

Social Habits: Their Role and Significance. . . . Because of the animal origin of all human society, and as a result of this force of inertia which exercises as powerful an action in the intellectual and moral world as in the material world, in every society which has not degenerated but keeps on progressing and advancing, bad habits, having priority in point of time, are more deeply rooted than good habits. This explains to us why, out of the total number of actual collective habits, in the more or less civilized countries, nine tenths of them are absolutely worthless.

Let no one imagine that I want to declare war upon the general tendency of society and men to let themselves be governed by *habit*. In this case, as in many other things, it is inevitable that men obey a natural law, and it would be absurd to revolt against natural laws. The action of habit in intellectual and moral life, of individuals as well as of societies, is the same as the action of vegetative forces in animal life. Both are conditions of existence and reality. The good as well as the evil, in order to take on reality, has to pass into habits, whether those of individual man or of society. All the exercises and studies which men go through have only this aim in view, and the better things take root within man and become second nature only because of this force of habit.

It would be sheer folly then to revolt against it, for it is an inexorable force over which neither human intelligence nor human will ever will be able to prevail. But if, enlightened by the rational ideas of our age and by the true concept of justice formed by us, we seriously want to become men, we have only one thing to do: constantly use our will-power, that is, the habit of willing developed within us by circumstances independent of ourselves, in order to uproot bad habits and replace them with good ones. In order to humanize society as a whole, it is necessary ruthlessly to destroy all the causes, and all the economic, political, and social conditions which produce within individuals the tradition of evil, and to replace them with conditions which will have for their necessary consequence the fostering and development within those individuals of the practice and habit of good.[8]

Poverty Is No All-Sufficient Factor of Revolution.   In Italy, as in any other country, there exists a single and indivisible world of rapacious persons, who, plundering the country in the name of the State, have led it, for the greater benefit of that State, to the utmost of poverty and despair.

But even the most terrible poverty afflicting the proletariat does not in itself guarantee the inevitability of revolution. Man is endowed by Nature with an astonishing and at times exasperating patience, and only the Devil knows the lengths to which a worker may go in tolerating those evils when, in addition to poverty which condemns him to untold privations and lingering death from starvation, he is endowed with stupidity, obtuseness, lack of realization of his rights, and unperturbed resignation and obedience. Such a man will never be roused; he would rather die than rebel.

Despair as a Revolutionary Factor.   When driven to extremes of despondency, he is liable to break forth in a fit of indignation. Despondency is a keen, passionate feeling. It shakes him out of the torpor of resigned suffering, and it already presupposes a more or less clear realization of the possibility of a better existence, which, however, he does not hope to attain.

Yet one cannot long remain in a state of despondency; it rapidly drives one to death or to espouse a cause. What cause? The cause of emancipation, of course, and the winning of better conditions of existence.

The Role of the Revolutionary Ideal.   But even poverty and despondency are not sufficient to provoke a social revolution. Though they may provoke a limited number of local revolts, they are inadequate to arouse whole masses of people. That can take place only when the people are stirred by a universal ideal evolving historically from the depths of the folk-instinct, and—developed, broadened, and clarified by a series of significant events, and distressing and bitter experiences—it can take place only when the people have a general idea of their rights and a deep, passionate, one might even say religious, faith in those rights. When this ideal and this popular faith meet poverty of the kind which drives man into despondency, then the Social Revolution is near and inevitable, and no power in the world will be able to stop it.[9]

Revolutions Can Be Waged Only at Definite Historic Moments.   I am going to explain the altogether special situation which may confront French Socialism following this war* if it ends with a shameful and disastrous peace for France. The workers will be much more dissatisfied than they have been until now. This of course is self-evident. But does it follow:

1. That they will become more revolutionary in temper and spirit, by

_____
* The Franco-Prussian war of 1870-71.

their will and decisions? And 2. Even if they become more revolutionary in temper, will it be easier for them, or just as easy as it is now, to wage a social revolution?[10]

Despair and Discontent Are Not Sufficient. I do not hesitate to give a negative answer here to both of these questions. First: As to the revolutionary temper of the working masses—and naturally it is not exceptional individuals that I have in mind—it does not depend only upon the greater or lesser extent of poverty and discontent, but also upon the faith or confidence which the working masses have in the justice of and the necessity for the triumph of their cause. Ever since political societies have been in existence, the masses always have been poverty-stricken and discontented, for all political societies, and all States—republican as well as monarchic—from the beginning of history down to our own days, were always and are exclusively based, differing only in the degree of candor, upon the poverty and the forced labor of the proletariat. Therefore social and political rights, like material blessings, have always been the exclusive privilege of the ruling classes; the laboring masses had for their part only material privations, and the contempt and violence of all politically organized societies. Hence their abiding discontent.[11]

Yet this discontent seldom produces revolutions. We see that even peoples who are reduced to the utmost misery do not show any signs of stirring. What is the reason for this? Are they content with their position? Not at all. The reason for this is that they are not aware of their rights, nor have they faith in their own power; and they remain hopeless slaves because they have neither one nor the other.[12]

The workers, as was the case after December, will be reduced to complete moral and intellectual isolation, and because of that they will be doomed to utter impotence. At the same time, in order to decapitate the working masses, a few hundreds, perhaps a few thousands, of the most energetic, most intelligent, most convinced and devoted among them will be arrested and deported to Cayenne, as was done in 1848 and 1851.

And what will the disorganized and beheaded working masses do? They will eat grass and, whipped by hunger, they will work furiously to enrich their employers. We shall have to wait a long time before the working people, reduced to such a position, wage a revolution![13]

Sheer Despair, Without the Organizing Power of Collective Will, Spells Disaster. But if, notwithstanding this miserable position, and driven on by this French energy which cannot easily resign itself to death, and driven to an even greater extent by despair, the French proletariat revolts—then of course rifles of the latest make will be put to use to teach reason to the workers; and against this terrible argument, which the workers will oppose not with intelligence, organization, or collective will, but only with the sheer power of their despair, the proletariat will be more impotent than before.[14]

What Constitutes the Strength of a Living Socialism. And then? Then French Socialism will cease to count among the active powers impelling the forward movement and the emancipation of the proletariat of Europe. There still may be left in France Socialist writers and Socialist newspapers, if the new government and the Chancellor of Germany, Count Bismarck, still deign to tolerate them. But neither authors, nor philosophers, nor their works, nor finally Socialist newspapers, yet constitute a living and powerful Socialism. The latter finds its real existence in the enlightened revolutionary instinct, in the collective will, and in the organization, of the working masses themselves; and when that instinct, that will, and that organization, are lacking, the best books in the world are nothing but theorizing in the void, impotent day-dreamings.[15]

CHAPTER 4 *Revolution and*
Revolutionary Violence

Revolution Means War. Revolutions are not child's play, nor are they academic debates in which only vanities are hurt in furious clashes, nor literary jousts wherein only ink is spilled profusely. Revolution means war, and that implies the destruction of men and things. Of course it is a pity that humanity has not yet invented a more peaceful means of progress, but until now every forward step in history has been achieved only after it has been baptized in blood. For that matter, reaction can hardly reproach revolution on this point; it has always shed more blood than the latter.[1]

Revolution is overthrow of the State.[2]

Political and Social Revolutions. Every political revolution which does not have economic equality as its *immediate* and *direct* aim is, from the point of view of popular interests and rights, only a hypocritical and disguised reaction.[3]

According to the almost unanimous opinion of the German Socialists, *a political revolution has to precede a social revolution*—which, in my opinion, is a grave and fatal error, because every political revolution which takes place prior to and consequently apart from a social revolution, necessarily will be a bourgeois revolution, and a bourgeois revolution can only further bourgeois Socialism; that is, it will necessarily end in new exploitation of the proletariat by the bourgeoisie—exploitation perhaps more skilful and hypocritical, but certainly no less oppressive.[4]

The Political Aspect of a Social Revolution. At one of the rallies of the Lefts held on August 23 or 24, [1870] a rally participated in by Thiers and a few *advanced* members of the Left Center, when the Lefts had expressed their intention to overthrow the existing government, and Thiers, who had besought them not to do it, finally asked: "But after all, whom will you put in place of the deposed Ministers, whom will you put in your Cabinet?" someone (I do not know who it was) answered: "There will be no Cabinet any more; the government will be entrusted to the armed nation acting through its delegates." Which, if it makes any sense at all, can mean only the following: *a national and limited Revolutionary Convention*—not a Constituent Assembly, rightfully and legally made up of delegates from all the cantons of France—*but a convention made up exclusively of delegates from cities who have waged a revolution.* I do not know whose mad voice it was that resounded in the midst of this council of sage men. Was it, perhaps, Balaam's ass, some innocent mount of the great prophet Gambetta? But it is certain that the ass spoke better than the prophet. What that ass announced was nothing less nor more than a social revolution, the saving of France by means of such a revolution.[5]

War to the finish! And not only in France, but throughout Europe—and that war can end only with decisive victory by one of the parties and the downfall of the other.

Military Dictatorship Versus Social Revolution. Either the bourgeois-educated world will subdue and then enslave the rebellious, elemental forces of the people in order, through the power of the knout and bayonets (consecrated, of course, by some sort of divinity and rationalized by science), to force the working masses to toil as they have been doing, which leads directly to re-establishment of the State in its most natural form, that is, the form of a military dictatorship or rule by an Emperor—or the working masses will throw off the hateful, age-long yoke, and will destroy to its very roots bourgeois exploitation and bourgeois civilization based upon that exploitation; and that would mean the triumph of the Social Revolution, the uprooting of all that is represented by the State.

Thus the State, on the one hand, and social revolution, on the other hand, are the two opposite poles, the antagonism which constitutes the very essence of the genuine social life of the whole continent of Europe.[6]

The New System of Organization. The Social Revolution must put an end to the old system of organization based upon violence, giving full liberty to the masses, groups, communes, and associations, and likewise to individuals themselves, and destroying once and for all the historic cause of all violences, the power and the very existence of the State, the downfall of which will carry down with it all the iniquities of juridical right, and all the falsehoods of the diverse religious cults—that right and those cults being simply the complaisant consecration (ideal as well as real) of all the violences represented, guaranteed, and furthered by the State.[7]

Within the depths of the proletariat itself—at first within the French and Austrian proletariat, and then in that of the rest of Europe—there began to crystalize and finally took shape an altogether new tendency which aims directly at sweeping away every form of exploitation and every kind of political and juridical as well as governmental oppression—that is, at the abolition of all classes by means of economic equality and the abolition of their last bulwark, the State.

Such is the program of the Social Revolution.

Thus at present there exists in all the civilized countries in the world only one universal problem—the fullest and final emancipation of the proletariat from economic exploitation and State oppression. It is clear then that this question cannot be solved without a terrible and bloody struggle, and that in view of that situation the right and the importance of every nation will depend upon the direction, character, and degree of its participation in this struggle.[8]

Social Revolution Is International in Character. But social revolution cannot be confined to a single people: it is international in its very essence.[9]

Under the historic, juridical, religious, and social organization of most civilized countries, the economic emancipation of the workers is a sheer impossibility—and consequently, in order to attain and fully carry out that emancipation, it is necessary to destroy all modern institutions: the State, Church, Courts, University, Army, and Police, all of which are ramparts erected by the privileged classes against the proletariat. And it is not enough to have them overthrown in one country only: it is essential to have them destroyed in all countries, for since the emergence of modern States—in the seventeenth and eighteenth centuries—there has existed among those countries and those institutions an ever-growing international solidarity and powerful international alliances.[10]

Revolutions Cannot Be Improvised. Revolutions are not improvised. They are not made at will by individuals, and not even by the most powerful associations. They come about through force of circumstances, and are independent of any deliberate will or conspiracy. They can be foreseen . . . but never can their explosion be accelerated.[11]

The Role of Individuals in the Revolution. The time of great political personalities is over. When it was a question of waging political revolutions, those individuals were in their place. Politics has for its object the foundation and preservation of the States; but he who says "the State" says domination on one hand and subjection on the other. Great dominant individuals are absolutely necessary in a political revolution; in a social revolution they are not only useless, they are positively harmful and are incompatible with the foremost aim of that revolution, the emancipation of the masses. At present, in revolutionary action as in modern labor, the collective must supplant the individual.[12]

In a social revolution, which is diametrically opposed in every way to a political revolution, the actions of individuals are virtually null while the spontaneous action of the masses should be everything. All that individuals can do is to elaborate, clarify, and propagate ideas corresponding to the popular instinct and contribute their incessant efforts to the revolutionary organization of the natural power of the masses, but nothing over and above that; the rest can and should be done by the masses themselves.[13]

Organization and Revolution.   [As to organization, it is necessary] in order that when the Revolution, brought about through the force of circumstances, breaks out in full power, there be a real force in the field, one that knows what should be done and by virtue thereof capable of taking hold of the Revolution and giving it a direction salutary for the people: a serious international organization of workers' associations in all countries, capable of replacing the departing political world of the States and the bourgeoisie.[14]

Universal public and private bankruptcy is the first condition for a social-economic revolution.[15]

Preliminary Conditions of a Revolution.   But States do not crumble by themselves; they are overthrown by a universal international social organization. And organizing popular forces to carry out that revolution—such is the only task of those who sincerely aim at emancipation.[16]

Industrial Workers and Peasants in the Revolution.   The initiative in the new movement will belong to the people . . . in Western Europe, to the city and factory workers—in Russia, Poland, and most of the Slavic countries, to the peasants.[17]

But in order that the peasants rise up, it is absolutely necessary that the initiative in this revolutionary movement be taken by the city workers, for it is the latter who combine in themselves the instincts, ideas, and conscious will of the Social Revolution. Consequently, the whole danger threatening the existence of the States is focused in the city proletariat.[18]

Revolution: An Act of Justice.   The social transformation to which we whole-heartedly aspire is the great act of justice, finding its basis in the rational organization of society with equal rights for all.[19]

Nowhere is the [Social] Revolution so near as in Italy, not even in Spain, where an official revolution is now taking place, while in Italy everything seems quiet. In Italy the whole populace awaits the social upheaval, and is consciously aiming toward it.[20]

The Proximity of Social Revolution.   Neither Spain nor Italy can be expected to embark upon a policy of foreign conquests; on the contrary, one can expect a social revolution [in both countries] in the near future.[21]

In England the Social Revolution is much nearer than it is generally thought, and nowhere will it assume such a terrible character, because in no other country will it meet with such a desperate and well-organized resistance as in England.[22]

One can confidently say that the need for an economic and social revolution is at present strongly felt by the masses of people in Europe, even in the less civilized countries—and it is precisely this which gives us faith in the near triumph of the Social Revolution. For if the collective interest of the masses did not pronounce itself so clearly, profoundly, and resolutely in this sense, no Socialists in the world, not even if they were men of the most outstanding genius, would be able to arouse those masses.[23]

Revolutionary Violence: Political Force Has to be Destroyed. Even profound historians and jurists have not understood the simple truth, the explanation and confirmation of which they could have read on every page of history, namely: that in order to render harmless any political force whatever, to pacify and subdue it, only one way is possible, and that is to proceed with its destruction. Philosophers have not understood that against political forces there can be no other guarantees but complete destruction; that in politics, as in the arena of mutually struggling forces and facts, words, promises, and vows mean nothing—and that is so because every political force, while it remains an actual force, even apart from and contrary to the will of the kings and other authorities who direct it, must steadfastly tend toward the realization of its own aims; this by virtue of its essential nature and because of the danger of self-destruction.[24]

Historic Right Is Consecration of Force. Upon assuming office, Chancellor Bismarck held a discourse in which he set forth his program [saying among other things that] "Great State problems are decided not by right but by force, force always antedating right."

Freedom Is Won by Force. Bismarck, with his usual boldness, cynicism, and scornful candor, expressed in these words the essence of the political history of nations, the *arcanum* of State wisdom. The predominance and the abiding triumph of force—that is the real core of the matter, and all that is called *right* in the language of politics is only the consecration of fact created by force. It is clear that the people, longing for emancipation, cannot expect it from the theoretical triumph of abstract right; they must win liberty by force, for which purpose they must organize their powers apart from and against the State.[25]

Power of Reaction Should Not Be Underestimated. The unprecedently easy triumph of popular rebellions over the troops in nearly all the capitals of Europe, which signified the beginning of the revolution of 1848, had a bad effect upon revolutionaries not only in Germany but in all other countries, for it gave rise to foolish confidence which made them regard the slightest demonstration of force by the people as sufficient to break down the resistance of any military power. Because of this the Prussian, and in general the German democrats and revolutionists, believing themselves ever able to hold the government in a state of permanent fright by threatening it with a popular rebellion, did not see that it was necessary to organize, direct, and intensify the revolutionary passions and forces of the people.

Bourgeois Democrats Fear Popular Revolution. On the contrary, the most revolutionary of them, as it behooves any well-behaved bourgeois, feared those passions and forces, and when it came to a showdown, they proved themselves ready to take the side of the State and the established order; and they generally agreed that the less frequently they fell back upon this dangerous expedient of popular rebellion, the better it would be for them.

Thus the official revolutionists of Prussia and Germany scorned the only means they had available to achieve a final and effective victory over the emergent reaction. Not only did they overlook this problem of organizing a popular revolution, but they even bent their efforts to hold it back and subdue it, thus wrecking the only potent weapon at their disposal.[26]

Can Justice Be Obtained Without Force? "And be on guard—a question reduced to terms of force remains a doubtful question."

But if force cannot obtain justice for the proletariat, what is capable of obtaining it? A miracle? We do not believe in miracles, and those who speak to the proletariat of such miracles are liars and corrupters. Moral propaganda? The moral conversion of the bourgeoisie under the influence of Mazzini's sermons? But it is utterly wrong on the part of Mazzini, who certainly should know history, to speak of such a conversion and to lull the proletariat with those ridiculous illusions. Was there ever, at any period, or in any country, a single example of a privileged and dominant class which granted concessions freely, spontaneously, and without being driven to it by force or fear?

Awareness of the Justice of a Cause Is Not Sufficient. The awareness of the justice of its own cause is no doubt vital to the proletariat in order to organize its own members into a power capable of attaining a triumph. And the proletariat now does not lack this awareness. Where such awareness is still lacking it is our duty to build it up among the workers; that justice has become incontestable even in the eyes of our adversaries. But the mere consciousnesss of such justice is not sufficient. It is necessary that the proletariat add to it the organization of its own forces, for the time is passed when the walls of Jericho would crumble at the blowing of trumpets; now force is necessary to vanquish and repulse other force.[27]

Humaneness in Revolutionary Tactics. We say to the workers: The justice of your cause is certain; only scoundrels can deny it. What you lack, however, is the organization of your own forces. Organize those forces and overthrow that which stands in the way of the realization of your justice. Begin by striking down all those who oppress you. And then, after having assured your victory and having destroyed the power of your enemies, show yourselves humane toward the unfortunate stricken-down foes, henceforth disarmed and harmless; recognize them as your brothers and invite them to live and work alongside of you upon the unshakable foundation of social equality.[28]

Organization Is Necessary.   The workers are great in number but numbers mean nothing if forces are not organized.[29]

And, indeed, what do we see? Spontaneous movements of the masses of people—and very serious movements like that of Palermo in 1866 and the even more formidable movement of the peasants in many provinces against the iniquities of the law of *macinato* (tax upon flour-grinding)— never found any sympathy, or very little of it, among this revolutionary youth of Italy. If the latter movement had been well organized and directed by intelligent people, it might have produced a formidable revolution. Lacking organization and leadership, it ended in a fiasco.[30]

Workers Are Socialists by Their Class Instinct.   Fortunately the proletariat of the cities, not excepting those who swear by the names of Mazzini and Garibaldi, never could let itself be completely converted to the ideas and cause of Mazzini and Garibaldi. And the workers could not do it for the simple reason that the proletariat—that is, the oppressed, despoiled, maltreated, miserable, starved mass of workers—necessarily possess the logic inherent in the historic role of labor.

Workers may accept the programs of Mazzini and Garibaldi; but deep down in their bellies, in the livid pallor of their children and their companions in poverty and suffering, in their everyday actual slavery, there is something which calls for a social revolution. They are all Socialists in spite of themselves, with the exception of a few individuals—perhaps one out of thousands—who, owing to a certain cleverness, to chance or knavery on their part, have entered, or hope to enter, the ranks of the bourgeoisie. All others—and I am referring to the masses of workers who follow Mazzini and Garibaldi—are such only in their imagination, and in reality they can be only revolutionary Socialists.

. . . If you will organize yourselves for this purpose throughout Italy, harmoniously, fraternally, without recognizing any leaders but your own young collective, I vow to you that within the year there will be no more Mazzinist or Garibaldist workers; they all will be revolutionary Socialists, and patriots, too, but in a very human sense of that word. That is, they will simultaneously be both patriots and internationalists. Thus you will create an unshakable foundation for the future of the Social Revolution.[31]

A Social Revolution Must Be a Simultaneous Revolution of City Workers and the Peasantry.   Organize the city proletariat in the name of revolutionary Socialism, and in doing this, unite it into one preparatory organization together with the peasantry. An uprising by the proletariat alone would not be enough; with that we would have only a political revolution which would necessarily produce a natural and legitimate reaction on the part of the peasants, and that reaction, or merely the indifference of the peasants, would strangle the revolution of the cities, as it happened recently in France.

Only a wide-sweeping revolution embracing both the city workers and peasants would be sufficiently strong to overthrow and break the organized power of the State, backed as it is by all the resources of the possessing classes. But an all-embracing revolution, that is, a social revolution, is a simultaneous revolution of the people of the cities and of the peasantry. It is this kind of revolution that must be organized—for without a preparatory organization, the most powerful elements are insignificant and impotent.[32] . . . The unions create that conscious power without which no victory is possible.[33]

CHAPTER 5 *Methods of the Preparatory Period*

You write me, my dear friend, that you are "the enemy of all statutes" and you maintain that "they are fit only for children's play." I do not altogether share your opinion on this point. Excessive regimentation is abhorrent, and, like you, I believe that "serious people should chart the course of their behavior and not swerve from it." Let us, however, try to understand each other.*

In order to establish a certain co-ordination in action, one which, in my opinion, is necessary among serious people striving toward the same goal, certain conditions are required, a definite set of rules equally binding upon all, certain agreements and understandings to be frequently renewed—lacking all that, if everyone is going to work as he pleases, even the most serious people will find themselves in a position whereby they will neutralize one another's efforts. The result will be disharmony and not the harmony and serene confidence at which we are aiming.

One has to know how, when, and where to find one another, and whom to turn to for possible co-operation. We are not rich, and it is only when we unite and co-ordinate our means and joint actions that we shall be able to create the capital [the power of organization] capable of competing with the combined capital [forces] of our adversaries. A small capital, well organized, is of greater value than a large but disorganized and ill-applied capital. [Here *capital* means the membership.]

I do not want the dictatorship of one capitalist [member of the organization] nor of a group of capitalists [a group of members] nor of one market over another. [By *market* a tendency, a party, apparently is meant.] I want to see order and serene confidence in our work, coming not as a

---

* The first four paragraphs in this chapter are from a letter written by Bakunin to Albert Richard; no date is given.

result of the dictates of a single will, but of a collective, well organized will of many of our comrades scattered through many countries. This means that we must put the secret but powerful action of all interested parties in place of a government emanating from a single center. But in order that this decentralization may become possible, it is necessary to have a real organization, and such an organization cannot exist without a certain degree of regimentation, which after all is simply the product of a mutual agreement or a contract.[1]

The Role of a Small Minority.   Three men united in an organization already form, in my opinion, a serious beginning of power. What will happen when you succeed in organizing several hundred of your followers throughout the country? . . . Several hundred well-intentioned young men, when organized apart from the people, of course do not constitute an adequate revolutionary force: this also is an illusion which should be left to Mazzini. And Mazzini himself seems to have become aware of this truth by now, for now he addresses himself directly to the masses of workers. But those several hundreds are sufficient to organize the revolutionary power of the people.[2]

The only army is the people, the whole people, in both the cities and the country. But how to approach these people? In the city you will be interfered with by the government, by the *consorteria,* and by the Mazzinists. In the country you will meet the priests on your way. Nevertheless, dear friends, there exists a power which is capable of overcoming all that. It is the collective. If you were isolated, if each of you were impelled to act on his own hook, certainly you would be powerless, but by being united and by organizing your own forces—however small they may be in the beginning—solely for joint action, being led by common thought and common attitude, and by striving toward a common goal, you will be invincible.[3]

At present, in revolutionary action as well as in work, the collective is to replace individuals. You should know that when you are organized you are stronger than all the Mazzinis and Garibaldis in the world. You will think, live, and act collectively, which, however, will in no way hinder the full development of the intellectual and moral faculties of every individual. Every one of you will contribute his own abilities, and in uniting you increase your value a hundred-fold. Such is the law of collective action.[4]

The Spirit of Rebellion.   The sentiment of rebellion, this satanic pride, which spurns subjection to any master whatever, whether of divine or human origin, alone produces in man a love for independence and freedom. . . .[5]

Destructive Character of Popular Rebellion.   A rebellion on the part of the people, which by nature is spontaneous, chaotic, and ruthless, always presupposes a vast destruction of property. The working masses are ever ready for such sacrifices: that is why they constitute the rude, savage force capable of heroic feats and of carrying out aims seemingly impossible of realization, and that is so because, having very little or no property, they have not been corrupted by it. When the exigencies of defense or victory demand it, they will not stop at the destruction of their own villages and cities, and inasmuch as property in most cases does not belong to the people, they very often evince a positive passion for destruction.

Role of the Destructive Passion. This negative passion, however, is far from rising to the great height of the revolutionary cause; but without that passion the revolutionary cause is impossible of realization, for there can be no revolution without a sweeping and passionate destruction, a salutary and fruitful destruction, since by means of such destruction new worlds are born and come into existence.[6]

Destruction Is Correlative With the Constructive Aspects of Revolution. [But] no one can aim at destruction without having at least a remote conception, whether true or false, of the new order which should succeed the one now existing; the more vividly that future is visualized, the more powerful is the force of destruction. And the nearer that visualization approaches the truth, that is, the more it conforms to the necessary development of the present social world, the more salutary and useful are the effects of the destructive action. For destructive action is ever determined —not only its essence and the degree of its intensity, but likewise the means used by it—by the positive ideal which constitutes its initial inspiration, its soul.[7]

Workers' Organizations Are Not Centers of Conspiracies. If the International were made up of central sections only, the latter probably would have succeeded by now in forming some conspiracies for the overthrow of the existing order of things. But those conspiracies would be confined to mere intentions, being too impotent to attain their goal since they would never be able to draw in more than a very small number of workers—the most intelligent, most energetic, most convinced, and most devoted among them. The vast majority, the millions of proletarians, would remain outside of such conspiracies, yet, in order to overthrow and destroy the political and social order which now crushes us, it will be necessary to have the co-operation of those millions.[8]

The now dominant system is strong not because of its idea and intrinsic moral force—of which it is totally devoid—but because of the whole organization of the State, mechanical, bureaucratic, military, and police, and by virtue of the science and the wealth of the classes interested in backing it. And one of Mazzini's abiding and most ludicrous illusions is precisely the fancied idea that it is possible to smash this power with the aid of a few handfuls of poorly armed young men. He holds onto and must hold onto this illusion, for inasmuch as his system precludes him from having recourse to a revolution waged by the great masses of people, no other way of action is left to him but conspiracies by handfuls of young people.[9]

This youth should now have the courage to recognize and proclaim its complete and definite break with politics, with conspiracies, and with the republican enterprises of Mazzini, under the pain of seeing itself annihilated and doomed to inertia and shameful helplessness.[10]

Economic Struggle Is the Prime Question; Strikes; Co-operation. The people, guided by their admirable sound sense as well as by their instincts, have realized that the first condition of their real emancipation, or of their *humanization*, was before all else a radical change in their economic situation. The question of daily bread is, justly, to them the prime question, for as it was noted by Aristotle, man, in order to think, in order to feel himself free, in order to become man, must be freed from the material cares of daily life. For that matter, the bourgeois, who are so vociferous in their outcries against the materialism of the people and who preach to them the abstinences of idealism, know it very well, for they themselves preach only by word and not by example.

The second question arising before the people—the question of leisure after work—is the *sine qua non* of humanity; but bread and leisure never can be obtained apart from a radical transformation of existing society, and that explains why the Revolution, impelled by the implications of its own principles, gave birth to *Socialism*.[11]

Apart from the great question of the final and complete emancipation of the workers by *the abolition of the right of inheritance, of political States*, and by the organization of collective property and production, as well as by other ways which subsequently will be passed upon by the Congress [of the International], the Section of the Alliance will undertake the study of and will try to put into practice all the provisional means or palliatives which might alleviate, at least in part, the existing situation of the workers.[12]

The prime question for the people is its economic emancipation, which necessarily and directly engenders its political—and following that—its intellectual and moral emancipation. Therefore we fully subscribe to the resolution adopted by the Congress in Brussels (1867):

"Recognizing that for the moment *it is impossible to organize a rational system of education*, the Congress urges its various sections to organize study courses which would follow a program of scientific, professional, and industrial education—that is, an integral program—in order to remedy as much as possible the lack of education among workers. And, of course, it stands to reason that a reduction of working hours is to be considered an indispensable preliminary condition."[13]

The Alliance of which I hereafter will speak is wholly different from the International Social Democratic Alliance [which Bakunin declared had committed suicide]. It is no longer an international organization; it is the *separate Section* of the Social Democratic Alliance of Geneva, recognized in July, 1869, by the General Council as the regular section of the International. . . . The best answer we can make to our detractors, to those who dare to say that we wish to dissolve the International Workingmen's Association is to [quote here] from the new rules:

". . . Article V. *The steadfast and real exercise of practical solidarity among the workers of all trades,* including, of course, the workers on the land, *is the surest guarantee of their impending deliverance.* To observe this solidarity in the private and public manifestations of the life of the workers and in their struggle against bourgeois capital shall be considered the supreme duty of every member of the Section of the Social Democratic Alliance. Any member who fails to observe this duty shall be immediately expelled."[14]

But without letting themselves be led astray by the siren voices of the bourgeoisie and of the bourgeois Socialists the workers, above all, should concentrate their efforts upon this great question of *economic emancipation,* which should be the source of all other emancipation.[15]

Revolutionary Significance of Strikes. The dominant news in the labor movement of Europe can be summed up in one word: *strikes.* . . . In the measure that we advance, strikes keep on spreading. What does it mean? It means that the struggle between labor and capital grows more and more accentuated, that economic anarchy grows with each day, and that we are marching with gigantic steps toward the inevitable end-point of this anarchy—toward social revolution. Most certainly the emancipation of the proletariat could be effected without any violent shocks, if the bourgeoisie were to have an August 4th* of its own, if it were willing to renounce its privileges, its escheatage rights of capital to labor. But bourgeois egoism and blindness are so inveterate that one must be an optimist even to hope that the social problem will be solved by a common understanding between the privileged and the disinherited. Therefore it is rather from the very excess of the present anarchy that the new social order may be expected to emerge.

The General Strike. When strikes begin to grow in scope and intensity, spreading from one place to another, it means that events are ripening for a general strike, and a general strike coming off at the present time, now that the proletariat is deeply permeated with ideas of emancipation, can only lead to a great cataclysm, which will regenerate society. Doubtless we have not yet come to that point, but everything leads toward it. Only it is necessary that the people should be ready, that they should not permit themselves to be eased out of it by chatter-boxes, windbags, and day-dreamers as in 1848, and that is why they must build up beforehand a strong and serious organization.[16]

---

* August 4, 1789, was the date on which the French nobles and the clergy in the Assembly in Paris purported to renounce their own feudal rights. But a new measure enacted there that night contained a provision which enslaved the peasants all the more.

Strikes Train Workers for the Ultimate Struggle.   Who does not know what every single strike means to the workers in terms of suffering and sacrifices? But strikes are necessary; indeed, they are necessary to such an extent that without them it would be impossible to arouse the masses for a social struggle, nor would it be possible to have them organized. Strikes spell war, and the masses of people become organized only during and by the means of war, which jolts the ordinary worker out of his humdrum existence, out of his meaningless, joyless, and hopeless isolation. War makes him band together with all the other workers in the name of the same passion and the same goal; it convinces all workers in the most graphic and perceptible manner of the necessity of a strict organization to attain victory. The aroused masses of the people are like molten metal, which fuses into one continuous mass, and which lends itself to shaping much more easily than non-molten metal—that is, if there are good craftsmen who know how to mold it in accordance with the properties and instrinsic laws of a given metal, in accordance with the people's needs and instincts.

Strikes awaken in the masses all the social-revolutionary instincts which reside deeply in the heart of every worker, which constitute, so to speak, his socio-physiological existence, but which ordinarily are consciously perceived by very few workers, most of whom are weighed down by slavish habits and a general spirit of resignation. But when those instincts, stimulated by the economic struggle, awaken in the heartened multitudes of workers, the propaganda of social-revolutionary ideas becomes quite easy. For these ideas are simply the purest and most faithful expression of the instincts of the people. If they do not correspond to those instincts, they are false; and in so far as they are false they will necessarily be rejected by the people. But if such ideas come as an honest expression of the instincts, if they represent *the genuine thought of the people*, they will quickly pervade the minds of the multitudes in rebellion; and once those ideas find their way to the minds of the people, they will swiftly proceed toward their full actualization.[17]

Every strike is the more valuable in that it broadens and deepens to an ever greater extent the gulf now separating the bourgeois class from the masses of the people; and in that it proves to the workers in the most perceptible manner that their interests are absolutely incompatible with the interests of the capitalists and property-owners. Strikes are valuable because they destroy in the minds of the now exploited and enslaved masses of people the possibility of any compromises or deals with the enemy; they destroy at its roots that which is called bourgeois Socialism, thus keeping the cause of the people free from any entanglements in the political and economic combinations of the propertied classes. There is no better means of detaching the workers from the political influence of the bourgeoisie than a strike.[18]

Yes, strikes are of enormous value; they create, organize, and form a

The serious economists of the two opposing schools—the liberal school and that of scientific Communists—who differ on all other points and agree only upon one point, have long ago stated their conviction (one based upon real science, that is, upon a rigorous study of the co-operative movement and the development of economic facts) that under the present organization of the social economy and production of commodities, and the increase, dominant control, and concentration of capital necessarily resulting from this organization of economy, no efforts on the part of labor associations will be able to free labor from the oppressive yoke of capital; and that labor banks, fed only by the meager savings of the toilers, will never be able to withstand the competition of the powerful, international, bourgeois, oligarchic banks.

They have long since concluded also that with the steady increase of the supply of labor and hungry stomachs, (an increase accelerated as a result of the concentration of capital into fewer hands and the concomitant proletarianization of the lower and even the middle layers of the bourgeoisie) the workers, in order to escape death from starvation, are bound to compete against one another, driving wages down to the lowest point required for their maintenance and subsistence; and that therefore all worker-consumers' associations, by diminishing the prices of the chief items in their budget, must invariably cause the driving down of the wage scale, thus making worse the situation of the workers.

The economists likewise have proved that producers' associations are feasible only in those branches of industry which have not yet been taken over by big capital, because no labor association can compete with the latter in the large-scale production of commodities. And inasmuch as big capital, by virtue of its inherent necessity, strives to put all branches of industry under its exclusive control, the ultimate fate of the producers' associations will be the same as that of the petty and middle bourgeoisie: inevitable general misery and slavish subjection to bourgeois oligarchic capital, and the absorption of every kind of small and middle sized property by the large-scaled property of the few hundreds of fortunate persons throughout Europe.[31]

The Iron Law of Wages. The freedom to exploit the labor of the proletariat, *forced* to sell itself to capital at the lowest possible price, forced not by any political or civil law whatever, but by the economic position in which the workers find themselves, and by the apprehension and fear of hunger; this freedom, I say, does not fear the competition of workers' associations—whether producers' or consumers' or mutual credit —and that is so for the simple reason that workers' associations, reduced to their own means, will never be able to build up the necessary capital capable of fighting bourgeois capital.[32]

The consumers' societies, organized on a small scale, can contribute their small share toward the amelioration of the hard lot of the workers; but as soon as they start growing, as soon as they succeed in lowering the prices of articles of prime necessity, there will come as an inevitable result a drop in the wage scale.[33]

Political Alliances and Blocs; Class Collaboration: At What Price? *Confidence produces union, and union creates power*—These are truths which no one will attempt to deny. But in order that these truths shall prevail, it is necessary to have two things: it is necessary that confidence should not turn into folly, and that the union, equally sincere on all sides, should not become an illusion, a falsehood, or a hypocritical exploitation of one party by another. It is necessary that all the united parties completely forget—not forever, of course, but for the duration of this union—their particular and necessarily opposing interests, the aims and interests which divide those parties in ordinary times; and that they become absorbed in the pursuit of the common purpose.

Otherwise, what will be the possible outcome? The sincere party necessarily becomes the victim and the dupe of another party which is less sincere or which completely lacks sincerity, and it will be sacrificed not to the triumph of the common cause but to the detriment of that cause, and for the exclusive benefit of that party which will have hypocritically exploited this union.[34]

In order that the union should be feasible and real in character, is it not necessary that the aim in the name of which the parties have to unite be the same? And is this the case at present? Can it be said that the bourgeoisie and the proletariat want absolutely the same thing? Not at all![35]

It is clear that the revolutionary Socialist section of the proletariat cannot ally itself with any faction, not even the most advanced faction, of bourgeois politics without immediately becoming, against its own will, an instrument of that politics.[36]

If the bourgeoisie and the proletariat of France pursue not only different but absolutely opposing purposes, by what miracle could a sincere and real union be established between them? It is clear that this so highly extolled and ardently advocated conciliation will be nothing but a sheer lie. It was this lie which destroyed France; can it be hoped that it will bring France back to life? Much as this division may be condemned, it nevertheless will not cease to exist in fact. And since it does exist, since it is bound to exist by the very nature of things, it would be puerile, I should even say fatal, from the point of view of France's salvation, to deny it, and not to recognize openly its existence. And also, since the safety of France calls upon you for union, forget, sacrifice all your interests, all your ambitions and all your personal divisions; forget and sacrifice, as much as it is possible, all the party differences; but in the name of this salvation steer clear of any illusions, for in this given situation illusions would be deadly. Seek union only with those who want just as seriously and passionately as yourselves to save France *at any price.*[37]

When a great danger has to be met, is it not better to march against it in small numbers but with the certainty of not being abandoned in the moment of struggle, rather than be trailed by a multitude of false allies who will betray you on the first battlefield?[38]

CHAPTER 6 *Jacobins of 1870 Feared Revolutionary Anarchy*

. . . The Imperial administration [of Napoleonic France in 1870] could not be destroyed with a single blow, because it would be impossible to replace it immediately with another. It that were to be attempted, there would ensue, in the midst of a terrible danger, a more or less prolonged interval during which France would find itself without any administration, and consequently with no trace of government—an interval in which the French populace, completely abandoned to itself, would become a prey to the most horrible anarchy. This might suit us all right—us, the revolutionary Socialists—but it does not enter into the plans of the Jacobins, State partisans beyond compare.[1]

In order to obviate this evil, Gambetta will no doubt send into all Departments [French provinces] proconsuls, extraordinary commissars endowed with complete powers.[2]

Sources of Revolutionary Strength of the Jacobins of 1793. It is now enough, [however], to be endowed with extraordinary powers in order to take extraordinary measures for public safety, in order to have the power to create new forces, to stimulate in a corrupted administration and within a populace systematically weaned away from any initiative, a salutary energy and activity. For that it is necessary also to possess what the bourgeois of 1792-1793 possessed to a high degree and what the bourgeoisie of today absolutely lacks—even its most radical representatives, the present-day republicans. In order to do that it is necessary to have revolutionary mind, will, and energy; it is necessary to have a demon within the flesh. . . .

Apart from those personal qualities, which put a truly heroic imprint upon the men of 1793, the success of the extraordinary commissars of the

Jacobins' National Convention was due to the fact that that convention in itself was genuinely revolutionary, and because, while depending in Paris upon the masses of the people, upon the vile populace, to the exclusion of the liberal bourgeoisie, it ordered all its proconsuls dispatched to the provinces to base themselves everywhere and always in their work upon the same rabble.[3]

The Commissars of the Great Revolution.   The antagonism between bourgeois revolution and popular revolution did not yet exist in 1793; it existed neither in the consciousness of the people nor even in the consciousness of the bourgeoisie. Historic experience had not yet brought out the timeless truth which states that the freedom of every privileged class—including, of course, that of the bourgeois—is essentially based upon the economic slavery of the proletariat. This truth has always existed as a fact, as a real consequence, but it was so greatly obscured by other facts and masked by so many interests and varied historical tendencies, (especially religious, national, and political tendencies), that it did not yet stand out in its great simplicity and present-day clarity, neither for the bourgeoisie, who invests money in enterprises, nor for the proletariat, whom the bourgeoisie exploits.

The bourgeoisie and the proletariat have always been natural, eternal enemies without being aware of it, and because of this ignorance they attributed—the bourgeoisie its fears and the proletariat its woes—to fictitious causes and not to their real antagonisms. They believed themselves to be friends, and because of that belief they all marched united against the monarchy, against the nobility, and against the priests. It was that which gave the bourgeois revolutionists of 1793 their great power. Not only were they not afraid to unleash popular passions, but they fomented such passions by all means at their disposal as the only way to save the country and themselves from foreign and domestic reaction.

When an extraordinary commissar delegated by the Convention arrived in a province he never addressed himself to the big-wigs of that region nor to the revolutionaries in white gloves; he devoted himself to the *sansculottes*, to the rabble, and it was upon these elements that he depended in order to carry out, against the will of the big-wigs and the well-bred revolutionists, the revolutionary decrees of the Convention. What these commissars did then was, properly speaking, not in the nature of centralization nor of building up a new administration; they aimed rather to evoke a popular movement.

Usually they did not come to any province with the intention of imposing upon it dictatorially the will of the National Convention. They did that only on rare occasions, when they went into provinces that were decidedly and unanimously reactionary and hostile. In such instances they did not go alone, but were accompanied by troops who added the argument of the bayonet to their civic eloquence. But ordinarily they went alone, without a single soldier to back them, and they sought their support among the masses, whose instincts invariably conformed to the ideas of the Convention.

Far from restraining the freedom of popular movements because of fear of anarchy, the commissars tried to foment it by all means at their disposal. The first thing they would do was to form a people's club, wherever none already existed; being themselves genuine revolutionists, they easily discovered the true revolutionists among the masses, and united with them in order to fan the revolutionary flames, to foment anarchy, to arouse the masses, and to *organize along revolutionary lines* this popular anarchy. That revolutionary organization was the sole administration and the sole executive force of which the extraordinary commissars availed themselves to revolutionize and terrorize the provinces.[4]

Such was the true secret of the power of those revolutionary giants whom the Jacobin pygmies of our own times admire without ever succeeding in coming near to them.[5]

As in 1792 France Could Be Saved from the Prussians Only by a Great Uprising of the People. The only thing that can save France in the face of the terrible, mortal dangers which menace it now is *a spontaneous, formidable, passionately energetic, anarchic, destructive, and savage uprising of the masses of people throughout France.*[6]

A Revolutionary Approach to the Peasants. I believe that right now in France, and probably in other countries as well, there exist only two classes capable of such a movement: *the workers* and *the peasants*. Do not wonder that I am speaking of peasants. The peasants, even those of France, sin only through ignorance and not from lack of temperament. Not having abused nor even used life, not having felt the deleterious effect of bourgeois civilization, which has affected them only superficially, they have preserved the energetic temperament, and all the nature of the people. Property, and the love and enjoyment not of pleasures but of gain, have made them egoistic to a considerable extent, but they have not abated their instinctive hatred for the "fine gentlemen," and above all, for the bourgeois land-owners, who enjoy income from the land without producing it with the work of their own hands. In addition, the peasants are deeply patriotic, and nationalistic, because they have built a cult around the land, because they have a passion for it, and I believe nothing should be easier than to stir them up against the foreign invaders who want to deprive France of two vast provinces.[7]

It is clear that in order to arouse and carry along the peasants it is necessary to use a great deal of prudence, in the sense that one must beware, in speaking of them, of enunciating ideas and employing phrases which exercise an all-powerful effect upon the city workers but which, having been interpreted for a long time for the peasants by all sorts of reactionaries (from the big land-owners to State functionaries and priests) in a manner which made them odious and threatening to the peasants, produced upon them an effect quite contrary to their intent. No, in speaking to the peasants one has to use at first the most simple language, words which correspond best to their instincts and level of understanding.

In those villages where the platonic and fictitious love for the Emperor [Napoleon III] really exists as a prejudice and a passionate habit, one should not even speak against the Emperor. It is necessary to *undermine in fact* the power of the State, and of the Emperor, without saying anything against him—by undermining the influence, the official organization, and as much as it is possible, by destroying the persons who act as functionaries for the Emperor: the mayors, justices of the peace, priests, gendarmes, and chiefs of village police—who, I believe, can be "Septemberized" by arousing the peasants against them. It is necessary to tell them that the Prussians must be driven out of France—this they will understand perfectly because they are patriots—and that for this they must arm themselves, organize themselves into battalions of volunteers, and march against the Prussians.

But before they begin marching it also is necessary that, following the example of the cities, which have rid themselves of all exploiting parasites and which have turned the task of their defense over to the sons of the people, to the workers,—the peasants, too, rid themselves of the "fine gentlemen" who exploit, dishonor, and exhaust the land by cultivating it with hired labor and not with their own hands. Then it is essential to arouse them to defiance of the village notables, the functionaries, and as much as possible, of the priest himself. Let them take whatever they want in the Church and of the land belonging to the Church—wherever the latter owns land—and let them take possession of the lands belonging to the State, as well as of the estates of the big land-owners, of the rich, utterly useless parasites.

And then the peasants will need to be told that since everywhere all payments have been suspended, they also must suspend their payments—payments on private debts, taxes, and mortgages—until perfect order has been established; that otherwise, all the money passing into the hands of the functionaries would remain with them or would pass into the hands of the Prussians. This done, let them march against the Prussians, but first let them organize, let them unite on the principles of federation, village with village, and with the cities too, for mutual support and for joint defense against both the foreign and domestic Prussians.[8]

Class Struggles in the Villages Will Rid the Peasantry of Its Political Prejudices. Here a question presents itself: The revolution of 1792 and 1793 could give the peasants—not gratis but at a very low price—the national estates, that is, the lands belonging to the Church and emigrant noblemen, all of which had been confiscated by the State. But now, it will be argued, the Revolution has nothing to give to the peasants. Has it not, though? Have not the Church and the religious orders of both sexes grown rich again owing to the criminal connivance of the legitimist monarchy, and above all of the Second Empire?

True, the greater part of their wealth was very prudently mobilized in anticipation of possible revolutions. The Church, which, though preoccupied with celestial matters, has never overlooked its material interests, (being notorious for its shrewd economic speculations), doubtless has placed the greater part of its earthly possessions, which it continues augmenting from day to day for the greater good of the poor and unfortunate, in all kinds of commercial, industrial, and banking enterprises, and in private bonds of every country.

Thus it would take a veritable universal bankruptcy—which will come as the inevitable consequence of a universal social revolution—to deprive the Church of that wealth which now constitutes the chief instrument of its power, alas, that still formidable power. But it remains no less certain that the Church now possesses, especially in the southern provinces of France, vast land holdings, and buildings, as well as ornaments and church plate which represent veritable treasures in silver, gold, or precious stones. Well, all of that can and should be confiscated, and not for the benefit of the State but for that of the communes.[9]

This then, as I see it, is the only effective way of influencing the peasants in two directions—in the direction of defending the country against Prussian invasion, and in the direction of destroying the State apparatus in the rural communes, where its principal roots are to be found—and consequently, toward the Social Revolution.

It is only by this kind of propaganda, only by a social revolution thus understood, that one can fight against the reactionary spirit of the villages, that one can succeed in overcoming it and transforming it into a revolutionary spirit.

The alleged Bonapartist sympathies of the French peasants do not alarm me. Such sympathies are merely the surface symptoms of the socialist instinct led astray by ignorance and exploited by malice, a skin disease which will yield to the heroic treatment of revolutionary Socialism. The peasants will not give away their own land, their money, nor their lives to preserve the power of Napoleon III, but they will willingly give for that purpose the lives and property of others, because they detest those others. They entertain the utmost, altogether socialistic hatred of men of labor against men of leisure, against the "fine gentlemen."[10]

Antagonism Between Peasants and City Workers Due to Misunderstanding. If we want to be practical, if, tired of day-dreaming, we make up our minds to fight in earnest in order to bring about a revolution, we shall have to start by ridding ourselves of a number of doctrinaire, bourgeois prejudices, unfortunately taken over to a great extent from the bourgeoisie by the city proletariat. The city worker, more highly developed than the peasant, too often despises the latter and speaks of him with an altogether bourgeois contempt. Nothing is more irritating than disdain and contempt—that is why the peasant answers this contempt on the part of the industrial workers with hatred. And this is nothing short of a misfortune, for such contempt and hatred divide the people into two camps, each of which paralyzes and undermines the other. Between these two parties there are in fact no conflicting interests; there is only a vast and baneful misunderstanding which should be smoothed out at any price.[11]

The more enlightened, more civilized Socialism of the city workers, a Socialism which because of this very circumstance takes on a somewhat bourgeois character, slights and scorns the primitive, natural, and much more savage Socialism of the villages, and since it distrusts the latter, it always tries to restrain it, to oppress it in the very name of equality and freedom, which naturally makes for dense ignorance about city Socialism on the part of the peasants, who confound this Socialism with the bourgeois spirit of the cities. The peasant regards the industrial worker as a bourgeois lackey or as a soldier of the bourgeoisie and he despises and detests the city worker as such. He hates the latter so much that he himself becomes the servant and blind tool of reaction.

Such is the fatal antagonism which hitherto has paralyzed the revolutionary efforts of France and of Europe. Whoever wants the triumph of the Social Revolution, must first of all smooth out this antagonism. Since the two camps are divided only by misunderstanding, it is necessary that one of them take the initiative in explaining and conciliating. The initiative by right belongs to the more enlightened party; that is, it rightfully belongs to the city workers. In order to bring about that conciliation, those workers should be the first to render an account to themselves of the nature of the grievances which they have against the peasants. What are their principal grievances?[12]

There are three of them: the first is that the peasants are ignorant, superstitious, and bigoted, and that they allow themselves to be led by priests. The second grievance is that the peasants are devoted to the Emperor. The third is that the peasants are ardent partisans of individual property.

Peasant Ignorance.   True, the French peasants are grossly ignorant. But is that their fault? Has anyone been concerned about providing them with schools? And is their ignorance a reason for despising and maltreating them? If so, then the bourgeois, who without doubt are more learned than the industrial workers, should have the right to despise and maltreat the latter; and we know a goodly number of bourgeois persons who say so, and who base on this superiority of education their right to dominate the city workers and to demand subordination from them. What constitutes the greatness of those workers as against the bourgeoisie is not their education, which is very small, indeed; it is their instinct and the fact that they stand for justice that make for their incontestable greatness. But do the peasants lack that instinct for justice? Look well and you will find among them this same instinct, though it is manifest in different forms. You will find in them alongside of ignorance a deep common sense, admirable shrewdness, and that energy of labor which spell the honor and the salvation of the proletariat.[13]

Religious Bigotry Among the Peasants Can Be Overcome by Correct Revolutionary Tactics. The peasants, you say, are superstitious and bigots, and they let themselves be led by the priests. Their superstition is the product of their ignorance, which is systematically and artifically fostered by all bourgeois governments. For that matter, the peasants are not so superstitious and bigoted as you make them out to be; it is their wives that are so. But then are all the wives of the city workers completely free from the superstitions and doctrines of the Roman Catholic religion?

As to the influence of the priests, it is only skin-deep; the peasants follow the priests inasmuch as domestic peace requires it and in so far as it does not run counter to their interests. Their religious superstition did not prevent them after 1789 from buying the properties of the Church which had been confiscated by the State, despite the curses hurled by the Church against the buyers as well as against the sellers of its properties. Hence it follows that in order to destroy definitely the influence of the priests in the villages, the Revolution has to do only one thing: to place the interests of the peasants in a position where they will necessarily clash with the interests of the Church.[14]

Realism and Sectarianism in the Struggle Against Religion. It has always annoyed me to have to listen not only to the revolutionary Jacobins but also to the Socialists brought up in the school of Blanqui and even to some of our intimate friends who have been indirectly influenced by the latter school, advancing the completely *anti-revolutionary* idea that the coming republic will have to abolish by decree all public cults and shall likewise decree the forcible expulsion of all priests. To begin with, I am *the absolute enemy of a revolution by decrees*, which is the application of the idea of a *revolutionary State* and a sequel of it; *that is, a reaction disguised by revolutionary appearances*. As against the system of revolutionary decrees *I oppose the system of revolutionary action*, the only effective, consistent, and true system. The authoritarian system of decrees, in seeking to *impose* freedom and equality, destroys them. *The Anarchist system of action evokes and creates them in an infallible manner*, without the intervention of any official or authoritarian violence whatever. The first leads inevitably to the ultimate triumph of an outspoken reaction. The second system establishes the Revolution on a natural and unshakable foundation.[15]

Religion Cannot Be Effectively Fought by Revolutionary Decrees. Thus, taking this example, we may say that if abolition of religious cults and expulsion of priests are going to be decreed by law, you can rest assured that even the least religious peasant will rise up in defense of the banned cult and the expelled priests; they may do it either because of a spirit of contradiction, or because a natural and legitimate sentiment—a sentiment which is the foundation of liberty—rises up in the heart of every man against any imposed measure, even if it be done in the name of freedom. One can be sure then that if the cities commit the folly of *decreeing* abolition of religious cults and expulsion of priests, the peasants will take the side of the priests, will rise in revolt against the cities, and will become a terrible instrument in the hands of reaction.

But does it follow that the priests should be left in full enjoyment of their power? Not at all. It is necessary to fight against them most energetically, not, however, because they are priests, nor because they are ministers of the Roman Catholic religion, but *because they are Prussian agents.* In the villages as well as in the cities, it should not be the revolutionary authorities, not even though they be a Revolutionary Committee of Public Safety, that should strike down the priests. *It should be the populace itself* (the workers in the cities and the peasants in the villages) which takes action against the priests, while the revolutionary authorities outwardly protect them in the name of respect for freedom of conscience. Let us copy the wisdom of our adversaries. See, for instance, how all governments expatiate on liberty while being thoroughly reactionary in their actions. Let the revolutionary authorities go easy on phrases, but while using as moderate and pacific language as possible, let them *create* the Revolution.[16]

In Time of Revolution Deeds Count More Than Theories. This is quite the opposite of what revolutionary authorities in all countries have hitherto been doing. Most frequently they have shown the greatest vigor and revolutionary quality in their language, while appearing very moderate, if not altogether reactionary, in their acts. It can even be said that *the vigor of their language,* in most cases, *has served them as a mask with which to fool the people, to disguise the feebleness and lack of consistency in their acts.* There are people, many of them among the so-called revolutionary bourgeoisie, who, by uttering some revolutionary phrases, believe that they are creating the Revolution, and once they have delivered themselves of those phrases and precisely because of that fact, they deem it permissible to be lax in action, to show a fatal inconsistency, and to indulge in acts of a purely reactionary character. We, who are truly revolutionaries, must act in quite a contrary manner. Let us speak less of revolution, and *do* a great deal more. Let us leave to others the task of developing theoretically the principles of social revolution and content ourselves with widely applying those principles, *with embodying them into facts.*[17]

Those among our allies and friends who know me well will perhaps be astonished at my using this language, I who have worked so much in theory, who have shown myself to be a jealous and ferocious guardian of revolutionary principles. But times have changed. A year ago we were preparing for a revolution, which some expected quickly, others at a later time—but now, whatever blind people may say, we are in the midst of a revolution. Then it was absolutely necessary to hold high the standard of theoretical principles, and to present those principles in all their purity, in order to form a party, small in numbers yet consisting exclusively of people sincerely, wholly, and passionately devoted to those principles, so that everyone of us, in time of crisis, could count upon all the others.

But now the issue is no longer that of recruiting people for such a party. We have succeeded, well or badly, in forming a small party—small in respect to the number of persons who are joining this party with full knowledge of what it stands for, but vast in respect to the great mass of people whom it represents better than any other party. Now all of us have to embark upon the revolutionary high seas, and henceforth we shall have to spread our principles not through words, but *through actions, for that is the most popular, the most potent, and the most irresistible form of propaganda.* Let us somehow keep silent about our principles whenever this may be required by policy; that is, whenever our temporary impotence in relation to a power hostile to us, demands it—*but let us ever be ruthlessly consistent in our actions.* Therein lies the salvation of the Revolution.[18]

CHAPTER 7 *Revolution by Decrees Doomed to Failure*

The principal reason why all the revolutionary authorities in the world have accomplished so little toward the Revolution *is that they always wanted to create the Revolution themselves, by their own authority and by their own power,* a circumstance which never failed to produce two results:

In the first place, it greatly narrowed down revolutionary activity, for it is impossible even for the most intelligent, most energetic, most candid revolutionary authority to encompass at once the great number of questions and interests stirred up by the Revolution. For every dictatorship (individual as well as collective, in so far as it is made up of several official persons) is necessarily very circumscribed, very blind, and is incapable of either penetrating the depths or comprehending the scope of the people's lives, just as it is impossible for the largest and most powerful sea-going vessel to measure the depth and expanse of the ocean. Second, every act of official authority, legally imposed, necessarily awakens within the masses a rebellious feeling, a legitimate counter-reaction.

What should revolutionary authorities—and let us try to have as few of them as possible—do in order to organize and extend the Revolution? *They must not do it themselves, by revolutionary decrees, by imposing this task upon the masses; rather their aim should be that of provoking the masses to action. They must not try to impose upon the masses any organization whatever, but rather should induce the people to set up autonomous organizations. This can be done by gaining influence over the most intelligent and advanced individuals of high standing in each locality,* so that these organizations will conform as much as possible to our principles. Therein lies the whole secret of our triumph.[1]

Jacobinism of 1793 Should Not Be Copied. Who doubts that this work is fraught with immense difficulties? Does anyone think that the Revolution is child's play, and that it can be carried out without surmounting innumerable obstacles? Revolutionary Socialists of our days could find nothing—or almost nothing—to imitate in the revolutionary tactics and proceedings of the Jacobins of 1793. Revolutionary routine would ruin them. They should work upon the basis of living experience; they must create everything anew.[2]

Peasants' Attachment to Property No Serious Obstacle to Revolution. To return to the subject of the peasantry. I have already said that the alleged attachment of the peasants to the Emperor does not frighten me. It is neither a deep nor a real attachment. It is simply a negative expression of their hatred against the landed gentry and the city bourgeoisie. That attachment therefore cannot be much in the way of the Social Revolution.

The final and chief argument of the city workers against the peasants is the cupidity of the latter, their gross egoism, and their attachment to individual ownership of land. The workers who level these reproaches at the peasants should ask themselves: Who is not an egoist? Who in present-day society is not grasping in the sense of passionately clinging to the little property he has succeeded in acquiring and which guarantees to him, in the prevailing economic chaos and in this society which shows no pity for those who die of starvation, his own existence and that of his near ones?

The peasants are not Communists, that is quite true; *they fear, they hate the protagonists of the division of property,* because they do have something to hold onto—in their imagination at least, and imagination is a great power which is generally underestimated in society. The workers, the great majority of whom do not have any property, are immeasurably more inclined toward Communism, which is quite natural. The Communism of the workers is just as natural as the individualism of the peasants—there is nothing here deserving of praise on one hand or of scorn on the other. Both, with their ideas, with all their passions, are the products of different environments. And then, are all city workers Communists?

Importance of Correct Tactics Toward the Peasants. There is no need to grumble nor to scorn or disparage the peasants. *It is necessary to lay down a line of revolutionary conduct which will obviate the difficulty of proselytizing the peasants and which will not only prevent the individualism of the peasants from pushing them into the camp of reaction but, on the contrary, will make it instrumental in the triumph of the Revolution.*[3]

Remember, my dear friends, and keep repeating to yourselves a hundred, a thousand times a day, that upon the establishment of this line of conduct depends the outcome of the Revolution: victory or defeat.

Revolutionary Terror Against Peasants Would Be Fatal to Revolution. You will agree with me that there is no more time left in which to convert the peasants by means of theoretical propaganda. There remains then, apart from the means I have already suggested, the following measure: *terrorism by the cities against the villages.* This excellent measure is cherished by all our friends, the workers of the big centers of France, who do not realize nor even suspect that they have borrowed this instrument of revolution—l was going to say of reaction—from the arsenal of revolutionary Jacobinism, and that if they ever have the misfortune to avail themselves of it, they will thus destroy themselves, and, what is more, they will have destroyed the Revolution itself. For what would be the inevitable, fatal consequence of that tactic? Simply that the whole rural population, ten million peasants, would be swept into the enemy camp of reaction, reinforcing the latter by their formidable and invincible masses.[4]

In this, as in many other respects, I deem the Prussian invasion a veritable piece of good fortune for France and for world social revolution. If that invasion had not taken place, and if the Revolution in France were to occur without such an invasion, the French Socialists themselves would attempt again, all on their own account, to carry out a revolution to seize the State. That would be utterly illogical, it would be a fatal step so far as Socialism is concerned, but the Socialists certainly would make an attempt at it—so greatly are they imbued and permeated with the principles of Jacobinism.

Consequently, among other measures of public safety decreed by a convention of city delegates, they would try to *impose* Communism or collectivism upon the peasants. They would arouse and arm against themselves the whole mass of peasants, and in order to put down the peasant revolt, they would find themselves compelled to have recourse to a vast armed force, well organized and well disciplined. As a result they would give an army to the reaction, and would beget, would form a caste of reactionary militarists, of ambitious generals, in their own midst. The State machine thus reinforced, they would soon have a leader to drive that machine—a dictator, an Emperor. All this inevitably would happen, for it is in the logic of things—not just in the capricious fancy of an individual—and this logic never errs.[5]

Fortunately the events themselves will open the eyes of the city workers and will compel them to give up the fatal system which they borrowed from the Jacobins. One must be mad to want to revert, under the present circumstances, to terrorism against the peasants. If the peasants rise up *now* against the cities, the latter, and France with them, will go down in ruin. . . . Under existing circumstances, the use of the terroristic method so beloved by the Jacobins, obviously has become impossible. And the French workers who do not know any other methods are now completely at a loss.[6]

Collectivism Imposed Upon the People Is the Negation of Humanity. . . . I do not believe that even under the most favorable circumstances the city workers will have sufficient power to impose Communism or collectivism upon the peasants; and I have never wanted this way of realizing Socialism, because I hate every system imposed by force, and because I sincerely and passionately love freedom. This false idea and this hope are destructive of liberty and they constitute the basic delusion of authoritarian Communism, which, because it needs the regularly organized violence of the State, and thus needs the State, necessarily leads to the re-establishment of the principle of authority and of a privileged class of the State.

Collectivism can be imposed only upon slaves—and then collectivism becomes the negation of humanity. Among a free people collectivism can come about only in the natural course of things, by force of circumstances, not by imposing it from above, but by a spontaneous movement from below, which springs forth freely and necessarily when the conditions of privileged individualism—State politics, the codes of civil and criminal law, the juridical family and inheritance rights—have been swept away by the Revolution.

Peasant Grievances Against the City Workers. One must be mad, I have said, to impose anything upon the peasants under present conditions: it would surely make enemies out of them and surely would ruin the Revolution. What are the principal grievances of the peasants, the main causes of their sullen and deep hatred for the cities?

1. The peasants feel that the cities despise them, and that contempt is felt directly, even by the children, and is never forgiven.

2. The peasants imagine, *not without plenty of reasons,* although lacking sufficient historic proofs and experiences to back up those assumptions, that the cities want to dominate and govern them, that they frequently want to exploit them, and that they always want to impose upon the peasants a political order which is very little to the liking of the latter.

3. In addition, the peasants consider the city workers *partisans of dividing up property,* and they fear that the Socialists will confiscate their land, which they love above everything else.[7]

A Friendly Attitude on the Part of the City Workers Necessary to Overcome the Peasants' Hatred. Then what should the city workers do in order to overcome this distrust and enmity of the peasants toward themselves? In the first place, they must cease displaying their contempt, stop despising the peasants. This is necessary for the salvation of the Revolution and of the workers themselves, for the hatred of the peasants constitutes an immense danger. Had it not been for this distrust and hatred, the Revolution would long ago have become an accomplished fact, for it is this animosity, which unfortunately the peasants have been showing toward the cities, that in all countries serves as the basis and the principal force of reaction. In the interest of the revolution which is to emancipate the industrial workers, the latter must get rid of their supercilious attitude toward the peasants. They also should do this for the sake of justice, for in reality they have no reason to despise or detest the peasants. The peasants are not idling parasites, they are rugged workers like the city proletariat. Only they toil under different conditions. In the presence of bourgeois exploitation, the city workers should feel themselves brothers of the peasants. . . .[8]

Workers' Dictatorship Over Peasants a Baneful Fallacy. The peasants will join cause with the city workers as soon as they become convinced that the latter do not pretend to impose upon them their will or some political and social order invented by the cities for the greater happiness of the villages; they will join cause as soon as they are assured that the industrial workers will not take their lands away.

It is altogether necessary at the present moment that the city workers really renounce this claim and this intention, and that they renounce it in such a manner that the peasants get to know and become convinced of it. Those workers must renounce it, for even when that claim and that intention seemed to lie within the bounds of realization, they were *highly unjust and reactionary*, and now when that realization becomes impossible, it would be no less than criminal folly to attempt it.

By what right would the city workers impose upon the peasants any form of government or economic organization whatever? By the right of revolution, we are told. But the Revolution ceases to be a revolution when it acts despotically, when, instead of promoting freedom among the masses, it promotes reaction. The means and condition, if not the principal aim of the Revolution, is the annihilation of the principle of authority in all of its possible manifestations—the abolition, the utter destruction, and, if necessary, the violent destruction of the State. For the State, the lesser brother of the Church, as Proudhon has proven it, is the historic consecration of all despotisms, of all privileges, the political reason for all economic and social enslavement, the very essence and focal point of all reaction. Therefore, whenever a State is built up in the name of the Revolution, it is reaction and despotism that are being furthered and not freedom, it is the establishment of privilege versus equality that comes as a result thereof.[9]

The Fatal Principle. This is as clear as daylight. But the Socialist workers of France, brought up in the political traditions of Jacobinism, have never wanted to understand it. Now they will be compelled to understand it, which is fortunate for the Revolution and for themselves. Whence this ridiculous as well as arrogant, unjust as well as baneful, claim on their part to impose their political and social ideal upon ten million peasants who do not want it? Manifestly this is one more bourgeois legacy, a political bequest of bourgeois revolutionism. What is the basis, the explanation, the underlying theory of this claim? It is the pretended or real superiority of intelligence, of education—in a word, of workers' civilization over that of the rural population.

But do you realize that with this principle one could easily justify any kind of conquest and oppression? The bourgeoisie have always fallen back upon that principle to prove their mission and their right to *govern* or, what amounts to the same thing, to exploit the world of labor. In conflicts between nations as well as between classes this fatal principle, which is simply the principle of authority, explains and poses as a right all invasions and conquests. Did not the Germans always put forth this principle by way of justifying their attempts upon the liberty and independence of the Slavic peoples, and of legitimizing the violent and forcible Germanization of the latter? That, they say, is the victory of civilization over barbarism.

Beware, the Germans already are remarking that the German Protestant civilization is much superior to the Catholic civilization of the peoples of the Latin race in general, and of the French civilization in particular. Beware lest the Germans soon imagine that their mission is to civilize you and to make you happy, just as you now imagine that it is your mission to civilize and forcibly free your compatriots, your brothers, the peasants of France. To me both claims are equally hateful, and I declare to you that in international relations, as well as in the relations of one class to another, I will be on the side of those who are to be civilized in this manner. Together with them I will revolt against all those arrogant civilizers—whether they call themselves Germans or workers—and in rebelling against them I shall serve the cause of revolution against reaction.[10]

The Hold of Reaction Upon the Peasants Cannot Be Destroyed by Decrees. But if this is the case, I shall be asked, must we then abandon the ignorant and superstitious peasants to all kinds of influences and intrigues, on the part of reaction? Not at all! Reaction must be destroyed in the villages just as it has to be destroyed in the cities. But in order to attain this goal, it is not enough to say: We want to destroy reaction; it must be destroyed and torn out by its roots, which can be done only by decrees. On the contrary—and I can prove it by citing history—decrees, and in general all acts of authority extirpate nothing; they perpetuate that which they set out to destroy.[11]

What follows? Since revolution cannot be *imposed* upon the villages,

*it must be generated right there, by promoting a revolutionary movement
among the peasants themselves, leading them on to destroy through their
own efforts the public order, all the political and civil institutions, and to
establish and organize anarchy in the villages.*[12]

But what is to be done? There is only one way—and that is, to revolutionize the villages as much as the cities. But who can do it? The only
class which is now the real outspoken agent of the Revolution is the
working class of the cities.[13]

**Workers' Delegations Should Not Act as Agents of Bourgeois Repub-
licanism in the Villages.** But how can the city workers undertake the
revolutionizing of villages? Shall they send individual workers into every
village as the apostles of the Republic? And where would they get the
money necessary to cover the expenses of this propaganda? True, the prefects, the sub-prefects, and the general commissars could send them at the
expense of the State. But then those emissaries would no longer be delegates of the world of labor but of the State, which circumstances would
completely alter their role and the very nature of their propaganda.

The latter would thus become not revolutionary but reactionary in
character, for the first thing they would have to do would be to inspire the
peasants with confidence in the newly established authority of the Republic or in those authorities which the Republic retained from the old
regime; that would mean inspiring confidence in the Bonapartist authorities, whose baneful activity still weighs heavily upon the villages. However,
it is clear that the prefects, the sub-prefects, and the general commissars,
acting in conformity with the natural law which makes everyone prefer
that which agrees with and not that which is contrary to his nature, would
select for this role of propagandists for the Republic the least revolutionary,
the most docile, and the most obliging workers. This again would be reaction parading under the banner of labor. But, as we have said, it is only
the Revolution that can revolutionize the villages.[14]

Finally, it must be added that individual propaganda, even when carried
on by the most revolutionary people in the world, cannot exercise too
great an influence upon the peasants. They do not respond much to
rhetoric, and words, when they do not come as a manifestation of force
and are not accompanied by deeds, remain mere words to them. A worker
who would simply confine himself to haranguing the peasants, would risk
being made the laughing stock of any village, and being chased out of it
as a bourgeois.[15]

CHAPTER 8 *Revolutionary Program for the Peasants*

It is necessary to send free detachments into the villages as propagandists for the Revolution.

There is a general rule to the effect that those who want to spread the Revolution by means of propaganda must be revolutionists themselves. One must have the Devil within himself in order to be able to arouse the masses; otherwise there can be only abortive speeches and empty clamor, but not revolutionary acts. Therefore, above all else the propagandistic free detachments have to be inspired and organized along revolutionary lines. They must carry the Revolution within themselves in order to be able to provoke and arouse it in their listeners. And then they have to draw up a plan, a line of conduct conforming to the aim which they have set for themselves.

What is this aim? It is not to impose the Revolution upon the peasants, but to provoke and arouse it among them.[1] A revolution that is imposed upon people—whether by official decree or by force of arms—is not a revolution but its opposite, for it necessarily provokes reaction. At the same time, those free detachments must appear in the villages as an impressive force, capable of making themselves respected; this show of strength, of course, is essential not for the purpose of using violence upon the peasants but in order to take away any desire to laugh at the detachments or maltreat them before giving them a chance to make themselves heard, which is liable to happen to individual propagandists when not accompanied by a showing of an impressive force. The peasants are somewhat rude and coarse, and rude natures are easily carried away by the prestige and manifestations of force, although later they may well revolt against that force if it imposes upon them conditions which run counter to their instincts and their interests.[2]

It is against this that the free detachments must be on their guard. They are not to impose anything but to stimulate and arouse. What they naturally can and must do at the beginning is to remove anything which stands in the way of successful propaganda. Thus their first task should be to break up without bloodshed the whole municipal administration, which is necessarily permeated with Bonapartist if not legitimist or Orleanist elements; and to seize, deport, or if necessary imprison, the municipal bureaucrats as well as all the reactionary large property owners—and the priests along with them—*for no other reason than their secret connivance with the Prussians.* The legal municipal administration should be replaced by a revolutionary committee comprising a small number of the most energetic peasants who are most sincerely converted to the cause of the Revolution.

But before such a committee is set up, it will be necessary to effect a real change in the sentiments of, if not all of the peasants, at least those of a great majority of them. It is essential that that majority become impassioned with the idea of revolution. How can this miracle be produced? By self-interest. The French peasant, we are told, is greedy for gain. And that cupidity should be harnessed in the interests of the Revolution. It is necessary to offer and give him immediately great material advantages.[3]

For there can be only one way of carrying out this program: to speak to the peasants and *push them in the direction of their own instincts.* They love the land; then let them take all of it and let them chase away all the proprietors who exploit the labor of others. They are reluctant to pay mortgages and taxes; so let them stop paying. Let those among them who do not want to pay their private debts be freed from the necessity of paying such debts. And finally, the peasants detest conscription—so let them be freed from the duty of furnishing soldiers for the Army.

Revolutionary Self-Interest Will Impel Peasants to Fight Invaders. But who will fight the Prussians? Let there be no fear on that score: when the peasants have felt and perceived the advantages of the Revolution, they will give more money and people for its defense than it would be possible to obtain from them by ordinary State policies or even by extraordinary State measures. The peasants will do against the Prussians what they did in 1792. For that they must become obsessed with the fury of resistance, and only an Anarchist revolution can imbue them with that spirit.

Property as a Simple Fact and Not a Right. But in letting them divide among themselves the land seized from the bourgeois owners, will this not lead to the establishment of private property upon a new and more solid foundation? Not at all, for that property will lack the juridical and political sanction of the State, inasmuch as the State and the whole juridical institution, the defense of property by the State, and family right, including the law of inheritance, necessarily will have to disappear in the terrific whirlwind of revolutionary anarchy. There will be no more political or juridical rights—there will be only revolutionary facts.[4]

Property will cease to be a right; it will be reduced to the status of a simple fact.[5]

But, you will say, in that case there will be civil war in the country. For if private property is not going to be guaranteed any more by any external political, administrative, juridical, or police power, but is to be defended only by the efforts of the owners of that property, everyone will want to take possession of the property of others, and the stronger will despoil the weaker.[6]

But what will prevent the weaker elements from uniting in order to plunder the stronger?[7]

To be sure, at the beginning things will not run altogether smoothly; there will ensue a period of strife and struggle. *Social order*, that holy of holies of the bourgeoisie, will be disturbed and the primary results flowing from this state of affairs may come very near to what is called civil war.[8]

Civil War in the Villages Is Not to be Feared. *Yes, that will be civil war.* But why do you attach a stigma to civil war, why do you fear it so much? I am asking this question with history as my guide: was it civil war or a social order imposed by some tutelary government that brought forth great thoughts, great characters, great nations? Because you were fortunate in having escaped civil war during the last twenty years, have you, a great nation, not fallen so low that the Prussians could swallow you in one mouthful?

To return to the topic of the villages, I am asking you: Do you want to see your ten million peasants unite against you in one solid and compact mass moved by a common hatred which is brought about by your decrees and revolutionary violence? Or would you prefer that a wide cleavage be effected in their ranks by this Anarchist revolution, which will enable you to build up a powerful party among them? But do you not see that the peasants are backward precisely because there has not yet come a civil war with its consequent strife in the villages? Their compact mass is simply a human herd, hardly capable of development and almost impervious to the propaganda of ideas. The civil war, on the contrary, by breaking up that compact mass, begets ideas, bringing forth a diversity of interests and aspirations. The peasants do not lack a soul, or human instincts; what they lack is spirit. The civil war will give them this spirit.

That war will open wide the door for the propaganda of your socialist and revolutionary ideas in the villages. You will have in the villages, I repeat, a party—something which you are now lacking—and you will be able widely to organize there a true Socialism, a collectivity inspired and animated by the ideas of complete liberty; you will organize it from below upward, by the action of the peasants themselves, a spontaneous action, *but one that at the same time will be brought about by the logic of things.* Your work shall then be true revolutionary Socialism.[9]

Civil War in the Villages Will Result in a Higher Social Order. Do not fear that civil war, and anarchy, will lead to the destruction of the villages. There is in every society a great deal of the instinct of self-preservation, of the power of collective inertia, which safeguards it against the danger of annihilation and which precisely renders the progress of revolutionary action so slow and difficult. Present-day European society, in the villages as well as in the cities—in the villages even more than in the cities—has fallen asleep, has, under the tutelage of the State, lost all energy, power, and independence of thought and action. A few more decades passed in that condition and this sleep may end in death. . . .

Do not fear that the peasants, once they are not restrained by public authority and respect for criminal and civil law, will cut one another's throats. They may at first try to do it, but they will not be slow in convincing themselves of the practical impossibility of continuing such a course, following which they will endeavor to come to a mutual understanding, with the view of putting an end to their strife and forming some kind of an organization. The need of eating and providing for their children—and consequently the necessity of cultivating the land and continuing work in the fields, the necessity of securing the safety of their houses, families, and their own lives against unforeseen attacks—all that will necessarily compel them to enter into some kind of mutual arrangements.

And do not believe that if these arrangements are concluded apart from the tutelage of any official authority and brought about by the force of circumstances, the stronger and wealthier peasants will exercise a predominant influence. Once the wealth of the rich people is not guaranteed by laws, it ceases to be a power. Rich peasants are now powerful because they are specially protected and courted by the functionaries of the State and because they are backed up by the State. With the disappearance of the State, this backing and power also will disappear. As to the more cunning and economically stronger peasants, they will have to give way before the collective power of the peasant mass, of the great number of poor and very poor peasants, as well as the rural proletarians—a mass which is now enslaved and reduced to silent suffering, but which revolutionary anarchy will bring back to life and will arm with an irresistible power.[10]

The Implicitly Progressive Role of Civil War. Civil war, so baneful for the power of the States, is on the contrary and by virtue of this very cause, always favorable to the awakening of popular initiative and the intellectual, moral, and even material development of the people. The reason thereof is quite simple: civil war upsets and disturbs in the masses the sheepish state so beloved of all governments, a state turning the people into herds to be tended and to be shorn at will by their shepherds. Civil war breaks up the brutalizing monotony of their daily existence, a mechanical existence devoid of thought, and compels them to reflect upon the claims of the various princes or parties contending for the right to oppress and exploit the masses of people. And it often leads them to the realization—if not conscious at least instinctive realization—of the profound truth that neither one of the contending parties has any claim upon them, and that both are equally bad.

Besides, from the moment that the people's collective mind, which is usually kept in a state of torpor, wakes up at one point, it necessarily asserts itself in other directions. It becomes stirred up, it breaks away from its worldly inertia, and, transcending the confines of a mechanical faith, shaking off the yoke of traditional and petrified representations which have served it in the place of genuine thoughts, it subjects all its idols of yesterday to a passionate and severe criticism, one that is guided by its own sound sense and upright conscience, which often are of greater value than science.

It is thus that the people's mind awakens. And with the awakening of that mind comes the sacred instinct, the essentially human instinct of revolt, the source of all emancipation; and simultaneously there develop within the people morality and material prosperity—those twin children of freedom. This freedom, so beneficial to the people, finds its support, guarantee, and encouragement in the civil war itself, which, by dividing the forces of the people's oppressors, exploiters, tutors, and masters, necessarily undermines the baneful power of one and the other.[11]

Civil War Does Not Detract From, But Adds to the External Power of a Nation. But will not this civil war paralyze the defense of France, even if it proves advantageous from any other points of view? Will not this internal struggle among the inhabitants of every community, aggravated by the strife among the communes, deliver France into the hands of the Prussians?[12]

Not at all. History shows that never did nations feel themselves so powerful in their foreign relations as when they were deeply agitated and troubled in their inner life; and on the contrary: never were they so weak as when they appeared united under one authority or when some kind of a harmonious order seemed to prevail among them. And this is quite natural: Struggle is life, and life is power.

To convince oneself of that, one has only to compare two epochs—or rather four epochs—of French history: First, France issuing from the Fronde, developed and tempered by the struggles of the Fronde, France of the early reign of the young Louis XIV as against the France of the last years of his reign, with the monarchy strongly established, united, and pacified by the Great King. Compare the first France, resplendent with victories, with the second France, marching from defeat to defeat, marching toward ruin.

Likewise compare France of 1792 with present-day France. In 1792 and 1793 France was torn by civil war: violent commotion, struggle, a life-and-death struggle, swept the whole republic. And yet France victoriously repelled the invasion of nearly all other European powers. [But] in 1870, France of the Empire, united and pacified, was defeated by the German armies and became demoralized to such an extent that one must tremble for its existence.[13]

CHAPTER 9   *On the Morrow of the Social Revolution*

Phases Passed By Humanity on Its Road to Socialism.   Men, pre-eminently carnivorous animals, began their history with cannibalism. Now they are aiming at universal association, at collective production and possession. But between those two points in historic time—what a ghastly and bloody tragedy! And the end of this tragedy is not yet in sight. Following cannibalism there came slavery; after slavery came serfdom; and that was followed by the system of wage-labor, after which are to come: first the terrible day of justice, and later, much later, the era of fraternity. Those are the phases through which must pass the animal struggle for life, a struggle which in the course of history gradually becomes transformed into human organization of life.[1]

International Union of Humanity Is Ultimate Goal.   The future, the far future, belongs in the first place to the European-American International. Later, much later indeed, this great European-American nation will merge organically with the Asiatic and African agglomeration. But that is too far distant in the future to be discussed here in a positive and precise fashion.[2]

Socialism Formulated.   Our demand proclaims anew this great principle of the French Revolution: That every man should have the material and moral means to develop all of his humanity. That principle, in our opinion, is to be translated into the following task:

To organize society in such a manner that every individual—man or woman—should find, on entering life, approximately equal means for the development of his [or her] various faculties and for their utilization in his work; to create a society which would place every individual, whoever he might be, in such a position that it would be impossible for him to exploit the labor of anyone else, and whereby he would be enabled to participate in the enjoyment of social wealth—which in reality is simply the product of human labor—only in so far as he contributed directly toward the production of that wealth.

Liberty Essential to Socialism.   Complete solution of this problem doubtless will be the work of successive centuries. But history has posed the problem and we cannot ignore it without condemning ourselves to utter impotence.

We hasten to add here that we vigorously reject any attempt at social organization which, being alien to the fullest liberty of individuals as well as of associations, would demand the establishment of a regimenting authority, of whatever character it might be. In the name of that freedom, which we recognize as the only foundation and the only legitimate creative principle of any organization—whether economic or political—we shall always protest against anything even remotely resembling State Communism or State Socialism.[3]

The Disappearance of Classes.　　All classes . . . are bound to disappear in the Social Revolution, with the exception of two—the city and the rural proletariat—who will become owners, probably collective owners, under various forms and conditions determined in every locality, in every region and every commune, by the prevailing degree of civilization in each and by the will of the populace. The city proletariat will become the owner of capital and of implements of labor, and the rural proletariat of the land which it cultivates with its own hands; both, impelled by their needs and mutual interests, will organize, and naturally and necessarily balance each other in an equal and at the same time perfectly free manner.[4]

Our program [includes]: . . . The organization of society through a free federation of workers' associations—industrial and agricultural as well as scientific, artistic, and literary—first into a commune; the federation of communes into regions, of regions into nations, and of nations into a fraternal international union.[5]

The land belongs to those who have cultivated it with their own hands —to the rural communes. The capital and all tools of labor belong to the city workers—to the workers' associations. The whole organization of the future should be nothing else but a free federation of workers—agricultural workers as well as factory workers and associations of craftsmen.[6]

Federalist Organization Will Progress Freely.　　I do not assert that the villages reorganized in this manner, freely reorganized from below upward, will immediately create an ideal organization, conforming in every respect to the kind of organization which we fancy and of which we dream. What I am convinced of, however, is that it will be a living organization, a thousand times superior to and more just than the one existing now. And moreover, that, while on one hand laying itself open to the active propaganda of the cities and on the other hand, being of a type of organization which cannot become fixed, or so to speak petrified, by the protection of the State and by that of the law—since there will then be neither State nor law in existence—each new local organization arising in the villages will be able to progress freely, and to keep on developing indefinitely, but at the same time ever remaining a living and free organization and not one brought into existence and sponsored by decree or by law—an organization capable of developing to any point that we may hope to achieve in our days.[7]

Since life and spontaneous action, suspended for centuries by the absorbing action of the all-powerful State, are going to be brought back to the communes by virtue of the abolition of the State, it is natural that every commune will take for the starting point of its new development not the intellectual and moral state ascribed to it by the official fiction but the real state of civilization. And since the degree of real civilization differs widely from one French commune to another, as well as among the communes of the rest of Europe, it will necessarily result in a wide latitude of difference in the rate of progressive development, which may at first lead to civil war among the communes, and inevitably to their effecting a mutual agreement, and in the development of a mutual understanding, harmony, and social equilibrium. There will come a new life and a new world.[8]

Integration of Manual and Intellectual Labor. The ideal appears to the people in the first place as the end of poverty and as the full satisfaction of all their material needs by means of collective labor, compulsory and equal for all.[9]

The isolated labor of the individual mind, as well as of all intellectual labor—in the field of original research and invention but not of application—should not be paid for. But then how will men of talent, men of genius, manage to live? Of course they will live by doing manual and collective labor like all the others. What? You want to submit the great minds to the "indignity" of manual labor, to the same labor as the inferior minds? Yes, we want it, and for two reasons: First, we are convinced that great minds, far from losing anything thereby, will on the contrary gain a great deal in health and mental vigor and above all in the spirit of solidarity and justice. Second, that this appears to us as the only means to elevate and humanize manual labor, and thereby establish real equality among men.[10]

Not Equal Degrees of Learning for All, But a General Scientific Education and Training. It seems to us that it is a mistake to believe, as some people do, that following the Social Revolution all will be equally learned. Science, as is the case at present, will then remain one of the numerous specialized fields, with this difference, however, that that field, now accessible only to persons belonging to the privileged classes, will in the future, when classes have been totally abolished, become easily accessible to all having the inclination and the will to devote themselves to it, with no prejudice toward the manual labor obligatory for all.

Only general scientific education will become the property of all, and chiefly so—a general knowledge of the scientific method, and training in scientific thought, that is, the ability to generalize from facts and to draw from them more or less valid conclusions.[11]

Labor and Science Both Will Profit by Integration of Manual and Mental Work. But, we are asked, if everyone is going to be educated, who will want to work? Our answer is simple: *Everyone will work and everyone will be educated.* . . . The knowledge of the savant will become more fruitful, useful, and broader in scope when the scientist ceases to be a stranger to manual toil, and the labor of the educated worker will be more intelligent and consequently more productive than that of an ignorant laborer.

Hence it follows that it is to the interest of both labor and science that there should be no more workers nor scientists but only men.[12]

Science in the Transitional Period. It is possible and even probable that in the more or less prolonged transitional period, which naturally will follow in the wake of the great social crisis, sciences of the highest standing will sink to a level much below those on which they are now.[13] . . . What science loses in sublime loftiness, will it not regain by broadening its base? Without doubt at first there will be fewer illustrious scientists, but at the same time there will also be fewer ignorant people. There will be no more of those gifted few who reach for the skies, but instead there will be millions who, now debased and crushed by the conditions of their lives, will then bestride the world like free and proud men; there will be no demi-gods, but neither will there be slaves. The demi-gods and the slaves alike will become humanized; the former will step down somewhat, and the latter will rise a great deal. There will be no place for deification nor for contempt. All will unite and march with fresh vigor toward new conquests in science as well as in life.[14]

Absorbing the Vanquished Bourgeoisie in the New Socialist Order. Socialism will wage a ruthless war upon "social positions," but it will not war against men. And once those positions have been destroyed, the people who had held them, now disarmed and deprived of any means of action, will become harmless and much weaker, I assure you, than the most ignorant worker; for their present power lies not in themselves as such, nor in their intrinsic qualities, but in their wealth and in the backing they get from the State.[15]

The Social Revolution then will not only spare them, but, having struck them down and deprived them of their arms, it will raise them up again and say to them: "And now, dear comrades, that you have become our equals, get ready to work alongside of us. In work, as in everything else, it is the first step that is difficult, and we will help you in a brotherly way to overcome that difficulty." Then any persons who, though robust and of good health, do not want to gain their livelihood by working, shall have the right to starve themselves to death, that is, if they do not resign themselves to a humble and miserable existence as wards of public charity, which certainly will not refuse them their base necessities.[16]

As to their children, there can be no doubt that they will become valiant workers, and free and equal men. There will certainly be less luxury in society, but unquestionably there will be more wealth; and still more, there will be the kind of luxury which is now ignored by all,—the luxury of humanity, the happiness of integral development and complete liberty for everyone in the equality of all.[17]

Terrorism Is Alien to a Genuine Social Revolution. All the other classes [except the city and rural proletariat] must vanish from the face of the earth; they must vanish not as individuals but as classes. Socialism is not cruel; it is a thousand times more humane than Jacobinism, that is, than the political revolution. It is not directed against individuals, not even against the most nefarious among them, since it realizes only too well that all individuals, good or bad, are the inevitable product of the social status created for them by society and history. True, Socialists will not be able to prevent the people in the early days of the Revolution from giving vent to their fury by doing away with a few hundreds of the most odious, the most rabid and dangerous enemies. But once that hurricane passes, the Socialists will oppose with all their might hypocritical—in a political and juridical sense—butchery perpetrated in cold blood.[18]

The Revolution, for that matter, is neither vindictive nor sanguinary. It demands neither the death, nor mass deportations, nor even individual deportations of the Bonapartist gang which, armed with powerful means and being much better organized than the Republic itself, conspires openly against that Republic, conspires against France. The Revolution demands only the imprisonment of all the Bonapartists, *simply as a measure of public safety*, until the end of the war and *until those scoundrels and their female counterparts disgorge at least nine tenths of the wealth which they have amassed by robbing France.* Following that, they shall be permitted to go wherever they wish; the Revolution will even grant a certain sum to every one of them to enable them to live out their days and hide their shame. As one can see, this hardly can be called a cruel measure, but obviously it will be very effective, just to the highest degree, and absolutely necessary from the standpoint of the welfare of France.[19]

As soon as the Revolution begins to take on a Socialist character, it will cease to be cruel and sanguinary. The people are not at all cruel; it is the ruling classes that have shown themselves to be cruel. At times the people rise up, raging against all the deceits, vexations, oppressions, and tortures, of which they are victims, and then they break forth like an enraged bull, seeing nothing ahead of them and demolishing everything in their way. But those are very rare and very brief moments. Ordinarily the people are good and humane. They suffer too much themselves not to sympathize with the sufferings of others.

But alas! too often have they served as instruments of the systematic fury of the privileged classes. All the national, political, and religious ideas, for the sake of which the people have shed their own blood and the blood of their brothers, the blood of foreign peoples, all these ideas have always served only the interests of those classes, ever turning into means of new oppression and exploitation of the people. In all the furious scenes in the history of all the countries wherein the masses of the people, enraged to the point of madness, have turned their energies to mutual destruction, you will invariably find that behind those masses are agitators and leaders belonging to the privileged classes: Army officers, noblemen, priests, and bourgeois. It is not among the people that one should look for cruelty and concentrated and systematically organized cold fury, but in the instincts, the passions, and the political and religious institutions of the privileged classes: in the Church and in the State, in their laws, and in the ruthless and iniquitous application of those laws.[20]

I have already shown the fury of the bourgeoisie in 1848. The fury of 1792, 1793, and 1794 likewise was an exclusively bourgeois fury. The famous Avignon massacres (in October, 1791), which opened the era of political assassinations in France were directed and partly perpetrated by priests and noblemen, and on the other hand, by the bourgeoisie.

The Vendee butcheries carried out by the peasants also were led by reactionary noblemen leagued with the Church. Without exception the instigators of the September massacres were all bourgeois, and what is less known: the initiators of those massacres, and most of the principal killers involved therein belonged to this class. Collot d'Herbois, Panis, the worshiper of Robespierre; Chaumette, Bourdon, Fourquier-Tinville, that personification of revolutionary hypocrisy and the guillotine; Carrier, who was responsible for the drownings at Nantes—all these were bourgeois. And the Committee of Public Safety, the calculated, cold, legal terror, the guillotine itself—all these also were bourgeois institutions. The people were in the role of spectators, and at times, alas! they foolishly applauded those exhibitions of hypocritical legality and political fury of the bourgeoisie. Following the execution of Danton, even the people became the victim of that fury.[21]

The Jacobin, bourgeois, exclusively political revolution of 1792-94 was bound to lead to legal hypocrisy and the solution of all difficulties and all questions by the victorious argument of the guillotine.

When, in order to extirpate reaction, we content ourselves with attacking its manifestations without touching its roots and the causes which continually produce it anew, we perforce arrive at the necessity of killing many people, of exterminating, with or without legal sanctions, many reactionaries.

It inevitably comes about that after killing many people, the revolutionaries see themselves driven to the melancholy conviction that nothing has been gained and that not a single step has been made toward the realization of their cause, but that, on the contrary, they did an ill turn to the Revolution by employing those methods, and that they prepared with their own hands the triumph of reaction. And that is so for two reasons: first, that the causes of the reaction having been left intact, the reaction is given a chance to reproduce and multiply itself in new forms; and second, that ere long all those bloody butcheries and massacres must arouse against them everything that is human in man.

The revolution of 1793, whatever one may say about it, was neither Socialist nor materialist, nor, using the pretentious expression of M. Gambetta, was it by any means a *positivist* revolution. It was essentially bourgeois, Jacobin, metaphysical, political, and idealist. Generous and sweeping in its aspirations, it reached out for an impossible thing: establishment of an ideal equality in the midst of material inequality. While preserving as *sacred foundations* all the conditions of economic inequality, it believed that it could unite and envelop all men in a sweeping sentiment of brotherly, humane, intellectual, moral, political, and social equality. That was its dream, its religion, manifested by the enthusiasm, by the grandly heroic acts of its best and greatest representatives. But the realization of that dream was impossible because it ran contrary to all natural and social laws.[22]

Source Bibliography

Maximoff prepared the original text of this volume in Russian, and drew the selections in it chiefly from the first Russian edition of Bakunin's collected works, five volumes of which appeared in 1919-1922, but also from the German edition (1921-1924) and from a few pamphlets and periodicals. For the convenience of readers, the French edition and one volume of the Spanish edition are included in the listing below, because they were consulted in the checking of the translation.

RUSSIAN EDITION, Petrograd and Moscow: published by *Golos Truda.*

    Vol.   I, 1919; 320 pp.
    Vol. II, 1919; 295 pp.
    Vol. III, 1920; 217 pp.
    Vol. IV, 1920; 267 pp.
    Vol. V, 1922; 214 pp.

GERMAN EDITION, Berlin: *Verlag Der Syndikalist.*

    Vol.   I, 1921; 306 pp.
    Vol. II, 1923; 281 pp.
    Vol. III, 1924; 274 pp.

FRENCH EDITION, Paris: P. V. Stock.

    Vol.   I, 1895; 327 pp.
    Vol. II, 1907; 456 pp.
    Vol. III, 1908; 406 pp.
    Vol. IV, 1910; 512 pp.
    Vol. V, 1911; 362 pp.
    Vol. VI, 1913; 434 pp.

SPANISH EDITION, Buenos Aires: *Editorial La Protesta.*

    Vol. V, *Statism and Anarchism,* 1929; 316 pp.

Source Notes

KEY TO ABBREVIATIONS in these notes:

Each source is indicated by a set of initials, and the language in which the source material was printed is shown by a single initial, followed by the volume number in a Roman numeral, and then by the page number. R means Russian; G German; F French; and S Spanish. Thus the designation "PHC; F III 216-218" means *Philosophical Considerations, French volume III, pages* 216-218. In some instances reference is made to sources in more than one language.

AM—*A Member of the International Answers Mazzini;* Russian volume V; French volume VI.

BB—*The Bear of Berne and the Bear of St. Petersburg;* Russian volume III; French volume II.

CL—*A Circular Letter to My Friends in Italy;* Russian volume V; French volume VI.

DS—*The Double Strike in Geneva;* German volume II; French volume V.

DV—*Drei Vortraege von den Arbeitern das Thals von St. Imier im Schweizer Jura, May,* 1871; German volume II.

FSAT—*Federalism, Socialism, and Anti-Theologism;* Russian volume III; French volume I.

GAS—*God and the State;* New York: Mother Earth Publishing Association, [*circa* 1915], 86 pp. See below, following the abbreviation KGE, a reference to a continuation of the essay embodied in this pamphlet.

IE—*Integral Education;* Russian volume IV; French volume V.

IR—*Report of the Commission on the Question of Inheritance Right;* French volume V.

IU—*The Intrigues of Mr. Utin;* in *Golos Truzenika,* a Russian periodical of the Industrial Workers of the World, Chicago, 1925; volume VII, No. 3, pp. 19-23; and volume VII, No. 4, pp. 9-12.

KGE—*The Knouto-Germanic Empire and the Social Revolution;* Russian volume II; French volumes II, III, and IV. Part of the text of this also appears in French volume I, under the heading of *God and the State.* That section, as Rudolf Rocker points out on page 25, was found among Bakunin's manuscripts by Max Nettlau, and is a logical continuation of the essay in the pamphlet bearing the same title.

LF—*Letters to a Frenchman;* Russian volume IV; French volumes II, IV.

LGS—*A Letter to the Geneva Section of the Alliance;* French volume VI.

LP—*Letters on Patriotism;* Russian volume IV; French volume I.

LU—*The Lullers;* Russian volume IV; French volume V.

OGS—*Organization and the General Strike;* German volume II; French volume V.

OI—*Organization of the International;* Russian volume IV.

OP—*Our Program;* Russian volume III.

PA—*Protestation of the Alliance;* Russian volume V; French volume VI.

PAIR—*The Program of the Alliance of International Revolution;* written in French and published in *Anarchichesky Vestnik,* Anarchist Courier, a Russian publication, in Berlin; volume V-VI, November, 1923; pp. 37-41; volume VII, May, 1924, pp. 38-41.

PC—*The Paris Commune and the State;* Russian volume IV; and in a pamphlet, *The Paris Commune and the Idea of the State,* Paris: Aux Bureaux des "Temps Noveau," 1899; 23 pp.

PHC—*Philosophical Considerations;* German volume I; French volume III.

PI—*The Politics of the International;* Russian volume IV; French volume V.

PSSI—*The Program of the Slavic Section of the International,* 1872. (Russian volume III.

PYR—*Pechat y Revoliutzia* (The Printed Word and Revolution); a Russian periodical, Moscow, 1921-June, 1930.

RA—*A Report on the Alliance;* Russian volume V; French volume VI.

SRT—*Science and the Urgent Revolutionary Task;* pamphlet in Russian; Geneva, Switzerland: Kolokol, 1870; 32 pp.

STA—*Statism and Anarchism;* Russian volume I; Spanish volume V. The Russian title of this volume is *Gosudarstvennost i Anarkhiia,* which literally means Statism and Anarchy. But from Bakunin's context therein it is evident that he was weighing one organized system against another, and not comparing a system with a condition of lawless confusion and disorder. So wherever this work is cited in these pages it is consistently referred to as *Statism and Anarchism.*

WRA—*World Revolutionary Alliance of Social Democracy;* pamphlet in Russian; Berlin: Hugo Steinitz Verlag, 1904; 86 pp.

PART I

Ch. 1–The World Outlook

1. PHC; F III 216-218.
2. *Ibid.*, 219.
3. *Ibid.*, 219-220.
4. *Ibid.*, 229.
5. FSAT; R III 157; F I 79.
6. FSAT; R III 157n; F I 79-80n.
7. FSAT; F I 79-80.
8. PHC; G I 224; F III 231.
9. PHC; G I 225; F III 234.
10. PHC; G I 267.
11. *Ibid.*, 267-268.
12. PC; R IV 261-262; F pamphlet 18.
13. PC; R IV 267.
14. KGE; R II 170.
15. PHC; F III 220.
16. *Ibid.*, 220-222.
17. *Ibid.*, 223.
18. *Ibid.*, 220.
19. FSAT; F I 123-124.
20. *Ibid.*, 124-125.
21. *Ibid.*, 126-127.
22. *Ibid.*, 125-126.
23. *Ibid.*, 127-128.

Ch. 2– Idealism and Materialism

1. KGE; R II 149; F III 26-27.
2. STA; R I 234.
3. KGE; R II 149-150.
4. *Ibid.*, 150-151.
5. *Ibid.*, R II 151; F III 29.
6. *Ibid.*, R II 162-163.
7. *Ibid.*, R II 163; F III 48.
8. *Ibid.*, R II 183-184; F III 76-77.
9. *Ibid.*, R II 184-185.
10. *Ibid.*, R II 185.
11. *Ibid.*, R II 185-186.
12. CL; R V 167.
13. *Ibid.*, 137-140.
14. *Ibid.*, 142-144.
15. *Ibid.*, 144.
16. AM; F VI 114-115.
17. *Ibid.*, 116-118.
18. *Ibid.*, 118.
19. *Ibid.*, 119.
20. *Ibid.*, 119-120.

Ch. 3– Science: General Outlook

1. PHC; G I 226.
2. KGE; R II 170.

3. PHC; G I 218.
4. *Ibid.*, 220.
5. *Ibid.*, 263.
6. PA; F VI 98.
7. PHC; G I 264; F III 316.
8. *Ibid.*, G I 264-265; F III 318-319.
9. *Ibid.*, G I 266.
10. *Ibid.*, G I 265; F III 319.
11. KGE; R II 192.
12. *Ibid.*, 192-193.
13. FSAT; F I 68-69.
14. PHC; G I 263.
15. *Ibid.*, G I 263-264; F III 315.
16. *Ibid.*, G I 266-267; F III 322-323.
17. KGE; R II 198.
18. FSAT; R III; 153; F I 69-71.
19. *Ibid.*, F I 71-72.
20. *Ibid.*, F I 72-73.
21. AM; R V 69; F VI 125-126.
22. FSAT; F I 73.
23. *Ibid.*, 73-75.
24. KGE; R II 199.

Ch. 4– Science and Authority

1. KGE; R II 167-168.
2. *Ibid.*, 193.
3. *Ibid.*, 197.
4. *Ibid.*, 194-195.
5. *Ibid.*, 196.
6. *Ibid.*, 197.
7. *Ibid.*, 203.
8. *Ibid.*, R II 166-167; F III 51-53.
9. STA; R I 187-188.
10. KGE; R II 200-201; F III 100-102.

Ch. 5–Modern Science Deals in Falsities

1. LU; R IV 32; F V 117-119.
2. *Ibid.*, R IV 39.
3. IE; R IV 44; F V 137.
4. *Ibid.*, R IV 45; F V 138.
5. LU; R IV 39-40; F V 132-133.

Ch. 6–Man: Animal and Human Nature

1. FSAT; F I 87.
2. *Ibid.*, 83-86.

3. *Ibid.*, 93.
4. KGE; R II 144-145; F III 19-20.
5. *Ibid.*, R II 146.
6. *Ibid.*, R II 202-204.
7. FSAT; F I 73.
8. *Ibid.*, 81-83.
9. *Ibid.*, 108.
10. *Ibid.*, 108-109n.
11. *Ibid.*, 109.
12. PHC; G I 246.
13. FSAT; F I 110-111.
14. PHC; G I 246; F III 280-281.
15. *Ibid.*, G I 248; F III 281.

Ch. 7–Man as Conqueror of Nature

1. PHC; G I 250.
2. *ibid.*, 250.
3. *Ibid.*, 225.
4. *Ibid.*, G I 250-251; F III 287-288.
5. *Ibid.*, G I 251-252.
6. *Ibid.*, 252.
7. *Ibid.*, G I 253; F III 293.
8. *Ibid.*, G I 254; F III 295.

Ch. 8–Mind and Will

1. PHC; G I 226-227; F III 238-243.
2. FSAT; F I 95-96.
3. *Ibid.*, 104-107.
4. PHC; G I 228-229.
5. *Ibid.*, 230-232.

Ch. 9–Man Subject to Universal Inevitability

1. PHC; G I 237-239; F III 262-266.
2. *Ibid.*, G I 242-245.
3. FSAT; F I 96-97.
4. IE; R IV 58-60; F V 160-162.
5. *Ibid.*, R IV 60-61.
6. PHC; G I 228; F III 245.
7. *Ibid.*, G I 232; F III 257-259.

Ch. 10– Religion in Man's Life

1. FSAT; F I 83-86.
2. *Ibid.*, 86-87.
3. *Ibid.*, 87-88.
4. *Ibid.*, 96-97.
5. *Ibid.*, R III 165-168; F I 97-104.
6. *Ibid.*, F I 112-121.

Ch. 11—Man Had to Look
for God Within Himself
1. FSAT; F I 128-134.
2. *Ibid.*, 61-64.
3. *Ibid.*, 64-68.
4. CL; F VI 398-399.

Ch. 12—Ethics: Divine or
Bourgeois Morality
1. FSAT; F I 133-136.
2. KGE; R II 279.
3. *Ibid.*, 279 et seq.

Ch. 13—Ethics:
Exploitation of the Masses
1. KGE; R II 286-294.
2. *Ibid.*, R II 250-253; F III 176.
3. *Ibid.*, R II 250-253n; F III 172-175n.
4. *Ibid.*, R II 294.

Ch. 14—Ethics:
Morality of the State
1. FSAT; F I 139-140.
2. *Ibid.*, 145-152.
3. BB; F II 61-62.
4. *Ibid.*, 62-65.
5. FSAT; F I 152-153.
6. BB; F II 24.
7. FSAT; F I 153-155.
8. *Ibid.*, 156.
9. *Ibid.*, 158-161.

10. KGE; R II 269-271.

Ch. 15—Ethics: Truly
Human or Anarchist
Morality
1. KGE; R II 294-295; F I 325-326.
2. FSAT; F I 136-137.
3. *Ibid.*, 177-190.
4. *Ibid.*, 195 et seq.

Ch. 16—Ethics: Man the
Product of Environment
1. FSAT; F I 198-204.
2. IE; F V 160-166.
3. FSAT; F I 54-55.
4. AM; F VI 122.
5. PAIR; R 40.
6. *Ibid.*, 39.
7. *Ibid.*, 40.
8. IE; F V 157.

Ch. 17—
Society and the Individual
1. KGE; R II 269-270.
2. IU; R 18-21.
3. *Ibid.*, R 17.
4. KGE; R II 262-263.
5. *Ibid.*, R II 256-261; F 267-273.
6. *Ibid.*, R II 263; F I 276-277.

Ch. 18—
Individuals Are Strictly
Determined
1. KGE; R II; 261-262; F I 273-275.
2. FSAT; F I 139-143.
3. IU; R 19.
4. OI; R IV 71.
5. IE; F V 158-159.
6. PC; R IV 264-265.

Ch. 19—
Philosophy of History
1. LP; F I 219.
2. PHC; G I 225-226; F III 236-237.
3. LP; F I 254-255.
4. *Ibid.*, 221.
5. *Ibid.*, 219-220.
6. *Ibid.*, 256-260.
7. WRA; R pamphlet 32-33.
8. KGE; R II 147.
9. *Ibid.*, 210.
10. *Ibid.*, 156.
11. *Ibid.*, R II 185-186; F III 79-80.
12. *Ibid.*, R II 195-196; F III 93-94.
13. *Ibid.*, R II 156-157.
14. LF; R IV 21-23.
15. KGE; R II 149.

PART II

Ch. 1—
Property Could Arise Only
in the State
1. KGE; R II 230.
2. *Ibid.*, 250-253.
3. PHC; G I 204-205.
4. IR; F V 199-202.

Ch. 2—
The Present Economic
Regime
1. STA; R I 69.
2. *Ibid.*, 109.
3. IE; F V 137-138.
4. KGE; R II 95.
5. PHC; G I 205-209.
6. *Ibid.*, 211-214.

Ch. 3—
Class Struggle in Society
Inevitable
1. FSAT; F I 22-24.
2. PI; F V 185-186.
3. STA; R I 78-79.

4. PA; F VI 35.
5. FSAT; F I 26-27.
6. *Ibid.*, 30-35.

Ch. 4—
Checkered History of the
Bourgeoisie
1. LP; FI 208-211.
2. *Ibid.*, 215-216.
3. STA; R I 209.
4. *Ibid.*, 94.
5. IE; F V 139-140.
6. CL; F VI 344-345.
7. STA; R I 125-126.
8. *Ibid.*, 307-308.
9. LF; R IV 87.
10. LU; F V 107-108.
11. *Ibid.*, R IV 29; F V 113.
12. PI; R IV 187-190.
13. PA; F VI 67-68.

Ch. 5—
Proletariat Long Enslaved
1. WRA; R pamphlet 33.
2. CL; F VI 390-391.

3. WRA; R 54-55.
4. KGE; R II 95-96.
5. WRA; R 61-67.
6. KGE; R II 81.
7. STA; R I 86.
8. *Ibid.*, 59-60.
9. LU; F V 115-116.

Ch. 6—
Peasants' Day Is Yet
To Come
1. LF; R IV 211-213.
2. STA; R I 254.
3. KGE; R II 54-55.
4. LF; R IV 183.
5. CL; F VI 399-400.

Ch. 7—
The State: General
Outlook
1. LP; F I 222-224.
2. PC; R IV 260; F pamphlet 16.
3. *Ibid.*, R IV 258-259; F 14.

4. LP; F I 224-227.
5. FSAT; R III 186-187.

Ch. 8–
The Modern State
Surveyed
1. STA; R I 68-70; S 77-79.
2. *Ibid.*, R 83-84.
3. *Ibid.*, R 98-99.
4. *Ibid.*, R 109.
5. *Ibid.*, R 124-125.
6. BB; F II 35-36.
7. PA; F VI 15.
8. *Ibid.*, 18.
9. *Ibid.*, 53-54.
10. BB; F II 36-37.
11. KGE; R II 33-34.
12. PI; R IV 193-194.
13. KGE; R II 35-36; F II 312-314.
14. PI; R IV 194-195.
15. KGE; R II 248; F III 169-170.
16. *Ibid.*, R II 248.

Ch. 9–
Representative System
Based on Fiction
1. BB; F II 35-42.
2. *Ibid.*, 46-47.
3. *Ibid.*, 43.
4. KGE; R II 43-46; F II 325-329.
5. WRA; R 10-12.
6. FSAT; F I 8-11.
7. *Ibid.*, R III 116-125.

Ch. 10–
Patriotism's Part in
Man's Struggle
1. LP; F I 227-231.
2. *Ibid.*, 231-246.

Ch. 11–
Class Interests in
Modern Patriotism
1. LP; F I 227.
2. FSAT; R III 251.
3. STA; R I 72.
4. FSAT; R III 20.
5. LF; R IV 216.
6. PA; F VI 38.
7. STA; R I 70-72.
8. *Ibid.*, 80-81.
9. *Ibid.*, 72-73.
10. *Ibid.*, 82.
11. *Ibid.*, 86-87.
12. *Ibid.*, 90.
13. KGE; R II 84-85.

Ch. 12–
Law, Natural and Invented
1. KGE; R II 262.
2. *Ibid.*, R II 272-274; F I, under *God and the State*, 290-294.
3. *Ibid.*, R II 164.
4. *Ibid*, 165.
5. *Ibid.*, R II 167; GAS (pamphlet in English) 31-32.
6. *Ibid.*, R II 168; GAS 32.
7. WRA; R 12.

8. KGE; R II 172; GAS 35.
9. KGE; R 171-172.
10. IR; F V 205.
11. STA; R I 285; S V 279.
12. LU; F V 131.
13. SRT; R 96.
14. PSSI; R III 70.
15. IR; F V 199-209.
16. OP; R III 97.
17. STA; R I 115.

Ch. 13–
Power and Authority
1. PA; F VI 16-18.
2. CL; F VI 343-344.
3. STA; R I 236.
4. *Ibid.*, 238.
5. KGE; R II 165-168; GAS 29-32.
6. KGE; R II 293; F I 320-322.
7. *Ibid.*, R II 171-172.
8. *Ibid.*, 177-178.
9. *Ibid.*, R II 172; F III 60.

Ch. 14–
State Centralization and
Its Effects
1. BB; F II 33-34.
2. *Ibid.*, 57.
3. STA; R I 270.
4. *Ibid.*, 312-313.
5. FSAT; F I 11-13.

Ch. 15–
The Element of Discipline
1. KGE; R II 23-25; F II 296-299.

PART III

Ch. 1–
Freedom and Equality
1. IE; R IV 57; F V 158.
2. PHC; G I 215-216.
3. *Ibid.*, 216.
4. *Ibid.*, 216.
5. IE; R IV 57; F V 158-159.
6. *Ibid.*, R 57.
7. PA; R V 48; F VI 87.
8. *Ibid.*, R V 49; F VI 88.
9. KGE; R II 166; F III 51.
10. *Ibid.*, R II 165; F III 49-50.
11. PHC; G I 229; F III 246.
12. KGE; R II 165.
13. *Ibid.*, 165-166.
14. *Ibid.*, 264.
15. *Ibid.*, 264-265.

16. *Ibid.*, R II 265; F I 279.
17. *Ibid.*, R II 265-266.
18. *Ibid.*, 266-267.
19. *Ibid.*, 267.
20. PC; R IV 260; F pamphlet 16.
21. *Ibid.*, R IV 260-261.
22. FSAT; R III 147; F I 58-59.
23. KGE; R II 167.
24. LU; R IV 27; F V 109-111.
25. PC; R IV 250; F pamphlet 4.
26. *Ibid.*, R IV 250-251.
27. *Ibid.*, 251.
28. IE; R IV 56-57; F V 165n.
29. *Ibid.*, R IV 61n.

30. STA; R I 306.
31. PHC; G I 214-215.

Ch. 2–
Federalism: Real and Sham
1. FSAT; R III 128; F I 16-17n.
2. CL; R V 191-192; F VI 385.
3. *Ibid.*, R V 192.
4. *Ibid.*, 192.
5. *Ibid.*, R V 193; F VI 387-389.
6. FSAT; R III 127.
7. *Ibid.*, 128.
8. *Ibid.*, 129.
9. *Ibid.*, 129-130.
10. *Ibid.*, 130.

11. FSAT; R III 130; F I 15-21.
12. BB; F II 57.
13. FSAT; R III 131 et. seq.; F I 21-22.
14. Ibid., R III 136; F I 33-35.

Ch. 3–
State Socialism Theories
Weighed

1. FSAT; R III 137; F I 36-37.
2. Ibid., R 137.
3. Ibid., R 138.
4. Ibid., R 138-139.
5. Ibid., R 139; F I 40.
6. Ibid., R 142; F 46-48.
7. Ibid., R 134.
8. Ibid., R 144-145; F 52-53.
9. WRA; R 18.
10. Ibid., 18-19.
11. Ibid., 19-20.
12. Ibid., 20-21.
13. KGE; R II 74; F II 369-370.
14. Ibid., R 74-75.
15. WRA; R 43-45.
16. Ibid., 44-45.
17. PI; R IV 17; F V 190.
18. CL; R V 170; F VI 350.

Ch. 4–
Criticism of Marxism

1. STA; R I 120-121.
2. Ibid., 238-239.
3. Ibid., 239.
4. Ibid., 239-240.
5. Ibid., 240.
6. Ibid., 290.
7. Ibid., 290-292.
8. Ibid., 291-292.
9. Ibid., 293.
10. PA; R V 19-20; F VI 38-39.
11. STA; R I 293-294; S V 287.
12. Ibid., R 294.
13. Ibid., R 294-295.
14. Ibid., R 295.
15. Ibid., R 295-296.
16. Ibid., R 296-297.
17. Ibid., R 298; S V 291.

Ch. 5–
Social-Democratic
Program Examined

1. LF; R IV 224-225; F IV 39-40.
2. Ibid., R 226; F 39-40.

3. Ibid., R 226; F 41-42.
4. Ibid., R 228.
5. Ibid., R 228-229.
6. Ibid., R 229.
7. Ibid., R 229-230; F IV 46-47.
8. Ibid., R 235-236.
9. Ibid., R 236; F IV 58.
10. Ibid., R 236-237.
11. Ibid., R 237.
12. Ibid., R 237-238.
13. Ibid., R 238.
14. Ibid., R 238-239; F IV 61-62.
15. PI; R IV 18; F V 191.
16. Ibid., R 18-19.
17. Ibid., R 19; F 192.

Ch. 6–
Stateless Socialism:
Anarchism

1. FSAT; R III 136; F I 33-35.
2. Ibid., R 145-146.
3. Ibid., 146-147.
4. Ibid., R 146-147.
5. BB; R III 22, F II 39.
6. STA; R I 114.
7. Ibid., 96.
8. CL; R V 171; F VI 351.
9. Ibid., R 167; F 345.
10. Ibid., R 197.
11. Ibid., R 197-198; F 395-396.
12. PC; R IV 257.
13. Ibid., 257-258.
14. Ibid., 258-259.
15. Ibid., 259.
16. Ibid., 251.
17. Ibid., R 251-252; F pamphlet 6.
18. Ibid., R 252.
19. STA; R I 320.
20. CL; R V 172; F VI 352.

Ch. 7–
Founding of Workers'
International

1. PA; R V 34-35; F VI 64.
2. Ibid., R 35.
3. Ibid., R 35-36.
4. Ibid., R 36; F 66.
5. Ibid., R 37-38.
6. Ibid., R 38.
7. Ibid., R 38-39.
8. Ibid., R 39-40; F 68-72.
9. Ibid., R 30; F 56.
10. Ibid., R 30-31.

11. Ibid., R 32.
12. Ibid., R 32.
13. Ibid., R 32-33.
14. Ibid., R 33; F 62.
15. Ibid., R 34; F 64.

Ch. 8–
Economic Solidarity
at Its Widest

1. PA; R V 40; F VI 73.
2. Ibid., R 40-41; F 73.
3. Ibid., R 41.
4. Ibid., R 41-42.
5. Ibid., R 42.
6. Ibid., R 43.
7. Ibid., R 41; F 73-80.
8. PI; R IV 7; F V 172.
9. Ibid., R 8; F 174-175.
10. CL; R V 162; F VI 336.
11. PA; R V 20; F VI 39-40.
12. CL; R V 171; F VI 351.
13. PI; R IV 9; F V 176.
14. Ibid., R 10; F 176-178.
15. Ibid., R 11.

Ch. 9–
What the Workers Lack

1. PI; R IV 11-12; F V 180-181.
2. Ibid., R 12.
3. Ibid., R 12-13.
4. Ibid., R 13; F 182.
5. PA; R V 46; F VI 82-83.
6. Ibid., R 46; F 84.
7. Ibid., R 46-47.
8. Ibid., R 47.
9. Ibid., R 47-48.
10. Ibid., R 48.
11. Ibid., R 48-49.
12. Ibid., R 49.
13. Ibid., R 49-50.
14. Ibid., R 50.
15. Ibid., R 50-51; F VI 90-91.
16. Ibid., R 53.
17. Ibid., R 53-54; F 96-97.
18. RA; R V 112; F VI 223-224.
19. CL; R V 198; F VI 396.
20. DS; G II 49; F V 45-46.
21. Ibid., G 49-50.
22. Ibid., G 50; F V 47.
23. PI; R IV 21; F V 198.
24. Ibid., R 22; F 199.

Ch. 10–
Fatherland and Nationality

1. CL; R V 189-190; F VI 382-383.
2. Ibid., R 190.

3. *Ibid.*, R 190.
4. *Ibid.*, R 191; F 384.
5. STA; R 114-115.
6. *Ibid.*, R 114-115.
7. KGE; R II 103.
8. FSAT; R III 102.

Ch. 11–
Women, Marriage, and
Family
1. RA; R V 97; F VI 198.
2. PSSI; R III 71.
3. OP; R III 96-97.
4. PSSI; R III 70.
5. CL; R V 191; F VI 385.
6. OP; R III 97.
7. PAIR; R V-VI 37-41; VII 38-41.

Ch. 12–
Upbringing and Education
1. CL; R V 173; F VI 354.

Ch. 1–
The Rationale of
Revolutionary Tactics
1. SRT; R 5 et seq.

Ch. 2–
Economic Problem
Underlies All Others
1. SRT; R 12-20.
2. *Ibid.*, 29.
3. *Ibid.*, 20.

Ch. 3–
Socio-Economic and
Psychological Factors
1. OI; R IV 68.
2. *Ibid.*, 68-69.
3. KGE; R II 35; F II 313-314.
4. *Ibid.*, R 35-36; F 314.
5. LF; F II 221.
6. KGE; R II 75; F II 371.
7. *Ibid.*, R 73-74; F 369.
8. LP; R IV 99; F I 242-243.
9. STA; R I 95.
10. LF; R IV 213.
11. *Ibid.*, 213-214.
12. *Ibid.*, R 214; F IV 19-20.
13. *Ibid.*, R 219.
14. *Ibid.*, R 219-220.
15. *Ibid.*, R 220; F IV 30-31.

Ch. 4–
Revolution and
Revolutionary Violence
1. BB; R III 12; F II 20-21.
2. KGE; R II 69; F II 363.

2. IE; R IV 43; F V 135.
3. *Ibid.*, R 44; F 136.
4. *Ibid.*, R 49.
5. *Ibid.*, R 49.
6. *Ibid.*, R 49-50.
7. *Ibid.*, R 50-51; F 147-148.
8. *Ibid.*, R 51-52.
9. *Ibid.*, R 52; F 150.
10. FSAT; R III 213-214; F I 199-200.
11. IU; R VII, No. 4, 10.
12. FSAT; R III 214; F I 200-201.
13. IE; R IV 54.
14. *Ibid.*, 54.
15. *Ibid.*, 54-55.
16. *Ibid.*, R 55; F V 155.
17. *Ibid.*, R 56; F 158.
18. KGE; R II 176-177; F III 68-69n.

PART IV

3. LP; R IV 82; F I 213.
4. LF; R IV 225; F IV 39.
5. *Ibid.*, R 147; F II 183-184.
6. STA; R I 79.
7. PC; R IV 258.
8. STA; R I 118.
9. *Ibid.*, 118-119.
10. OI; R IV 67.
11. PI; R IV 21; F V 197.
12. CL; R V 211-212; F VI 419-420.
13. PC; R IV 257.
14. PI; R IV 22; F V 198.
15. STA; R I 92.
16. *Ibid.*, 114.
17. FSAT; R III 144; F I 53.
18. LF; R IV 213; F IV 18.
19. PI; R IV 15; F V 184-185.
20. STA; R I 60-61.
21. *Ibid.*, 97.
22. *Ibid.*, 88.
23. PA; R V 45; F VI 82.
24. STA; R I 257.
25. *Ibid.*, R 285; S V 279.
26. *Ibid.*, R 266; S 260.
27. CL; R V 175; F VI 359-360.
28. *Ibid.*, R 177; F 362.
29. LF; R IV 197.
30. CL; R V 349; F VI 348-349.
31. *Ibid.*, R 196-197; F VI 394.

19. IU; R 13.
20. KGE; R II 177n; F III 69n.
21. *Ibid.*, R 177-178n.
22. IE; R IV 61-62; F V 165-166.
23. CL; R V 173-174; F VI 355.
24. IU; R VII, No. 4, 10-11.
25. IE; R IV 62.
26. *Ibid.*, R 62; F V 166-168.
27. FSAT; R III 132.
28. *Ibid.*, 132.
29. KGE; R II 176.
30. IE; R IV 63; F V 168.

Ch. 13–Summation
1. PAIR; R.

32. *Ibid.*, R 202; F 402-403.
33. STA; R I 60.

Ch. 5–
Methods of the
Preparatory Period
1. PYR; R.
2. CL; R V 211; F VI 418-419.
3. *Ibid.*, R 211; F 418.
4. *Ibid.*, R 212; F VI 420.
5. KGE; R II 108; F II 418-419.
6. STA; R I 90.
7. PA; R V 36; F VI 66-67.
8. *Ibid.*, R 38; F 70.
9. CL; R V 172; F VI 352-353.
10. *Ibid.*, R 171; F 351.
11. FSAT; R III 136; F I 34-35.
12. RA; R V 102; F VI 207.
13. IE; R IV 62-63; F V 168.
14. RA; R V 101-102; F VI 206-207.
15. IE; R IV 63; F V 168.
16. OGS; G II 50-51; also in French volume V.
17. WRA; R 77-79.
18. *Ibid.*, 79-80.
19. *Ibid.*, 86.
20. PA; R V 24; F VI 45-46.
21. WRA; R 21.
22. *Ibid.*, 21-22.
23. *Ibid.*, 22.
24. *Ibid.*, 22-23.

25. *Ibid.*, 23.
26. *Ibid.*, 24.
27. STA; R I 289-290.
28. *Ibid.*, 290.
29. WRA; R 24.
30. *Ibid.*, 25.
31. *Ibid.*, 29-31.
32. LF; R IV 238; F IV 61.
33. CL; R V 204; F VI 406.
34. KGE; R II 20-21; F II 292-293.
35. *Ibid.*, R 21; F 293.
36. PA; R V 16; F VI 33.
37. KGE; R II 22; F II 294-295.
38. *Ibid.*, R 22-23; F 295.

Ch. 6–
Jacobins of 1870 Feared
Revolutionary Anarchy
1. LF; R IV 146; F II 182-183.
2. *Ibid.*, R 148; F 186.
3. *Ibid.*, R 149; F 186-187.
4. *Ibid.*, R 150-151; F 188-189.
5. *Ibid.*, R 151; F 190.
6. *Ibid.*, R 169; F 215.
7. *Ibid.*, R 169-170; F II 216-217.
8. *Ibid.*, R 170-171; F 216-218.
9. KGE; R II 61-62; F II 351-352.
10. LF; R IV 171; F II 219.
11. *Ibid.*, R 173.
12. *Ibid.*, 173-174.
13. *Ibid.*, 174.
14. *Ibid.*, 174-175.

15. *Ibid.*, 175.
16. *Ibid.*, 175-176.
17. *Ibid.*, 176.
18. *Ibid.*, 176-177.

Ch. 7–
Revolution by Decrees
Doomed to Failure
1. LF; R IV 177; F II 227-228.
2. *Ibid.*, R 177-178.
3. *Ibid.*, 178.
4. *Ibid.*, 179.
5. *Ibid.*, 179-180.
6. *Ibid.*, 180.
7. *Ibid.*, 182.
8. *Ibid.*, 182-183.
9. *Ibid.*, 185.
10. *Ibid.*, 185-186.
11. *Ibid.*, 186.
12. *Ibid.*, 186-187; F II 242.
13. KGE; R II 48; F II 332-333.
14. *Ibid.*, R 48-49; F 333.
15. *Ibid.*, R 49; F 334.

Ch. 8–
Revolutionary Program
for Peasants
1. KGE; R II 49; F II 334.
2. *Ibid.*, R 49-50; F 335.
3. *Ibid.*, R 50; F 335-336.
4. LF; R IV 187; F II 242-243.
5. KGE; R II 58; F II 347.
6. *Ibid.*, R 58; F II 347-348.
7. LF; R IV 187; F II 243.
8. KGE; R II 58; F II 348.
9. LF; R IV 187-188; F II 243-244.

10. *Ibid.*, R 189; F 246.
11. KGE; R II 111-112; F II 423-424.
12. LF; R IV 190.
13. *Ibid.*, R 190-191; F II 247-248.

Ch. 9–
On the Morrow of the
Revolution
1. LP; R IV 86; F I 219-220.
2. CL; R V 195; F VI 392.
3. FSAT; R III 146; F I 55-56.
4. CL; R V 201; F VI 401-402.
5. *Ibid.*, R 197-198; F 396.
6. OP; R III 97.
7. LF; R IV 189-190.
8. *Ibid.*, R 190; F II 246-247.
9. STA; R I 236.
10. LU; R IV 37; F V 127-128.
11. STA; R I 236.
12. IE; R IV 49.
13. *Ibid.*, R 49; F V 146.
14. *Ibid.*, R 50; F 146.
15. CL; R V 200.
16. *Ibid.*, 200-201.
17. *Ibid.*, R 201; F VI 401.
18. *Ibid.*, R 200; F 400.
19. PHC; G I 201-202; F III 183-184.
20. *Ibid.*, G 202-204.
21. *Ibid.*, G 202-204.
22. *Ibid.*, G 204; F 189-191.

Index